Legal Framework for North Carolina's

ELDER PROTECTION SYSTEM

Meredith S. Smith and Aimee N. Wall

The School of Government at the University of North Carolina at Chapel Hill works to improve the lives of North Carolinians by engaging in practical scholarship that helps public officials and citizens understand and improve state and local government. Established in 1931 as the Institute of Government, the School provides educational, advisory, and research services for state and local governments. The School of Government is also home to a nationally ranked Master of Public Administration program, the North Carolina Judicial College, and specialized centers focused on community and economic development, information technology, and environmental finance.

As the largest university-based local government training, advisory, and research organization in the United States, the School of Government offers up to 200 courses, webinars, and specialized conferences for more than 12,000 public officials each year. In addition, faculty members annually publish approximately 50 books, manuals, reports, articles, bulletins, and other print and online content related to state and local government. The School also produces the *Daily Bulletin Online* each day the General Assembly is in session, reporting on activities for members of the legislature and others who need to follow the course of legislation.

Operating support for the School of Government's programs and activities comes from many sources, including state appropriations, local government membership dues, private contributions, publication sales, course fees, and service contracts.

Visit sog.unc.edu or call 919.966.5381 for more information on the School's courses, publications, programs, and services.

Michael R. Smith, DEAN
Thomas H. Thornburg, SENIOR ASSOCIATE DEAN
Jen Willis, ASSOCIATE DEAN FOR DEVELOPMENT
Michael Vollmer, ASSOCIATE DEAN FOR ADMINISTRATION

FACULTY

Whitney Afonso
Trey Allen
Gregory S. Allison
Lydian Altman
David N. Ammons
Ann M. Anderson
Maureen Berner
Frayda S. Bluestein
Kirk Boone
Mark F. Botts
Anita R. Brown-Graham
Peg Carlson
Connor Crews
Leisha DeHart-Davis
Shea Riggsbee Denning
Sara DePasquale
Jacquelyn Greene
Margaret F. Henderson
Norma Houston
Cheryl Daniels Howell
Willow S. Jacobson
Robert P. Joyce
Diane M. Juffras

Dona G. Lewandowski
Adam Lovelady
James M. Markham
Christopher B. McLaughlin
Kara A. Millonzi
Jill D. Moore
Jonathan Q. Morgan
Ricardo S. Morse
C. Tyler Mulligan
Kimberly L. Nelson
David W. Owens
William C. Rivenbark
Dale J. Roenigk
John Rubin
Jessica Smith
Meredith Smith
Carl W. Stenberg III
John B. Stephens
Charles Szypszak
Shannon H. Tufts
Aimee N. Wall
Jeffrey B. Welty (on leave)
Richard B. Whisnant

CONTENTS

Introduction

While there are two authors listed on the cover of this publication, this project was truly informed, supported, and improved by many individuals in different ways. The North Carolina Conference of Superior Court Clerks and the Executive Director, Jamie Lassiter, provided not only financial support but also the impetus for creating the manual. The clerks, who are at the center of adult guardianship cases, recognized a need for more information and resources. In response, Jamie Lassiter applied for elder abuse grant funding through the Governor's Crime Commission and contracted with the School of Government (SOG) to assist with the development of resources and training.

At the outset of the project, we recognized that in order to create useful, practical resources we had to start with the professionals who are involved with elder abuse work around the state. Throughout the summer of 2018, we met with individuals and teams in six counties around the state: Alamance, Ashe, Cumberland, Johnston, Mecklenburg, and Pitt. The insight provided by the clerks, social services staff, guardian ad litem attorneys, law enforcement officials, prosecutors, community members, and others was invaluable. Their knowledge and experiences informed every page of this manual.

As the project progressed further, we invited several individuals to join the Elder Abuse Advisory Committee (EAAC). We have called on this group to brainstorm ideas for website design and content, review draft chapters and other resources, and provide quick turn-around feedback about ideas and questions. Committee members include the following individuals.

- Hon. Michelle Ball, Clerk of Superior Court, Johnston County

- Hon. Mandana Vidwan, Assistant Clerk of Superior Court, Mecklenburg County

- Loann Meekins, Attorney, Cleveland County

- Marjorie Brown, Public Guardian, Cabarrus County

- Detective Scott Sluder, Financial Crimes Section, Winston-Salem Police Department

- Kayley Taber, Managing Assistant District Attorney, Chatham County

- Janet Coleman, Assistant District Attorney, New Hanover County

- Karey Perez, Adult Services Section Chief, Division of Aging and Adult Services

- Kim Lassiter-Fisher, Adult Services Supervisor, Orange County

- Felissa Ferrell, Social Services Director, Rockingham County

- Preston Craddock, Protective Services Social Worker, Greene County

We also called on several attorneys, clerks, agency staff, and other professionals outside the EAAC to review chapter drafts and materials throughout the process. We are grateful for their candid feedback and suggestions for improvement.

At about the same time we started working on this project, the North Carolina Conference of District Attorneys also began work on a manual designed specifically for prosecutors. Our work overlapped to a certain degree, and we greatly appreciate the collaboration, resource-sharing, and support from the team involved with that manual. Special thanks to Kim Spahos and the project lead, Nancy Warren.

Within the SOG, this project was supported and improved by many different professionals. Research attorneys Aly Chen and Caitlin Little gathered information, participated in meetings, synthesized content, and did careful citation reviews. Mistyre Bonds made outstanding contributions with her vision, organization, and technical skills related to the website design, roadmap, tools, and other resources. Lindsay Hoyt was the mastermind behind the website, and Stefanie Panke, the overall project lead for the IT team.

A special thanks must go out to the publications and design team, including Melissa Twomey, Robby Poore, Emily Hinkle, Kevin Justice, Jennifer Henderson, and Sonja Matanovic. Work on this manual, in particular, evolved and changed in ways that were not typical for SOG publications. The patience, flexibility, professionalism, and expertise of the publications team have been remarkable and much appreciated.

Finally, we must thank our families for their support as we immersed ourselves in this work for a few years and leaned on their guidance and patience along the way.

Meredith S. Smith
Aimee N. Wall

Preface

When choosing a title for this manual, we recognized that we were taking a bit of a leap of faith. Our research and experiences related to elder abuse suggested that there may not actually be a "system" in place. Rather, we recognized that there are many agencies, organizations, and individuals who are dedicated to this work and are doing everything within their powers to help older adults who may be at risk of or victims of abuse, neglect, or exploitation. In some parts of the state, these groups and individuals work together on a regular basis. But we learned that in most parts of the state, time and resources are so scarce that they are often struggling to connect, collaborate, and create a local elder protection system.

This project, which includes not only this manual but also a website, additional online resources and tools, and workshops, was designed to support connectivity and understanding among the various components of North Carolina's elder protection professionals and organizations.

- **Manual.** The *Legal Framework for North Carolina's Elder Protection System* (*The Legal Framework*) is the foundation for the entire project. One of the key challenges we identified in our preliminary research was that the components of the system understood their own roles within the system, but they did not necessarily understand the roles that others played. Each chapter provides a relatively high-level overview of one component. For example, Chapter 2 describes the work of adult protective services (APS). The first part of each chapter provides an overview of the work of the component and will primarily be helpful for those who work outside the component (e.g., those who are not social workers involved with APS work). The latter part of each chapter includes a "call and response" section that explores challenges faced by the component and possible options for overcoming those challenges.

- **Website.** The project website, protectadults.sog.unc.edu, integrates content from the manual and builds on it to make a more robust and interactive platform to support education and connectivity. The site has several sections.

  - **Resources:** A collection of resources, including the full text of the manual; an interactive roadmap that links out to sections of the manual; and various tools, reference guides, and other materials designed to support local elder protection professionals.

  - **Forum:** A discussion forum for professionals involved with elder protection. The forum is grouped by subjects such as powers of attorney, confidentiality, and adult protective services.

- **Find Your Peers:** A digital map and directory of professionals across the state involved with elder protection. Professionals are added to the map and directory after joining the website.

- **MDT Administrative Space:** This space is designed to support communities as they establish and grow local multidisciplinary teams (MDTs). Each county has one MDT space, which they can use to organize administrative information about their team, such as contact information, meeting calendar, and policies and procedures. For security reasons, the space must not be used to share case-specific or identifiable information.

We plan to revise, update, and expand the site over time as we learn more about and from the elder protection community.

- **Workshops and Training.** In connection with this project, the School of Government (SOG) hosted a two-day workshop for MDTs in Fall 2019. We also expect to host a webinar in Spring 2020 to provide an overview of the project and help clerks and other public officials involved with elder protection offer local training about the law and resources available in their communities. We will continue to look for opportunities to offer training, webinars, and workshops over time that will build on the collaborative learning that is essential to making an elder protection system operate.

We encourage you to use the *Legal Framework* as a reference guide but to also consider consulting additional resources available from the SOG and from others involved in this field when exploring some of the challenging legal and practical questions facing the elder protection community.

Chapter 1
Background and Overview

CONTENTS

I.   PURPOSE OF MANUAL

The primary purpose of this manual is to provide a solid base of information to help different public officials work together as part of a coherent whole to address cases involving suspected elder abuse, neglect, or exploitation. It includes overviews of several key governmental functions related to this field, including adult protective services, criminal investigation and prosecution, and guardianship, as well as focused summaries of related areas of law such as powers of attorney, protective orders, and civil actions. Because these areas of the law are so complex and involve different groups of public officials, they are often addressed separately in training and written materials. We integrated them in this manual so that public officials, such as clerks of court, social services staff and attorneys, and law enforcement officials, could develop a more comprehensive understanding of the different components of the elder protection system in North Carolina and identify opportunities for collaboration and cooperation. The manual should also be useful for others, such as private attorneys, advocates, and family members, as they try to identify options for assisting victims of elder abuse and navigate the sometimes-fragmented system.

II.   SCOPE OF CHAPTER

This chapter will provide some foundational context for the rest of the manual. It opens by defining two key terms: elder abuse and older adult. It then identifies trends that indicate the likelihood that elder abuse will increase dramatically in the future and highlights the impacts of elder abuse on individuals, families, and society. The chapter also provides some background on why elder abuse has been such a challenging issue for public officials to address. Finally, it includes a brief, high-level overview of the chief elements of the elder protection system in the state—including its three key governmental components, adult protective services, criminal investigation and prosecution, and guardianship—and explores the role that other legal tools and components—such as civil remedies (e.g., powers of attorney), state agencies (e.g., long-term care ombudsman program), health care providers, and financial institutions—play in the system.

III.   WHAT IS ELDER ABUSE?

Organizations and government agencies use different terminology in the context of abuse, neglect, and exploitation of older adults. They may use words such as elders, elderly, older adults, seniors, or geriatric to refer to the population affected. They may refer to the actions causing harm as abuse, neglect, exploitation, maltreatment, or mistreatment. Throughout this manual, the terms older adult and elder abuse will be used. Below are brief overviews of how these terms may be understood and applied.

A. ELDER ABUSE

1. TYPES OF ABUSE

When addressing the topic of elder abuse generally, this manual will rely primarily on definitions developed by the U.S. Centers for Disease Control and Prevention (CDC) in 2016. The CDC studied definitions from various organizations in order to develop common uniform definitions of elder abuse that could be adopted across different jurisdictions and fields of study. The CDC defines elder abuse in general as "an intentional act, or failure to act, by a caregiver or another person in a relationship involving an expectation of trust that causes or creates a risk of harm to an older adult."[1] Table 1.1 provides more detailed overviews of the most common types of elder abuse.

Table 1.1. **Types of Elder Abuse (as Defined by the CDC)**

TYPE OF ABUSE	DESCRIPTION	EXAMPLES
Physical abuse	The intentional use of physical force that results in acute or chronic illness, bodily injury, physical pain, functional impairment, distress, or death.	Includes violent acts such as striking (with or without an object or weapon), hitting, beating, scratching, biting, choking, suffocation, pushing, shoving, shaking, slapping, kicking, stomping, pinching, and burning.
Sexual abuse or abusive sexual contact	Forced or unwanted sexual interaction (touching and non-touching acts) of any kind with an older adult.	Includes forced or unwanted <ul><li>completed or attempted contact between a penis and a vulva or a penis and an anus involving penetration;</li><li>contact between a mouth and a penis, vulva, or anus;</li><li>penetration of the anal or genital opening of another person by a hand, finger, or other object; and</li><li>intentional touching, either directly or through clothing, of a person's genitalia, anus, groin, breast, inner thigh, or buttocks.</li></ul> These acts also qualify as sexual abuse if they are committed against a person who is not competent to give informed approval.

---

1. U.S. Dep't of Health & Human Servs., Ctrs. for Disease Control & Prevention (CDC), *Violence Prevention*, "Elder Abuse: Definitions," CDC.GOV (last visited May 28, 2019), https://www.cdc.gov/violenceprevention/elderabuse/definitions.html. *See also* Lori Stiegel & Ellen Klem, ABA Comm'n on Law & Aging, Types of Abuse: Comparison Chart of Provisions in Adult Protective Services Laws, by State (2007), https://aemqa.americanbar.org/content/dam/aba/administrative/law_aging/Abuse_Types_by_State_and_Category_Chart.pdf.

Table 1.1, *cont'd*

TYPE OF ABUSE	DESCRIPTION	EXAMPLES
Emotional or psychological abuse	Verbal or nonverbal behavior that results in the infliction of anguish, mental pain, fear, or distress.	Includes behaviors intended to • humiliate (e.g., calling names or insults); • threaten (e.g., expressing an intent to initiate nursing home placement); • isolate (e.g., secluding a person from family or friends); or • control (e.g., prohibiting or limiting access to transportation, telephone, money, or other resources) another person.
Caregiver neglect	A failure by a caregiver or other responsible person to (1) protect an elder from harm or (2) meet an elder's needs for essential medical care, nutrition, hydration, hygiene, clothing, basic activities of daily living or shelter, which results in a serious risk of compromised health and safety.[2]	Includes • not providing adequate nutrition, hygiene, clothing, shelter, or access to necessary health care and • failing to prevent exposure to unsafe activities and environments.
Financial abuse or exploitation[3]	The illegal, unauthorized, or improper use of an older individual's resources by a caregiver or other person in a trusting relationship, for the benefit of someone other than the older individual. This includes depriving an older person of rightful access to, information about, or use of, personal benefits, resources, belongings, or assets.[4]	Includes • forgery, misuse, or theft of money or possessions; • use of coercion or deception to get elder to surrender finances or property; and • improper use of guardianship or power of attorney.

2. *See* Nat'l Adult Protective Servs. Ass'n (NAPSA), *Get Informed*, "What is Neglect?," NAPSA-NOW.ORG, http://www.napsa-now.org/get-informed/what-is-neglect/ (last visited July 5, 2019). Abandonment is considered by some to be a distinct form of abuse. Nat'l Ctr. on Elder Abuse (NCEA), *Types of Abuse*, "Abandonment," NCEANCL.GOV, https://ncea.acl.gov/Suspect-Abuse/Abuse-Types.aspx#abandonment (last visited July 5, 2019).

3. *See* Nat'l Council on Aging (NCOA), *Elder Abuse Facts*, "What Is Elder Abuse?," NCOA.ORG, https://www.ncoa.org/public-policy-action/elder-justice/elder-abuse-facts/ (last visited July 5, 2019).

4. NAPSA, *Get Informed*, "What Is Financial Exploitation?," NAPSA-NOW.ORG, http://www.napsa-now.org/get-informed/what-is-financial-exploitation/ (last visited July 5, 2019).

Some also consider abandonment to be a distinct form of abuse, but it is often directly connected with caregiver neglect.[5] Examples of abandonment include leaving a cognitively impaired older adult at a hospital emergency room without identification or caregiver contact information or buying an older adult a one-way bus ticket to another town or state.

Self-neglect is also often classified as elder abuse.[6] It involves an adult's lack of self-care, such as failing to seek needed medical care. It can also involve living in conditions that may be unsafe or unsanitary. It is different from other types of elder abuse in a couple of key ways. First, there is not necessarily a "perpetrator." It is possible that the self-neglect could arise as a result of caregiver neglect or abandonment, but that is not always the case. Second, adults may make choices about their food, living conditions, or medical care that differ from those that a social worker, law enforcement official, family member, or friend may make. "It is sometimes difficult to differentiate between an eccentric lifestyle and one that poses an immediate danger to the elder or other people."[7] The goal of protecting adults must be balanced carefully against the importance of preserving an adult's right to self-determination.[8]

Table 1.2. **Some Signs and Symptoms of Abuse[9]**

TYPE OF ABUSE	EXAMPLES OF SIGNS AND SYMPTOMS
Physical abuse	• Bruises, welts, burns, lacerations, and rope marks • Broken bones, sprains, dislocations, and internal injuries • Open wounds, cuts, punctures, and untreated injuries • Broken eyeglasses, physical signs of being subjected to punishment, and signs of being restrained • Overdose or under-use of prescribed drugs • An older adult's report of being hit, slapped, kicked, or mistreated • An older adult's sudden change in behavior • A caregiver's refusal to allow visitors to see an older adult alone • Changes in speaking, breathing, or swallowing that may be the result of strangulation
Sexual abuse or abusive sexual contact	• Difficulty in walking or sitting • Pain or itching in genital area • Unexplained venereal disease or genital infections • Bruises around the breasts, inner thighs, or genital areas • Unexplained vaginal or anal bleeding • Torn, stained, or bloody underclothing

5. BONNIE BRANDL ET AL., ELDER ABUSE DETECTION AND INTERVENTION: A COLLABORATIVE APPROACH 72 (2006); NCEA, *supra* note 2; Stiegel & Klem, *supra* note 1.

6. Jason Burnett et al., *Four Subtypes of Self-Neglect in Older Adults: Results of a Latent Class Analysis*, 62 J. AM. GERIATRICS SOC'Y 1127–32 (2014); NAPSA, *Get Informed*, "Other Safety Concerns and Self-Neglect," NAPSA-NOW.ORG, http://www.napsa-now.org/get-informed/other-safety-concerns-2/ (last visited July 5, 2019).

7. BRANDL ET AL., *supra* note 5, at 72.

8. *Id.*

9. Examples adapted from Lori A. Stiegel, LEGAL ISSUES RELATED TO ELDER ABUSE: A DESK GUIDE FOR LAW ENFORCEMENT, 9-15, American Bar Association Commission on Law and Aging (2015).

Table 1.2, *cont'd*

TYPE OF ABUSE	EXAMPLES OF SIGNS AND SYMPTOMS
Emotional or psychological abuse	• Being emotionally agitated • Being extremely withdrawn and nonresponsive • Depression or suicidal ideation • Signs of self-mutilation • Hypervigilance when in the presence of the abuser • Unusual behavior usually attributed to dementia (e.g., sucking, biting, rocking) • An older adult's report of being verbally or emotionally mistreated
Caregiver neglect	• Dehydration • Malnutrition • Hyperthermia or hypothermia • Hazardous or unsafe living conditions/arrangements • Inadequate or inappropriate clothing • Absence of eyeglasses, hearing aids, dentures, or prostheses • Unexpected or unexplained deterioration of health • Untreated bed sores and other health conditions • Failure to thrive • Lack of routine medical care and/or medications
Financial abuse or exploitation[10]	• Changes in banking practice, including an unexplained withdrawal of large sums of money • Abrupt changes in a will or other financial documents • Unexplained disappearance of funds or property • Substandard care being provided or bills unpaid despite the availability of adequate financial resources • Unexplained sudden transfer of property • Extraordinary interest by family member or "new friend" in older person's assets • Execution of a legal document or transaction that an elder does not understand or was rushed to complete

2. SIGNS AND SYMPTOMS OF ABUSE

Indications that an older adult has been or is being abused may be subtle or they may be glaringly obvious. Individuals who work with older adults should be aware of the different types of abuse and remain alert to potential signs or symptoms.[11] In many cases, the older adult is a victim of more than one type of abuse at the same time.[12] Therefore, if a sign or symptom of one type of abuse is identified, it is essential to search for others. Table 1.2, above, sets out several signs and symptoms that may be associated with the different types of elder abuse. The list should not be viewed as exhaustive but, rather, as a starting point for evaluating individual circumstances.

---

10. *See* NCOA, *supra* note 3.

11. John M. Halphen & Jason Burnett, *Elder Abuse and Neglect: Appearances Can Be Deceptive*, 31 PSYCHIATRIC TIMES 14 (2014).

12. *See* Valory N. Pavlik et al., *Quantifying the Problem of Abuse and Neglect in Adults—Analysis of a Statewide Database*, 49 J. AM. GERIATICS SOC'Y 47 (2001) (finding that almost 30 percent of the abuse and neglect reports related to older adults in Texas in a specified period involved more than one type of report).

3. PERPETRATORS OF ABUSE

Perpetrators of elder abuse, other than self-neglect, may be anyone, including family members, friends, informal or formal caregivers, home health workers or in-home aides, guardians, and strangers. Research indicates that perpetrators are "most likely to be adult children or spouses" and have challenges related to behavioral health, substance abuse, social isolation, financial stress, or unemployment.[13] Specifically with respect to financial exploitation, one study found that perpetrators were usually

- family members (in almost 60 percent of cases),

- friends and neighbors (almost 17 percent), and

- home care aides (almost 15 percent).[14]

Potential predictors of elder abuse include poverty, functional and cognitive impairment, worsening cognitive impairment, and living with someone.[15] These risk factors are associated not only with the demographics and abilities of the older adult but also of the perpetrator. Elder abuse is more likely when (1) the perpetrator is suffering from caregiver stress, mental illness or psychological problems, substance abuse, or cognitive impairment and (2) relational issues, such as family disharmony or conflictual relationships, are involved.[16] An abuser's dependency on the older person (often financial) also increases the risk of abuse.[17]

B. OLDER ADULT

Both the CDC and the National Council on Aging (NCOA) consider adults aged 60 and over to be "older adults."[18] In North Carolina, however, some statutes recognize 60 as the age threshold, while others use 65 as a definitional guide.

Two state criminal statutes include the age of an older adult as an element of the particular crime. One law applies to adults aged 60 and older, the other applies to adults 65 and older.

- Domestic abuse, neglect, and exploitation of disabled or elder adults (Chapter 14, Section 32.3 of the North Carolina General Statutes (hereinafter G.S.)): This statute governs abuse of "elder adults," which is defined as persons aged 60 or older who are

---

13. Mark S. Lachs & Karl A. Pillemer, *Elder Abuse*, 373 NEW ENG. J. MED., 1947–56 (2015).

14. Janey C. Peterson et al., *Financial Exploitation of Older Adults: a Population-Based Prevalence Study*, 29 J. GEN. INTERNAL MED. 1615–23, 1620 (Dec. 2014).

15. RON ACIERNO ET AL., NAT'L INST. OF JUST., NATIONAL ELDER MISTREATMENT STUDY 73–74 (Mar. 2009), https://www.ncjrs.gov/pdffiles1/nij/grants/226456.pdf.

16. CDC, *Violence Prevention*, "Risk and Protective Factors," CDC.GOV (last visited May 28, 2019), https://www.cdc.gov/violenceprevention/elderabuse/riskprotectivefactors.html.

17. *Id.*

18. CDC, *supra* note 1; NCOA, *supra* note 3.

"not able to provide for the social, medical, psychiatric, psychological, financial, or legal services necessary to safeguard [their] rights and resources and to maintain [their] physical or mental well-being."

- Exploitation of an older or disabled adult (G.S. 14-112.2): This law defines the term "older adult" to mean a person who is 65 or older.

These two laws represent only a small fraction of the potential crimes that a person abusing an older adult may be committing. The full universe of potential crimes is quite expansive and includes assault, battery, and kidnapping (in cases involving physical abuse or neglect) and forgery, theft, and embezzlement (in financial crimes cases). See Chapter 3 for a list of crimes that may involve elder abuse.

The adult protective services law does not apply exclusively to "older adults" but, rather, it applies to all adults (aged 18 and older) who are disabled.[19] An adult's disability may relate to age, but not necessarily. That body of law is more expansive because it is intended to protect all adults who may be vulnerable due to disability. See Chapter 2 for a discussion of the definition of "disabled" in the context of adult protective services.

Similarly, incompetency and adult guardianship law does not apply exclusively to "older adults" but instead covers all adults (aged 17.5 and older) who lack the ability to make and communicate decisions or manage their affairs.[20] An adult's lack of competency may relate to age, but not necessarily. That body of law is more expansive because it is intended to protect all adults who may be vulnerable due to incompetency. See Chapter 4 for a discussion of the definition of "incompetency" in the context of guardianship.

IV. WHY IS IT SO IMPORTANT TO ADDRESS ELDER ABUSE?

A. PREVALENCE OF ELDER ABUSE

Many studies and reports related to the prevalence of elder abuse are based on estimates and extrapolations because research and data related to elder abuse lag behind other fields such as child abuse and domestic violence.[21] In addition, experts agree that elder abuse is drastically underreported.[22] One study estimated that only one in fourteen cases of elder abuse is reported to authorities, while another estimated that only one in twenty-four cases is reported.[23]

---

19. Chapter 108A, Section 101(d) of the North Carolina General Statutes (hereinafter G.S.) (defining "disabled adult").

20. G.S. 35A-1101(7) (defining "incompetent adult").

21. NCEA, *Research*, NCEANCL.GOV, https://ncea.acl.gov/About-Us/What-We-Do/Research.aspx (last visited July 5, 2019).

22. UNDER THE RADAR: NEW YORK STATE ELDER ABUSE PREVALENCE STUDY, SELF-REPORTED PREVALENCE AND DOCUMENTED CASE SURVEYS, FINAL REPORT 52 (May 2011), https://ocfs.ny.gov/main/reports/Under%20the%20Radar%2005%2012%2011%20final%20report.pdf; Ron Acierno, et al., *Prevalence and Correlates of Emotional, Physical, Sexual, and Financial Abuse and Potential Neglect in the United States: The National Elder Mistreatment Study,* 100(2) AM. J. PUB. HEALTH 292, 292–97 (2010).

23. Nat'l Ctr. for Elder Abuse, *Statistics and Data*, "What Is Known about the Incidence and Prevalence of Elder Abuse in the Community Setting?: Prevalence," NCEANCL.GOV, https://ncea.acl.gov/What-We-Do/Research/Statistics-and-Data.aspx (referring to a 2011 New York State Elder Abuse Prevalence Study, which found that only

Despite these limitations, it is still important to examine the data that exists to recognize the scope of the current problem and consider the potential impact of future demographic changes. According to the National Center on Elder Abuse (NCEA), approximately one in ten Americans aged 60 and over have experienced some form of elder abuse.[24] Another study suggests that as many as 5 million older adults are abused each year.[25] The rates are likely higher in institutions such as long-term care facilities.[26]

Like most other states, North Carolina lacks comprehensive state-level data about the prevalence of elder abuse. Some data related to adult protective services is available from the state's Division of Aging and Adult Services (DAAS) within the Department of Health and Human Services. According to DAAS, in state fiscal year 2017–2018, county social services agencies received 30,128 adult protective services reports.[27] Of those reports, 15,563 were screened in and evaluated by social services staff. Of those that were evaluated, 73 percent of the affected adults were 60 years of age or older.[28]

There is some data available regarding criminal charges and convictions under G.S. 14-32.3 and 14-112.2, two state laws that specifically address older adults.[29] See Table 1.3, below, for data from calendar year 2018. There are two important limitations to keep in mind when evaluating this data. First, the statutes also apply to abuse and exploitation of disabled adults who may or may not be older adults. The data does not specify whether the victim was disabled, older, or both. Second, many elder abuse prosecutions in North Carolina and other states rely on other criminal statutes. Therefore, this data is certainly not an accurate representation of the full scope of criminal cases involving elder abuse.

one of twenty-four cases of elder abuse gets reported) (last visited July 19, 2019); NCOA, *supra* note 3; NAT'L RESEARCH COUNCIL, ELDER MISTREATMENT: ABUSE, NEGLECT, AND EXPLOITATION IN AN AGING AMERICA (2003), *available through the National Center for Biotechnology Information at* http://www.ncbi.nlm.nih.gov/books/NBK98802/ (estimating that one in fourteen cases of elder abuse is reported).

24. NCOA, *supra* note 3. *See also* NCEA, *Statistics and Data*, "What Is Known about the Incidence and Prevalence of Elder Abuse in the Community Setting?," NCEANCL.GOV, https://ncea.acl.gov/About-Us/What-We-Do/Research/Statistics-and-Data.aspx#prevalence (last visited July 5, 2019).

25. NCOA, *supra* note 3.

26. World Health Org. (WHO), *Elder Abuse*, WHOINT (June 8, 2018), https://www.who.int/news-room/fact-sheets/detail/elder-abuse. *See also* NCEA, *Statistics and Data*, "Abuse in Nursing Homes and Other Long-Term Care Facilities," NCEANCL.GOV, https://ncea.acl.gov/About-Us/What-We-Do/Research/Statistics-and-Data#ltc (last visited Oct. 16, 2019).

27. N.C. DEP'T OF HEALTH & HUMAN SERVS. (NCDHHS), DIV. OF AGING & ADULT SERVS. (DAAS), ANNUAL ADULT PROTECTIVE SERVICES (APS) SURVEY, SFY 2017–2018 (on file at DAAS) (hereinafter APS SURVEY); NCDHHS, DAAS, CLIENT SERVICES DATA WAREHOUSE (CSDW), APS 110 CLIENT DEMOGRAPHICS (on file at DAAS) (hereinafter CSDW APS 110 REPORT). *See also* Thomas Goldsmith, *Mistreated Adults Need Support from State, Not Just Counties and Feds, Advocates Say*, NORTH CAROLINA HEALTH NEWS (Feb. 7, 2019), https://www.northcarolinahealthnews.org/2019/02/07/advocates-want-more-funds-for-adult-protective-services/.

28. APS SURVEY, *supra* note 27; CSDW APS 110 REPORT, *supra* note 27.

29. N.C. ADMIN. OFFICE OF THE CTS., 2018 TALLY OF CRIMINAL CHARGES AND CONVICTIONS (on file with authors).

Table 1.3. **2018 Charges and Convictions for Elder-Specific Crimes**

CRIME	STATUTE (G.S.)	TOTAL # OF CHARGES
Abuse disabled/elderly with injury	14-32.3(a)	27
Abuse disabled/elderly with serious injury	14-32.3(a)	21
Neglect disabled/elderly with injury	14-32.3(b)	16
Neglect disabled/elderly with serious injury	14-32.3(b)	16
Exploit disabled/elderly trust	14-112.2(b)	317
Exploit disabled/elderly capacity	14-112.2(c)	370

Source: N.C. ADMIN. OFFICE OF THE CTS., *supra* note 29.

B. AGING AND DEMOGRAPHICS

Lower fertility rates and increased longevity have led to the rapid growth of the older population across the world and in the United States.[30] In 2015, among the estimated 7.3 billion worldwide population, 617.1 million (9 percent) were aged 65 and older.[31] By 2030, the older population will total roughly 1 billion (12 percent of the projected total world population); by 2050, 1.6 billion (17 percent) of the total world population of 9.4 billion will be 65 and older.[32] The United States will experience further expansion of its older population for many decades to come, fueled by the baby boom cohort that began turning 65 years old in 2011.[33]

Of the more than 10 million people living in North Carolina in 2017, about 16 percent were aged 65 and older.[34] According to the Office of State Management and Budget, this percentage is expected to continue increasing over the next two decades, reaching an estimated 21 percent of the population by 2037.[35] In other words, one in five people will be 65 or older in 2037. The fastest-growing age group will be those 85 and older.[36]

The balance between the older and younger population is also clearly shifting in North Carolina. In 2017, approximately 40 percent of the population was 60 and older.[37] In 2037, it is expected that almost 50 percent of the population will be in that age group.[38] In 2019, it is expected that the state will have more people aged 60 and older than people who are 18 years and younger.[39] (See Figure 1.1, below.)

---

30. WAN HE ET AL., U.S. CENSUS BUREAU, INTERNATIONAL POPULATION REPORTS, AN AGING WORLD: 2015 1 (2016), https://www.census.gov/content/dam/Census/library/publications/2016/demo/p95-16-1.pdf.

31. *Id.* at 3.

32. *Id.*

33. *Id.* at 9.

34. NCDHHS, DAAS, *North Carolina Is Aging!*, https://files.nc.gov/ncdhhs/documents/files/NC%20State%20Aging%20Profile%202017_0.pdf (last visited July 5, 2019).

35. *Id.*

36. *Id.*

37. *Id.*

38. *Id.*

39. *Id.*

Figure 1.1. **Projected Growth (in Percentages) of Age Groups in N.C. Population from 2017 to 2037**

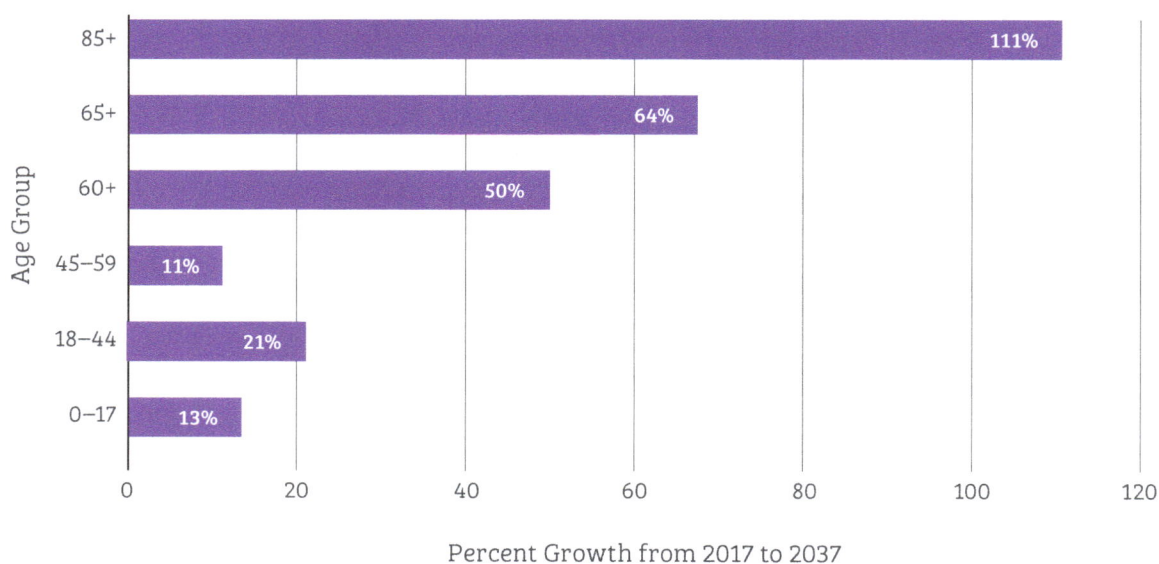

Source: NCDHHS, DAAS, *supra* note 34.

With such a tremendous population expansion on the horizon for older adults in North Carolina, it is reasonable to expect that elder abuse has the potential to increase as well.

C. HEALTH IMPLICATIONS

Elder abuse can lead to physical harm ranging from minor scratches and bruises to broken bones and disabling injuries. It can also lead to serious, sometimes long-lasting, psychological consequences, including depression and anxiety. For older adults, even relatively minor injuries can cause serious and permanent harm or even death. Studies indicate that elder abuse is "predictive of later disability among persons who initially displayed no disability and is associated with increased rates of emergency department utilization, increased risks for hospitalization, and increased risk for mortality."[40] One study found that victims of elder abuse are twice as likely to die prematurely as people who are not victims of elder abuse.[41] Another study found that victims of elder abuse have a 300 percent higher risk of death when compared to those who have not been mistreated.[42]

---

40. NCEA, *Statistics and Data*, "What Is the Impact of Elder Abuse?," NCEANCL.GOV, https://ncea.acl.gov/About-Us/What-We-Do/Research/Statistics-and-Data#impact (citing Mark S. Lachs et al., *ED Use by Older Victims of Family Violence*, 30 ANNALS EMERGENCY MED. 448–54 (1997); M.W. Baker et al., *Mortality Risk Associated with Physical and Verbal Abuse in Women Aged 50 to 79*, 57 J. AM. GERIATRICS SOC'Y 1799–1809 (2009)) (last visited July 5, 2019).
41. WHO, *supra* note 26.
42. NCOA, *supra* note 3.

D. ECONOMIC IMPACT

It is difficult to estimate the economic impact of elder abuse because such abuse is underreported and there are not consistent definitions and reliable data sources to draw on.[43] When trying to estimate economic impact, one element to consider is direct loss tied to financial exploitation and fraud. These losses are estimated to range anywhere from $2.9 billion to $36.5 billion annually.[44] There are also the financial implications of other types of abuse, which can include medical costs, increased costs related to caregiving for victims, and the decreased financial security of caregivers.[45] Other societal costs may include expenses associated with the prosecution, punishment, and rehabilitation of perpetrators.

V. WHY IS ELDER ABUSE DIFFICULT TO ADDRESS?

Recognizing the need to address elder abuse is relatively easy. Protecting older adults, preserving assets, preventing future abuse, and punishing perpetrators can be much more complicated. Below is a snapshot of some of the potential barriers facing public officials and others trying to address elder abuse, along with at least one suggestion to help make it easier to do.

A. MANY INVOLVED

The various agencies, officials, and organizations involved with elder abuse approach the issue of elder abuse from different perspectives and are governed by different bodies of law. It can be difficult to know who is responsible for what, who has taken which steps, and what the respective roles should be in each situation. Public officials may not fully understand all of the components of the elder protection system in their communities. A concerned family member, neighbor, churchgoer, or professional may not necessarily know where to turn for help.

---

43. Tobie Stanger, *Financial Elder Abuse Costs $3 Billion a Year or Is it $36 Billion?*, CONSUMER REPORTS.ORG (Sept. 29, 2015), https://www.consumerreports.org/cro/consumer-protection/financial-elder-abuse-costs--3-billion-----or-is-it--30-billion-.

44. NCOA, *supra* note 3; True Link Fin., *The True Link Report on Elder Financial Abuse 2015* (Jan. 2015), http://documents.truelinkfinancial.com/True-Link-Report-On-Elder-Financial-Abuse-012815.pdf; NCEA, *Elder Abuse and its Impact: What You Must Know* (last revised Feb. 2015), https://ncea.acl.gov/NCEA/media/Publication/Elder-Abuse-and-Its-Impact-What-You-Must-Know-2013.pdf.

45. NCEA, *Statistics and Data*, NCEANCL.GOV, https://ncea.acl.gov/About-Us/What-We-Do/Research/Statistics-and-Data#impact (last visited July 5, 2019); MetLife Mature Mkt. Inst., *The MetLife Study of Caregiving Costs to Working Caregivers: Double Jeopardy for Baby Boomers Caring for Their Parents* (June 2011), http://www.caregiving.org/wp-content/uploads/2011/06/mmi-caregiving-costs-working-caregivers.pdf.

> **IDENTIFY PARTNERS AND BUILD STRATEGIC RELATIONSHIPS IN YOUR LOCAL ELDER PROTECTION COMMUNITY. CREATE A COMMON UNDERSTANDING OF THE VARIOUS ROLES OF THE PARTNERS AND THE RESOURCES AVAILABLE IN THE COMMUNITY.**
>
> - Identify others in the community who are involved with elder abuse protection. Learn about their missions, the limitations on their roles, and the opportunities presented by their involvement. Build relationships and develop plans for collaboration and coordination. Strive for a no-wrong-door model to ensure that potential victims and reporters are directed to the appropriate resources within the community.
> - Consider developing a formalized multidisciplinary team in your community. (See Section VII, below.)
> - Develop a public education campaign that simplifies concepts and reporting. (See www.protectadults.sog.unc.edu for more information and resources, including sample training and written materials.)

B. COMPLEX PSYCHOLOGICAL AND EMOTIONAL CONSIDERATIONS

Victims of elder abuse may not be willing to share information or cooperate fully, or they may recant testimony because they are afraid for their own safety or are ashamed to be the subject of an abusive situation or exploitation. They may want to protect a potential abuser who may be a family member or friend. Victims also may be reluctant to seek change because they may be worried about the disruption that would come from reporting abuse, changing living arrangements, or losing a caregiver.

C. DIMINISHED CAPACITY

Older adults may suffer from cognitive impairments, such as dementia, that may prevent them from (1) remaining aware the abuse, (2) providing helpful information to social workers or law enforcement officers, or (3) testifying in proceedings. The presence of cognitive impairments may also present challenges to determining whether an older adult gave consent to a perpetrator's acts.

📖 RESOURCE

What Is Dementia?

Dementia is not a specific disease. It is a general term used to describe conditions that cause losses of memory so severe that they may impact a person's ability to carry out daily activities.[46] It is caused by damage to brain cells.[47] The primary risk factor for dementia is age.[48]

A recent study found that in the United States in 2017, a total of 261,914 reported deaths had dementia as an underlying cause of death.[49] The number of dementia-related deaths has more than doubled in recent years, increasing from 30.5 deaths per 100,000 people in 2000 to 66.7 deaths in 2017.[50] Forty-six percent of these dementia-related deaths were due to Alzheimer's disease,[51] which is the most common form of dementia.[52]

There is no cure and no treatment to stop the progression of Alzheimer's disease.[53] There are drugs and therapies that temporarily improve symptoms.[54]

EARLY SIGNS AND SYMPTOMS OF ALZHEIMER'S DISEASE	TYPICAL AGE-RELATED CHANGES
• Memory loss that disrupts daily life	• Sometimes forgetting names or appointments but remembering them later
• Challenges in planning or solving problems	• Making occasional errors when balancing a checkbook
• Difficulty completing familiar tasks at home, work, or leisure	• Occasionally needing help to use the settings on a microwave
• Confusion with time or place	• Getting confused about the day of the week but figuring it out later
• Trouble understanding visual images and spatial relationships	• Vision changes related to cataracts
• New problems with words in speaking or writing	• Sometimes having trouble finding the right word
• Misplacing things and losing the ability to retrace steps	• Misplacing things from time to time and retracing steps to find them
• Decreased or poor judgment	• Making a bad decision once in a while
• Withdrawal from work or social activities	• Sometimes feeling weary of work, family, and social obligations
• Changes in mood and personality	• Developing very specific ways of doing things and becoming irritable when a routine is disrupted

Note: Adapted from the Alzheimer's Association, *10 Early Signs and Symptoms of Alzheimer's*, "What Is the Difference between Alzheimer's and Typical Age-Related Changes?, ALZ.ORG, https://www.alz.org/alzheimers-dementia/10_signs (last visited July 3, 2019).

---

46. CDC, *Alzheimer's Disease and Related Dementias*, CDC.ORG (last visited Oct. 9, 2018), https://www.cdc.gov/features/alzheimers-disease-dementia/index.html.

47. Alzheimer's Ass'n, *What Is Dementia?*, ALZ.ORG, https://www.alz.org/alzheimers-dementia/what-is-dementia (last visited July 5, 2019).

48. *Id.*

49. CDC, Nat'l Ctr. for Health Statistics, *Dementia Mortality in the United States, 2000–2017*, NAT'L VITAL STATISTICS REPS., vol. 68, no. 2, at 3 (Mar. 14, 2019), https://www.cdc.gov/nchs/data/nvsr/nvsr68/nvsr68_02-508.pdf.

50. *Id.* at 9.

51. *Id.* at 5.

52. *Id.* at 1.

53. Alzheimer's Ass'n, *supra* note 47.

54. *Id.*

INVEST TIME IN DEVELOPING THE EXPERTISE NECESSARY TO COMMUNICATE APPROPRIATELY WITH AND PROVIDE SUPPORT FOR OLDER ADULTS WHO MAY BE VICTIMS OF ABUSE.

Adopt interviewing and information-gathering techniques that are sensitive to potential psychological and emotional barriers, as well as potential limitations related to typical age-related changes in memory or behavior (see Appendix B for more information).

D. LIMITED RESOURCES

All of the public and private agencies involved with the elder protection system have limited financial and human resources. At the same time, they are intensely dedicated to their mission and carrying out their role in protecting older adults.

DEVELOP STRATEGIC PARTNERSHIPS THAT MAXIMIZE THE IMPACT OF EACH PARTNER'S LIMITED RESOURCES.

Each component of a community's elder protection system brings with it opportunities and limitations. They have different missions, expertise, legal authority, and resources. The rest of this manual and the accompanying resources are designed to provide information to help each component understand how the various pieces of the elder protection puzzle fit together. With better understanding, these public and private agencies may be able to find ways to work together to make the most efficient and effective use of the limited resources available.

VI. WHAT ARE THE KEY COMPONENTS OF NORTH CAROLINA'S ELDER PROTECTION SYSTEM?

Elder abuse is a problem that cannot be adequately addressed by over-reliance on one governmental system alone. Rather, it is a societal problem that is cross-cutting in nature. It is therefore useful to take a wider, multidisciplinary view of elder abuse as a topic when trying to ascertain best efforts to combat it. Below is a high-level overview of the chief elements of North Carolina's elder protection system (each is addressed in more detail in the chapters that follow in this manual), including its three key governmental components: adult protective services (APS) (covered in Chapter 2), criminal investigation and prosecution (Chapter 3), and guardianship (Chapter 4). The discussion below also summarizes the roles that other legal tools and components—such as civil remedies (e.g., powers of attorney), state agencies (e.g., long-term care ombudsman program), health care providers, and financial institutions—play in the system (Chapters 4 through 7). Each heading in the subsections immediately below cross-references the manual chapter where readers can find more in-depth information.

A. ADULT PROTECTIVE SERVICES (CHAPTER 2)

Social work is the foundation for adult protective services. According to the National Adult Protective Services Association (NAPSA), the term "adult protective services" (APS) is defined as "a social services program provided by state and/or local governments nation-wide serving older adults and adults with disabilities who are in need of assistance" due to abuse, neglect, self-neglect, and/or exploitation.[55] The term "assistance" as used in this definition is vague by necessity because the circumstances in each case are unique and the affected adult's needs will vary tremendously from person to person.

The primary goal of APS is "ensuring that protective services are provided to disabled adults who have been abused, neglected or exploited rather than determining whether a particular abusive incident occurred or punishing the perpetrator."[56] APS social workers are focused on ensuring the well-being of disabled adults. While this goal differs from the one underlying criminal prosecution, it is often essential to involve both APS and law enforcement officials when an older adult has been abused. APS may be able to protect an older adult from abuse, neglect, or exploitation, but law enforcement officials are able to investigate potential crimes, punish a perpetrator, and possibly deter future abuse.

In North Carolina, APS is a governmental function, and front-line APS workers are county government employees. APS workers are often the first people to have contact with a disabled adult, the adult's caregivers, and sometimes with the perpetrators of the alleged abuse. These social workers are not law enforcement officers, they do not carry weapons, and they are limited in their ability to collect evidence, so they may be seen as somewhat less intimidating than sworn officers.

APS involvement begins with a report to a county social services agency. The primary way APS protects and supports older adults is by delivering or arranging for the provision of services that are custom-tailored to address the particular concerns that are putting the older adult at risk. An older adult may consent to the provision of services or a court may order APS to provide them.

B. CRIMINAL INVESTIGATION AND PROSECUTION (CHAPTER 3)

North Carolina law does not establish a specific crime of "elder abuse." Instead, several crimes may be implicated if an older adult is being abused or exploited. Only two crimes focus specifically on older or disabled adults, but many other generally applicable

---

55. NAPSA, *Get Help*, "What is Adult Protective Services?," NAPSA-NOW.ORG, http://www.napsa-now.org/get-help/how-aps-helps/ (last visited July 5, 2019).

56. NCDHHS, DAAS, DIV. OF AGING & ADULT SERVS. MANUAL I-2 (Apr. 1, 2011), https://files.nc.gov/ncdhhs/documents/files/APS_Manual.pdf.

crimes—such as assault, battery, rape, fraud, forgery, obtaining property by false pretenses, embezzlement, or robbery—may be implicated when a victim is an elder adult. A combination of local, state, and federal officials are involved in both investigating and prosecuting these crimes.

Criminal investigation and prosecution is unique in that it allows for the punishment of perpetrators. The other bodies of law discussed in this manual focus primarily on protecting or providing redress to the affected older person. But punishing a perpetrator can actually prevent further victimization of a particular elder and also potentially deter abuse of other adults in the future.

C. GUARDIANSHIP (CHAPTER 4)

The third governmental component of the elder protection system in North Carolina, guardianship, exists to help individuals who lack capacity to exercise their rights, including the right to remain free from abuse.[57] Guardianship is a "legal relationship under which a person or agency (the guardian) is appointed by a court to make decisions and act on behalf of a minor or an incapacitated adult (the ward) with respect to the ward's personal affairs, financial affairs, or both."[58] A guardian may be appointed for the person, for property, or for both. In North Carolina, clerks of superior court have the exclusive authority to adjudicate incompetency and appoint a guardian. They also have the authority to remove a guardian if the guardian is abusing the older adult.

If an incompetent adult is abused by someone other than a guardian, the appointment of a guardian could help protect the adult in several ways. For example, the guardian could

- move the adult to a different living space or health care facility,

- secure or recover assets that have been stolen or compromised, and

- identify and consent to physical or behavioral health care needed to help the adult recover from the abuse.

A guardian may be appointed relatively quickly in emergency situations or in cases where an imminent risk exists to the older adult or to the older adult's property. A guardian may have broad powers or, if the older adult is determined to have capacity in some areas, the authority of a guardian can be limited. A family member or friend may be appointed to serve as an older adult's guardian or the guardian may be the director of social services or a private guardianship corporation. The court has a continuing role in overseeing the guardianship after the guardian is appointed. Guardianship is seen as a remedy of last resort because of the impact it has on the autonomy of the older adult. Thus, limiting through guardianship the rights of an older adult who lacks capacity should not be undertaken unless it is clear that the guardian will give the older adult a fuller capacity for exercising his or her rights.[59]

---

57. G.S. 35A-1201(a).
58. JOHN L. SAXON, N.C. GUARDIANSHIP MANUAL § 1.3, at 5 (UNC School of Government, 2008).
59. G.S. 35A-1201(a)(4).

D. POWERS OF ATTORNEY (CHAPTER 5)

A power of attorney (POA) is a legal writing or other record that grants authority to an agent to act in the place of the principal.[60] POAs intersect with all other areas of the elder protection system. A law enforcement officer may be presented with a POA as a defense to a crime. An APS social worker may be presented with a POA as evidence that the older adult does not need protective services. A court may appoint a guardian with the authority to terminate a POA or may enter an order removing an agent.

A POA may grant an agent authority with respect to property and property interests or as to health care. This manual discusses POAs related to property and property interests, sometimes referred to in practice as **durable POAs**. A POA is durable if the incapacity of the principal does not terminate the agent's authority to act. An older adult may execute a POA for any number of reasons, including convenience or as part of planning for future incapacity. Unlike guardianship, which requires a court action, a POA is largely a private arrangement and preserves the self-determination of the older adult. The older adult selects the agent and determines in the POA the extent of the agent's authority to act on his or her behalf.

POAs are regularly used by and often recommended to older adults as a way to avoid guardianship. But POAs may be—and often are—a source of abuse. Because they are private arrangements, unscrupulous individuals may use undue influence or other abusive tactics to get an older adult who lacks capacity to sign a POA. In other cases an older adult with capacity may sign a POA free from undue influence but the agent appointed under the POA may abuse or exceed the authority granted under the POA. Fortunately, there are actions that may be taken by the older adult, by others acting with or on behalf of the older adult, or by the court to protect the older adult from abuse under a POA.

E. CIVIL ACTIONS, DOMESTIC VIOLENCE, AND HOUSING (CHAPTER 6)

In addition to APS, guardianship, and POAs, there are additional civil remedies an older adult or a caregiver may call upon to protect the older adult and provide him or her redress in the event of abuse. Some of these are briefly described below.

- **Private civil actions.** Private civil actions instituted to recover property, seek monetary damages, or rescind a document executed by an older adult include actions alleging breach of fiduciary duty, fraud, conversion, intentional infliction of emotional distress, and civil assault.

- **Domestic violence protective orders.** A victim of domestic violence may be able to obtain an ex parte order of protection in situations involving physical harm or harassment. The terms "domestic violence" and "personal relationship" are defined broadly enough in state law to encompass many of the family relationships that may

---

60. *See* G.S. 32C-1-102(9) (defining "power of attorney"), (1) (defining "agent"), (11) (defining "principal").

involve elder abuse, such as when abuse is perpetrated by an elder's adult children, grandchildren, or spouses or ex-spouses.[61] The law also applies to situations where people of the opposite sex live together, which may be the case with some in-home aides.[62]

- **Civil no-contact orders.** A victim of unlawful conduct may petition the court for a no-contact order. Under this body of law, "unlawful conduct" is limited to nonconsensual sexual conduct and stalking.[63] These orders apply in situations where an older adult victim has been subjected to unlawful conduct by someone with whom he or she is not in a personal relationship.

- **Housing actions.** Depending on the facts of a particular case, an older adult who is a property owner may bring (1) an action for summary ejectment to remove an abuser or exploiter from his or her home or (2) an action for civil or criminal trespass. An older adult who is a tenant has protections under state and federal law.

If the older adult victim has a low income, Legal Aid of North Carolina may be able to assist the victim in pursuing some of these remedies. Alternatively, private attorneys and elder law clinics may be an option for the older adult to explore.

F. OTHER CRITICAL GOVERNMENTAL COMPONENTS (CHAPTER 7)

While local law enforcement and social services agencies often take the lead in elder abuse cases, it may be possible to collaborate with or transition a case to other government agencies with specific areas of expertise and statutory authority. Several other state agencies are involved in the protection of adults. Some of these organizations are listed below.

- The Division of Health Services Regulation within the Department of Health and Human Services will become involved if an older adult has been abused or neglected in a licensed facility.

- The Department of Justice may become involved if an older adult is the victim of a scam or other consumer fraud.

- The Department of Insurance has law enforcement officers who may become involved if the case involves insurance fraud.

- The Secretary of State's office may become involved if the case involves securities or investment fraud.

---

61. G.S. 50B-1.
62. G.S. 50B-1(b)(2).
63. G.S. 50C-1(7) (defining "unlawful conduct").

VII. HOW CAN THESE KEY COMPONENTS COLLABORATE TO PROTECT ELDERS?

The term "elder protection system" suggests more connectivity and integration than actually exists in many communities. The various components are often trying to find better ways to collaborate and develop a stronger, more systematic approach to elder protection. One way professionals in various disciplines can collaborate to address elder abuse is through the formation of multidisciplinary teams (MDTs). An MDT is a group of professionals in a geographic region who commit to working together toward a common goal. Elder abuse MDTs have gained traction because the problems they seek to tackle are complex and difficult for any single actor to detect, prevent, and resolve.[64]

For example, APS may intervene in a case to provide protective services to an older adult and to resolve the crisis for that particular adult. However, APS does not have authority to prosecute the perpetrator of the abuse and, therefore, after APS involvement, if no other actor steps in to offer assistance the perpetrator may move on to another victim. Alternatively, an older adult who is the victim of elder abuse may be unable to consent to the protective services offered by APS. In such a case, APS must seek a court-appointed guardian to help implement changes that will protect the older adult from further abuse. APS will then work with that guardian to ensure that protective action is taken on behalf of the older adult.

Some jurisdictions are mandated by law to establish MDTs or protocols for collaboration.[65] Other states expressly authorize public officials to coordinate and provide a collaborative response to elder abuse cases, addressing issues such as information-sharing and confidentiality.[66] The National Adult Protective Services Association's *Recommended Minimum Program Standards* encourage APS systems to form intentional and specific collaborations in order "to provide comprehensive services to alleged victims by building

---

64. U.S. Gov't Accountability Off., Elder Justice: Stronger Federal Leadership Could Enhance National Response to Elder Abuse (Mar. 2011), https://www.gao.gov/assets/320/316224.pdf; U.S. Dep't of Just., The Elder Justice Roadmap: A Stakeholder Initiative to Respond to an Emerging Health, Justice, Financial and Social Crisis 5, https://www.justice.gov/file/852856/download (last visited July 5, 2019). Elder Abuse: Research, Practice and Policy ch. 19, at 417 (Xin Qui ed., 1st ed. 2017). *See* Bureau of Consumer Fin. Prot., Off. of Fin. Prot. for Older Americans, Report and Recommendations: Fighting Elder Financial Exploitation through Community Networks 4 (May 2018), https://files.consumerfinance.gov/f/documents/bcfp_fighting-elder-financial-exploitation_community-networks_report.pdf (recommending the creation of networks to combat financial exploitation of older adults). *See also* Deborah Cox-Roush, *Senior Corps and the Department of Justice: Working Together to Prevent Elder Fraud and Abuse*, Dep't Just. J. Fed. L. & Prac., vol. 66, no. 7, at 270 n.22 (Dec. 2018), https://www.justice.gov/usao/page/file/1121446/download (stating that "[m]ultidisciplinary teams are a hallmark of elder abuse prevention programs that reflect the consensus that no single agency has all the resources or expertise needed to effectively resolve all forms of abuse and neglect. Teams may be involved in a variety of collaborative activities, including advocacy, service coordination, professional training, resource development and outreach.").

65. *See* Cal. Welf. & Inst. Code § 15763(a) (requiring adult protective services agencies to lead MDTs in every county).

66. *See, e.g.,* Fla. Stat. §§ 415.1102 (authorizing the state APS agency to establish adult protection teams); 415.106 (requiring the state APS agency to enter into collaborative agreements with others involved with elder protection); 415.107 (specifying when the state APS agency may share confidential information with others involved in elder protection).

on the strengths, and compensating for the weaknesses, of the service delivery system available in the community, and by avoiding working at cross-purposes."[67]

North Carolina does not have specific laws that address elder abuse MDTs. While they are not specifically required or authorized by statute, they are also not prohibited or discouraged.

A. TYPES OF MDTs

There are as many different types of MDTs as there are groups that work together to form them. One of the benefits of an MDT is its flexibility; each group in the MDT is able to decide what approaches and actions will work best for its team or community based on the composition of the community and its resources. That being said, MDTs generally break down in two main types: (1) case-review MDTs and (2) systemic-review MDTs.[68]

1. CASE-REVIEW MDTs

In a case-review MDT, team members recommend specific, complex cases for review by the MDT and collaborate on resolving each selected case. A case-review MDT is typically comprised of the people doing the work out in the field, responding to and resolving reports of abuse on a day-to-day basis. A case-review team may have an information-sharing agreement in place that allows members to share information about specific cases. A case-review MDT may specialize in particular types of cases.[69] Examples of specialized case-review MDTs are set out below.

- **Fiduciary Abuse Specialist Team (FAST).** This type of team specializes in financial exploitation, with an emphasis on early intervention.[70] The team's membership is typically drawn from private sector organizations, such as financial institutions and accountants, and from state and federal regulatory agencies with authority over the investigation and enforcement of financial exploitation.[71]

- **Fatality Review Team.** This kind of team focuses on investigating and sometimes prosecuting elder abuse–related deaths and makes recommendations to improve service systems and professional roles.[72] In addition to traditional MDT members,

67. NAPSA, *Adult Protective Services, Recommended Minimum Program Standards*, at 6 (2013), http://www. napsa-now.org/wp-content/uploads/2014/04/Recommended-Program-Standards.pdf ("The goal of these intentional and specific collaborations is to provide comprehensive services to vulnerable adults in need of protection by building on the strengths, and compensating for the weaknesses, of the service delivery system available in the community, and by avoiding working at cross-purposes. One method to enhance community collaboration is to develop Multidisciplinary Teams as needed or required.").

68. Georgia J. Anetzberger, *The Evolution of a Multidisciplinary Response to Elder Abuse*, MARQUETTE ELDER'S ADVISOR, vol. 13, no. 1, at 119 (2011), https://scholarship.law.marquette.edu/elders/vol13/iss1/1.

69. ELDER ABUSE: RESEARCH, PRACTICE AND POLICY, *supra* note 64, at ch. 19, 419.

70. *Id.* at 420. *See* BUREAU OF CONSUMER FIN. PROT., *supra* note 64 (noting that only 6 percent of known elder abuse networks specialize in financial exploitation).

71. *See* SANTA CLARA CTY. (CAL.), FINANCIAL ABUSE SPECIALIST TEAM PRACTICE GUIDE (v. 2.0, Apr. 2016), https://www. sccgov.org/sites/ssa/daas/aps/Documents/fast_practice_guide.pdf.

72. Lori A. Stiegel, ELDER ABUSE FATALITY REVIEW TEAMS: A REPLICATION MANUAL, AMERICAN BAR ASSOCIATION COMMISSION ON LAW AND AGING (2005), https://www.americanbar.org/content/dam/aba/administrative/law_aging/fatalitymanual.authcheckdam.pdf.

Fatality Review Teams may also include representatives from coroner's offices, funeral homes, state licensing agencies, and hospice agencies.[73]

- **Hoarding Team.** This variety of case-review MDT focuses specifically on older adults who display hoarding behaviors and on the related mental health concerns associated with those behaviors.[74]

- **Elder Abuse Forensic Centers.** These centers/teams focus on conducting investigations and gathering evidence to allow for more efficient prosecution of elder abuse cases by collaborating with health care providers and adult protective services.[75] They may also conduct evidentiary investigations, tape victim interviews, consult on cases, and perform research.[76]

2. SYSTEMIC-REVIEW MDTs

In a systemic-review MDT, team members work together to address systemic problems and service gaps and to develop information networks. A systemic-review MDT is generally staffed by people within organizations who are more senior in rank and who have decisional authority. Examples of actions undertaken by systemic-review MDTs are set out below.

- Disseminating information about new services, legislation, and policy changes to members of the MDT

- Increasing community awareness of elder abuse by offering trainings to the community, including to older adults, caregivers, clergy, financial institutions, and others

- Establishing practical reporting protocols among MDT members

- Forming partnerships and increasing understanding of the various roles, responsibilities, and limitations of each of the professionals on the MDT

- Creating self-help materials for dissemination in the community, such as a community resource guide

- Obtaining and sharing resources

A systemic-review MDT may be organized into separate divisions that carry out each of these actions.

---

73. *Id.*

74. *Id.* For an analysis of hoarding trends in elders, refer to *Hoarding and Elders: Current Trends, Dilemmas, and Solutions*, J. GERIATRIC CARE MGMT. (SPECIAL ISSUE), vol. 20, no. 2 (2010), https://www.aginglifecare.org/ALCA_Web_Docs/memberonly/gcmjournal/GCMJournal-fall10.pdf.

75. See generally the website of the University of California-Irvine Medical Center's Center of Excellence on Elder Abuse & Neglect at http://www.centeronelderabuse.org/EAFC.asp.

76. *Id.*

B. PARTICIPANTS IN MDTs

 The question of who should participate on an MDT will depend on the needs and resources of the particular community, as well as on the purpose of the MDT.[77] Some MDTs have members authorized to conduct case reviews and other members that only serve to address systemic issues. Some MDTs engage technical advisors to consult on issues that require specialized knowledge, such as forensic accountants, geriatricians, and neuro-psychologists. The composition of an MDT may grow and change over time. It may be preferable, when starting out, for an MDT to have a small group upon which it can build a strong foundation.[78] Figure 1.2 lists possible agencies/organizations/sectors from which MDT members might be drawn.

Figure 1.2. **Possible Members of an MDT**

Domestic Violence	Geriatrician	GAL Attorney
Ombudsman	Legal Aid	Hospital	Housing
Area Agency on Aging		Law Enforcement
Private Attorney	Mental Health	Court
Public Guardian	Financial Institution
Adult Protective Services	District Attorney

---

77. U.S. DEP'T OF JUST., ELDER JUST. INITIATIVE, MDT GUIDE ch. 3, "Selecting Team Members," https://www.justice.gov/elderjustice/selecting-team-members (last visited July 5, 2019).

78. *Id.*

Judges, including clerks of superior court who serve as probate judges in North Carolina, are limited in their ability to serve on MDTs. A judge or clerk could serve on a systemic-review MDT but not on a case-review MDT. This is because judges and clerks must remain impartial and should not be involved in responding to specific cases that come before them outside of a hearing. Judges and clerks may participate, and are important actors, on systemic-review MDTs in order to improve the administration of justice. Judges and clerks can be effective community conveners. Judicial leadership gives a sense of urgency to a matter and emphasizes the importance of an issue.[79] Participation in systemic-review MDTs may help the court to better assess capacity issues, craft more dynamic and responsive court orders, and more effectively oversee cases.[80]

C. POTENTIAL BENEFITS OF MDTs

MDTs provide professionals with an opportunity to step out of their silos and coordinate on the detection, prevention, and resolution of elder abuse in their communities.[81] While research efforts related to the use of MDTs in elder abuse is limited, there have been some studies with positive findings. Below are some examples.

- Staff from agencies involved with the MDT reported believing that they are more efficient and effective when they collaborate with a forensic center.

- Financial exploitation cases that involved collaboration with MDTs or forensic centers were more likely to be referred for prosecution, to result in the filing of charges, and to have an outcome that established the perpetrator's guilt.[82]

- Older adults who received services from an MDT that involved social workers and attorneys were less likely to face future mistreatment.[83]

- Forensic centers were shown to be an effective approach for determining whether a petition for guardianship should be filed in order to protect an older adult.[84]

---

79. NAT'L CTR. FOR STATE CTS., COURT GUIDE TO EFFECTIVE COLLABORATION ON ELDER ABUSE (2012), http://www.eldersandcourts.org/~/media/microsites/files/cec/court%20collaboration.ashx.

80. *Id.*

81. *See* BUREAU OF CONSUMER FIN. PROT., *supra* note 64; U.S. DEP'T OF HEALTH & HUMAN SERVS., ADMIN. FOR CMTY. LIVING, FINAL VOLUNTARY CONSENSUS GUIDELINES FOR STATE ADULT PROTECTIVE SERVICES SYSTEMS 4–6 (Sept. 2016), https://acl.gov/sites/default/files/programs/2017-03/APS-Guidelines-Document-2017.pdf (guidelines developed in 2016, proposed updates to be incorporated in 2019).

82. Adria Navarro et al., *Holding Abusers Accountable: An Elder Abuse Forensic Center Increases Criminal Prosecution of Financial Exploitation*, GERONTOLOGIST, vol. 53, no. 2, at 303–12 (Apr. 2013), http://gerontologist.oxfordjournals.org/content/early/2012/05/15/geront.gns075; KATHLEEN H. WILBER ET AL., EVALUATING THE ELDER ABUSE FORENSIC CENTER MODEL vii–viii (submitted to U.S. Department of Justice Apr. 3, 2014), https://www.ncjrs.gov/pdffiles1/nij/grants/246428.pdf; Mary S. Twomey et al., *The Successes and Challenges of Seven Multidisciplinary Teams*, J. ELDER ABUSE & NEGLECT, vol. 22, no. 3-4, at 291–305 (2010).

83. Victoria Marie Rizzo et al., *A Systematic Evaluation of a Multidisciplinary Social Work-Lawyer Elder Mistreatment Intervention Model*, J. ELDER ABUSE & NEGLECT, vol. 27, no. 1 (2015).

84. Zachary D. Gassoumis et al., *Protecting Victims of Elder Financial Exploitation: The Role of an Elder Abuse Forensic Center in Referring Victims for Conservatorship*, J. AGING & MENT. HEALTH, vol. 19, no. 9, at 790–98 (2015).

Table 1.4 outlines potential benefits that an MDT may be able to bring to its team members, to victims of elder abuse, and to the community as a whole.

Table 1.4. **Potential Benefits of a Formalized MDT**[85]

BENEFIT TO THE MDT MEMBERS	BENEFIT TO THE VICTIM	BENEFIT TO THE COMMUNITY
• Increased understanding of the elder protection system in North Carolina • Reduced duplication in the investigation of and response to elder abuse • Strengthened community networks • Better access to information; improved communication among disciplines • Relieved tensions and frustrations	• Improved access to services and supports • Enhanced coordination and efficiency of services • Creation of a "no-wrong-door" system • More complete information about the victim is gathered • Greater expertise is applied to respond to the victim • Increased array of resolutions that are acceptable to the victim	• Increased awareness of the signs of elder abuse • Increased participation in elder abuse prevention • Broadening of the public and private networks that support older adults • Extended reach of limited resources

D. CHALLENGES FOR MDTs

Common challenges faced by MDTs in creating and implementing actions and approaches include[86]

- the establishment of a clear and legal process for information-sharing and confidentiality;

- a lack of participation from key disciplines, such as law enforcement and medical and mental health professionals;

- a failure to get the right people, with necessary authority to make decisions, to the table;

- a lack of legal expertise on teams;

- communication problems across disciplines;

- different goals and expectations among team members;

---

85. Anetzberger, *supra* note 68, at 126, 143 (noting the importance of a multidisciplinary approach).

86. *Id.* at 127–28. *See also* NCEA, *Multidisciplinary Teams*, NCEANCL.GOV, https://ncea.acl.gov/What-We-Do/Practice/Multidisciplinary-Teams.aspx (last visited July 5, 2019); U.S. DEP'T OF JUST., ELDER JUST. INITIATIVE, Developing an Elder Abuse Case Review Multidisciplinary Team in Your Community (revised Sept. 2016), https://www.justice.gov/elderjustice/file/938921/download.

- mistrust or misperceptions among team members;

- the existence of interpersonal bias or conflicts on teams;

- competition among team members for recognition;

- insufficient administrative support and/or resources;

- competition among team members regarding work demands;

- sustaining interest in the MDT over time;

- unrealistic expectations on the part of team members, the victim, or members of the community; and

- turnover of key team members.

In 2016, the U.S. Department of Justice published a guide called *Developing an Elder Abuse Case Review Multidisciplinary Team in Your Community*. This guide provides a number of solutions for overcoming common obstacles to the creation, effectiveness, and sustainability of MDTs.[87]

📖 **RESOURCE**

MDT Guide and Toolkit

The U.S. Department of Justice published an MDT guide and toolkit to encourage and facilitate the development and growth of elder abuse MDTs. The toolkit provides general information, checklists, and forms on elder abuse case-review MDTs. The guide and toolkit are accessible at https://www.justice.gov/elderjustice/mdt-toolkit.

---

87. U.S. DEP'T OF JUST., ELDER JUST. INITIATIVE, *supra* note 77, at ch. 9, "Anticipating Challenges and Troubleshooting," https://www.justice.gov/elderjustice/9-anticipating-challenges-troubleshooting (last visited July 5, 2019).

Chapter 2
Adult Protective Services

CONTENTS

I. SCOPE OF CHAPTER

This chapter describes the role of the county department of social services (DSS) in providing protective services to disabled adults. In addition to protective services, counties provide support to older adults in other ways, such as financial support and in-home assistance to help the adults stay at home rather than move into facilities. This chapter will focus, however, on the agency's statutory mandate related to protective services—which includes receiving reports of abuse, neglect, and exploitation; conducting an evaluation; and, if necessary, providing or arranging for services for the adult.

II. OVERVIEW OF ADULT PROTECTIVE SERVICES

Social work is the foundation for adult protective services (APS). These services, which are provided by government programs and agencies, serve "older persons and adults with disabilities who are in need of assistance due to abuse, neglect, self-neglect and/or exploitation."[1]

In North Carolina, the term "protective services" is defined broadly to encompass evaluating a disabled adult's needs and mobilizing those services necessary to protect the adult from abuse, neglect, or exploitation.[2] This definition is intentionally vague because the circumstances in each APS case are unique and the needs will vary tremendously from person to person.

The primary goal of APS is to ensure "that protective services are provided to disabled adults who have been abused, neglected or exploited rather than determining whether a particular abusive incident occurred or punishing the perpetrator."[3] Because the goals of APS and criminal prosecution are different, it is often essential to involve both APS and law enforcement when an older adult has been abused. APS may be able to protect an older adult from abuse, neglect, or exploitation, while law enforcement officials are able to investigate potential crimes, punish perpetrators, and possibly deter future abuse.

In order to effectively protect and provide services to adults, APS must collaborate with others in the community. For example, they must work with meal delivery services, in-home aide organizations, adult day-care providers, residential placement facilities, and health care providers.

1. NAT'L ADULT PROTECTIVE SERVS. ASS'N (NAPSA), ADULT PROTECTIVE SERVICES RECOMMENDED MINIMUM PROGRAM STANDARDS 5 (2013), http://www.napsa-now.org/wp-content/uploads/2014/04/Recommended-Program-Standards.pdf.

2. Chapter 108A, Section 101(n) of the North Carolina General Statutes (hereinafter G.S.).

3. N.C. DEP'T OF HEALTH & HUMAN SERVS. (DHHS), DIV. OF AGING & ADULT SERVICES (DAAS), DIV. OF AGING & ADULT SERVS. MANUAL I-2 (Apr. 1, 2011) (hereinafter APS MANUAL), https://files.nc.gov/ncdhhs/documents/files/APS_Manual.pdf.

A. WHO IS RESPONSIBLE?

APS is a governmental function. The front-line APS workers are local government employees. Every county is served by an agency that has responsibility for APS. The agency may be a county department of social services (DSS), a regional department of social services, or a consolidated human services agency.[4] To simplify things, this chapter will refer to all three types of agencies as the "local DSS." State law directs these agencies to carry out certain responsibilities involved with APS. In addition, these agencies provide other services for adults, such as helping an adult find a placement in a facility or serving as an adult's representative payee for public benefits.

At the state level, the Division of Aging and Adult Services (DASS), which is part of the N.C. Department of Health and Human Services, is responsible for oversight and supervision of the locally-administered APS programs.

At the local DSS level, APS functions are typically carried out by the individuals listed below.

- **Social services director.** The director has primary responsibility for oversight of the agency and staff. The state APS statutes assign responsibilities to the director, who then delegates authority to staff to carry out the day-to-day APS functions.[5]

- **Adult services supervisor.** This person typically supervises all of the social workers and other staff involved with adult services, including APS.

- **APS social workers.** These staff members are responsible for responding to APS reports; conducting evaluations; and, if a report is substantiated, for offering, providing, or coordinating protective services.

- **Social services attorney.** Every local agency has access to an attorney. The role of the attorney varies from county to county, but he or she typically is available to advise the agency and represent it in judicial proceedings, such as those involving guardianship and protective services. In some counties, the attorney is employed by DSS and reports to the social services director. In others, the attorney is part of the county attorney's office or may be a contractor in private practice.

In North Carolina, most of the APS laws are located in Chapter 108A, Articles 6 and 6A of the North Carolina General Statutes (hereinafter G.S.).[6] These laws require the reporting of suspected elder abuse, outline the scope of DSS's authority to take action, and provide some tools for a county to use when evaluating an abuse report and providing services in response to it. Regulations governing the APS system are found in Title 10A, Chapter 71, Subchapter A of the North Carolina Administrative Code.[7] Important guidance about the program and the scope of DSS's authority can also be found in the state's Division of Aging and Adult Services Manual (*APS Manual*).[8]

---

4. *See* G.S. 108A-1.
5. G.S. 108A-12 (appointment of director of social services); -14 (duties and responsibilities of director of social services).
6. G.S. Ch. 108A, Arts. 6, 6A.
7. Title 10A, Chapter 71, Subchapter A of the North Carolina Administrative Code (N.C.A.C.).
8. APS MANUAL, *supra* note 3.

B. HOW DOES APS PROTECT OLDER ADULTS?

The primary way APS protects older adults is by delivering tailored services to address the particular concerns that put a certain adult at risk. Specifically, when authorized by law, APS staff is able to mobilize essential services for an older adult who is in need of protective services. The term "essential services" is defined broadly in the law to mean:

> those social, medical, psychiatric, psychological or legal services necessary to safeguard the disabled adult's rights and resources and to maintain the physical or mental well-being of the individual. These services shall include, but not be limited to,
>
> - the provision of medical care for physical and mental health needs,
>
> - assistance in personal hygiene, food, clothing,
>
> - adequately heated and ventilated shelter,
>
> - protection from health and safety hazards,
>
> - protection from physical mistreatment, and
>
> - protection from exploitation.[9]

While this definition includes examples of services, it is not an exhaustive list. APS social workers have wide latitude to determine what services are needed for older adults.

Under state APS laws, a "disabled adult" is a person who is

- 18 years of age or older or a lawfully emancipated minor,

- present in the state of North Carolina, and

- physically or mentally incapacitated.[10]

According to G.S. 108A-101, a person may be physically or mentally incapacitated as a result of "an intellectual disability, cerebral palsy, epilepsy or autism; organic brain damage caused by advanced age or other physical degeneration in connection therewith; or due to conditions incurred at any age which are the result of accident, organic brain damage, mental or physical illness, or continued consumption or absorption of substances."[11]

---

9. G.S. 108A-101(i).
10. G.S. 108A-101(d).
11. *Id.*

◇ **EXAMPLE**

Two sisters retired from their professional careers and were living together. Scammers contacted the sisters by phone and convinced them to transfer signifi-cant amounts of money, rapidly depleting their assets. A report was made to DSS. Social workers visited the home and found it to be in terrible condition and found that the utilities had been disconnected due to non-payment. DSS took the follow-ing steps:

- *obtained a protective order and froze the sisters' remaining financial assets;*
- *contacted family members;*
- *filed petitions for incompetency and guardianship, which resulted in a family member being appointed guardian of the person and a local attorney being appointed guardian of the estate for each sister; and*
- *worked with family to identify community resources to assist the sisters, including helping to find a residential facility for them that was close to family.[12]*

There are limits on the types of assistance or intervention that DSS can provide. For example, unless APS staff has an emergency order from a court specifically directing it to do so, staff may not assume physical custody of the adult without the adult's consent.[13]

C. HOW DOES APS WORK?

APS involvement begins with a report to the county social services agency. In general, an APS case will follow the path outlined below.

- **Reporting.** A report of suspected abuse, neglect, or exploitation is received by DSS.

- **Screening.** DSS then screens the report to determine if it has authority to conduct an APS evaluation.

- **Evaluation.** If DSS has such authority, it is supposed to "screen in" the report and conduct an evaluation that will include meeting with the adult and, possibly, reviewing records and interviewing caretakers, family, and other contacts.

- **Freeze and inspect financial records.** If the case involves potential financial exploitation, the evaluation will likely include a review of the older adult's financial records.

12. Interview with Assistant District Attorney Lori Wickline, Alamance County District Attorney's Office, in Chapel Hill, North Carolina (June 28, 2018).
13. *See* G.S. 108A-101(h), (i) (definitions of "emergency services" and "essential services," respectively). These defini-tions indicate that DSS can take custody of an adult pursuant to an emergency order issued pursuant to G.S. 108A-106. Another option for assuming physical custody of an older adult is through an involuntary commitment proceeding pursuant to G.S. Chapter 122C, Article 5, Part 7.

- **Provision of services.** If DSS concludes that an older adult is in need of "protective services" and the adult has the capacity to consent to the provision of these services, APS staff will ask the adult to consent. If DSS concludes that the older adult is in need of protective services but does not have the capacity to consent, APS staff will seek a court order authorizing it to provide essential services.

> (")) **KEY TERMS**
>
> - *Protective services* means "services provided by the State or other government or private organizations or individuals which are **necessary to protect the disabled adult from abuse, neglect, or exploitation**. They shall consist of evaluation of the need for service and mobilization of essential services on behalf of the disabled adult."[14]
> - *Essential services* are "those social, medical, psychiatric, psychological or legal services necessary to safeguard the disabled adult's rights and resources and to maintain the physical or mental well-being of the individual."[15]

If, during the screening process, DSS determines that it does not have the legal authority under the APS laws to proceed, the abuse report will be "screened out," which means that the agency will not conduct an APS evaluation. The reporter will be notified of the agency's decision. Depending on the circumstances, DSS may reach out to the affected adult to offer other services it provides or it may try to connect the adult with appropriate services available in the community. For example, DSS may conclude that the adult is not disabled but that he or she may still benefit from assistance with meals, transportation, or in-home assistance. APS may offer to help the adult identify needs and locate resources, but the adult may always refuse.

Below are more details about each of the five steps in the path of an APS case: reporting, screening, evaluation, freezing and inspecting financial records, and provision of services.

1. REPORTING

There is one universal APS reporting requirement in state law: Any person who has reasonable cause to believe that a disabled adult is in need of protective services must make a report to DSS.[16] With one exception, this reporting requirement applies to everyone—including law enforcement officials, court officials, and health care providers. Regional staff working with the State Long-Term Care Ombudsman Program, which

---

14. G.S. 108A-101(n) (emphasis added).

15. G.S. 108A-101(i). The definition goes on to provide a non-exhaustive list of examples, including "the provision of medical care for physical and mental health needs, assistance in personal hygiene, food, clothing, adequately heated and ventilated shelter, protection from health and safety hazards, protection from physical mistreatment, and protection from exploitation." The term does "not include taking the person into physical custody without his consent except as provided for in G.S. 108A-106 and in Chapter 122C of the General Statutes."

16. G.S. 108A-102.

provides advocacy for long-term care facility residents, are excepted from the mandatory reporting requirement. They are allowed to report abuse, neglect, or exploitation to APS with the consent of the long-term care resident or the State Ombudsman (see Chapter 7 for an overview of the ombudsman program).[17]

> ### 📖 RESOURCE
>
> Call a county social services agency to file an APS report. Contact information for each agency is available online:
>
> > http://www.ncdhhs.gov/divisions/dss/local-county-social-services-offices
>
> If it is not appropriate for the contacted county to respond, the case may be referred to another county.

In addition to this universal reporting requirement, there are two reporting requirements that apply to certain types of organizations and individuals.

1. **Financial institutions, including officers and employees.**[18] If any of these parties has reasonable cause to believe that a disabled adult or older adult is the victim or target of financial exploitation, they must report it to

   - any person identified by the customer as a "trusted person";

   - the appropriate local law enforcement agency; and

   - the appropriate county department of social services, if the adult is a disabled adult.

   This report can be oral or in writing. It must include the name and address of the disabled adult or older adult, the nature of the suspected financial exploitation, and any other pertinent information.

2. **Employees and volunteers at mental health, developmental disability, or substance abuse treatment facilities (MH/DD/SA).**[19] These employees and volunteers are subject to the reporting rules set out below.

   - If an employee or volunteer at such a facility witnesses another employee or volunteer knowingly causing pain or injury to a client (other than as a part of generally accepted medical or therapeutic procedure), under G.S. 122C-66, he or she must report the incident.[20] This particular statute requires that reports

---

17. G.S. 143B-181.20(f) ("If the subject of the complaint involves suspected abuse, neglect, or exploitation, the Regional Ombudsman shall only with the written informed consent of the resident or authorization by the State Ombudsman notify the Adult Protection Services section of the county department of social services. Except as provided herein, the State or Regional Ombudsman is not subject to the reporting requirements of Article 6 of Chapter 108A of the General Statutes.").

18. G.S. 108A-115.

19. G.S. 122C-3(14) (definition of "facility"); -66 (reporting requirements).

20. G.S. 122C-66(b).

be made to authorized personnel designated by the facility. It is important to remember, however, that the universal reporting requirement still applies and that, therefore, a report must also be made to DSS if the victim is a disabled adult and the action constitutes abuse or neglect.[21]

- If an employee or volunteer at such a facility witnesses a client becoming a victim of one of many specific crimes, most of which involve sexual violence or abuse, under G.S. 122C-66, he or she must report it within twenty-four hours.[22] See Table 2.1, below, for a list of the different crimes included within the scope of this reporting requirement. The statute allows the reports to be made to DSS, law enforcement, or the district attorney. Again, the universal reporting requirement still applies in these circumstances, so the employee must also file a report with DSS if the victim is a disabled adult.[23]

Reading these reporting laws together, an employee or volunteer in an MH/DD/SA facility should always report the types of incidents described above to DSS if a disabled adult is involved. By doing so, they will have satisfied both reporting laws. If they report only to law enforcement and the victim is a disabled adult, they will not have satisfied the universal reporting requirement.

A facility employee or volunteer could be charged with a crime (misdemeanor) for failing to make one of these required reports.[24]

---

21. G.S. 122C-66(e).

22. G.S. 122C-66(b1). Subsection (b1) refers to G.S. Chapter 14, Article 7A; all of the statutes in that Article were recodified into Article 7B, which lists rape and other sexual offenses.

23. G.S. 122C-66(e).

24. G.S. 122C-66(b) (Class 1 misdemeanor for failure to properly report abuse, exploitation, or accidental injury); -66(b1) (Class A1 misdemeanor for failure to properly report sexual violence or abuse).

Table 2.1. **Selected Crimes Subject to the Specific Reporting Requirement Applicable to MH/DD/SA Employees and Volunteers**[25]

CRIME	STATUTORY CITATION
Forcible rape	G.S. 14-27.21 (First-degree) G.S. 14-27.22 (Second-degree)
Forcible sexual offense	G.S. 14-27.26 (First-degree) G.S. 14-27.27 (Second-degree)
Sexual battery	G.S. 14-27.33
Crime against nature	G.S. 14-177
Incest	G.S. 14-178
Fornication and adultery	G.S. 14-184
Obscene literature and exhibitions	G.S. 14-190.1
Coercing acceptance of obscene articles or publications	G.S. 14-190.4
Preparation of obscene photographs, slides, and motion pictures	G.S. 14-190.5
Disclosure of private images	G.S. 14-190.5A
Indecent exposure	G.S. 14-190.9
Using profane, indecent, or threatening language to any person over telephone; annoying or harassing by repeated telephoning or making false statements over telephone	G.S. 14-196
Cyberstalking	G.S. 14-196.3
Secretly peeping into room occupied by another person	G.S. 14-202

Under all three reporting laws, reporters have some level of immunity from liability.[26] The immunity provisions are slightly different in scope, as illustrated in Table 2.2.

---

25. Because this manual is limited to older adults, Table 2.1 does not include several crimes subject to the reporting requirement because they involve child victims. For example, the table does not include statutory rape, but MH/DD/SA employees and volunteers are required to report those crimes.

26. G.S. 108A-102(c) ("Anyone who makes a report pursuant to this statute, who testifies in any judicial proceeding arising from the report, or who participates in a required evaluation shall be immune from any civil or criminal liability on account of such report or testimony or participation, unless such person acted in bad faith or with a malicious purpose."); -115(c) ("No financial institution, or officer or employee thereof, who acts in good faith in making a report under this section may be held liable in any action for doing so."); 122C-66(d) ("An employee who makes a report in good faith under this section is immune from any civil liability that might otherwise occur for the report. In any case involving liability, making of a report under this section is prima facie evidence that the maker acted in good faith.").

Table 2.2. **Immunity from Liability for Reporting**

REPORTING REQUIREMENT	PERSON WITH IMMUNITY	SCOPE OF IMMUNITY	LIMITATIONS
Universal reporting	Anyone who makes a report, testifies in a proceeding, or participates in an evaluation	Immune from civil or criminal liability	Person must not act in bad faith or for a malicious purpose
Financial institutions	Financial institution or officer or employee of that institution	May not be held liable in any action	Person must act in good faith
MH/DD/SA facilities	Employee of the facility	Immune from any civil liability	Person must act in good faith. Making a report under the statute is prima facie evidence that the reporter acted in good faith.

2. SCREENING

When DSS receives a report, APS staff is required to screen the report to determine whether it falls within the scope of DSS's authority. In some circumstances, DSS may screen out a report because the agency does not have legal authority under the protective services law to take action. Three types of situations in which DSS lacks the authority to proceed with the provision of protective services are discussed below.

a. Not a "Disabled Adult"

North Carolina's child protective services are available to every child in the state. Adult protective services, on the other hand, are available only to a limited population of adults—those who are "disabled" and are in need of protective services. Some older adults will satisfy the definition of "disabled" but many others will not. Social workers are thus encouraged to consider the level of an adult's functioning by asking themselves the following question: "Does [the adult's] non- or reduced functioning necessitate reliance on others to meet his or her basic needs[?]"[27] Age alone is not enough to authorize DSS to screen in a report. For example, a 50-year-old with dementia or significant physical limitations will be considered disabled but a person who is 80 years old and in good physical and mental health will not. Similarly, diagnosis alone is not sufficient to determine disability. As the *APS Manual* explains:

A physical condition, disease, or diagnosis that limits one person may not limit another. For example, arthritis and heart disease in one person may not impair

---

27. *See* APS MANUAL, *supra* note 3, at III-3.

that individual's functioning while in another it keeps them confined to bed. Each person and situation is unique.[28]

Finally, DSS must not rely only on a person's health or physical status, or on his or her living conditions, when deciding whether the adult is disabled. For example, an adult who is homeless but generally healthy and able would not meet the definition of disabled.[29]

When DSS receives a report, the social work staff will gather as much information as possible from the reporter about the adult's situation and condition in order to determine whether the agency has the authority to follow up on the report. If DSS concludes that the adult is not disabled, the agency is not authorized to provide protective services. It may, however, provide other support services to the adult depending on his or her situation and needs.

b. Someone Else Available to Help

One of the initial questions DSS will explore with the reporter is whether the affected adult needs services to protect him or her from abuse, neglect, or exploitation. In order to move forward with the evaluation or provision of services, the agency must conclude that

- the adult is unable to perform or obtain essential services because of his or her physical or mental incapacity and

- no able, responsible, and willing person is able to perform or obtain the essential services for the adult.[30]

As stated above, a service is considered "essential" if it is necessary to safeguard the adult's rights and resources and maintain his or her physical or mental well-being. Essential services could include medical care, food, clothing, shelter, protection from physical mistreatment, and protection from exploitation.

In some situations, DSS will determine that an older adult needs essential services but that a family member or friend is willing to help obtain those services for the adult. Before ceding responsibility, DSS must determine that the volunteer is not only willing to help but also able to provide the required assistance and responsible enough to provide the needed services.

c. Abuse or Neglect by Someone Other Than a Caretaker

DSS's authority extends to allegations of abuse, neglect, and exploitation. For exploitation, this authority reaches and covers any alleged perpetrator. For abuse or neglect, however, DSS has authority to act only (1) if the alleged perpetrator is the disabled adult's "caretaker" or (2) in cases that may involve self-neglect.[31] In order to understand how this all fits together, it is important to understand a few key definitions.

---

28. *Id.* at III-17.
29. *See id.* at III-43 (stating that some clients, such as those who are homeless, may not reach true stability and that such cases "should not be kept open for APS indefinitely.").
30. G.S. 108A-101(e).
31. G.S. 108A-101(a) (definition of "abuse"); (m) (definition of "neglect").

- A "**caretaker**" is "an individual who has the responsibility for the care of the disabled adult as a result of family relationship or who has assumed the responsibility for the care of the disabled adult voluntarily or by contract."[32] The *APS Manual* further clarifies that the term "does not include individuals or organizations that provide specific, limited services to the adult voluntarily or by contract, such as an in-home aide and adult day care program, home health aide, or general hospital."[33]

- "**Abuse**" is "the willful infliction of physical pain, injury or mental anguish, unreasonable confinement, or the willful deprivation by a caretaker of services which are necessary to maintain mental and physical health."[34]

- " '**[N]eglect**' refers to a disabled adult who is either living alone and not able to provide for himself or herself the services which are necessary to maintain the person's mental or physical health or is not receiving services from the person's caretaker."[35]

If these three definitions are woven together with the scope of authority granted to DSS, it seems that one type of case that may fall outside DSS's authority is the willful infliction of pain, injury, or anguish upon, or the confinement of, a disabled adult by someone other than a caretaker. However, depending on the circumstances, DSS may be able to screen in these types of cases if they rise to the level of self-neglect. In other words, the agency may determine that the disabled adult is not able to protect him- or herself from the abuse and may therefore proceed with the protective services evaluation.

> ◇ **EXAMPLE**
>
> *Nancy is 90 years old and disabled. She lives alone and is generally able to take care of her own needs. She gets into a dispute with her next-door neighbor about trashcans and the neighbor pushes Nancy down. This type of physical assault would not be considered abuse by a caretaker and, therefore, would fall outside the scope of DSS's authority.*

Even though such cases may not be within DSS's authority, they may easily fall within the scope of generally applicable criminal laws, such as assault, embezzlement, and larceny.

3. EVALUATION

Once DSS has received a report and screened it in, a social worker will meet with the affected adult as soon as possible; confer with other people connected to the adult, such as family members, neighbors, friends, and medical professionals; and gather records from

---

32. G.S. 108A-101(b).
33. APS MANUAL, *supra* note 3, at III-4. The manual further explains that "[s]uch services may assist to a limited degree with the adult's care, but the individual or organization providing the services does not have comprehensive responsibility for the adult's well-being." *Id.*
34. G.S. 108A-101(a).
35. G.S. 108A-101(m).

providers and/or financial institutions in an effort to properly evaluate the report. The purpose of the evaluation is to determine whether the case should be "substantiated"—in other words, to answer the question, "Are protective services necessary and appropriate?" DSS must initiate and complete this evaluation within statutorily prescribed time-frames (see Table 2.3).

Table 2.3. **Statutory Timelines for APS Evaluation**[36]

INITIATE EVALUATION		COMPLETE EVALUATION	
WHEN?	**IN WHAT CIRCUMSTANCES?**	**WHEN?**	**IN WHAT CIRCUMSTANCES?**
Immediately	If complaint alleges danger of death in an emergency[37]	**Within 30 days**	For allegations of abuse or neglect
Within 24 hours	If complaint alleges danger of irreparable harm in an emergency	**Within 30 days**	For allegations of exploitation
Within 72 hours	If complaint does not allege either of the above		

In the course of this evaluation, DSS has the authority to interview the affected adult alone, to obtain records related to the adult's care, and to request assistance with the evaluation from the local public health department and other public and private providers.[38] DSS may also contract with private providers to conduct medical assessments.[39]

During this process, DSS will compile a wealth of information about the adult, ranging from the social worker's interview notes to medical and, possibly, financial records. In addition, the social worker is required to complete a detailed report about the evaluation.[40] While the information gathered by DSS in the course of the evaluation is confidential pursuant to state law,[41] this information may be extremely useful in a guardianship proceeding, a law enforcement investigation, or in other legal proceedings. Despite the strict confidentiality laws that apply, there are opportunities for others involved with protecting the adult to obtain access to these records.

a. No Need for Protective Services

If, after the evaluation, DSS concludes that the adult does not need protective services from the agency, it may not proceed any further with regard to such services under the protective services law. Staff may, however, decide to offer other DSS services to the adult or may look into whether DSS should connect the adult with other agencies that could provide support.

36. G.S. 108A-103(d).
37. G.S. 108A-101(g) (defining "emergency").
38. G.S. 108A-103(a), (b).
39. G.S. 108A-103(c).
40. G.S. 108A-103(a).
41. G.S. 108A-80; 10A N.C.A.C. Ch. 69 ("Confidentiality and Access to Client Records").

Andy's neighbor contacts DSS because she is worried that Andy is not taking care of himself (i.e., that self-neglect may be an issue). A DSS social worker conducts an evaluation and concludes that Andy has decisional capacity and seems to be caring for himself adequately. However, Andy's apartment is quite untidy and he is a little unkempt in appearance. And while he does not appear malnourished, he does not have a lot of food in his kitchen. He visited his primary care doctor recently for a check-up and received a good report. The social worker does not believe that Andy is neglecting his own care but does think he might benefit from some supports. She shares information with him about available community resources (e.g., meal delivery from a nonprofit organization, in-home aides to assist with food preparation and cleaning) and economic services (such as SNAP, or food stamp, benefits from DSS). The social worker also offers to help Andy sign up for any of the community resources of interest to him and to connect with an economic services specialist at DSS to determine if he is eligible for any economic services.

This example helps illustrate how APS is just a subset of the services that DSS can provide to older adults. Even if a situation does not meet the statutory threshold for APS, DSS may still offer assistance and support or it may be able to help identify other supports available in the community.

Figure 2.1. **Adult Protective Services (APS) as a Subset of Overall Community Social Services for Older Adults**

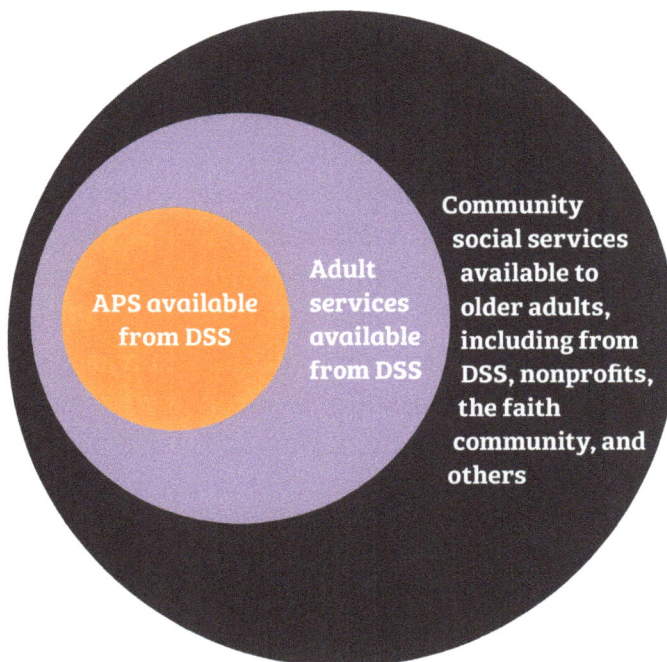

APS available from DSS

Adult services available from DSS

Community social services available to older adults, including from DSS, nonprofits, the faith community, and others

b. Need for Protective Services

If DSS concludes that an older adult needs protectives services (i.e., that the case is "substantiated"), the agency must then determine whether the disabled adult has capacity to consent to those services. The APS Manual provides some guidance for DSS staff when evaluating this type of capacity. It states that the focus should be on the adult's ability to perceive and understand his or her situation, including his or her physical limitations, the resources and assistance that are available to him or her, and the consequences of not getting such assistance.[42] It also emphasizes a few other points.

- **Capacity is different than competency.** The former is determined by DSS for the limited purpose of assessing ability to consent to services, while the latter is determined by a judicial official in the context of a guardianship case (see Chapter 4).[43]

- **Capacity may be intermittent**. Someone with an acute illness, such as a urinary tract infection, may temporarily lack decisional capacity. Once treated, the person's capacity may be restored, and DSS should recognize that change and adapt to it.[44]

- **Professional evaluations may be helpful but they are not determinative**. If DSS is unsure about an adult's capacity, it may consult with a medical or behavioral health professional. The decision about capacity, however, rests with DSS.[45]

If DSS concludes that an older adult has capacity, it must ask the adult for his or her consent to provide protective services.[46] If, on the other hand, DSS concludes that the older adult lacks capacity to consent, the agency must ask a court to order it to provide these services. DSS may choose to ask the court for a standard order or it may request an emergency ex parte order.

c. Capacity to Consent to Provision of Services

If an adult has been determined to have capacity to consent to DSS protective services and ultimately refuses the agency's offer to provide such services, DSS must close the protective services case.[47] The agency does not have the authority to compel an adult with decisional capacity to accept services. Similarly, if the adult initially consents to the services and then later withdraws that consent, DSS must abide by that decision.[48] By recognizing that an adult who has capacity must be allowed to refuse services, state law is clearly trying to find the appropriate balance between protecting individuals and preserving their independence and autonomy. DSS may still offer an adult with capacity who has refused its services other services that are consistent with policy and practice, but it may not provide protective services to that adult pursuant to law.

---

42. APS MANUAL, *supra* note 3, at III-28.
43. *Id.* at III-29.
44. *Id.*
45. *Id.*
46. G.S. 108A-104(a).
47. G.S. 108A-104(c).
48. *Id.*

d. Lacks Capacity to Consent to Provision of Services

If DSS concludes that an adult needs protective services but lacks the capacity to consent, the agency may file a petition in district court requesting permission to provide those services.[49] If the court finds by clear, cogent, and convincing evidence that the disabled adult (1) is in need of protective services and (2) lacks capacity to consent, under G.S. 108A-105, it will issue an order authorizing DSS to provide such services.[50] A determination by the court that the adult lacks capacity "shall in no way affect incompetency proceedings."[51]

G.S. 108A-106 allows for a more expedited process in emergency situations as well as for an ex parte order.[52] To issue one of these orders, the court must find that[53]

- the adult lacks capacity to consent,

- the adult is in need of protective services,

- an emergency exists, and

- no other person authorized by law or order to give consent for the adult is available and willing to arrange for emergency services.

The key to this type of order is the definition of "emergency." This term refers to a situation where

- the adult "is in **substantial danger of death or irreparable harm** if protective services are not provided immediately";[54]

- the adult is not able to consent to the provision of services;

- "no responsible, able, or willing caretaker is available to consent to emergency services";[55] and

- there is insufficient time to use the statutory procedure for obtaining a standard APS order.[56] (See Table 2.4, below, for a comparison of standard vs. emergency orders.)

If the court denies DSS's petition for either a standard or an emergency order, the agency may not proceed with its plan to provide protective services. Depending on the circumstances, DSS may still decide to offer some other services to the adult, such as referrals for nutrition programs or caregiver support, but it may not provide protective services.

---

49. G.S. 108A-105(a). If an adult lacks the capacity to consent to services and also has a guardian, the guardian could provide consent on the adult's behalf. See Chapter 4 for more details regarding the authority of a guardian.

50. G.S. 108A-105(c).

51. G.S. 108A-105(d). This subsection refers to incompetency proceedings as set forth in G.S. Chapters 33, 35, or 122. Note that all three chapters have been repealed and that the laws regarding incompetency proceedings are now codified in G.S. Chapter 35A.

52. G.S. 108A-106.

53. G.S. 108A-106(a).

54. G.S. 108A-101(g) (emphasis added).

55. *Id.*

56. *Id.*

Table 2.4. **Comparing Standard and Emergency APS Orders**

TYPE OF APS ORDER	TIMELINE	NOTICE TO CLIENT	DURATION OF AWARD
Standard[57]	Hearing must be held within 14 days of filing of petition	Affected adult must be given at least 5 days' notice of hearing	• No more than 120 days • Within 60 days, court must review to determine if there is a need to pursue guardianship or, for good cause shown, to extend APS order for an additional 60 days
Emergency[58]	Hearing must be held immediately	Affected adult, guardian, child, or next of kin must be given notice at least 24 hours prior to hearing OR No notice (ex parte) required if court makes certain findings	• Up to 14 days • Unless dissolved for good cause, ex parte order remains in effect until hearing is held on petition for emergency services • May order only such services as are necessary to remove the conditions creating the emergency

e. Freezing Assets and Inspecting Financial Records

> ◇ **EXAMPLE**
>
> *Betty is a 90-year-old woman who has dementia. She owns a home and has significant monthly income from Social Security and retirement benefits. Her next-door neighbor, Stan, takes her to an attorney to complete a power of attorney granting Stan plenary authority. On the same day, Stan sells Betty's home and moves her to a skilled nursing facility. The proceeds from the sale of her home and her other assets are quickly depleted. The facility is never paid for providing Betty care and her taxes fall into arrears. If someone had made an APS report, DSS would have been able to take action quickly to freeze Betty's assets and conduct an evaluation.*

If an APS report relates to financial exploitation, DSS will almost certainly need to obtain access to financial records. The older adult or the adult's guardian or agent may have some of the records available. If DSS needs to obtain access to records from a financial institution, such as a bank or credit union, it will need to either have valid written

---

57. G.S. 108A-105(b), (c).
58. G.S. 108A-106(b), (d).

consent from the adult or the adult's guardian or agent, or it will need to ask a court for permission to gain access. This is because financial institutions are subject to extraordinarily strict federal and state confidentiality laws.[59]

Table 2.5. **DSS Tools for Accessing a Disabled Adult's Financial Records**

TOOL	WHO CAN REQUEST?	WHAT DOES IT ALLOW?	WHEN IS IT ALLOWED?
Freeze and inspect order[60]	Social services officials	May ask a judge to issue an order (1) freezing the assets of a disabled adult who is a suspected victim of financial exploitation and (2) directing a financial institution to provide access to the adult's financial records	When social services has received a report of suspected financial exploitation of a disabled adult and a judge finds that (1) the adult is in need of protective services, (2) the adult lacks the capacity to consent to the release of financial records, and (3) the alleged exploitation was committed by the adult's caretaker
Subpoena for financial records[61]	Law enforcement and social services officials	May ask a judge to issue a subpoena directing a financial institution to provide access to the financial records of a disabled adult or older adult who may be the victim of financial exploitation	When a judge finds that (1) the official is investigating a credible report of financial exploitation, (2) financial records are needed for the investigation, and (3) time is of the essence in order to prevent further exploitation
Search warrant[62] (rare)	Any applicant may request but only a law enforcement official may execute[63]	May request a search warrant directing a law enforcement officer to seize financial records necessary to investigate suspected exploitation of a disabled adult or older adult	When the official issuing the warrant (1) finds probable cause to believe that the financial records constitute evidence of the crime of financial exploitation under G.S. 14-112.2 or (2) discovers the identity of a person participating in the crime

---

59. *See generally* G.S. Chapter 53B (Financial Privacy Act); 15 U.S.C. §§ 6801, 6803 (Gramm-Leach-Bliley Act).
60. G.S. 108A-106(f).
61. G.S. Ch. 108A, Art. 6A ("Protection of Disabled and Older Adults From Financial Exploitation"); 108A-116(a).
62. G.S. Ch. 15A, Art. 11 ("Search Warrants").
63. G.S. 15A-247. *See* Jeff Welty, *Non-Officers Applying for Search Warrants*, N.C. Crim. L.: A UNC Sch. of Gov't Blog (June 19, 2013), https://nccriminallaw.sog.unc.edu/non-officers-applying-for-search-warrants/.

It may be impractical to rely on the affected adult's consent in some situations involving access to financial records. For example, the adult's social worker may have concerns about

- the adult's capacity to consent,

- the adult being coerced by a caretaker who is benefiting from the suspected exploitation, or

- the guardian acting as the adult's exploiter.

If consent is impractical, DSS has three tools available for accessing financial records. The first is a freeze and inspect order authorized specifically for social services investigations. The second is a subpoena that is available for both social services and law enforcement investigations. The third is a traditional search warrant, which social services staff may apply for but not execute. While a search warrant would not be used to gather information for the APS investigation, DSS staff may nonetheless find it appropriate to apply for a warrant if it appears that a crime has been committed. This tool is rarely, if ever, used by DSS staff. Table 2.5, above, provides a brief overview of each of the three tools.[64]

There are several important differences between the two commonly used access tools, the freeze and inspect order and the subpoena for financial records. Some of these are set out below.

- **Differences as to the potential victim.** Law enforcement officials are authorized to investigate crimes involving both older adults and disabled adults. Social services officials may only investigate reports involving disabled adults. Under the applicable criminal law, an older adult is any person over 65 years of age.[65] Under the APS law, a disabled adult is any person 18 years of age or older (or a lawfully emancipated minor) who is physically or mentally incapacitated due to one more reasons, such as illness, accident, advanced age, and substance abuse.[66] Therefore, law enforcement officials using the subpoena tool have greater authority to act than does APS, as law enforcement is not limited to only using subpoenas for disabled adults. This difference may be a good reason to involve law enforcement early in the process if there is an emergency situation involving suspected financial exploitation of an older adult.

- **Differences as to the potential exploiter.** The freeze and inspect order is available only if the suspected exploitation is being committed by the disabled adult's caretaker.[67]

- **Differences as to notice.** The freeze and inspect order requires that notice of the order be provided to the adult and to his or her caretaker. With the subpoena,

---

64. For more details, see Aimee N. Wall, *Financial Exploitation of Older Adults and Disabled Adults: An Overview of North Carolina Law*, SOC. SERVS. L. BULL. No. 43 (Oct. 2014), https://www.sog.unc.edu/sites/www.sog.unc.edu/files/reports/sslb43_0.pdf.

65. G.S. 14-112.2(a)(2) (defining "older adult" as a person 65 or older).

66. G.S. 108A-101(d).

67. *See* G.S. 108A-101(b) (definition of "caretaker").

notice is required, but the investigating entity (law enforcement or social services) may request a delay in the notice in some circumstances.

- **Differences as to consent.** The freeze and inspect order is available only if the disabled adult lacks the capacity to consent. The laws governing the other two tools are silent in this regard.

- **Differences as to freezing the affected adult's assets.** The freeze and inspect order is the only tool that authorizes a judge to freeze the older adult's assets. In a criminal investigation, the district attorney may ask a judge to freeze the defendant's assets if the defendant is charged with a financial exploitation crime that involves assets valued at more than $5,000.[68]

- **Differences as to confidentiality of court records.** The law authorizing the subpoena provides that records of proceedings where a subpoena for access to a disabled or older adult's financial records is sought (1) are not a matter of public record, (2) must be maintained separately from other records, and (3) may be examined only pursuant to a court order.[69] Because of this heightened confidentiality requirement, the Administrative Office of the Courts (AOC) has established such a proceeding as a Special Proceeding Confidential.[70] The freeze and inspect order and search warrant tools are not subject to the same level of confidentiality protection.

D. PROVISION OF SERVICES

If DSS is authorized to provide protective services, pursuant to either consent or court order, the types of services that are appropriate will vary tremendously from person to person. As mentioned above, the law defines the term "essential services" broadly to include "those social, medical, psychiatric, psychological or legal services necessary to safeguard the disabled adult's rights and resources and to maintain the physical or mental well-being of the individual."[71]

1. EMERGENCY SERVICES

If a situation involving a disabled adult or an older adult rises to the level of an "emergency" as that term is defined above, and if DSS obtains an emergency ex parte order, the agency may provide only those services "necessary to maintain the person's vital functions and without which there is reasonable belief that the person would suffer irreparable harm or death."[72] In extraordinary circumstances, it may involve taking custody of the adult.

---

68. G.S. 14-112.2(f).
69. G.S. 108A-116(g).
70. *See* N.C. Admin. Off. of the Cts. (AOC), Form AOC-SP-630, "Petition and Order for Issuance of Subpoena Directing Release of Financial Records" (caption indicates that it is a special proceeding confidential), https://www.nccourts.gov/assets/documents/forms/sp630-en.pdf?yK8fIemirJJ3YFWnwMVoB.260aDfJUZ4.
71. G.S. 108A-101(i).
72. G.S. 108A-101(h).

This narrowly defined service scope is trying to strike a balance, weighing the need to provide immediate protection to the older adult against the need to ensure that the adult and others are provided with appropriate due process. Because a court may issue this type of order quickly and with limited judicial proceedings, DSS must limit its response to addressing only the issue that gave rise to the emergency.[73] If additional protective services are necessary, DSS must petition the court for a non-emergency protective order.[74]

2. ENTERING PROPERTY

A social worker may need to enter a person's private property without the person's consent. There are two possible legal avenues for lawfully gaining entry to property without consent. First, after a court has issued an order directing DSS to provide short-term emergency services, staff members from the agency may enter property without consent if they determine that doing so is necessary to protect the affected adult.

Second, DSS may find it necessary to enter property without consent in the absence of an emergency order. For example, a social worker may want to enter an apartment to interview an adult who is the subject of a report but the adult's roommate may refuse to open the door. In such a situation, the social worker may ask a court to issue an administrative search and inspection warrant.[75] These warrants are not the same as the search warrants used by sworn law enforcement officers.[76] Instead, these are orders that authorize non-sworn public officials to enter property and conduct an inspection if

- the inspection is elsewhere authorized by law (such as DSS's authority to conduct an evaluation and interview the older adult);

- a warrant is constitutionally required to enter the property (which it would be, without the resident's consent); and

- there is probable cause to believe that there is a condition, object, activity, or circumstance that legally justifies the inspection (such as a report that the older adult has been abused or neglected).[77]

In order to obtain an administrative search and inspection warrant, DSS must file an affidavit.[78] The AOC has developed forms for both the affidavit and the warrant.[79] These

---

73. *See* G.S. 108A-106(b).

74. *Id.; id.* § 108A-105.

75. *See* G.S. 15-27.2 (administrative search and inspection warrants); 108A-106(e) (allowing entry into disabled adult's premises by DSS worker if necessary after entry of court order for emergency services).

76. G.S. 15-27.2(g) ("The warrants authorized under this section shall not be regarded as search warrants.").

77. G.S. 15-27.2(a), (c)(1). There is another type of administrative warrant that is available when there is a "legally authorized program of inspection which naturally includes that property." *See id.* § 15-27.2(c)(1).

78. G.S. 15-27.2(c).

79. AOC, Form AOC-CR-913M, "Affidavit to Obtain Administrative Inspection Warrant for Particular Condition or Activity," https://www.nccourts.gov/assets/documents/forms/cr913m-en.pdf?68gKaFqSOC3ASvY0bHvoFLgJvzdg1T7c.

types of warrants may be issued by a magistrate, judge, clerk, or an assistant or deputy clerk of court.[80] Once the administrative warrant is issued, the social worker who has obtained it will need to act quickly, as this warrant is valid for only twenty-four hours.[81]

3. DEVELOPMENT OF A SERVICE PLAN

Once a report is substantiated, DSS must develop a service plan for the disabled adult based on the findings from and recommendations made in its evaluation of the adult. The purpose of the plan is to establish goals and a time line for resolving the abuse, neglect, or exploitation identified in the evaluation, as well as to identify services needed by the disabled adult.[82] The *APS Manual* recommends that the service plan should

- flow from the evaluation,

- be client- and family-focused,

- contain function-oriented goals,

- be time-limited, and

- consider a wide range of services.[83]

The manual notes that the services "will vary according to factors such as community resources available and the client's personal needs and choices." It goes on to explain that protection may

> be provided on a continuum ranging from a very protective plan, such as placement, to a less protective plan, such as provision of in-home aide services several days per week. Often a compromise must be reached between the level of protection the worker considers optimal and the level of protection the client is willing to accept.[84]

In planning services, APS is expected to focus on identifying the least restrictive alternatives and respecting the adult's right to self-determination.[85]

---

80. G.S. 15-27.2(b).
81. G.S. 15-27.2(e).
82. APS MANUAL, *supra* note 3, at III-39.
83. *Id.*
84. *Id.*
85. *Id.* at III-39 through -40.

Table 2.6. **Available Adult Protective Services Forms**

FORM NO.	FORM NAME
CV-770	Petition for Order Authorizing Protective Services, Emergency Services, or Ex Parte Emergency Services and Appointment of a Guardian Ad Litem
CV-771	Certificate of Services (Adult Protective Services)
CV-772	Notice of Hearing in Adult Protective Services Proceedings
CV-773	Order Authorizing Protective Services
CV-774	Notice of Hearing in Emergency Protective Services Proceedings
CV-775	Order Authorizing Emergency or Ex Parte Emergency Protective Services
CV-776	Petition for Order to Inspect Financial Records and to Freeze Assets
CV-777	Order to Authorize Inspection of Financial Records and to Freeze Assets
CV-778	Notice of Order to Inspect Financial Records and Freeze Assets
CV-779	Certification to Financial Institution as Required by G.S. 53B-5
CV-781	Notice of Hearing to Enjoin Interference with Protective Services (Consenting Adult)
CV-782	Order to Enjoin Interference with Protective Services (Consenting Adult)
SP-630	Petition and Order for Issuance of Subpoena Directing Release of Financial Records

III.   CHALLENGES FOR APS

A. DETERMINING WHICH COUNTY IS RESPONSIBLE

Sometimes multiple counties may be involved in an APS case. Consider the following example.

> ◇ **EXAMPLE**
>
> *A disabled older adult owns a home in County A and has lived there independently for fifty years. The adult's grown child assists him with chores, shopping, and medication administration. The adult is hospitalized in County B after an injury and is discharged to a rehabilitation unit in County B; the adult may not be able to live independently in the future. An APS report is filed in County B related to potential abuse of the adult by his child.*

In the example described above, both County A and County B have legal authority to take action with respect to this adult. The APS law grants authority to the director in the county in which the older adult resides (County A) and the one in the county in which the older adult is currently present (County B).[86]

---

86. The legal framework for APS grants authority to the DSS "director." In the context of the APS law, the term "director" is defined as "the director of the county [DSS] in the county in which the person resides or is present."

Because state statutes do not provide clear direction in these types of situations, counties rely primarily on state regulations and on guidance from the Division of Aging and Adult Services.[87] In most instances, the county in which the older adult is located (for purposes of our example, County B) will contact the county of residence (County A) after receiving a report about the adult. County A would then assume responsibility for the evaluation of the adult and for the provision of services to the adult. Exceptional circumstances may exist that make it more appropriate for County B to take the lead. Some examples are set out below.

- **Emergencies.** If there is an emergency and the older adult is in substantial danger, County B will likely try to obtain the adult's consent for protective services or pursue an emergency order. Once the older adult is out of danger, the two counties may decide that County A should assume responsibility going forward.

- **Residential facilities.** If an older adult moves into a residential facility, such as a nursing home, in a county other than the one in which he or she legally resides, a state regulation authorizes the county of residence to transfer responsibility to the county in which the adult is located.[88] This regulation provides that the county in which a residential facility is located has primary responsibility for providing protective services to adults in that facility. Questions may arise if an adult is in the facility for a short-term placement.

- **Conflicts of interest.** There are times when the DSS in an older adult's county of residence should not take the lead on an APS case because the agency has a conflict of interest. For example, a report could allege abuse, neglect, or exploitation of a disabled adult by a county commissioner or a DSS employee. Or the DSS director may be serving as the guardian of the disabled adult who is the subject of the report. In these instances, DSS will need to enlist assistance from a neighboring county to manage the adult's evaluation and possibly the provision of services to the adult.[89]

These situations and others require counties to communicate with one another regularly and remain flexible to meet the needs of the disabled adult.

B. DECIDING BETWEEN APS AND GUARDIANSHIP

Some may consider APS and guardianship, particularly interim guardianship, to be interchangeable tools available to help an older adult who may lack capacity and is in need of assistance. The APS tools available to DSS are unique and should be used carefully to

---

G.S. 108A-101(c). Therefore, both directors have the legal authority to act, and each director may delegate that authority to DSS staff. *Id.* § 108A-14(b).

87. 10A N.C.A.C. 71A, § .0504.

88. *Id.*

89. APS MANUAL, *supra* note 3, at III-2, III-7 to -8, III-24, III-37, and III-42.

carry out the purposes for which they are intended. The purposes of protective services, interim guardianship, and guardianship overlap to some extent, but they are also distinctive. Table 2.7, below, provides a high-level summary comparison of the essential elements and purposes of each APS tool.

One of the challenges facing DSS is that it may be more expedient to pursue interim guardianship if a disabled adult needs immediate assistance. This is, in part, because a clerk of superior court—the official who presides over guardianship proceedings—may be more readily accessible in some counties than a district court judge (who presides over APS proceedings).

MAKE CASE-SPECIFIC DECISIONS AFTER CAREFUL EVALUATION OF OBJECTIVES AND AVAILABLE OPTIONS.

Table 2.7. **Comparison: Protective Services, Interim Guardianship, and Guardianship**

	PROTECTIVE SERVICES	INTERIM GUARDIANSHIP	GUARDIANSHIP
Timeframe	Short-term	Short-term	Long-term
Function	Protection of a disabled adult from abuse, neglect, or exploitation; provision of essential services	Decision making and/or action on behalf of an adult who is probably incompetent	Decision making and/or action on behalf of an adult who has been adjudicated incompetent
Means of initiation	DSS can initiate following a report to APS	Petitioner, GAL, or clerk in a guardianship proceeding	Any person, including DSS, can initiate by filing a petition with clerk
Presiding official	District court judge	Elected clerk of superior court or an assistant clerk	Elected clerk of superior court or an assistant clerk
Standard of capacity applied	Lack capacity to consent to services (limited)	Inability to make or communicate decisions (more expansive)	Inability to make or communicate decisions (more expansive)

Table 2.7. *cont'd*

	PROTECTIVE SERVICES	**INTERIM GUARDIANSHIP**	**GUARDIANSHIP**
Duration of tool	Up to 120 days (initial order may be in effect for up to 60 days; may request additional 60 days)	Up to 90 days (initial order may be in effect for up to 45 days; may request additional 45 days)	Continues until death of the older adult or until clerk issues an order to restore competency

C. CARETAKER OR FAMILY INTERFERENCE

In some situations, an older adult's caretaker or family member may try to intervene or disrupt either the evaluation of the adult or the provision of services to him or her.

The law provides some options for addressing these challenges, but there may be times when DSS staff members will need to rely primarily on their social work skills to navigate such difficult situations.

CONSIDER WHETHER DSS SHOULD SEEK AN INJUNCTION TO PREVENT A CARETAKER FROM INTERFERING.

When an older adult has consented to the provision of protective services but his or her caretaker interferes with those services, DSS has the authority "to petition the district court for an order enjoining the caretaker from interfering."[90] Forms are available for both the petition and the order. If the caretaker continues to interfere after an order enjoining interference is issued, DSS may ask the court to hold the caretaker in contempt.[91]

Note that this type of court order is applicable only to a "caretaker," defined under statute to mean "an individual who has the responsibility for the care of the disabled adult as a result of family relationship or who has assumed the responsibility for the care of the disabled adult voluntarily or by contract."[92] If the person interfering is not a caretaker, options for DSS staff are more limited.

---

90. G.S. 108A-104(b).
91. G.S. 5A-21 (civil contempt).
92. G.S. 108A-101(b).

D. OBTAINING MEDICAL RECORDS FROM NON-CARETAKER MEDICAL PROVIDERS

In order to conduct a thorough evaluation in an APS case, social workers will often need to review medical records or talk with care providers. The state statute addressing the issue, G.S. 108A-103, is not entirely clear about DSS's right of access to otherwise confidential records. Subsection (a) of that law provides:

> When necessary for a complete evaluation of the report, the director shall have the authority to review and copy any and all records, or any part of such records, related to the care and treatment of the disabled adult that have been maintained by any individual, facility or agency acting as a caretaker for the disabled adult. This shall include but not be limited to records maintained by facilities licensed by the North Carolina Department of Health and Human Services.[93]

Some health care providers interpret this provision narrowly, arguing that it only allows DSS to have access to records if the involved provider was a "caretaker" of the adult. As discussed above, the term "caretaker" is defined in the law to mean someone who "has responsibility for the care of the disabled adult as a result of family relationship or who has assumed the responsibility for the care of the disabled adult voluntarily or by contract."[94] Some argue that the provision of medical services does not necessarily rise to the level of "assuming responsibility" for an adult's care. Others argue that such a narrow interpretation would defeat the purpose of the law and unnecessarily limit DSS's authority to conduct a thorough evaluation.

Subsection (b) of the same statute appears to support the latter argument. It states:

> The staff and physicians of local health departments, area mental health, developmental disabilities, and substance abuse authorities, and other public or private agencies shall cooperate fully with the director in the performance of his duties. These duties include immediate accessible evaluations and in-home evaluations where the director deems this necessary.[95]

Health care providers are subject to many different and complex confidentiality laws. Attorneys advising them may wish to see different language in the law to assure the providers that information-sharing is mandated. Typically, if a state law mandates disclosure, other medical confidentiality laws allow such disclosure.[96]

---

93. G.S. 108A-103(a).
94. G.S. 108A-101(b).
95. G.S. 108A-103(b).
96. *See, e.g.,* 45 C.F.R. § 164.512(a) (HIPAA Privacy Regulation allowing disclosures of protected health information if otherwise required by law). *But see* 42 C.F.R. pt. 2 (not allowing the disclosure of records from substance abuse treatment facilities when required by state law).

E. ADULT WITH CAPACITY REFUSES SERVICES

Older adults with decisional capacity have the right to refuse protective services. This fundamental concept can at times be frustrating for DSS because its social workers may recognize that an adult who has made such a refusal will suffer physical or financial harm if the agency does not intervene.

EXAMPLE

Jacob is 85 years old, is in a wheelchair, and has full decisional capacity. His son, along with his son's girlfriend, her children, and her children's spouses, all live in Jacob's large home. Jacob pays for all of the housing expenses and food for the entire group. Jacob primarily stays in one or two rooms in the house, while the group uses the rest of the space. His son's girlfriend provides Jacob with regular meals. Jacob's resources are being rapidly depleted but he tells DSS that he does not want anything to change because he wants to stay in his home and that this arrangement allows him to do so.

◇ **EXAMPLE**

John is 85 years old, is homebound, is in a wheelchair, and has full decisional capacity. His son, David, serves as his representative payee for Social Security benefits. David uses about one-quarter of the money each month to buy his father a few groceries and pay for his father's utilities. He uses the rest of the money for his own purposes. John refuses DSS's offer to serve as his representative payee and to either (1) locate an in-home aide for him or (2) find him a placement in a facility. John explains that he knows exactly what his son is doing but that he does not mind. He believes that if he changes the arrangement, his son will stop visiting him.

TRAIN DSS STAFF TO CAREFULLY BALANCE THE NEED TO PROTECT AGAINST THE NEED TO PRESERVE THE ADULT'S RIGHT TO SELF-DETERMINATION.

In each of these two examples, a social worker is going to have to spend a significant amount of time explaining potential consequences to the older adult. The social worker will carefully evaluate each situation to determine whether the older adult is being coerced or threatened and, if coercion or threats are found, will take steps to intervene. But if the older adult's decision to refuse services is truly one that the adult is making freely and with full knowledge of the potential consequences, it is essential that the social worker respect that decision.

Figure 2.2. **APS Process Overview**

Report
→ Screening
  → Screen out → Refer services and terminate
  → Screen in → Evaluation
    → No need for protective services → Refer services and terminate
    → Substantiated report
      → Capacity to consent
        → Consents → Provide services
        → Refuses → Refer and terminate
      → Lacks capacity to consent
        → Protective order → Provide services
        → Guardianship order → Provide services

Chapter 3
Criminal Investigation and Prosecution

CONTENTS

I.   SCOPE OF CHAPTER

This chapter provides an overview of the general landscape of criminal prosecution of elder abuse. It highlights some of the primary crimes implicated and provides an introduction to the actors involved in the prosecution of cases. Finally, it explores some of the challenges to prosecuting criminal cases involving older adults.

This chapter is not an in-depth guide to investigating and prosecuting an elder abuse case. Other resources have been developed specifically for law enforcement officials and prosecutors to support them in this work.[1] Rather, this chapter is designed to orient others involved with the elder protection system to the tools, processes, and challenges involved with criminal investigations and prosecutions.

In the context of crimes against older adults, criminal investigation and prosecution is unique in that it allows for the punishment of perpetrators. The other bodies of law discussed in this manual focus primarily on tools available through the civil legal system to protect an older adult or provide redress to the older adult or the adult's family. But criminal remedies are extremely important to the overall system of elder protection because they not only punish perpetrators but also possibly prevent further victimization of affected older adults and deter abuse of other older adults in the future.

North Carolina law does not establish a specific crime of "elder abuse." Instead, several crimes may be implicated if an older adult is being abused or exploited. While only two crimes focus specifically on older or disabled adults, many other generally applicable crimes—such as assault, rape, fraud, forgery, obtaining property by false pretenses, embezzlement, or robbery—may be applicable when a victim is an elder adult. A combination of local, state, and federal officials may be involved in both investigating and prosecuting these crimes.

II.   OVERVIEW OF CRIMINAL INVESTIGATION AND PROSECUTION

This section provides some context for understanding the landscape for criminal investigation and prosecution of elder abuse cases. Why is it important? Who is involved in this work? What are they able to do?

---

1. AEQUITAS, THE PROSECUTOR'S RESOURCE: ELDER ABUSE (current as of Apr. 2017), https://aequitasresource.org/wp-content/uploads/2018/09/Prosecutors-Resource-on-Elder-Abuse.pdf; Lori A. Stiegel, ABA Comm'n on Law & Aging, Legal Issues Related to Elder Abuse: A Pocket Guide for Law Enforcement (2014), https://www.americanbar.org/content/dam/aba/administrative/law_aging/2014_ElderAbusePocketGuides.authcheckdam.pdf; Ctr. for Elders and the Cts., *Toolkits for Prosecutors and Courts*, "Elder Abuse Toolkit for Prosecutors," http://www.eldersandcourts.org/Elder-Abuse/Toolkits-for-Prosecutors-and-Courts.aspx (last visited July 17, 2019); NAT'L CTR. FOR STATE CTS., PROSECUTING ELDER ABUSE CASES: BASIC TOOLS AND STRATEGIES (2012), https://www.bja.gov/Publications/NCSC-Prosecuting-Elder-Abuse-Cases-Basic-Tools-and-Strategies.pdf; U.S. Dep't of Justice, *Elder Justice Initiative (EJI)*, https://www.justice.gov/elderjustice (including resources for law enforcement and prosecutors) (last visited July 17, 2019); EAGLE (Elder Abuse Guide for Law Enforcement), http://eagle.trea.usc.edu/.

A. HOW DOES CRIMINAL INVESTIGATION AND PROSECUTION PROTECT ELDERS?

Criminal investigation and prosecution plays several important roles in the elder protection system, including

- gathering essential information during the course of the investigation that may be useful in the criminal proceeding as well as in other proceedings necessary to help the adult, such as protective services, guardianship, and other civil proceedings;

- taking immediate action to protect an adult in an emergent or urgent situation, such as taking a perpetrator into custody;

- holding perpetrators accountable;

- protecting the community by deterring perpetrators from targeting other victims;

- preserving and possibly restoring assets taken from victims of exploitation by obtaining an order to freeze assets of the perpetrator and seeking court-ordered restitution; and

- treating or otherwise rehabilitating perpetrators.[2]

B. WHAT ARE SOME OF THE POTENTIAL CRIMES THAT MAY BE INVOLVED WITH ELDER ABUSE?

Two criminal statutes, Chapter 14, Sections 32.3 and 112.2 of the North Carolina General Statutes (hereinafter G.S.), focus specifically on harms caused to disabled and older adults. The first addresses domestic abuse and neglect and the second addresses exploitation. Many other criminal statutes that apply regardless of the age of the victim, such as assault, theft, and embezzlement, may also be implicated in a particular case. Below is a detailed review of the specific crimes that focus on older adults and a general overview of the other potential crimes that may be appropriate to consider.

1. G.S. 14-32.3: DOMESTIC ABUSE AND NEGLECT OF DISABLED OR ELDER ADULTS

There are two separate crimes under G.S. 14-32.3: (1) abuse and (2) neglect. Previously the law addressed exploitation as well, but that crime has been moved to a separate statute (G.S. 14-112.2, discussed below). However, the title of G.S. 14-32.3 was not amended to conform to the change and still includes the word "exploitation."

---

2. *See* Arlene M. Markarian, "Protecting Elder Abuse Victims: Building the Case, Building the Team," presentation at National Center for Victims of Crime 2012 National Conference (2012), https://victimsofcrime.org/docs/Toolkit%20 Bulletins/natl-center-for-victims-of-crime-conf-ea-handouts.pdf?sfvrsn=0.

A person may be guilty of **abuse** if

- the person is a caretaker of a disabled[3] or elder adult who is residing in a domestic setting;

- the person, with malice aforethought, knowingly and willfully

  - assaults the adult,

  - fails to provide the adult with medical or hygienic care, or

  - confines or restrains the adult in a place or under a condition that is cruel or unsafe, and

- the adult suffers mental or physical injury as a result.[4]

A person may be guilty of **neglect** if

- the person is a caretaker of a disabled or elder adult who is residing in a domestic setting;

- the person wantonly, recklessly, or with gross carelessness

  - fails to provide the adult with medical or hygienic care or

  - confines or restrains the adult in a place or under a condition that is unsafe; and

- the adult suffers mental or physical injury as a result.[5]

For both of these crimes—abuse and neglect—the statute includes some definitions that are key to establishing a sound case.

---

3. Chapter 14, Section 32.3(d)(2) of the North Carolina General Statutes (hereinafter G.S.) (This statute defines "disabled adult" as someone who is "18 years of age or older or a lawfully emancipated minor who is present in the State of North Carolina and who is physically or mentally incapacitated as defined in G.S. 108A-101(d)." G.S. 108A-101(d) defines physical or mental incapacitation as being caused by "an intellectual disability, cerebral palsy, epilepsy or autism; organic brain damage caused by advanced age or other physical degeneration in connection therewith; or due to conditions incurred at any age which are the result of accident, organic brain damage, mental or physical illness, or continued consumption or absorption of substances." Some older adults will satisfy the definition of "disabled," but many others will not.).

4. G.S. 14-32.3(a).

5. G.S. 14-32.3(b).

Caretaker *is defined in the law as a "person who has the responsibility for the care of a disabled or elder adult as a result of family relationship or who has assumed the responsibility for the care of a disabled or elder adult voluntarily or by contract."[6] If the perpetrator of the abuse is a stranger, family member, or friend who is not actually responsible for the care of the older adult, prosecutors will not be able to charge this crime.*

Elder adult *is defined as a "person 60 years of age or older who is not able to provide for the social, medical, psychiatric, psychological, financial, or legal services necessary to safeguard the person's rights and resources and to maintain the person's physical and mental well-being."[7] In some cases, older adults may be subject to abuse or neglect but they may still be able to provide for their own needs. If so, prosecutors will not be able to charge this crime.*

Domestic setting *is defined as "any residential setting except for a health care facility or residential care facility. . . ."[8] This means that prosecutors will not be able to charge this particular crime if the abuse occurred in places such as hospitals, nursing homes, or rehabilitation or assisted living facilities. The crime also does not apply to abuse or neglect by staff of home health agencies.*

While these definitions are somewhat limiting, it is important to remember that other crimes of general applicability may be options for prosecutors. For example, abuse or neglect by a home health worker or a staff person in an assisted living facility is subject to a separate criminal law governing patient abuse and neglect.[9]

G.S. 14-32.3 requires a different state of mind for each of the two crimes it covers. Abuse requires the prosecutor to prove that the perpetrator acted "with malice aforethought, knowingly and willfully."[10] Neglect, on the other hand, will likely be easier to establish because it requires the prosecutor to prove that the perpetrator acted wantonly, recklessly, or with gross carelessness, a lower standard of proof than malice aforethought.[11] Briefly, a malicious state of mind may be proved by showing that a perpetrator's conduct

---

6. G.S. 14-32.3(d)(1).
7. G.S. 14-32.3(d)(4).
8. G.S. 14-32.3(d)(3).
9. G.S. 14-32.2.
10. *See* JESSICA SMITH, NORTH CAROLINA CRIMES: A GUIDEBOOK ON THE ELEMENTS OF CRIME 3–10 (7th ed. 2012) (discussing states of mind from intentional to negligent conduct).
11. *See id.*

was intentional and done with ill will or hatred, while wanton, reckless, or gross careless-ness is indicated by conduct exhibiting a thoughtless disregard of consequences or an indifference to the harm that may be done to others.[12]

Both crimes require that the older adult suffer mental or physical injury. The conse-quences of conviction will be more severe if the injury suffered by the older adult was *seri-ous*. (See Table 3.1, below.) According to the pattern jury instructions used by judges and attorneys, an injury is "serious" if it "causes great pain and suffering."[13] A mental injury may be sufficient to meet the definition of a "serious personal injury" if (1) it extends for an "appreciable" period of time beyond the circumstances of the crime and (2) it is a mental injury beyond that normally experienced in other crimes of the same type.[14] Examples of evidence of mental injuries that were found to have risen to the level of a "serious personal injury" include nightmares, difficulty sleeping, severe disruption to normal life activities, and the victim's need for therapy to overcome the lingering trauma from the crime.[15]

Both crimes—abuse and neglect—include an exception for situations in which a care-taker acted or failed to act in a manner that was consistent with state law related to a "natural death."[16] In this context, a natural death is one resulting from the withholding or discontinuation of life-prolonging measures. North Carolina has two separate laws that govern situations involving a natural death—one law addresses when a person has declared his or her wishes related to natural death and the second addresses when a per-son has not made a specific declaration.[17]

12. *See* State v. Sexton, 357 N.C. 235, 237–38 (2003) (discussing malice); State v. Jones, 353 N.C. 159, 165 (2000) (defining criminal negligence in terms of reckless and careless conduct).

13. N.C.P.I.—CRIM. 120.12; State v. Boone, 307 N.C. 198 (1982), *overruled on other grounds by* State v. Richmond, 347 N.C. 412, *cert. denied*, 525 U.S. 843 (1998).

14. State v. Baker, 336 N.C. 58, 64 (1994); *Boone*, 307 N.C. at 590.

15. *See, e.g.*, State v. Lilly, 117 N.C. App. 192 (1994), *aff'd per curiam*, 342 N.C. 409 (1995); State v. Davis, 101 N.C. App. 12 (1990). *See also* State v. Ackerman, 144 N.C. App. 452 (2001) (involving a combination of physical and mental injuries).

16. G.S. 14-32.3(a), (b) (both subsections provide that a caretaker is not guilty of a crime if the act or failure to act is in accordance with G.S. 90-321 or -322, which describe procedures for withholding or discontinuing life-prolonging measures).

17. G.S. 90-321 (declaration); -322 (no declaration).

Table 3.1. **Comparing Abuse and Neglect under G.S. 14-32.3**

	ABUSE	NEGLECT
Is perpetrator a caretaker of a disabled or elder adult in a domestic setting?	Yes	Yes
State of mind	With malice aforethought, knowingly and willfully	Wantonly, recklessly, or with gross carelessness
Acts or omissions	The perpetrator assaults the adult, fails to provide the adult with medical or hygienic care, or confines or restrains the adult in a place or under a condition that is cruel or unsafe.	The perpetrator fails to provide the adult with medical or hygienic care or confines or restrains the adult in a place or under a condition that is unsafe.
Did adult suffer mental or physical injury as a result of perpetrator's actions?	Yes	Yes
Exception for health care facilities and residential facilities?	Yes	Yes
Exception for acts complying with laws related to natural death?	Yes	Yes
Penalty[18]	• Class H (not serious injury) • Class F (serious injury)	• Class I (not serious injury) • Class G (serious injury)

See Section III.H. of this chapter for more discussion of the limitations of the abuse and neglect statutes.

In addition to the elder-specific abuse crimes set out in G.S. 14-32.3 and described above, several other crimes may be relevant when an older adult is physically abused. See Section II.B.3, below, for a list of possible crimes and Appendix C for more detailed summaries of

---

18. A number of factors determine the type and length of punishment a perpetrator may receive, including the class of offense, the perpetrator's prior record level, and possible enhancements or aggravating or mitigating factors. A perpetrator could receive an active sentence or a suspended sentence with either supervised or unsupervised probation. In addition, a perpetrator may be required to pay fines, costs, other fees, or restitution to the victim. For more information on sentencing factors and guidelines, see JAMES M. MARKHAM & SHEA RIGGSBEE DENNING, NORTH CAROLINA SENTENCING HANDBOOK (2018 ed.).

each. Two crimes in particular focus on specific populations that may be relevant in a case involving an older adult.

- **Assault on an individual with a disability (G.S. 14-32.1).** Under this law, the term "individual with a disability" is defined so broadly that it likely encompasses many older adults. The term refers to any individual who has a physical disability, a mental disability, or an infirmity "that would substantially impair the ability to defend oneself."[19] A simple assault under this law is a Class A1 misdemeanor.[20] The penalty increases to a Class F felony if the assault was aggravated (i.e., if the person used a deadly weapon or force likely to inflict serious injury or serious damage, inflicted serious injury or serious damage to the victim, or intended to kill the victim).[21]

- **Patient abuse or neglect (G.S. 14-32.2).** Under this law, it is a crime to physically abuse a patient when that abuse results in death or bodily injury.[22] "Abuse" is defined broadly enough to capture neglect in some circumstances because it includes conduct that is "culpably negligent," which means the conduct was "of a willful, gross and flagrant character, evincing reckless disregard of human life."[23] This law applies (1) to patients in medical facilities, such as hospitals and skilled nursing facilities (nursing homes), or in residential care facilities, such as adult care homes, and (2) to care by home health agencies.[24] Penalties range from Class C to Class H felonies, depending on the perpetrator's state of mind and the harm caused.[25]

Because the specific crime related to abuse and neglect of an older adult is somewhat narrow in scope, it is essential to think creatively about other possible crimes that may be involved in these cases.

2. G.S. 14-112.2: EXPLOITATION OF AN OLDER ADULT OR DISABLED ADULT

G.S. 14-112.2 includes two separate crimes of exploitation of an elder: one requires a specific relationship with the disabled or older adult and the other does not. At the outset, it should be noted that this law applies to adults who are 65 years of age or older, which is different from the other "elder adult" criminal law (G.S. 14-32.3), which applies to adults 60 years of age or older.[26]

A person may be guilty of **relationship-based exploitation** if

- the person either

  - stands in a position of trust and confidence with the adult or

  - has a business relationship with the adult;

---

19. G.S. 14-32.1(a).
20. G.S. 14-32.1(f). Note that a simple assault on a non-disabled person is a Class 2 misdemeanor. *Id.* § 14-33(a).
21. G.S. 14-32.1(e).
22. G.S. 14-32.2(a).
23. G.S. 14-32.2(e).
24. G.S. 14-32.2(a), (c), (c1).
25. G.S. 14-32.2(b).
26. G.S. 14-112.2(a)(2).

- the person
  - knowingly,
  - by deception or intimidation,
  - obtained, used, or endeavored to obtain or use
  - the adult's funds, assets or property; and
- the person intended to
  - temporarily or permanently deprive the adult or
  - benefit someone other than the adult.[27]

A person may otherwise be guilty of **exploitation** under this statute if

- the person
  - knowingly,
  - by deception or intimidation,
  - obtained, used, endeavored to obtain or use, or conspired to obtain or use
  - the adult's funds, assets, or property;
- the person intended to
  - temporarily or permanently deprive the adult or
  - benefit someone other than the adult; and
- the person was not acting within the scope of his or her lawful authority as agent for the adult.[28]

Table 3.2. **Comparing Penalties for Exploitation**[29]

VALUE OF FUNDS, ASSETS, OR PROPERTY	RELATIONSHIP-BASED EXPLOITATION	OTHER EXPLOITATION
< $20,000	Class H felony	Class I felony
$20,000 to $100,000	Class G felony	Class H felony
$100,000+	Class F felony	Class G felony

---

27. G.S. 14-112.2(b).
28. G.S. 14-112.2(c).
29. G.S. 14-112.2(d), (e).

If a person (defendant) is charged with either of the two exploitation crimes listed in G.S. 14-112.2 and the amount involved is valued at more than $5,000, the prosecutor may ask the court to freeze or seize enough of the defendant's assets to preserve them for potential restitution to the victim.[30] Key points to consider about "freeze and seize" orders are set out below.

> ## ✎ PRACTICE NOTE
> ### *"Freeze and Seize" Orders*
>
> - Only the prosecutor has the authority to request this type of order.
> - Procedurally, the prosecutor must file a petition in the pending criminal proceeding consistent with state rules governing injunctions as well as the specific rules governing these particular types of orders.[31]
> - In order to succeed, the prosecutor must prove by clear and convincing evidence that the defendant is about to or intends to "divest himself or herself of assets in a manner that would render the defendant insolvent for purposes of restitution."[32]
> - The court may issue an order affecting the defendant's assets in an amount equal to up to 150 percent of the value of the victim's potentially exploited assets.[33]

In practice, it is still somewhat unusual for prosecutors to rely on this tool for preserving assets. According to a recent elder abuse prosecution manual produced by the North Carolina Conference of District Attorneys, the requirement that the prosecutor prove that the defendant "is about to or intends to divest" the assets may be so difficult to establish that it serves as a significant deterrent for prosecutors.

3. OTHER CRIMES THAT MAY BE APPLICABLE IN ELDER ABUSE CASES

There are many other crimes that may be appropriate for prosecutors to consider in cases involving elder abuse. While a full summary and analysis of every possible law is beyond the scope of this manual, Table 3.3, below, includes a list of some of the potentially relevant crimes and Appendix C includes a more detailed review of each crime, including the elements associated with each.

---

30. G.S. 14-112.2(f).
31. G.S. 14-112.3(b) (referencing G.S. 1A-1, Rule 65, regarding injunctions).
32. G.S. 14-112.3(d).
33. G.S. 14-112.2(f).

Table 3.3. Crimes That May Be Charged in Elder Abuse Cases

RAPE AND OTHER SEX OFFENSES	
Crime	**Statute (G.S.)**
First-Degree Forcible Rape	14-27.21
Second-Degree Forcible Rape	14-27.22
First-Degree Forcible Sexual Offense	14-27.26
Second-Degree Forcible Sexual Offense	14-27.27
Sexual Battery	14-27.33
Crime Against Nature	14-177
ASSAULTS	
Crime	**Statute (G.S.)**
Assault with a Deadly Weapon with Intent to Kill Inflicting Serious Injury	14-32(a)
Assault with a Deadly Weapon Inflicting Serious Injury	14-32(b)
Assault with a Deadly Weapon with Intent to Kill	14-32(c)
Assault on an Individual with a Disability	14-32.1
Patient Abuse or Neglect	14-32.2
Assault Inflicting Serious Bodily Injury	14-32.4(a)
Assault by Strangulation	14-32.4(b)
Simple Assault	14-33(a)
Assault Inflicting Serious Injury	14-33(c)(1)
Assault on a Female	14-33(c)(2)
Habitual Misdemeanor Assault	14-33.2
KIDNAPPINGS	
Crime	**Statute (G.S.)**
First-Degree Kidnapping	14-39
Second-Degree Kidnapping	14-39
False Imprisonment	Common law
Felonious Restraint	14-43.3
BURGLARY AND OTHER HOUSEBREAKINGS	
Crime	**Statute (G.S.)**
First-Degree Burglary	14-51
Second-Degree Burglary	14-51
Breaking or Entering a Building with Intent to Commit Felony or Larceny	14-54(a)
Breaking or Entering a Building with Intent to Terrorize or Injure Occupant	14-54(a1)
Misdemeanor Breaking or Entering	14-54(b)
Break or Enter Motor Vehicle with Intent to Commit Felony or Larceny	14-56

Table 3.3. *cont'd*

LARCENY AND ROBBERY	
Crime	**Statute (G.S.)**
Felony Larceny	14-72
Misdemeanor Larceny	14-72
Larceny, Concealment or Destruction of Wills	14-77
Robbery with a Dangerous Weapon	14-87
Common Law Robbery	Common law; *see* 14-87.1
Extortion	14-118.4
OTHER FINANCIAL AND RELATED CRIMES	
Crime	**Statute (G.S.)**
Embezzlement by an Agent or Fiduciary	14-90
Obtain Property by False Pretenses	14-100
Obtain Signature by False Pretenses	14-101
Obtain Advance by False Promise to Work	14-104
Financial Transaction Card Theft	14-113.9(a)(1)
Forgery of Financial Transaction Card	14-113.11
Financial Transaction Card Fraud	14-113.13
Financial Identity Theft	14-113.20
Common Law Forgery	See 14-119, -120
Common Law Uttering	See 14-120
Forgery and Counterfeiting of Instruments	14-119
Uttering Forged Instruments	14-120
Forging an Endorsement on Checks and Securities	14-120
MISCELLANEOUS	
Crime	**Statute (G.S.)**
Indecent Exposure	14-190
Using Threatening Language on the Telephone	14-196(a)(2)
Repeated Telephone Calls to Harass, etc.	14-196(a)(3)
Using Electronic Mail or Communication to Threaten or Extort	14-196(b)(1)
Communicating Threats	14-277.1
Stalking	14-277.3A
Interfering with Emergency Communication	14-286.2
Violation of a Domestic Violence Protective Order	50B-4.1

C. WHO IS RESPONSIBLE FOR CRIMINAL INVESTIGATION OF ELDER ABUSE?

Many agencies and officials are involved in the investigation of potential criminal activity involving elder abuse, including

- local law enforcement officials, such as police officers and sheriff's deputies;

- state law enforcement officials, such as the N.C. Department of Justice and the N.C. Secretary of State; and

- federal law enforcement officials, such as the U.S. Department of Justice, the Internal Revenue Service, and the U.S. Postal Service.

Law enforcement officials will become involved in elder abuse cases only if their agencies have jurisdiction. An agency will have jurisdiction in certain geographic areas and in certain types of cases. Occasionally, jurisdiction is limited to one type of agency, but most often agencies have overlapping and concurrent authority. (See Table 3.4.)

Table 3.4. **Law Enforcement Officials Involved with Elder Abuse Investigations—Territorial Jurisdiction**

LAW ENFORCEMENT OFFICER	JURISDICTION TO ARREST	AUTHORIZING STATUTE (G.S.)
State officers	At any place within the state	15A-402(a)
County and city officers	Within the officer's particular city or county and on any property and rights-of-way owned by the city or county outside its territorial limits	15A-402(b)
	May pursue someone outside the territory for a crime committed within the territory if arrest is made during the person's immediate and continuous flight from that territory	15A-402(d)
City officers	If outside the city: within one mile or less from the nearest point in the boundary of that city	15A-402(c)
County officers[34]	At any place within the state for a felony committed within the officer's territory	15A-402(e)
Federal officer[35]	May enforce criminal laws anywhere in the state when a state or local law enforcement agency or officer has asked for temporary assistance and the request is within the scope of that agency's or officer's subject matter and territorial jurisdiction	15A-406(a)–(b)

---

34. For felonies, the term "county officer" includes officers of consolidated city-county law enforcement agencies. G.S. 15A-402(e).

35. Includes certain types of law enforcement officers if they are employed full-time by the federal government.

Typically, municipal and county law enforcement officials work closely together to refer cases to each other and to federal or state agencies when it is appropriate to do so. Chapter 7 describes many of the state and federal agencies that could be involved in an elder abuse case and their respective areas of authority.

Examples include Federal Bureau of Investigation special agents, Drug Enforcement Administration special agents, United States Customs Service officers, United States Postal Service inspectors, Internal Revenue Service special agents, United States Marshals Service marshals and deputies, and Immigration and Naturalization Service officers. G.S. 15A-406(a).

Figure 3.1. **N.C. Prosecutorial Districts**

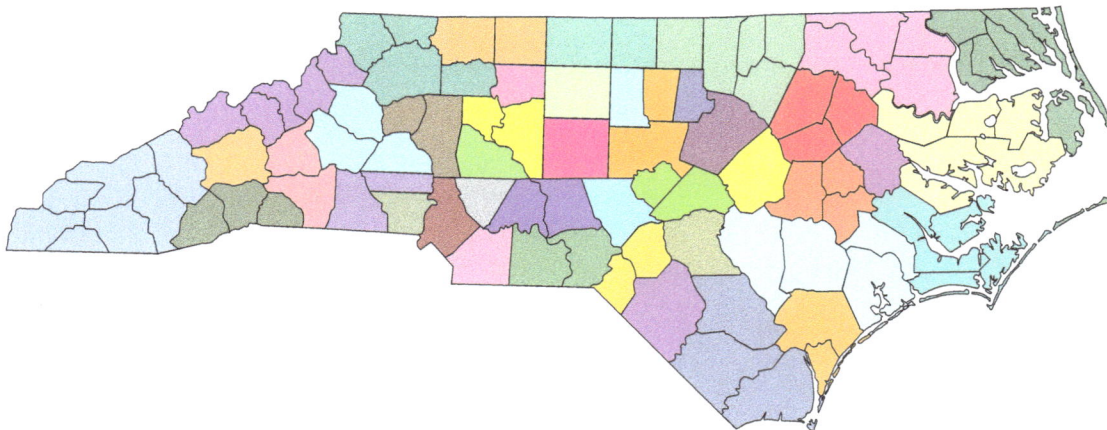

D. WHO IS RESPONSIBLE FOR CRIMINAL PROSECUTION IN ELDER ABUSE CASES?

District attorneys (DAs) are elected public officials who are responsible for prosecuting all state criminal actions in their respective prosecutorial districts.[36] While North Carolina has one hundred counties, the state is divided into forty-three prosecutorial districts, meaning that some district attorney offices have jurisdiction in more than one county.[37] (See Figure 3.1.)

Each DA's office employs a number of assistant district attorneys (ADAs), who typically are involved with the daily work of prosecuting elder abuse cases. The offices also have their own investigators, victim witness legal assistants, and other administrative staff who support the office's work.

The DA's office prosecutes criminal matters on behalf of the State. DAs work closely with the local law enforcement officials in their districts, who refer cases to the DA for prosecution and coordinate with the DA's office on case management. Because the DA represents the State rather than the individual victims of crime, the office may proceed with a case without the express cooperation of the victim.

With regard to federal law, the United States Attorney's Office serves as the prosecutor.[38] North Carolina has three federal prosecutorial districts: Eastern, Middle, and Western.[39] Some state and federal agencies also have prosecutorial authority and often coordinate efforts for both investigations and prosecutions. For example, the U.S. Department of

---

36. N.C. CONST. art. IV, § 18; G.S. 7A-61 (describing general duties of district attorneys); -63 (describing general duties of assistant district attorneys).

37. G.S. 7A-60. Note that effective January 1, 2023, prosecutorial districts will increase by one, to forty-four districts. *Id.* § 7A-60 (a1) (this statute has multiple subsections designated as (a1), each with a different effective time period).

38. U.S. Dep't of Just., Offices of the U.S. Att'ys, *Mission* (updated Sept. 22, 2016), https://www.justice.gov/usao/mission.

39. *See* U.S. Cts., *Court Website Links*, USCOURTS.GOV, https://www.uscourts.gov/about-federal-courts/federal-courts-public/court-website-links (showing a map of geographic boundaries of all U.S. Courts of Appeals and U.S. District Courts) (last visited July 19, 2019); U.S. Dist. Ct., E. Dist. of N.C., *County List,* NCED.USCOURTS.GOV, http://www.nced.uscourts.gov/counties/Default.aspx (showing a map and a list of counties in this district) (last visited July 19, 2019).

Justice issued a press release in February 2018 highlighting a nationwide "sweep" of elder abuse cases.[40] The cases involved a wide range of federal authorities and state attorneys general. One case in North Carolina related to a lottery scam. The defendant was a mail carrier who accepted cash for diverting packages.[41]

E. HOW DOES CRIMINAL INVESTIGATION AND PROSECUTION WORK IN ELDER ABUSE CASES?

A criminal case involving elder abuse may begin in several different ways.

- **Reporting.** A member of the public, such as a victim or a family member of a victim, or a representative of an organization, such as a bank or health care provider, makes a report of suspected elder abuse directly to 911 or law enforcement.

- **Agency referral.** Another government agency, such as the county department of social services, notifies law enforcement officials of suspected abuse.

- **Other investigations.** Officers, investigators, or prosecutors uncover evidence of elder abuse when investigating another crime.

Below is a brief overview of each possible path for initiating a criminal elder abuse case.

1. REPORTING

In almost all situations, a person who suspects that an older adult is being abused, neglected, or exploited is allowed to report those suspicions to law enforcement directly. Some professionals, such as social workers and medical professionals, may be subject to confidentiality laws that limit voluntary reporting. In addition to voluntary reporting, North Carolina has four mandatory reporting laws that may come into play in an elder abuse case. (See Table 3.5, below.)

---

40. Press Release, U.S. Dep't of Just., Justice Department Coordinates Nationwide Elder Fraud Sweep of More Than 250 Defendants (Feb. 22, 2018), https://www.justice.gov/opa/pr/justice-department-coordinates-nationwide-elder-fraud-sweep-more-250-defendants.

41. Bill of Indictment, United States v. Brown, No. 3:17-cr-00047-RJC-DCK (W.D.N.C. Feb. 22, 2017), https://www.justice.gov/opa/page/file/1037356/download; Press Release, U.S. Att'y's Off., W. Dist. of N.C., Former Charlotte-Area Mail Carrier Pleads Guilty to Mail Theft in Connection with Jamaican-Based Lottery Fraud Scheme (Apr. 3, 2017), https://www.justice.gov/usao-wdnc/pr/former-charlotte-area-mail-carrier-pleads-guilty-mail-theft-connection-jamaican-based.

Table 3.5. **Selected North Carolina Mandatory Reporting Laws**

WHO REPORTS?	WHEN/WHAT TO REPORT?	WHO TO REPORT TO?
Any person[42]	Report if there is reason to believe that a disabled adult needs protection from potential abuse, neglect, or exploitation	County DSS DSS must share information with the district attorney in certain situations[43]
Financial institutions and their officers and employees[44]	Report if there is reason to suspect that a disabled or older adult (65 or over) is the target or the victim of financial exploitation	Local law enforcement County DSS if the adult is disabled
Physicians and hospitals[45]	Report if physicians/hospitals treat wounds, injuries, or illnesses that arise from a gunshot wound, poisoning, knife, or sharp instrument (1) if it appears that a criminal act was involved or (2) that cause grave bodily harm or grave illness if it appears that the harm or illness resulted from a criminal act of violence	Local law enforcement
Licensed adult care homes[46]	Report any incidents of abuse, neglect, or exploitation of a resident by a person certified as an assisted living administrator	Health Care Personnel Registry

If a report is made to law enforcement, it can go to either the police or the sheriff. The law enforcement agency responsible for responding to and following up on the report will vary depending on whether the older adult is within a city (police) or in an unincorporated area of a county (sheriff). It may be that other law enforcement officials, such as campus police or private security, receive the report or are involved in the response. These law enforcement agencies typically communicate and coordinate regularly to determine which agency will be primarily responsible for the initial investigation. For the reporter, it is a matter of simply getting the report submitted as fast as possible so that the appropriate unit can respond quickly.

---

42. G.S. 108A-102(a), (b). There is one exception to this reporting requirement. If the subject of a complaint filed with the Long Term Care Ombudsman Program relates to potential abuse, neglect, or exploitation, regional program staff may submit a report to the county DSS only with (1) permission from the state or (2) the written, informed consent of the adult. G.S. 143B-181.20(f).

43. G.S. 108A-109.

44. G.S. 108A-115.

45. G.S. 90-21.20.

46. G.S. 90-288.19.

2. AGENCY REFERRAL

As mentioned above, state law requires every person who has "reasonable cause to believe that a disabled adult is in need of protective services" to report that belief to the county social services agency (DSS).[47] The agency will then screen and act on such a report in accordance with the adult protective services (APS) law. See Chapter 1 for more details about APS. While APS is subject to many confidentiality laws, those laws also recognize the importance of sharing information with law enforcement officials. The statutes address this exchange of information in several ways.

- **Immediate notification.** APS may contact the district attorney or law enforcement officials immediately after receiving a report if there is reason to believe that physical harm to the disabled adult may occur. In this situation, APS may share information that would otherwise be confidential, including most health information.[48]

- **After an evaluation.** If the county social services agency finds evidence of abuse, neglect, or exploitation of a disabled (possibly older) adult, it is required to notify the district attorney in writing.[49] The notification is required to include

  - the name, address, age, and condition of the adult;

  - the allegations (excluding the identity of the reporter);

  - the agency's evaluation, including findings and supporting documents such as medical records;

  - the agency's conclusions and recommendations for action.[50]

  While conducting a criminal investigation or prosecution, law enforcement officials may want to know the identity of the person who made the report or the identities of other people who provided information to DSS in the course of the protective services evaluation. In this situation, DSS may share this information with law enforcement officials or prosecutors upon request.[51]

In some jurisdictions, a single individual or unit within the DA's office may be responsible for coordinating with APS or receiving these agency referrals. Once received, staff with the DA's office will likely then follow a protocol for initiating potential criminal investigations.

---

47. G.S. 108A-102.

48. Title 10A, Chapter 71A, Section .0201(c) of the North Carolina Administrative Code (N.C.A.C.). DSS would not be able to share information subject to the Federal Substance Abuse Confidentiality regulation. 42 C.F.R. pt. 2 ("Confidentiality of Substance Use Disorder Patient Records").

49. G.S. 108A-109 (requires reporting); 10A N.C.A.C. 71A, § .0906 (requires that the report be in writing).

50. 10A N.C.A.C. 71A, § .0901.

51. 10A N.C.A.C. 71A, § .0802(2).

3. OTHER INVESTIGATIONS

As discussed in Chapter 1, one of the most challenging issues facing the professionals involved in elder protection is underreporting. Fortunately, law enforcement officials and prosecutors may be able to look for clues of elder abuse, neglect, or exploitation in other reports and cases to which they have access.

> ◇ **EXAMPLE**
>
> *A case involving an 80-year-old widowed woman first came to the attention of the DA's office when a man was charged with obtaining property by false pretenses after stealing the woman's lawnmower. As part of the criminal case, the victim's daughter offered a five-page impact statement detailing how the man had exploited her mother, who was suffering from dementia. He had insinuated himself into her life by doing chores for her. Over the course of two years, he ended up obtaining $140,000 in loans and a land transfer from the victim, which required her to take out two mortgages on her home. The man was successfully prosecuted and sentenced to five years for exploitation of an elder.*[52]

With this access and with increased awareness of elder abuse generally, law enforcement officials and prosecutors can take the time to dig deeper and ask questions that will help identify these difficult and sometimes hidden crimes.

Once potential elder abuse comes to the attention of law enforcement, local officers (police, sheriff) will typically conduct an investigation. A full review of the investigatory process is beyond the scope of this manual. In 2019, the North Carolina Conference of District Attorneys was finalizing an elder abuse manual for prosecutors. Once available, it should be able to provide additional information and support for law enforcement officials. Some key concepts for others involved with the elder protection system to understand about the investigatory process are listed below.

- Local law enforcement officials have expansive authority to investigate suspected criminal violations. Other components of the elder protection system have more narrowly tailored authority. For example, APS focuses on serving adults who are disabled, guardianship is limited to those who are found to be incompetent by a court, and legal aid is typically available to lower-income clients. The broader authority of law enforcement serves as an essential safeguard for older adults.

- While law enforcement officials have expansive authority to investigate criminal activity, they are somewhat limited in their ability to provide direct assistance to the older adults who have been harmed or are at risk.

---

52. Interview with Lori Wickline, Assistant District Attorney, Alamance County District Attorney's Office, in Chapel Hill, N.C. (June 28, 2018).

- Victim assistance advocates will be able to provide support and services to any older adult who has been the victim of or who witnesses a violent crime.

- Law enforcement may reach out to other components of the system for help. For example, APS may be able to help the affected adult find alternative housing or residential care. A private attorney may need to help the older adult obtain a protective order.

- Some communities have a "Family Justice Center" that serves as a coordinating hub for many of the services and supports an older adult may need after experiencing abuse. (See sidebar below.)

- Information-sharing and collaboration at the early stages of an investigation involving an older adult can be especially important. For example, a law enforcement official may have concerns that an older adult is being financially exploited. The official may reach out to APS to ask the agency to take immediate steps to freeze the adult's assets. Each component of the elder protection system should have a clear understanding of the laws and policies that govern the sharing of information with law enforcement officials to minimize delay and maximize cooperation.

📖 RESOURCE

Family Justice Centers in North Carolina

At least three counties in North Carolina have established Family Justice Centers that incorporate supports and services for elder abuse.

- Family Justice Center of Alamance County, https://www.alamance-nc.com/fjc/
- Buncombe County Family Justice Center, https://www.buncombecounty.org/law-safety/family-justice-center/
- Guilford County Family Justice Center, https://www.guilfordcountync.gov/our-county/family-justice-center

While there are differences between the centers, they are all designed to provide centralized access to coordinated services from a wide array of professionals, such as law enforcement officials, social workers, health care providers, victim advocates, and attorneys.

Once law enforcement officials have investigated a case alleging elder abuse, neglect, or exploitation, they refer it to the DA's office for prosecution. A law enforcement officer explained that "[i]t's like a hand off in a football play. . . . We developed the investigation, collected the evidence and the facts. Once we hit that point and established probable cause exists, we charge the appropriate charges and hand it over to the prosecution."[53]

---

53. Abigail Margulis, *Cases of Elder Abuse Hard to Prosecute*, BLUERIDGENOW.COM (Times-News Online) (Jan. 31, 2016), https://www.blueridgenow.com/news/20160131/cases-of-elder-abuse-hard-to-prosecute.

The DA's office decides whether to prosecute a named person criminally and, if so, with what charges.[54] As the North Carolina Supreme Court has stated,

> District attorneys have wide discretion in performing the duties of their office. This encompasses the discretion to decide who will or will not be prosecuted. In making such decisions, district attorneys must weigh many factors such as "the likelihood of successful prosecution, the social value of obtaining a conviction as against the time and expense to the State, and his own sense of justice in the particular case."[55]

Perhaps the most important issue a prosecutor will wrestle with is the last one that arises: How will justice best be served in this particular case?

◇ **EXAMPLE**

A young man was charged with financial card theft after taking his grandmother's credit card and using it for his own purposes. The grandmother asked the prosecutor to dismiss the charges, arguing that he didn't mean to do it. Taking the matter at face value, the prosecutor could have simply charged the grandson with a misdemeanor. However, having received elder abuse training, she spent a little extra time, no more than fifteen to twenty minutes, asking the grandmother for more information. She discovered that the grandson had forcefully stolen the credit card by throwing the victim down and taking the card out of her back pocket. The grandmother admitted that her grandson had also assaulted her in the past and that he had drug problems. She was afraid of anything bad happening to her grandson, though, noting that she had mostly raised him since his mother had committed suicide and that his father was a drug addict who abandoned the family. The prosecutor considered the situation and allowed some time for the grandson to attend rehab and look for work. He followed through on both of these things, and the prosecutor considered proceeding with a misdemeanor, thereby avoiding subjecting the grandson to a felony, which would have more serious collateral consequences for him throughout his life. Taking into account the twin goals of victim safety and offender accountability, the prosecutor considers the matter to be a rare success in trying to achieve justice for all involved.[56]

If a prosecutor elects to proceed with an elder abuse case, the decisions he or she makes (e.g., with regard to strategy, witnesses, evidence, plea deals, etc.) could have a significant impact on the potential outcomes.

---

54. State v. Spicer, 299 N.C. 309, 311 (1980). A prosecutor also has an ethical duty not to bring charges he or she knows are not supported by probable cause. N.C. R. PROF'L CONDUCT. 3.8 (N.C. State Bar 1997) (last amended Mar. 16, 2017), https://www.ncbar.gov/for-lawyers/ethics/rules-of-professional-conduct/rule-38-special-responsibilities-of-a-prosecutor/.

55. *Spicer*, 299 N.C. at 311.

56. Interview with Lori Wickline, *supra* note 52.

While a detailed review of the process of prosecuting a criminal case is beyond the scope of this manual, other resources tailored to prosecutors and other participants in the criminal justice system are available.[57]

> ### ✏️ PRACTICE NOTE
>
> The state of North Carolina has a special fund dedicated to reimbursing crime victims for medical expenses and lost wages associated with certain crimes such as assault and rape.[58] In order to be eligible for reimbursement, the crime must be reported to law enforcement within seventy-two hours and a claim must be filed within two years.[59] Applications are available online at https://www.ncdps.gov/DPS-Services/Victim-Services. Alternatively, a victim or a representative may contact Victim Services at the N.C. Department of Public Safety at 800-826-6200 or 919-733-7974.

III. CHALLENGES TO CRIMINAL INVESTIGATION AND PROSECUTION

A. NATURE OF THE VICTIM

Investigators and prosecutors may be deterred from pursuing an elder abuse case because the victim (and possibly some witnesses) are older. They may have concerns about the reliability of an older adult's memory or the ability of the adult to physically participate in an investigation or trial.[60] When these concerns are not grounded in reality but are generalized to the population of older adults as a whole, they are biases. The American Bar Association's Criminal Justice Standards for the Prosecution Function include an explicit prohibition on manifesting or exercising "by words or conduct, bias or prejudice based upon race, sex, religion, national origin, disability, age, sexual orientation, gender identity, or socioeconomic status." The Standards also direct the prosecutor's office to be "proactive in efforts to detect, investigate, and eliminate improper biases . . . ."[61] Therefore, it is essential that investigators and prosecutors avoid age-related biases and assumptions.

---

57. OFF. OF KY. ATT'Y GEN., PROSECUTION MANUAL FOR CRIMES AGAINST THE ELDERLY (2018); Lori A. Stiegel, ABA Comm'n on Law & Aging, Legal Issues Related to Elder Abuse: A Desk Guide for Law Enforcement (2015), available for download at https://www.americanbar.org/groups/law_aging/resources/elder_abuse/legal_issues_related_to_elder_abuse_guides/.

58. G.S. Ch. 15B, Art. 1 (Crime Victims Compensation Act).

59. G.S. 15B-11(a)(1), (3).

60. Paul R. Greenwood, *Our Graying Society: Issues of Elder Abuse and Age Bias*, 31(4)/32(1) PROSECUTOR'S BRIEF 40 (California District Attorneys Association, 2010), https://d3n8a8pro7vhmx.cloudfront.net/kasemcares/pages/70/attachments/original/1510772835/Our_Graying_Society_Issues_of_Elder__Abuse_and_Age_Bias_by_Paul_Greenwood.pdf?1510772835.

61. CRIM. JUST. STANDARDS FOR THE PROSECUTION FUNCTION STANDARD 3-1.6 (Am. Bar Ass'n, 4th ed., Nov. 2018), https://www.americanbar.org/groups/criminal_justice/standards/ProsecutionFunctionFourthEdition/.

It is certainly true that some older adults may have cognitive impairments resulting from age or disability. These impairments may make it difficult for the adult to participate in an interview, testify in court, or be productively involved with other aspects of an investigation. Some older adults may die before the case proceeds to trial. The vulnerability of these victims is one reason why they are targeted.

While age and cognitive or physical impairment may present real challenges in some cases, there are deliberate steps that can be taken in the course of an investigation to gather useful and credible information from older adults and preserve testimony for use in the criminal proceeding.

TIPS FOR INTERVIEWING OLDER ADULT VICTIMS OR WITNESSES IN ELDER ABUSE CASES.

- Avoid making assumptions based on a person's age. Older witnesses often make excellent and compelling witnesses.

- Be thoughtful about interviewing older adults. Appendix B includes a detailed discussion of general interviewing techniques for older adults.

- Consider developing a protocol for joint investigations and/or interviews by APS and law enforcement.[62]

- Record interviews throughout the investigation. A taped interview will likely not be admissible to prove the truth of the matter asserted; however, it may be used in some situations for other reasons.[63] For example, one prosecutor recorded an interview with an older adult immediately after a caretaker neglect investigation began and recorded another interview with the same elder several months later. If the older adult were to be unable to testify, the prosecutor was planning to use the recordings to demonstrate the victim's improved condition. In a case from California, recorded interviews were allowed to be admitted as evidence to demonstrate the mental capacity of the older adult who had been a victim of exploitation and was deceased at the time of trial.[64]

62. *See, e.g.*, SANTA CLARA CTY., CAL., ELDER AND DEPENDENT ADULT ABUSE PROTOCOL FOR SANTA CLARA COUNTY LAW ENFORCEMENT (July 2010), https://www.sccgov.org/sites/ssa/daas/aps/Documents/daas_elder_dependent_adult_protocol.pdf ("While an officer has a duty to cross report any known or suspected instance of abuse or neglect immediately or as soon as practically possible to the appropriate agency, the need for a joint investigation may not be immediately apparent. Therefore, the decision to conduct a joint investigation may be made prior to, in conjunction with or after cross reporting obligations are satisfied. In some instances, the elder/dependent adult may be in need of immediate emergency services. In such cases it will be clear that an agency such as APS [Adult Protective Services] or OMB [Ombudsman] should be immediately contacted for the dual purpose of providing a cross report and beginning a joint investigation. . . . Whenever possible, the investigating officer shall coordinate the investigation with the appropriate agency while mindful that the officer's investigative focus may differ from that of the other agency. For instance, while the officer is responsible for the criminal documentation of the crime, the APS social worker and/or OMB are there to provide supportive services and to ensure the elder is safe.").

63. ROBERT L. FARB, ARREST, SEARCH, AND INVESTIGATION IN NORTH CAROLINA 726–30 (5th ed. 2016) (discussing hearsay and exceptions to the hearsay rule).

64. People v. Cooper, 56 Cal. Rptr. 3d 6 (Cal. Ct. App. 2007). *See* AEQUITAS, *supra* note 1, at 45–47 (discussing the preservation of witness testimony).

- Take depositions from the victim and from older witnesses. While depositions may be unusual in criminal cases, they can be useful for preserving testimony that ultimately may be admissible as evidence for the truth of the matter asserted.[65] An important difference between a deposition and a taped interview is that the defendant and the defendant's attorney would have an opportunity to participate in the former.[66] Even though North Carolina lacks a statutory framework for pretrial depositions in criminal cases, one author recommends several key features to consider:

  - The defendant should have a right to be present, with counsel, when the deposition is taken.

  - The defendant should be afforded full discovery far enough in advance of the deposition so that there will be a meaningful opportunity for cross-examination at the deposition.

  - The deposition should be recorded using audio and visual equipment. The addition of a visual component will allow the fact-finder to observe the witness's demeanor, an observation that is not possible with a written transcript.

  - The recording of the deposition must be of sufficient quality for in-court presentation.

  - While objections may be made at the time of the deposition, the witness should be required to answer all questions. Or, as an alternative, a judge could attend by remote video connection and rule on objections as they arise.[67]

  The author further emphasizes the importance of allowing the defendant to be present during any such deposition.

- Gather as much information as possible from the victim and from older witnesses during the probable cause hearing or at other preliminary hearings.[68] If the victim or witness is later unavailable, the prosecutor may be able to introduce testimony from the hearing to support the State's case.[69]

65. *See* Jessica Smith, *Two-Way Remote Testimony: Will It Pass Muster? (Part III)*, N.C. CRIM. L.: A UNC SCH. OF GOV'T BLOG (Feb. 10, 2011), https://nccriminallaw.sog.unc.edu/two-way-remote-testimony-will-it-pass-muster-part-iii/ ("Although North Carolina does not have a statutory procedure for the State to take pretrial depositions in a criminal case, procedures for doing so exist in other jurisdictions. *See, e.g.*, FED. R. CRIM. PRO. 15 (authorizing depositions in 'exceptional circumstances'). Additionally, the procedure is not unheard of in North Carolina; in extreme situations, such as when a key witness is ill and cannot travel to trial or is not expected to survive until trial, North Carolina trial judges have exercised their inherent authority and ordered pretrial depositions.").

66. Jessica Smith, *Understanding the New Confrontation Clause Analysis: Crawford, Davis, and Melendez-Diaz*, ADMIN. OF JUST. BULL. No. 2010/2 (Apr. 2010), https://www.sog.unc.edu/sites/www.sog.unc.edu/files/reports/aojb1002.pdf.

67. Smith, *supra* note 66.

68. *See* G.S. 15A-611.

69. State v. Ross, 216 N.C. App. 337, 345 (2011). *See also* Jessica Smith, *Court Holds That Probable Cause Hearing Provides a Prior Opportunity to Cross Examine*, N.C. CRIM. L.: A UNC SCH. OF GOV'T BLOG (Nov. 7, 2011), https://nccriminallaw.sog.unc.edu/court-holds-that-probable-cause-hearing-provides-a-prior-opportunity-to-cross-examine/.

B. POWERS OF ATTORNEY

Many cases of financial exploitation involve a family member, friend, or acquaintance who has secured a power of attorney (POA) from the older adult. Law enforcement officials may find these cases frustrating to investigate and prosecute.[70] It can be challenging to evaluate the validity and scope of the POA documents involved in an exploitation case. For example, the documents may be drafted broadly enough to allow the agent to use the older adult's funds to give the agent and others gifts. An investigator may in such circumstances face the following questions:

- Did the older adult have capacity to sign the document(s)?

- Is the gifting clause valid?

- Did the agent's actions exceed the scope of his or her authority?

Fortunately, it is possible to find answers to these questions, which may allow a criminal case to proceed when appropriate. In February 2019, for example, the Chatham County Sheriff's Office charged an older man's daughter with felony embezzlement and other crimes related to her abuse of a power of attorney.[71]

Because many older adults are completing POAs, and because so many exploitation cases involve them, it is important for law enforcement officials and prosecutors to become comfortable with the law governing POAs and to develop strategies for investigating their misuse and abuse.

> ### TIPS FOR APPROACHING ELDER ABUSE CASES INVOLVING POWERS OF ATTORNEY.
>
> - Remember that the existence of a POA does not automatically preclude prosecution.
> - Learn the foundational law governing POAs. Some deficiencies and abuses will be relatively easy to identify.
> - Develop relationships with local elder law attorneys. They may be willing to review and advise on the scope and limitations of specific POAs.
> - See Chapter 5 for a fuller discussion of POAs.

---

70. As one district attorney explained: "I can't help them when I see [a power of attorney document] . . . To prove a crime in a case like this is a real, real challenge. While these crimes appear suspicious on the face, it does not mean that I can prove a crime." Margulis, *supra* note 53.

71. Blake Hodge, *Chatham County Woman Accused of Embezzling from Elderly Victim*, CHAPELBORO.COM (Feb. 25, 2019), https://chapelboro.com/news/crime/chatham-county-woman-accused-of-embezzling-from-elderly-victim; Donaldson Funeral Home & Cremation, "Lindo Marion Webster," https://www.donaldsonfunerals.com/notices/Lindo-Webster (identifying daughter as Deborah Bowes) (last visited July 19, 2019).

C. LIMITED FINANCIAL HARM

Investigators or prosecutors may choose not to pursue a financial exploitation case because the victim ultimately recovered the funds at the root of the charge. For example,

- a bank or credit card company might have detected the criminal activity and refunded the stolen money to the older adult customer or

- a guardian of the estate might have misused a ward's funds but the ward's estate might have recovered on the guardian's bond, thereby making the estate whole.

Recoveries like these may indicate that the harm caused was minimal or that the exploitation case was resolved. Some may also be concerned that the investment of time and money required for a criminal investigation is not appropriate when the financial loss to the older adult is relatively minimal or the money has already been recovered or restored. However, one should be mindful of a greater community concern, namely, that without criminal consequences for the perpetrator, it seems likely that other older adults will be victimized.

TIPS FOR APPROACHING ELDER ABUSE CASES WHERE LIMITED FINANCIAL HARM RESULTED.

- Become familiar with the civil remedies for restoring assets in financial crimes cases and encourage victims and their families to pursue them.
- Consider using these civil recovery methods to support the criminal financial exploitation case. Gather detailed information from fraud investigation units in financial institutions and, in cases involving guardianship, gather from the clerk of superior court the incompetency and guardianship court files. This information will likely make the criminal case stronger.

D. RELUCTANT OR RECANTING VICTIMS

Victims are often protective of family members and caretakers who are abusing them. For example, a grandchild may be stealing money from a grandparent in order to support a drug habit. The grandparent may not want to get the grandchild in trouble so is reluctant to report the abuse or participate in an investigation.

> **TIPS FOR APPROACHING ELDER ABUSE CASES INVOLVING RELUCTANT VICTIMS.**
>
> - Work with APS to encourage other family members and friends to support the older adult's participation in the criminal investigation and prosecution. A broader network of support may reduce the older adult's perceived dependence on the abuser.
> - If necessary, consider using prior inconsistent statements, 911 recordings, or other evidence to impeach the victim.[72]

E. OBTAINING MEDICAL, APS, AND FINANCIAL RECORDS

Compiling records to build a strong elder abuse case can be challenging because some of the most helpful records—medical, APS, and financial—are subject to confidentiality laws that may be interpreted by the record holders as prohibiting or limiting disclosure. The bottom line is that all three types of records may be shared with law enforcement officials, including prosecutors, who are investigating or prosecuting elder abuse. There may be procedures to follow or exceptions that apply but, in general, law enforcement officials should not be discouraged by the need to obtain these types of records.

> **BECOME FAMILIAR WITH CONFIDENTIALITY LAWS GOVERNING ALL COMPONENTS OF THE ELDER PROTECTION SYSTEM.**
>
> For a brief summary of the law governing information sharing between DSS, law enforcement, health care providers, and clerks of court in guardianship proceedings, review "Quick Reference: Information Sharing in Elder Abuse Cases," available at protectadults.sog.unc.edu.

F. COMPLEXITY OF FINANCIAL EXPLOITATION CASES

Cases involving financial exploitation are resource-intensive and sometimes require specific knowledge, such as of financial privacy laws, or expertise. For example, some law enforcement agencies employ or work with forensic accountants. These experts will review financial records to identify patterns and aberrations. The review typically will go back at least one year.[73] Law enforcement officials may find the investigatory demands too daunting when other demands on their time and resources are so high.

---

72. Greenwood, *supra* note 60, at 46.
73. OFF. OF KY. ATT'Y GEN., *supra* note 57, at, 66.

> **TIPS FOR HANDLING COMPLEX FINANCIAL RECORDS AND ISSUES IN EXPLOITATION CASES.**
>
> - Invest in specialized training for selected investigators and prosecutors.
> - Consider developing a regional support model. This could be accomplished informally, by relying on others who have developed specialized expertise, or it could be done more formally through the development of regional centers or teams. Formalized regional initiatives could provide support to local law enforcement officials or, in some cases, assume responsibility for the investigation entirely.

G. FREEZING ASSETS

As discussed above in Section II.B.2, after a person (the defendant) is charged with financial exploitation of an older or disabled adult, the district attorney (DA) may ask the court to freeze the defendant's funds, assets, or property.[74] The goal is to preserve some assets so that the defendant can provide restitution to the victim if the court so orders. There are at least two reasons why this tool may not be used very often.

- The tool is available only after a person has been charged with financial exploitation. In many cases, a perpetrator will sell property or expend funds soon after exploiting an older or disabled adult or as soon as the perpetrator suspects an investigation is underway.

- The law requires the DA to prove that the defendant "is about to or intends to divest himself or herself of assets in a manner that would render the defendant insolvent for purposes of restitution."[75] It may be difficult for a DA to establish this by "clear and convincing" evidence, which is the standard the court will apply in these proceedings.[76]

---

74. G.S. 14-112.3.
75. G.S. 14-112.3(b).
76. *Id.*

> **DISCUSS WITH APS THE POTENTIAL BENEFITS OF FREEZING THE OLDER ADULT'S ASSETS EARLY IN AN EXPLOITATION INVESTIGATION.**
>
> Communicate early with APS about the possibility of freezing the older adult's assets during the investigation stage. If this step is appropriate and is taken early enough, it may protect the remaining assets of the older adult. For example, if the exploiter has the older adult's power of attorney and suspects that an investigation is underway, the exploiter may try to transfer or expend most or all of the older adult's assets. It may be difficult at this point to recover those funds even if the exploiter is later convicted. See Chapter 2 for more details about the authority of APS to request a court order to freeze the older adult's assets.

H. LIMITATIONS OF ABUSE AND NEGLECT STATUTES

While there is a specific statute addressing abuse and neglect of disabled and older adults (G.S. 14-32.3) and another addressing exploitation (G.S. 14-112.2), a few concepts and terms integral to the laws make them more difficult to use effectively in elder abuse cases.

- **Caretaker.** In order for a person to be guilty of abuse or neglect of an older or disabled adult, the person must be a "caretaker" for the adult. G.S. 14-32.3(d)(1) defines the term to mean a "person who has the responsibility for the care of a disabled or elder adult as a result of family relationship or who has assumed the responsibility for the care of a disabled or elder adult voluntarily or by contract."[77] If a prosecutor is not able to establish such a relationship, this statute will not be useful in addressing abuse or neglect. For example, a son is visiting his father from another state for the weekend. During that time, he slaps his father and his father falls down and breaks his hip. While the son could be charged under another criminal law, such as assault, he could not be charged under the statute specific to abuse of older adults because he is not a caretaker.

- **Injury.** In order for a person to be guilty of abuse or neglect of a disabled or older adult, the adult must have suffered an injury.[78] In some situations, the adult may have been abused but does not ultimately suffer an injury. For example, in one case an in-home nursing assistant was overmedicating an older woman in order to make the woman less alert and sleep more. The nursing assistant could not be charged with domestic abuse of an older adult because the woman did not suffer any injury.[79] In this situation, other crimes may be applicable, such as patient abuse, but the penalties may be less severe.

---

77. G.S. 14-32.3(d)(1).
78. G.S. 14-32.3(a) (abuse), (b) (neglect).
79. Interview with Lori Wickline, *supra* note 52.

- **Malice aforethought.** The portion of G.S. 14-32.3 addressing abuse, subsection (a), requires that the prosecutor show that the perpetrator had "malice aforethought." That is a high bar, requiring proof that the perpetrator's conduct was done intentionally, either with ill will or hatred or without just cause or excuse.[80]

- **Deception or intimidation.** In order for a person to be guilty of exploitation of an older or disabled adult, the prosecutor must be able to show that the person employed "deception or intimidation" when depriving the adult of funds, assets, or property. This element may be difficult to prove where family members or close friends insinuate themselves into the older adult's life, express love and concern for them, and promise to take care of them. The older adult may even agree to allow the other person to use their funds, assets, or property, not realizing the potential for misuse or exploitation. Often the exploiter does provide some benefit to the older adult, blurring the line between assistance and exploitation. While a situation may look like someone is manipulating or taking advantage of an older adult, there may be insufficient evidence of lying or intimidation to meet the requirements of G.S. 14-112.2.

> ### EXPLORE ALL OPTIONS WHEN DECIDING WHAT KINDS OF CHARGES TO BRING IN CASES INVOLVING OLDER ADULTS.
>
> Do not rely entirely on the elder-specific criminal statutes. Remember that there are many crimes of general applicability that may be more appropriate and useful in a particular case involving elder abuse, neglect, or exploitation. For a summary of some potentially relevant crimes, see Appendix C.

---

80. *See* State v. Sexton, 357 N.C. 235 (2003). For a discussion of malicious conduct, and other criminal states of mind, *see* SMITH, *supra* note 10, at 3–10.

I. SCAMS

Some consumer scams that target older adults are local in nature, such as those involving home improvement or storm recovery. These local scams can often be investigated and prosecuted successfully.[81] But many consumer scams originate in other states or countries, making them extremely difficult to investigate. They may involve an older adult wiring money or purchasing gift cards, which can be impossible to trace and recover. As a result, local law enforcement officials often find these investigations frustrating or even futile.

TIPS FOR HANDLING SCAMS INVOLVING OLDER OR DISABLED ADULTS.

- Work with community partners to educate the public and retail outlets about consumer scams.
- Seek assistance from state and federal law enforcement officials, especially for scams that may be multi-state or international. See Chapter 7 for more information about the roles played by other state and federal agencies.

---

81. *See, e.g.*, Dalisa Robles, *Man Accused of Obtaining $3,500 as Part of Roofing Scam*, WNCT.COM (Aug. 17, 2018), https://www.wnct.com/local-news/man-accused-of-obtaining-3500-as-part-of-roofing-scam/.

Chapter 4
Adult Guardianship

CONTENTS

I. SCOPE OF CHAPTER

This chapter describes adult guardianship, a component of the elder protection system in North Carolina that exists to help individuals who lack capacity to exercise their rights and remain free from abuse.[1] Guardianship is the legal relationship created by a state court that gives a person or entity (the guardian) the authority to make decisions for an individual who lacks capacity (the ward) with respect to the individual's personal affairs, financial affairs, or both.[2] Adult guardianship is governed by state law in G.S. Chapters 35A and 35B and is available for incompetent persons aged 17.5 or older. This chapter focuses on guardianship as it applies to older adults in cases involving elder abuse. It provides an overview of guardianship in North Carolina, including

- A. how guardianship protects older adults,
- B. who is responsible for guardianship,
- C. how the legal process for appointment of a guardian for an older adult works,
- D. the role of the guardian appointed by the court, and
- E. the role of the court in overseeing the guardianship.

This chapter concludes by identifying some of the common challenges related to guardianship, including the fact that the guardian may be the perpetrator of elder abuse.

II. OVERVIEW OF GUARDIANSHIP

A. HOW DOES GUARDIANSHIP PROTECT OLDER ADULTS?

A family member who is a caregiver for an older adult gets access to the older adult's bank account and withdraws money for her own benefit. She also leaves the older adult alone for long periods of time and the older adult becomes dehydrated and malnourished. A person concerned for the older adult wants to take action to stop the abuse and support the older adult. Or a county department of social services (DSS) in response to an adult protective services report is required to take action to provide protective services to the older adult.[3] The older adult is unable to take action on his own behalf or consent to protective services because he lacks capacity. There is no other surrogate decision maker, such as an agent under a power of attorney, authorized to act on the older adult's behalf. Or the agent authorized to act on behalf of the older adult is the perpetrator of the abuse.

Guardianship is a tool that may be used to stop such ongoing abuse and safeguard against future abuse. To appoint a guardian for an older adult, two proceedings are filed before the court: an incompetency proceeding and a guardianship proceeding.

---

1. Chapter 35A, Section 1201, of the North Carolina General Statutes (hereinafter G.S.).

2. JOHN L. SAXON, NORTH CAROLINA GUARDIANSHIP MANUAL § 1.3, at 4 (2008).

3. For further discussion of the role of the county department of social services (DSS) in providing protective services to disabled adults, including disabled older adults, refer to Chapter 2 of this manual.

In the incompetency proceeding, the court[4] determines, based on the evidence presented, whether the older adult is incompetent.[5] The term "incompetent adult" is defined under North Carolina law as an adult or emancipated minor who lacks sufficient capacity to

1. manage his or her own affairs or
2. make or communicate important decisions concerning his or her person, family, or property.[6]

If the court finds that an older adult is incompetent, the court must appoint a guardian to act on his or her behalf.[7] The court's role during the guardianship proceeding is to determine (1) the type of guardianship needed by the older adult based on the older adult's capacity, assets, needs, and liabilities and (2) who can most suitably serve as guardian.[8] There are three main types of guardians under North Carolina law: a guardian of the person (GOP), a guardian of the estate (GOE), and a general guardian (GG).[9] (See Table 4.1.) If there is or reasonably appears to be an imminent or foreseeable risk of harm to the older adult or to the older adult's property that requires immediate intervention, and if there is reasonable cause to believe that the older adult is incompetent, the court may appoint a temporary guardian, known as an interim guardian, to act on the older adult's behalf while the incompetency proceeding is pending before the court.[10]

Table 4.1. **Primary Types of Guardians for Adults in North Carolina**

GUARDIAN TYPE	RELEVANT STATUTE (G.S.)	NATURE OF GUARDIANSHIP
Guardian of the Person	35A-1202(10)	A guardian appointed solely for the purpose of performing duties relating to the care, custody, and control of a ward.
Guardian of the Estate	35A-1202(9)	A guardian appointed solely for the purpose of managing the property, estate, and business affairs of a ward.
General Guardian	35A-1202(7)	A guardian of both the estate and the person.

---

4. While the older adult who is the subject of the incompetency proceeding has a right to a jury trial, in practice, the decision of whether the adult is incompetent or not is most frequently made by the court. G.S. 35A-1110 (establishing the right to a jury trial in an incompetency proceeding). The right to a jury trial is discussed further in Section II.C.1.g, *infra*.

5. G.S. 35A-1112(c), (d).

6. G.S. 35A-1101(7). The older adult's lack of capacity may be because of a condition such as dementia, mental illness, intellectual disability, autism, inebriety, or other cause or condition. *See id.* However, evidence of a specific condition or diagnosis is not required for a court to find that an older adult is incompetent, and evidence of a specific condition or diagnosis is not determinative of incompetency. JOAN G. BRANNON & ANN E. ANDERSON, NORTH CAROLINA CLERK OF SUPERIOR COURT PROCEDURES MANUAL 85.1 (2012) (hereinafter CSC MANUAL).

7. G.S. 35A-1120.

8. G.S. 35A-1212(a). If the court determines that the nature and extent of the older adult's capacity justifies ordering a limited guardianship, the court may do so. *Id.*

9. G.S. 35A-1202(10), (9), (7).

10. Refer to Section II.C.3.b, *infra*, for a discussion of interim guardianship.

Once a guardian is appointed, the guardian has a duty to take actions, depending on the type of guardianship created, to protect the older adult and the older adult's property from abuse.[11] The court oversees the guardianship to ensure that the guardian carries out his or her duties.[12] This includes reviewing and responding to reports filed with the court, such as status reports filed by a GOP or accountings filed by a GOE. If the court detects abuse based on information it receives, the court has legal tools available to stop the abuse and protect the older adult. Examples include holding a status report hearing, modifying the guardianship, or removing the guardian.[13]

> ### ✎ PRACTICE NOTE
>
> ***When an Older Adult May Need a Guardian to Protect against or Remedy Abuse***
>
> The older adult is **incompetent** and . . .
>
> - has no power of attorney (POA), health care power of attorney, or other surrogate decision-maker authorized to act on the adult's behalf.
> - is the victim of financial exploitation and continues to pay money over to perpetrators of scams.
> - the adult's agent under a POA misuses the adult's property or fails/is unable to carry out the duties of the agent under the POA and there is no successor agent identified in the POA.
> - the agent under a health care POA fails/is unable to act on the adult's behalf or acts in a way that is inconsistent with the health care POA.
> - the family members or caretakers of the adult argue over the adult's care and subject the adult to emotional abuse, placing the adult in the middle of a push-and-pull of decision-making, and a guardian is needed to provide consistency and certainty to the decisions made on the adult's behalf.
> - has the financial means to pay for care or services but is unable to consent to services or care that would help to rectify the abuse.
> - is unable to maintain a safe and accessible home environment.
> - is unable to manage medications and/or seek health care treatment and has no other supports available to help guide health care decisions and care.
> - is the victim of physical, emotional, sexual, or verbal abuse and is unable to stop or report the abuse.

---

11. Refer to Section II.D, *infra*, for a discussion of the role of the guardian.
12. G.S. 35A-1203(b).
13. Refer to Section II.E, *infra*, for further discussion of court oversight of the guardian.

B. WHO IS RESPONSIBLE FOR GUARDIANSHIP?

Various actors have roles in the legal process of determining incompetency and appointing a guardian for an allegedly incompetent older adult, including

- the clerk of superior court,

- the petitioner,

- the respondent/ward,

- the guardian ad litem attorney,

- next of kin of the older adult and other interested persons,

- the applicant for appointment of guardian, and

- guardian(s).

Unlike civil actions, where the parties are frequently adversarial and focused on their own interests, incompetency and guardianship proceedings are about the older adult, the capacity of the older adult, and what is in the best interests of an incompetent older adult. Guardianship can be effective in protecting incompetent older adults from abuse when each actor fulfills his or her legally prescribed role. Below is a brief overview of each of these actors' roles in these proceedings.

1. CLERK OF SUPERIOR COURT

The clerk of superior court is the judicial official who presides over incompetency and adult guardianship proceedings in North Carolina.[14] The duties of clerks include both administrative as well as judicial functions.[15] These judicial functions include adjudicating incompetence and appointing and overseeing guardians for adults.[16] The clerk decides all issues of fact and law raised in the incompetency and adult guardianship proceedings, unless there is a jury trial in the incompetency proceeding (discussed more in Section II.C.1.g, *infra*) or the clerk is disqualified from hearing either proceeding.[17]

Each of North Carolina's 100 counties has an elected clerk of superior court. Each clerk has a staff of assistant and deputy clerks. Assistant clerks are authorized to perform all of the duties and functions of the clerk.[18] This is unlike deputy clerks, who, except in limited criminal matters, only perform ministerial acts of the clerk.[19] An assistant clerk has the same judicial authority as the clerk and may preside over and enter orders as the judge in incompetency and guardianship proceedings.[20]

---

14. G.S. 35A-1103(a); 35A-1203(a).

15. *See* G.S. 1-13 (jurisdiction of clerk); 7A-40 (judicial powers of clerk); -109 (record-keeping procedures); -103 (authority of clerk of superior court).

16. G.S. 35A-1103(a); -1203.

17. G.S. 1-301.2(d), (g)(1); 1-301.3(b); 7A-104.

18. G.S. 7A-102(b).

19. *Id.*

20. G.S. 7A-102(b), -103.

Figure 4.1. Who May Hear a Guardianship Case in North Carolina?

Clerk of Superior Court	√
Assistant Clerk of Superior Court	√
Deputy Clerk of Superior Court	X
Superior Court Judge*	X
District Court Judge	X
Magistrate	X

* A superior court judge may hear the case if the clerk is disqualified under G.S. 7A-104; also, a superior court judge hears an appeal of the clerk's decision.

Under North Carolina law, a clerk's office may have no fewer than five staff positions plus the elected clerk.[21] There is no statutory maximum. As a result, some small counties, such as Perquimans, may have six people in the clerk's office, while other larger counties, like Mecklenburg, may have more than 200 people in the office. The staff in smaller counties tends to be comprised of generalists who have to fulfill every role in the clerk's office. The staff in larger counties tends to be more specialized. A clerk in a smaller county may preside over an incompetency and adult guardianship hearing as the judge, accept papers for filing at the front counter, and staff the district or superior court courtroom all in the same day. In many larger counties, there are assistant clerks designated as hearing officers whose sole role it is to preside over court proceedings such as those involving incompetency and guardianship.

Practices with respect to incompetency and guardianship proceedings differ across the state depending on the needs and demands of a particular clerk's office. Hearings may be held in a courtroom, a conference room, or a clerk's office. The clerk may wear a robe or dress in business casual clothes when presiding over a hearing. Regardless, the clerk is the judge in the proceedings, and valid orders of the clerk have the full force and effect as if they were entered by a district or superior court judge.[22]

2. PETITIONER

The petitioner brings an incompetency proceeding by filing a petition. The petition may be filed by "any person."[23] "Person" in this context includes individuals such as family members, caregivers, friends, or neighbors. It also includes entities such as nursing homes, county departments of social services (DSS), hospitals, or financial institutions.

There is no requirement that a person have a certain degree of kinship or particular relationship with the older adult to file an incompetency petition. This means that a low barrier exists to getting these types of proceeding before the court, which may be particularly important in cases involving elder abuse. For example, a family member may be

---

21. G.S. 7A-102(a).
22. *See* G.S. 7A-103.
23. G.S. 35A-1105.

the one who is financially exploiting an older adult who lacks capacity. A neighbor, friend, or DSS could file an incompetency petition and seek the appointment of a guardian to cut off the financial exploitation by the family member.

The petitioner may, but is not required to, apply to be appointed as the guardian for the older adult. Someone may have concerns about the abuse of an older adult and seek the appointment of a guardian to protect the adult, but he or she may be unwilling or unable to serve as guardian. If the petitioner does not want to apply to be a guardian for the older adult, the petitioner may recommend another person or entity in the petition to serve as guardian.

> 💬 **KEY TERMS**
>
> A **petitioner** files an incompetency proceeding against a **respondent**, who is the alleged incompetent person.

3. RESPONDENT/WARD

The respondent is the person who is alleged to be incompetent in a proceeding filed before the clerk.[24] If the respondent is adjudicated incompetent and a guardian is appointed by a court, the respondent is then referred to as the ward.[25]

> 💬 **KEY TERM**
>
> Once the respondent is adjudicated incompetent and a guardian is appointed on his or her behalf, the respondent is known as the **ward**.

4. GUARDIAN AD LITEM ATTORNEY

Every older adult who is a respondent in an incompetency proceeding is entitled to be represented by counsel of his or her choice or by an appointed guardian ad litem attorney (GAL).[26] Upon the filing of a petition, the court appoints a GAL to represent the older adult.[27] Clerks typically use N.C. Administrative Office of the Courts (AOC) Form AOC-SP-201, "Notice of Hearing on Incompetence/Motion in the Cause and Order Appointing Guardian ad Litem," to do this. The GAL is required to personally visit the respondent as soon as possible after being appointed by the court.[28] The GAL represents the older adult until the GAL is discharged by the court, the petition is dismissed, or a guardian is appointed.[29]

---

24. G.S. 35A-1101(15).
25. G.S. 35A-1101(17).
26. G.S. 35A-1107(a).
27. *Id.*
28. G.S. 35A-1107(b).
29. G.S. 35A-1107(a), (b).

The GAL serves a dual role. The GAL's primary role is to make every reasonable effort to determine the older adult's wishes regarding the incompetency proceeding and any proposed guardianship.[30] The GAL must present those wishes to the court at all relevant stages of the proceedings.[31] The GAL also makes recommendations to the clerk regarding the older adult's best interests to the extent those recommendations differ from the older adult's wishes.[32]

The appointment of the GAL does not preclude the older adult from hiring his or her own attorney.[33] If the older adult does choose to hire an attorney, the GAL may be discharged by the court.[34] In practice, the court rarely discharges the GAL.

The GAL, as the respondent's counsel, plays an important role in protecting against and preventing elder abuse. Through his or her representation of the respondent, the GAL may (1) identify and take action to protect the respondent if the respondent is the subject of abuse, such as filing a motion for interim guardianship, and (2) investigate and screen potential guardians to enable the court to appoint a guardian who will not later subject the older adult to abuse.

5. NEXT OF KIN OF THE OLDER ADULT AND OTHER INTERESTED PERSONS

Every petition filed initiating an incompetency proceeding must contain, to the extent known, the name, address, and county of residence of the older adult's next of kin[35] and other persons known to have an interest in the proceeding, such as neighbors, friends, employees at a care facility, or other persons who play an important role in the older adult's life.[36] Next of kin and other interested persons often play an important role in providing a complete picture of the older adult's capacity, assets, needs, and liabilities to the court. A petitioner may present only one side of the story or, in extreme cases, actually mislead or hide information from the court. Next of kin and other interested persons may have critical information the court needs to assess the older adult's capacity and ensure that a guardian is appointed who will keep the older adult safe from abuse.

---

30. G.S. 35A-1107(b).

31. *Id.*

32. *Id.*

33. G.S. 35A-1107(a). *See also* N.C. State Bar, Formal Ethics Op. 16, Representation of Client Resisting an Incompetency Petition (Jan. 15, 1999), https://www.ncbar.gov/for-lawyers/ethics/adopted-opinions/98-formal-ethics-opinion-16/?opinionSearchTerm=Copy%20file.

34. *Id.*

35. The term "next of kin" is not defined in the law related to incompetency and adult guardianship proceedings. However, it has been construed in other contexts to mean heirs or persons entitled to inherit property from a decedent who did not leave a will. CSC MANUAL, at 85.4.

36. G.S. 35A-1106(5).

6. APPLICANT FOR APPOINTMENT OF GUARDIAN

Any person or entity that files an application for guardianship is known as the applicant and is a party to the guardianship proceeding.[37] Frequently, the applicant is a family member, such as an adult child, or a friend of the older adult. There may be more than one applicant in the guardianship proceeding or there may be no applicants—or no suitable applicants—in the proceeding. In the absence of a suitable applicant, the clerk of superior court will likely appoint DSS or a corporation as the older adult's GOP and a local attorney or public guardian as GOE if the court determines that the older adult is incompetent and needs both a GOP and a GOE.

> ### 💬 KEY TERMS
>
> An **applicant** files an application to be appointed as a guardian for the **respondent**.

7. GUARDIAN(S)

The guardian is appointed by the court to make decisions on behalf of an incompetent older adult. After a petition is filed and before the formal adjudication of incompetence, the clerk may appoint an interim guardian of the person, an interim guardian of the estate, or an interim general guardian to immediately intervene if (1) there is or reasonably appears to be an imminent or foreseeable risk of harm to the older adult or to the older adult's property that requires immediate interverntion and (2) there is reasonable cause to believe that the older adult is incompetent.[38]

After an older adult is adjudicated incompetent, the court has the discretion to appoint a guardian of the person, guardian of the estate, or a general guardian, depending on the capacity, assets, needs, and liabilities of the older adult. If the older adult has capacity with regard to certain decisions, the court may order a limited guardianship.[39] A limited guardianship allows an older adult to retain certain rights and privileges.[40] For example, a clerk may order that the older adult retains the right to make decisions related to expenditures of up to $50 a week or that the older adult retains the right to make decisions about what church to attend or who may visit him or her. The court may appoint a limited guardian of the person, a limited guardian of the estate, or a limited general guardian for an incompetent older adult.

C. HOW DOES GUARDIANSHIP WORK?

There are two separate court proceedings involved in the appointment of a guardian: an incompetency proceeding and a guardianship proceeding. As a practical matter, however, the adjudication of incompetency and appointment of a guardian are often combined into

---

37. G.S. 35A-1210; SAXON, *supra* note 2, at § 4.1, p. 46.
38. G.S. 35A-1114.
39. G.S. 35A-1212(a).
40. *Id.*

Figure 4.2. **Overview of the Court Procedure to Appoint a Guardian for an Incompetent Adult**

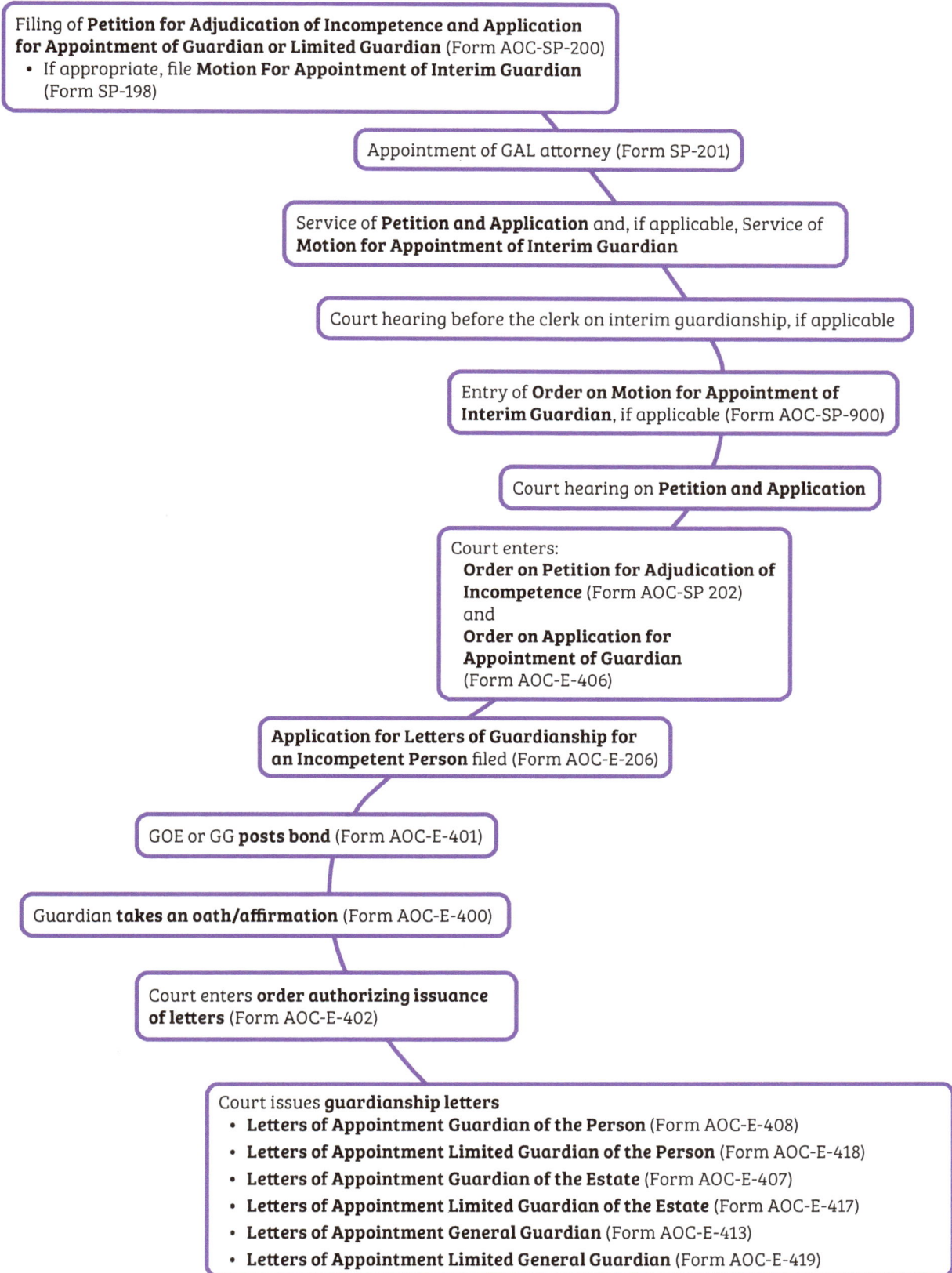

Filing of **Petition for Adjudication of Incompetence and Application for Appointment of Guardian or Limited Guardian** (Form AOC-SP-200)
- If appropriate, file **Motion For Appointment of Interim Guardian** (Form SP-198)

Appointment of GAL attorney (Form SP-201)

Service of **Petition and Application** and, if applicable, Service of **Motion for Appointment of Interim Guardian**

Court hearing before the clerk on interim guardianship, if applicable

Entry of **Order on Motion for Appointment of Interim Guardian**, if applicable (Form AOC-SP-900)

Court hearing on **Petition and Application**

Court enters:
Order on Petition for Adjudication of Incompetence (Form AOC-SP 202)
and
Order on Application for Appointment of Guardian (Form AOC-E-406)

Application for Letters of Guardianship for an Incompetent Person filed (Form AOC-E-206)

GOE or GG **posts bond** (Form AOC-E-401)

Guardian **takes an oath/affirmation** (Form AOC-E-400)

Court enters **order authorizing issuance of letters** (Form AOC-E-402)

Court issues **guardianship letters**
- **Letters of Appointment Guardian of the Person** (Form AOC-E-408)
- **Letters of Appointment Limited Guardian of the Person** (Form AOC-E-418)
- **Letters of Appointment Guardian of the Estate** (Form AOC-E-407)
- **Letters of Appointment Limited Guardian of the Estate** (Form AOC-E-417)
- **Letters of Appointment General Guardian** (Form AOC-E-413)
- **Letters of Appointment Limited General Guardian** (Form AOC-E-419)

one hearing before the clerk. The subsections below provide an overview of each of these proceedings, with particular emphasis placed on opportunities to protect older adults from abuse. While the process may vary from case to case, Figure 4.2 presents a snapshot of some of the key steps in the process for appointing a guardian.

1. INCOMPETENCY PROCEEDING

a. Filing the Petition

The incompetency proceeding is initiated by the filing of a verified petition.[41] Through this petition, a person (the petitioner) is asking the court to determine whether an older adult (the respondent) is incompetent.[42] Typically, the petitioner completes and files N.C. Administrative Office of the Courts (AOC) Form AOC-SP-200, "Petition for Adjudication of Incompetence and Application for Appointment of Guardian or Limited Guardian," to initiate the action. The form satisfies state law requirements for initiating an incompetency proceeding. A petitioner may also write his or her own petition and file it to initiate the proceeding, provided the writing meets minimum legal requirements. While the AOC form is not required, petitioners rarely initiate proceedings without using it.

b. Notice of Hearing; Timing of the Hearing

Within five days after the filing of a petition, the clerk of superior court must issue a written notice of hearing.[43] Clerks typically use Form AOC-SP-201, "Notice of Hearing on Incompetence/Motion in the Cause and Order Appointing Guardian ad Litem," to do this. The notice must include the date, time, and place for the hearing.[44]

The hearing must take place not less than ten but no more than thirty days from the service of the petition on the older adult/respondent, unless the clerk extends the time for good cause, such as to allow time for mediation or for the completion of a medical, mental health, social work, or other multidisciplinary evaluation.[45] This time frame (from the filing of the action to the hearing) is much shorter than other court proceedings, such as civil actions, that may take up to two years or more to complete. It ensures that where an older adult is incompetent and needs the assistance of a guardian, one can be appointed relatively quickly. This is particularly true where there is no dispute as to the older adult's incapacity, such as where the older adult has advanced dementia. In cases involving ongoing elder abuse, the ability to go from the filing of a petition to a hearing within a short period of time is critical. If the thirty-day deadline must be extended for good cause, there are other tools, such as interim guardianship, that may be employed to stop or protect an older adult from abuse while the incompetency proceeding is pending. Interim guardianship is discussed further below.

---

41. G.S. 35A-1105.
42. *Id.*
43. G.S. 35A-1108(a).
44. *Id.*
45. *Id.*

c. Service of the Petition

The incompetency petition and the notice of hearing must be served personally on the respondent.[46] Because the use of private process servers is very limited in North Carolina, personal service is completed on the respondent by the sheriff in most cases.[47] Service is not proper if the notice and petition are sent by FedEx, UPS, or regular mail or left with a family member at the respondent's home. This heightened requirement of service on the respondent ensures that the respondent knows of the proceeding and knows the location, date, and time of the hearing. It reflects the significant impact an adjudication of incompetency has on a person's rights to make decisions about his or her life and property. The return of service located on the back of the Form AOC-SP-201, "Notice of Hearing," is typically completed to show proof of service on the respondent.

> ### 🖊 PRACTICE NOTE
>
> For an older adult who may never have had an interaction with the court system before the filing of the incompetency petition, service by the sheriff may cause fear or anxiety. The petitioner may wish to speak with the sheriff's office prior to service on the older adult/respondent so that the petitioner may be present when the petition is served. The petitioner may also request that the sheriff send a plain-clothes officer to serve the older adult. These practices may minimize the older adult's fear and anxiety upon being served by the sheriff.

The GAL appointed to represent the respondent in the proceeding must be served with copies of the petition and notice of hearing in accordance with Rule 4 of the N.C. Rules of Civil Procedure.[48] In practice, the GAL often accepts service by signing the back of the Form AOC-SP-201.

The petitioner is required to serve copies of the notice of hearing and the petition on the respondent's next of kin identified in the petition and on any other persons the clerk may designate.[49] If, for example, the GAL determines through the GAL's representation of the older adult that the petitioner left next of kin or other interested persons off the petition and did not serve them with the notice of hearing, the GAL may request that the clerk direct the petitioner to serve them with notice. The petitioner completes service by mailing the copies by first-class mail within five days after the filing of the petition, unless the next of kin or other interested person accepted notice.[50] The petitioner files proof of service by filing a certificate with the court.[51] Typically, the petitioner uses Form AOC-SP-207, "Certificate of Service (Incompetent Proceeding)." Subsequent notices to next of kin and other persons are sent by the clerk via first-class mail.[52]

---

46. G.S. 35A-1109.
47. *See* Locklear v. Cummings, 822 S.E.2d 587, 593 (N.C. Ct. App. 2018); N.C. State Bar v. Hunter, 217 N.C. App. 216, 224 (2011). *See also* G.S. 1A-1, Rule 4(h), (h1).
48. G.S. 35A-1109.
49. *Id.*
50. *Id.*
51. *Id.*
52. *Id.*

d. Evidence at the Hearing

At the hearing on the incompetency petition, the burden is on the petitioner to present testimony and other evidence regarding the older adult/respondent's incapacity.[53] Both the petitioner and the respondent are entitled to present evidence.[54] Evidence related to the respondent's capacity typically includes testimony from the respondent, the petitioner, next of kin, and other interested persons. Additional evidence may include medical, mental health, and substance abuse records; adult protective services (APS) records; and financial records. The guardian ad litem attorney (GAL) presents the older adult's express wishes and may make recommendations concerning the respondent's best interests if those interests differ from the older adult's express wishes.[55]

The evidence may include a court-ordered multidisciplinary evaluation (MDE).[56] Any party may request, and the court may order, an MDE of the older adult.[57] A request for an MDE must be made in writing and filed with the clerk of superior court within ten days after service of the incompetency petition on the older adult.[58] The court may order an MDE at any time.[59] An MDE is an important tool that assists the court in (1) determining the nature and extent of the older adult's disability and (2) developing an appropriate guardianship plan and program.[60] The MDE may contain a current psychological, social work, and medical evaluation or other evaluations as directed by the court.[61] The MDE may be helpful in identifying areas in which the older adult is vulnerable to abuse, such as if a decline in an older adult's cognitive capacity tends to make him or her less able to identify scams or renders the older adult dependent upon a perpetrator of abuse.[62]

e. Respondent's Presence at the Hearing

The older adult (the respondent in this context) has a right to attend the hearing, but the respondent's presence is not required.[63] Frequently, the respondent does not appear at the hearing. This may be due to a number of factors, including inability to travel to the courthouse due to incapacity or other disability; lack of access to transportation; or fear, given that it may be the first time the older adult has ever been involved in a court proceeding. If the respondent is unable to make it to the hearing, the court may inquire as to whether he or she wants to be at the hearing but is being prevented from being there by something or

---

53. CSC MANUAL, at 85.15.
54. G.S. 35A-1112(b).
55. G.S. 35A-1107(b).
56. G.S. 35A-1111(e).
57. G.S. 35A-1111(a).
58. *Id.*
59. *Id..*
60. *Id.*
61. *See* G.S. 35A-1111(c).
62. For further discussion of MDEs in incompetency and adult guardianship proceedings, refer to Meredith Smith, *Ordering, Preparing, and Paying for Multidisciplinary Evaluations in Incompetency and Adult Guardianship Proceedings*, SOC. SERVS. L. BULL. No. 47 (Dec. 2016), https://www.sog.unc.edu/publications/bulletins/ordering-preparing-and-paying-multidisciplinary-evaluations-incompetency-and-adult-guardianship.
63. SAXON, *supra* note 2, at § 5.11, p.64.

someone. The court may continue the hearing to allow the respondent to be present. The court may make an accommodation to provide the older adult access to the courthouse. Each North Carolina courthouse has a disability access coordinator who can assist the public with questions about and requests for accommodations.[64] The court may, instead, hold the hearing where the older adult is located, such as a mental health facility or adult care home.

> ### ✎ PRACTICE NOTE
>
> A list of disability access coordinators in each county is available at https://www.nccourts.gov/documents/publications/disability-access-coordinator.

The respondent's appearance at the hearing is important because it enables the court to observe and hear from the respondent to help the court make a determination as to the respondent's capacity. Often a clerk will ask questions of the respondent to better understand the nature and extent of the respondent's lack of capacity.[65] At times an older adult with dementia may begin a conversation in a coherent manner but then start to repeat himself or herself and forget commonly known information or what he or she just told the court.

The respondent's presence also helps ensure that his or her express wishes are made known to the court. This includes, for example, where the respondent wants to live, activities in which the respondent wants to participate, the type of guardian needed, and who the respondent wants to be appointed as guardian.

Finally, the respondent's presence at the hearing can be helpful because it gives the court an opportunity to look for signs of elder abuse. For example, the court will look for bruises on the respondent or for other signs of physical abuse, such as sprains or burns; signs of emotional abuse, such as acting in a frightened or withdrawn manner; and signs of neglect, such as poor hygiene, dirty clothes, unkempt hair, or absence of necessary aids, such as a walker, a hearing aid, or an oxygen tank. Note that if the older adult has concerns about testifying in open court, the older adult, the older adult's counsel, or the GAL may request that the court close the hearing. Upon such request, the court must close the hearing to the public so that only those persons directly involved in or testifying at the hearing are present.[66] This may be particularly helpful in cases where the perpetrator of the abuse appears at the hearing as a means of intimidating the older adult or in order to continue exerting influence over the older adult.

---

64. N.C. Jud. Branch, *Disability Access*, NCCOURTS.GOV, https://www.nccourts.gov/help-topics/disability-and-special-needs/disability-access (describing how to request reasonable accommodation in court proceedings).

65. The court has the authority to call and interrogate witnesses. G.S. 8C-1, Rule 614.

66. G.S. 35A-1112(a).

f. Burden of Proof

The burden of proof, or standard the petitioner must meet to prove the claim that the respondent is incompetent, is *clear, cogent, and convincing evidence.*[67] This is a high standard. It is higher than a preponderance of the evidence, typically seen as 51 percent or more likely than not, but not quite as high as beyond a reasonable doubt, the standard most frequently applied in criminal proceedings.

Figure 4.3. **Burdens of Proof under North Carolina Law**

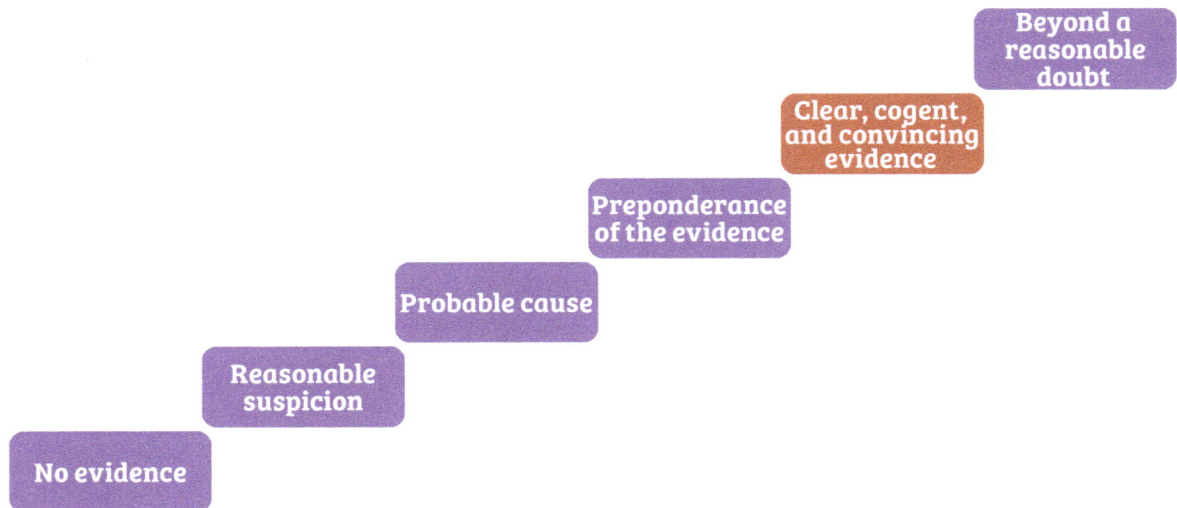

Beyond a reasonable doubt

Clear, cogent, and convincing evidence

Preponderance of the evidence

Probable cause

Reasonable suspicion

No evidence

g. Right to Jury Trial

Typically, the decision about a respondent's competency is made by the clerk. However, a respondent has a right to a jury trial on the issue of his or her competency.[68] A jury trial may be requested by the respondent, the respondent's counsel, or the GAL.[69] Failure to request a jury trial constitutes a waiver of the right.[70]

h. Order

If the clerk or a jury does not find, based on the evidence presented, that the respondent is incompetent, then the court enters an order dismissing the proceeding.[71] If the court or a jury finds that the respondent is incompetent, then the court enters an order to that effect.[72] The court may also find that the respondent is incompetent to a limited extent and appoint a limited guardian.

---

67. CSC MANUAL, at 85.15; G.S. 35A-1112(d).
68. G.S. 35A-1110.
69. *Id.*
70. *Id.*
71. G.S. 35A-1112(c).
72. G.S. 35A-1112(d).

Figure 4.4. Excerpt from Form AOC-SP-202, Order on Petition for Adjudication of Incompetence

ORDER
☐ The clerk/the jury did not find the respondent to be incompetent by clear, cogent, and convincing evidence and it is ORDERED that the proceeding is dismissed.
☐ No hearing was held due to the death of the respondent and it is ORDERED that the proceeding is dismissed.
It is adjudged that:
☐ the respondent is incompetent.
☐ the respondent is incompetent to a limited extent.
☐ It is ORDERED that a guardian be appointed by this court.

2. GUARDIANSHIP PROCEEDING AND APPOINTMENT OF THE GUARDIAN

An incompetent older adult who is not able to act effectively on his or her own behalf has a right to a qualified, responsible guardian.[73] Once the court adjudicates an older adult incompetent or incompetent to a limited extent, it must appoint a guardian to act on the older adult's behalf.[74] The guardianship proceeding is initiated by an application and is in the nature of an estate matter.[75] The application may be joined with or filed subsequent to the petition for the adjudication of incompetence.[76] That petition and the application for the appointment of a guardian are, in practice, typically filed together. Form AOC-SP-200 is both a petition for adjudication of incompetence and an application for guardianship.[77]

During the guardianship proceeding, the court examines both the type of guardian needed by the older adult and who to appoint as a guardian. Once the guardian is appointed, the guardian must then qualify and obtain letters of appointment from the court. The "letters" evidence the guardian's authority to act on behalf of the older adult.

a. Type of Guardianship

In the guardianship proceeding, the court has a duty to make inquiries and to receive evidence necessary to determine the type of guardian to appoint.[78] This is different in each case and depends on the older adult's capacity, needs, assets, and liabilities. For example, if the older adult does not own any property and the only income he receives is from a federal benefit program, such as Social Security, then the clerk may decide to only appoint a guardian of the person because the adult's assets (or lack thereof) do not warrant appointing a guardian of the estate, who will have to post a bond and file annual accountings. The federal benefit may be managed by a representative payee appointed by the federal agency in charge of distributing the benefit, such as the Social Security

---

73. G.S. 35A-1201(a)(2).
74. G.S. 35A-1120.
75. *In re* Winstead, 189 N.C. App. 145, 151 (2008).
76. G.S. 35A-1210.
77. *See* N.C. ADMIN. OFF. OF THE CTS. (AOC), Form SP-200, "Petition for Adjudication of Incompetence and Application for Appointment of Guardian or Limited Guardian," available at https://www.nccourts.gov/assets/documents/forms/sp200-en_0.pdf?fENlxiBSNjB5NUdaKi9J.d4H04dFAjIU.
78. G.S. 35A-1212(a).

Administration. The three main types of guardians—guardian of the estate, guardian of the person, and general guardian—and the different roles of each are discussed further in Section II.D, *infra*.

b. Selection of a Suitable Guardian

The court has a duty to make inquiries and to receive evidence it deems necessary to determine who can most suitably serve as guardian for an older adult.[79] An individual, a corporation, or a county department of social services (DSS) director or assistant director (known as a disinterested public agent guardian) may be appointed as guardian for an older adult in North Carolina.[80] The clerk of superior court must by statute consider who to appoint in a certain order of priority. Specific preferences are given to certain recommendations made in a will, power of attorney, or health care power of attorney. Next, a general preference is given to individuals, then to corporations, and finally, as a last resort, to DSS.[81] Notwithstanding the priority set out in the statute, the clerk is always charged with basing the appointment of the guardian on the best interests of the ward.[82]

> ### ✐ PRACTICE NOTE
>
> *Appointing a Guardian: Order of Priority*
>
> 1. An individual recommended under certain wills (G.S. 35A-1212.1) or a nominee under a power of attorney (G.S. 32C-1-108(a)) or a health care power of attorney (G.S. 32A-22)
> 2. An individual
> 3. A corporation
> 4. A disinterested public agent (DSS)

To determine who can most suitably serve as guardian, the clerk may consider recommendations of next of kin and other persons. Even if it is clear that the older adult lacks capacity, the court may still order a multidisciplinary evaluation (*see* Section II.C.1.d, *supra*) to help with issues related to the guardianship proceeding, including a recommended guardianship plan and program, an evaluation of the suitability of a prospective guardian, and recommendations as to an appropriate party to serve as guardian.[83]

---

79. G.S. 35A-1212(a)(3). The clerk has exclusive authority to appoint the guardian; the issue may not be determined by a jury. *Id.* § 35A-1203. *See also id.* §§ 1-301.3(a), (b).

80. G.S. 35A-1213, -1214. The only disinterested public agent qualified to serve as a guardian in North Carolina is the director or assistant director of a county department of social services (DSS). *Id.* §§ 35A-1214; -1202(4). The DSS director or assistant director is appointed as guardian by the court in its order, but a social worker employed by the county DSS carries out the day-to-day powers and duties of guardian.

81. G.S. 35A-1214 (general order of priority); 35A-1212.1 (effect of a recommendation in a will); 32C-1-108(a) (effect of a nomination of a guardian in a power of attorney); 32A-22 (effect of a nomination of a guardian of the person in a health care power of attorney).

82. G.S. 35A-1214.

83. G.S. 35A-1111; -1212(b), (c).

The risk of abuse of an older adult under guardianship may be reduced by effective court screening of potential guardians.[84] This includes

1. appointing an effective GAL to represent the older adult who conducts civil and criminal background checks on potential guardians and takes other steps to screen potential guardians, such as interviewing the potential guardian prior to the hearing;
2. asking any potential guardian at the hearing questions similar to those questions set out in the *Preventing, Identifying, and Responding to Elder Abuse in Incompetency and Adult Guardianship Cases: A Bench Card for North Carolina Clerks of Superior Court*, available at protectadults.sog.unc.edu;
3. asking the older adult at the hearing who he or she wants to serve as guardian by employing interviewing techniques and tips similar to those set out in Appendix B; and
4. asking next of kin and other interested persons present at the hearing questions about the potential guardian's relationship with the older adult.

c. Qualification of a Guardian

After the clerk of superior court adjudicates incompetence and appoints a guardian, the guardian appointed by the clerk's order must then qualify with the court to obtain letters. The guardian initiates this process by submitting an application for letters (Form AOC-E-206). The form application contains a preliminary inventory—a listing/statement of the assets and liabilities of the ward—that is completed if a person is to act as a guardian with authority over the ward's property.[85]

Figure 4.5. **Steps to Qualify as a Guardian**

1. Guardian applies for letters (Form AOC-E-206) and submits bond, if GOE or GG (Form AOC-E-401)
2. Guardian takes an oath/affirmation (Form AOC-E-400)
3. Clerk enters order authorizing issuance of letters (Form AOC-E-402) and the clerk issues letters depending on the type of guardian appointed:
   - Letters of Appointment Guardian of the Person: Form AOC-E-408
   - Letters of Appointment Limited Guardian of the Person: Form AOC-E-418
   - Letters of Appointment Guardian of the Estate: Form AOC-E-407
   - Letters of Appointment Limited Guardian of the Estate: Form AOC-E-417
   - Letters of Appointment General Guardian: Form AOC-E-413
   - Letters of Appointment Limited General Guardian: Form AOC-E-419

---

84. U.S. Gov't Accountability Off., GAO-17-33, Elder Abuse: The Extent of Abuse by Guardians Is Unknown, but Some Measures Exist to Help Protect Older Adults 19–20 (2016) (hereinafter GAO Elder Abuse Report).

85. AOC, Form E-206, "Application for Letters," available at https://www.nccourts.gov/documents/forms/application-for-letters-of-guardianship-for-an-incompetent-person.

A critical step in the qualification process involves the posting of a bond. If a guardian of the estate (GOE) or general guardian (GG) is appointed by the clerk, then the GOE or GG must post a bond before receiving any property and before the clerk will issue letters of appointment.[86] A guardian of the person (GOP) typically does not have to post a bond.[87] The amount of the bond is calculated based on the value of the ward's personal property and the rents and profits of the ward's real estate.[88] Typically, the guardian uses Form AOC-E-401 to post the bond, which contains forms for both a corporate surety bond and a personal surety bond.

> ### ✏ PRACTICE NOTE
>
> **Critical Tool to Protect against Elder Abuse**
>
> A bond from an appropriate surety in the appropriate amount throughout the guardianship is a critically important tool to protect an older adult from financial exploitation by a guardian. The purpose of the bond is to protect the ward's estate and to compensate the ward if the ward suffers a financial loss as a result of the guardian's failure to properly exercise his or her duties to the ward.[89]

The bonding company will do a credit check on the potential guardian before issuing the bond. The ability to be bonded is often a challenge for potential guardians and may result in someone otherwise qualified to serve being unable to serve as a GOE or GG. The individual may still be appointed as GOP if otherwise qualified, and frequently the public guardian or a local attorney is appointed as GOE when no other suitable person qualifies.

The bond is conditioned on the guardian faithfully executing the trust placed in the guardian and obeying all lawful orders relating to the guardianship committed to the guardian.[90] If, for example, the guardian uses funds in the ward/older adult's bank account for the guardian's own personal purpose, the guardian may be removed and a successor guardian may make a claim against the bond on the older adult's behalf. If the surety company pays out on a bond claim, the surety company may then file a civil action against the former guardian for recovery of the amounts owed to the surety company.

After the bond is posted, to ensure that the older adult's property remains adequately protected, the guardian is charged with two critical responsibilities.

---

86. G.S. 35A-1230. There are exceptions to the guardian's duty to post a bond. For example, if a parent's will makes a recommendation for a guardian of an unmarried child adjudicated incompetent, the parent may also direct in the will that the guardian may qualify and serve without giving bond; the guardian may serve without a bond unless the clerk determines that the best interests of the ward require otherwise. *Id.* § 35A-1212.1.

87. G.S. 35A-1230. The clerk may require a nonresident guardian of the person to post a bond or other security. *Id.* The Secretary of the N.C. Department of Health and Human Services is required to purchase individual or blanket bonds that cover all disinterested public agents appointed as guardians of the estate, guardians of the person, and general guardians. *Id.* § 35A-1239. The bonds are conditioned on the faithful performance of their duties as guardians and are made payable to the State of North Carolina. *Id.* The premiums are paid by the State. *Id.*

88. G.S. 35A-1231(a).

89. CSC MANUAL, at 86.27.

90. G.S. 35A-1231(a).

1. **Renew the bond.** If the bond is from a personal surety, the guardian must renew the bond every three years.[91]
2. **Adjust the bond.** The guardian is required to increase the bond, as appropriate. The guardian must increase the amount of the bond before he or she receives the proceeds from the sale of real or personal property owned by the older adult if the value is believed to be greater than the value used in determining the amount of the bond.[92] The amount of the bond may be decreased in the discretion of the clerk if the amount of assets held by the guardian are reduced.[93]

While the duties to renew and adjust the bond fall on the guardian, the clerk may be liable to the ward's estate if the clerk fails to

- take a good and sufficient security for the bond,
- require an increase in the amount of the bond to cover an increase in the ward's assets, or
- compel the timely renewal of a personal surety bond.[94]

After the guardian submits an application for letters and the clerk approves the bond, the guardian takes an oath or affirmation (see Form AOC-E-400). In the oath, the guardian swears or affirms (1) to faithfully and honestly discharge the duties imposed on him or her to the best of his or her skill and abilities and according to law and (2) to support and maintain the laws of the United States and the State of North Carolina.[95] The clerk then enters an order authorizing the issuance of letters (see Form AOC-E-402) and issues letters.[96] The letters issued depend on the type of guardian appointed by the clerk. The N.C. Administrative Office of the Courts maintains the form letters referenced in Figure 4.5, *supra*. The letters attest to the authority granted to the guardian by the court and provide that the guardian's authority is in full force and effect. The letters also prescribe the nature and extent of the guardian's authority to act on the ward's behalf.

3. EMERGENCY CIRCUMSTANCES

Three tools are available under North Carolina guardianship law to address an emergency situation involving an older adult who lacks capacity. Examples of such emergency situations include (1) where someone has access to an older adult's bank accounts and is presently taking money from the account and (2) where an older adult is in need of an immediate medical procedure and is unable to consent to treatment. These tools are available prior to an adjudication of incompetency by the court. They may be critical to protecting an adult from ongoing elder abuse. The tools require a lower standard of proof, have truncated notice requirements, and enable the court to enter time-limited orders to respond to specific emergencies.

---

91. G.S. 35A-1236.
92. G.S. 35A-1231(b).
93. G.S. 35A-1233.
94. G.S. 35A-1238, -1231, -1236.
95. *See* G.S. 11-11.
96. G.S. 35A-1203, -1206, -1215.

Figure 4.6. **Emergency Guardianship, Special Protective Orders, and Interim Guardianship**

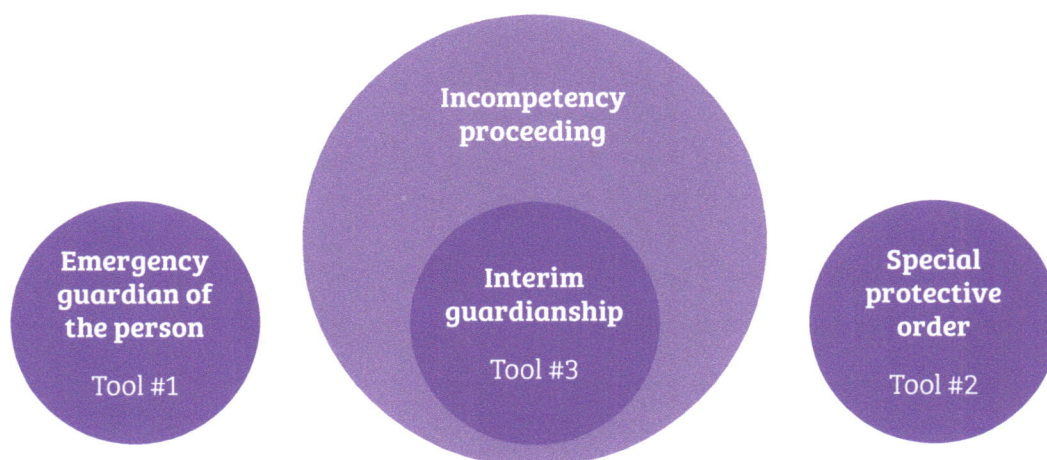

The first two tools fall under a court's "special jurisdiction" and are referred to in this manual as (1) emergency guardianship of the person and (2) special protective orders.[97] These types of emergency orders are appropriate when a North Carolina court's authority (jurisdiction) to decide a particular case is unclear, undetermined, or otherwise lacking because the respondent (the older adult) has contacts with multiple states. The third tool, interim guardianship, is available when a North Carolina court has the jurisdiction to hear the case.[98] It is available when there is or reasonably appears to be an imminent or foreseeable risk of harm to the respondent or the respondent's property.[99]

a. Emergency Guardianship of the Person and Special Protective Orders

An older adult may have lived in North Carolina for many years preceding the filing of a petition of incompetence in this state and may have few to no contacts with other states beyond visits for vacation or business. Under these circumstances, it is clear that North Carolina is the most appropriate state for the filing of an incompetency petition and the appointment and oversight of a guardian. There are no concerns about whether a North Carolina court has the authority to hear a particular case.

There may be other cases when an older adult has contacts with multiple states prior to the filing of the incompetency petition. This will most often be evidenced on the first page of the "Petition for Adjudication of Incompetence and Application for Appointment of Guardian or Limited Guardian," Form AOC-SP-200.

---

97. G.S. 35B-18(a).
98. G.S. 35A-1114(a).
99. G.S. 35A-1114(d).

Figure 4.7. Excerpt from Petition for Adjudication of Incompetence and Application for Appointment of Guardian or Limited Guardian (Form AOC-SP-200)

In support of this Petition, the undersigned states:

1. During the past twelve (12) months, the above-named respondent was physically present as follows:

Period of Physical Presence *(include up to the 12 months prior to the filing date of the petition; do not list periods of temporary absence)*		Address
From	**To**	
	Present	

For example, the older adult may live in North Carolina during the summer and Florida during the winter. Or the older adult may move from another state where he had lived his entire life to live with an adult child in North Carolina. There may also be more nefarious circumstances at play, such as when a family member or caregiver moves the older adult to North Carolina to isolate her from other family and friends and to take control of her finances through a guardianship proceeding (also known as "granny snatching"). Or one family member of an older adult may file a petition for guardianship in North Carolina and another may file a petition for guardianship in another state, creating dueling petitions in two different state courts. There may be confusion or conflict over which state is the most appropriate one to hear the incompetency proceeding and appoint a guardian to act on behalf of the older adult, if needed. The older adult is caught in the push and pull of the conflict and incurs unnecessary costs related to multiple proceedings or to a proceeding filed in an inappropriate state.

The Uniform Adult Guardianship and Protective Proceedings Jurisdiction Act (UAGPPJA) in G.S. Chapter 35B applies to North Carolina incompetency and adult guardianship proceedings. It provides the exclusive jurisdictional basis for a North Carolina court to adjudicate incompetence and appoint a guardian for an adult.[100] The purpose of UAGPPJA is to ensure that jurisdiction to hear a guardianship case exists in one and only one state, except when an emergency exists or an individual owns property in multiple states.[101]

---

100. G.S. 35B-16.
101. G.S. 35B-1(d)(1).

Before adjudicating incompetence and appointing a guardian for an older adult under G.S. Chapter 35A, a North Carolina court must first determine that it has jurisdiction under Chapter 35B to hear the case over other states because it is (1) the respondent's "home state," [102] (2) a "significant-connection state,"[103] or (3) an "other" state.[104]

The North Carolina court may need to (1) communicate with a court in another state to determine which court will hear the case or (2) take additional evidence at a hearing on jurisdiction here in North Carolina.[105] While the North Carolina court sorts out the jurisdictional questions, there may be an emergency with regard to the older adult or the older adult's property.

i. Emergency Guardianship of the Person

UAGPPJA provides that a clerk of superior court has special jurisdiction to appoint a guardian of the person (GOP) in an emergency for a term not exceeding ninety days for a respondent/older adult who is physically present in North Carolina.[106]

💬 **KEY TERM**

Emergency is defined as a circumstance that likely will result in substantial harm to a respondent's health, safety, or welfare, and for which the appointment of a guardian of the person is necessary because no other person has authority and is willing to act on the respondent's behalf.[107]

---

102. G.S. 35B-15(a)(2) (defining "home state" as "[t]he state in which the respondent was physically present, including any period of temporary absence, for at least six consecutive months immediately before the filing of a petition for the adjudication of incompetence; or if none, the state in which the respondent was physically present, including any period of temporary absence, for at least six consecutive months ending within the six months prior to the filing of the petition for the adjudication of incompetence").

103. G.S. 35B-15(a)(3) (defining "significant-connection state" as "[a] state, other than the home state, with which the respondent has a significant connection other than mere physical presence and in which substantial evidence about the respondent is available"). Factors to consider when determining whether a respondent has a significant connection with a state are listed in G.S. 35B-15(b) and include location of the respondent's family members and property, the length of time the respondent was present in that state, and civic ties such as voter and motor vehicle registration.

104. G.S. 35B-17(3).

105. *See* G.S. 35B-5, -23(2).

106. G.S. 35B-18(a)(1).

107. G.S. 35B-15(a)(1).

An emergency GOP may make decisions related to the care, custody, and control of the respondent. There are no forms available for the petition for emergency guardianship, the court's order appointing the emergency GOP, or letters authorizing the emergency GOP to act on the respondent's behalf.

The appointment of an emergency GOP may provide a bridge to allow the court to resolve any jurisdictional questions while ensuring that the respondent's health, safety, and welfare are protected. An emergency guardianship of the person does not grant authority over the respondent's property.

◇ EXAMPLE

Emergency Guardianship of the Person

Alice moves her 88-year-old mother, Jane, to North Carolina to live with her. Jane has lived her entire life in Georgia—her extended family and friends are there, as is her house, car, and personal property, except for a vacation home she owns in the North Carolina mountains. Jane was diagnosed with dementia and there has been a recent severe decline in her condition. Alice petitions to have Jane adjudicated incompetent and seeks to be Jane's appointed guardian in North Carolina. Jane's son, Tom, contests the petition in North Carolina and states that North Carolina does not have jurisdiction to hear the case; the appropriate state to hear the case is Georgia, he argues. There are allegations that Alice keeps the refrigerator and pantry in her house locked and that she has not taken Jane to see a doctor since moving her to North Carolina five months ago. The North Carolina court appoints Tom as emergency guardian of the person to allow him to seek treatment on behalf of his mother and move her to a stable residence while the jurisdictional questions are addressed by the court. Tom plans to file a petition for guardianship in Georgia.

ii. Special Protective Order for Certain Property

Similar to the appointment of an emergency guardian, a special protective order is available when there is a question as to a North Carolina court's jurisdiction to hear a case.[108] The North Carolina clerk of superior court always has the authority to issue a special protective order with respect to real or tangible personal property owned by a respondent located in North Carolina.[109] This is an important tool when an older adult who owns real or tangible personal property located in this state is the subject of financial exploitation. The clerk's order grants a GG or GOE the authority to take control of and protect the real and tangible personal property of the older adult located in North Carolina while the jurisdictional questions are sorted out between North Carolina and some other state or states.

---

108. G.S. 35B-18(a)(2).
109. *Id.*

b. Interim Guardianship

One of the most important tools available in guardianship to stop the abuse or exploitation of an older adult is interim guardianship.[110] An interim guardian is a temporary guardian appointed prior to an adjudication of incompetence.[111] The purpose of the interim guardianship is to provide temporary protection for a person who requires immediate intervention to address conditions that constitute imminent or foreseeable risk of harm to the person's physical well-being or to the person's estate.[112]

A verified motion for interim guardianship (Form AOC-SP-198) may be filed at the time of or subsequent to the filing of a petition for the adjudication of incompetence by the petitioner or the guardian ad litem.[113] The clerk may also appoint an interim guardian on his or her own motion at the incompetency hearing.[114] Unlike emergency guardianship of the person or special protective orders, the court must have jurisdiction of the underlying incompetency and guardianship proceeding as a home state, a significant connecting state, or other state to appoint an interim guardian.[115]

Upon the filing of a motion for an interim guardian, the clerk immediately sets a date, time, and place for a hearing on the motion.[116] The motion and notice of hearing on interim guardianship must be served promptly on the petitioner, respondent, guardian ad litem attorney, and anyone else designated by the clerk.[117]

If at the hearing the clerk finds that (i) there is reasonable cause to believe that the older adult is incompetent, and (ii) there is or reasonably appears to be an imminent or foreseeable risk of harm to the older adult's physical well-being or estate that requires immediate intervention, the clerk immediately enters an order appointing an interim guardian.[118] Once the court holds a hearing on the motion for appointment of an interim guardian, the petitioner may not voluntarily dismiss the petition for adjudication of incompetence.[119]

The clerk's order appointing an interim guardian sets forth the interim guardian's powers and duties.[120] These powers and duties are limited and extend only so far and so long as necessary to meet the conditions necessitating the appointment of an interim guardian.[121]

---

110. For additional information on interim guardianship, refer to Meredith Smith, *Some Things to Remember About Interim Guardianship*, ON THE CIVIL SIDE: A UNC SCH. OF GOV'T BLOG (May 4, 2016), https://civil.sog.unc.edu/some-things-to-remember-about-interim-guardianship/.

111. G.S. 35A-1101(11) (defining "interim guardian" as a guardian, appointed prior to adjudication of incompetence and for a temporary period, for a person who requires immediate intervention to address conditions that constitute imminent or foreseeable risk of harm to the person's physical well-being or to the person's estate").

112. G.S. 35A-1114(b).

113. G.S. 35A-1114(a).

114. G.S. 35A-1112(b1).

115. G.S. 35A-1114(a).

116. G.S. 35A-1114(c).

117. G.S. 35A-1114(c1).

118. G.S. 35A-1114(d).

119. G.S. 35A-1114(f).

120. G.S. 35A-1114(e).

121. *Id.*

An interim guardian's authority does not continue indefinitely. An interim guardianship terminates on the earliest of[122]

- the date specified in the clerk's order;

- forty-five days after entry of the clerk's order unless the clerk, for good cause shown, extends that period for up to forty-five additional days;

- when any guardians are appointed following an adjudication of incompetence; or

- when the incompetency petition is dismissed by the court.

As a practical matter, the longest period of time that an interim guardianship could possibly be in place is ninety days from entry of the clerk's order. After that time, the interim guardian no longer has authority to act because the interim guardianship terminates.

An interim guardian whose authority relates only to the person of the respondent does not have to post a bond.[123] However, an interim guardian of the respondent's estate must post a bond in an amount determined by the clerk and submit an account to the clerk.[124]

◇ EXAMPLE

Interim Guardianship and Elder Abuse

Mary, an 89-year-old woman, fell in her yard one day. A younger man was driving by and stopped to help her up. He befriended Mary and began spending time with her by helping her with chores, paying bills, and administering her medication. After a few weeks, he had Mary sign a power of attorney (POA) naming him as her agent. Mary wrote several large checks for tens of thousands of dollars to the man, purportedly for home renovations that were only partially started but never completed, and Mary co-signed a car loan with him. After Mary's family became concerned about the nature of the relationship, her daughter filed an incompetency petition (AOC-SP-200) together with a motion for interim guardianship (AOC-SP-198). The interim guardian of the estate revoked the POA and put a freeze on Mary's accounts to stop further access to them by the man.

D. WHAT IS THE ROLE OF THE GUARDIAN?

A guardian is charged with making decisions for an older adult who lacks capacity. The guardian must make decisions that are in the best interests of the older adult.[125] This means that a guardian may first consider any express directions set out by the older adult on the issue underlying a particular decision. If there are no express directions,

---

122. *Id.*
123. *Id.*
124. *Id.*
125. G.S. 35A-1241(a)(3); *id.* § 35A-1251.

then the guardian may look to make a decision that aligns with the older adult's history of decision-making, including the adult's lifestyle, values, desires, and needs. Finally, if there are no express directions or guidance based on the adult's history, the guardian then makes a decision that the guardian determines is reasonable and prudent and in the older adult's best interests, which is the lodestar of guardianship decision-making.[126]

The extent of a guardian's decision-making powers and, thus, the guardian's duties, depends on the type of guardian appointed by the court. There are three primary types of guardians under North Carolina law: a guardian of the estate (GOE), a guardian of the person (GOP), and a general guardian (GG). For purposes of this section, references to a GOE and a GOP include a GG.

1. GUARDIAN OF THE ESTATE (GOE)

a. Powers of the GOE

A GOE's powers are broad. The GOE has the power to perform in a reasonable and prudent manner every act that a reasonable and prudent person would perform incident to the collection, preservation, management, and use of the older adult's estate to administer the older adult's estate (1) legally and (2) in the older adult's best interests.[127] These powers continue until the guardianship is terminated.[128]

North Carolina statutory law lists some of the specific powers of a GOE but makes clear that the list is not exhaustive.[129] The list includes the power to take possession of the older adult's estate, to receive assets, to maintain actions to recover property, to complete contracts, to abandon property, to renounce an interest in property, to insure property against loss, to pay necessary expenses of administering the older adult's estate, to employ professionals such as attorneys and accountants, and to pay taxes and expenses to protect the estate.[130] A GOE has the power to authorize a financial institution to provide access to the older adult's financial records and may also have the authority to place a security freeze with a credit reporting agency. Both actions are discussed in greater detail in Chapter 7.

---

126. G.S. 35A-1251, -1242(a2).
127. G.S. 35A-1251.
128. G.S. 35A-1295(a).
129. G.S. 35A-1251.
130. *Id.*

PRACTICE NOTE

It is important for the GOE to know what property the older adult owns so that the GOE can plan for the older adult's care and secure the older adult's real and personal property. The GOE is required to file an inventory with the court within three months of being appointed by the court but should begin taking action to identify and secure the older adult's property immediately after being appointed. This may include the following.

- Filing a change of address for the older adult to redirect mail to the GOE for at least six months to ensure that the GOE receives all bills and other notices related to the older adult's property. It also may help prevent consumer scam letters from reaching the older adult. The GOE should be sure to provide the older adult with any personal mail items received in a timely manner.
- Printing out copies of the older adult's bank and other financial statements for at least the last year and review what income has been coming in and what drafts have been going out to identify the scope of the older adult's property as well as whether there have been any suspicious transactions.

The default rule is that a GOE may exercise decision-making powers on behalf of the older adult without prior court approval.[131] There are exceptions to this rule. The GOE must initiate a proceeding before the court seeking court approval before taking any of the below-listed actions related to the older adult's property. Failure to obtain court approval of any of these actions may result in removal of the GOE.[132]

Actions by a GOE that require court approval include

- any action for which court approval is mandated by court order;

- expending estate principal;[133]

- selling, mortgaging, or exchanging real property;[134]

- leasing real estate for more than three years;[135]

- exercising certain powers with respect to revocable trusts;[136]

- selling, leasing, or exchanging any personal property in the aggregate value of more than $5,000 per accounting period (typically, one year);[137]

---

131. *See Id.*
132. *See* G.S. 35A-1290.
133. G.S. 35A-1251(12), (21).
134. *See generally* G.S. Ch. 35A, Art. 14 (Sale, Mortgage, Exchange or Lease of Ward's Estate).
135. G.S. 35A-1251(17)a. *See also id.* § 35A-1301(b).
136. G.S. 35A-1251(24).
137. G.S. 35A-1251(17)a.

- making gifts of the older adult's property;[138] and

- paying commissions to the guardian.[139]

A guardian may not receive a commission until the clerk enters an order allowing the commission and setting the amount of the commission. A GOE is entitled to receive commissions for the time and trouble spent in managing the older adult's estate, subject to court approval.[140] The commission may not exceed 5 percent of the receipts and expenditures of personal property made by the guardian.[141] In determining the amount of a commission, the clerk will consider the time, responsibility, trouble, and skill involved in the management of the older adult's estate.[142] The clerk may also take into account fees paid for professional services performed in the ordinary course of estate administration, including services performed by attorneys and accountants.[143] A petition for commissions is generally filed with an annual account so that the clerk may review the commissionable receipts and expenditures made by the guardian during the previous year.

A GOE may employ an attorney to advise or assist the guardian in the performance of the guardian's duties.[144] Attorneys' fees are a proper expense to be charged in the guardian's account if the fees are reasonable in amount and expended in connection with the proper administration of the estate.[145] The guardian may be individually liable for attorneys' fees not approved by the court.[146]

b. Duties of the GOE

A GOE is charged with certain duties, both as to the older adult and to the court. These include

- involving the older adult in decision-making to the extent possible;[147]

- permitting the older adult to exercise those rights within his or her comprehension and judgment, allowing for the possibility of error to the same degree as is allowed for persons who are not incompetent;[148]

- taking reasonable and prudent actions on the older adult's behalf;[149]

- administering the older adult's estate legally and in the older adult's best interests;[150]

---

138. *See generally* G.S. Ch. 35A, Art. 17 (Gifts from Income for Certain Purposes), Art. 18 (Gifts from Principal for Certain Purposes).

139. G.S. 35A-1269.

140. *Id.*

141. G.S. 28A-23-3(a) (G.S. 35A-1269 states that commissions shall be determined in the same manner and under the same rules and restrictions pursuant to G.S. 28A-23-3 and -4).

142. G.S. 28A-23-3(b).

143. G.S. 28A-23-3(a).

144. G.S. 35A-1251(14).

145. Md. Cas. Co. v. Lawing, 225 N.C. 103 (1945).

146. *Id.*

147. G.S. 35A-1201(a)(5).

148. *Id.*

149. G.S. 35A-1251.

150. *Id.*

- taking possession of the older adult's property and using it for the older adult's benefit;[151]

- diligently attempting to collect money and other obligations due to the older adult by lawful means;[152]

- paying taxes and other assessments owed by the older adult out of the older adult's estate;[153]

- observing "a standard of judgment and care under the circumstances then prevailing that an ordinarily prudent person of discretion and intelligence" would observe when serving as a fiduciary of the property of another person;[154]

- using any special skills or expertise for the benefit of the older adult;[155]

- obeying lawful court orders pertaining to the guardianship;[156]

- obtaining, renewing, and modifying any bond, as required by law;[157] and

- timely filing inventories and accountings with the court.[158]

The GOE's duties terminate when the guardianship is terminated, with one exception.[159] The GOE has a continued duty to file accountings after the guardianship is terminated until discharged by an order of the clerk.[160]

2. GUARDIAN OF THE PERSON (GOP)

a. Powers of the GOP

A GOP has far-reaching powers over an older adult, including custody.[161] Unless the court order appointing the GOP provides otherwise, the GOP has the power to make decisions relating to the following matters:

- Where the older adult lives. The GOP must give preference to locations in North Carolina that are not treatment facilities.[162] If the only available and appropriate location is a treatment facility, the GOP must give preference to community-based treatment facilities, such as group homes or nursing homes, over treatment facilities that are not community-based.[163]

---

151. G.S. 35A-1253(1).
152. G.S. 35A-1253(2).
153. G.S. 35A-1253(3).
154. G.S. 35A-1253(4).
155. *Id.*
156. G.S. 35A-1253(5).
157. G.S. 35A-1230, -1231, -1232.
158. G.S. 35A-1253(5).
159. G.S. 35A-1295(a).
160. G.S. 35A-1295(b).
161. G.S. 35A-1241 (listing powers and duties of a guardian of the person). *See also* Corbett v. Lynch, 251 N.C. App. 40 (2016).
162. G.S. 35A-1241(a)(2).
163. *Id.*

- Social interactions and visitation. This includes the power to impose limits if interactions would be deleterious to the older adult.

- Day-to-day needs. This includes arranging for the older adult's meals and grocery delivery, hygiene, and clothing, as necessary.

- Training, education, employment, rehabilitation, and habilitation for the older adult.[164]

- Consent to medical, psychological, or other professional care needed by the older adult.[165]

- Consent for the older adult to receive necessary legal or other professional counsel.[166]

The default rule is that the GOP may exercise decision-making powers on behalf of the older adult without prior court approval. There are exceptions to this rule. Decisions that require court approval include those involving

- any action for which court approval is mandated by court order; and

- consenting to sterilization of an older adult with a mental illness or intellectual disability, which requires a separate proceeding initiated pursuant to G.S. 35A-1245.[167]

Unlike a GOE, a GOP is not entitled to receive a fee for services performed and time spent carrying out guardianship duties.[168] The GOP is entitled to reimbursement from the older adult's estate for reasonable and proper expenses incurred in carrying out guardianship duties.[169]

There are legal limitations on the liability of the GOP to the older adult and to the older adult's estate. The GOP may not be held liable for damages to the older adult or to the older adult's estate if[170]

- the GOP authorizes or gives consent or approval for the older adult to receive legal, psychological, or other professional care and damages result from negligence or other acts of a third party or

- the GOP authorizes medical treatment or surgery for the older adult and does so acting in good faith and without negligence.

---

164. G.S. 35A-1241(a)(1).

165. G.S. 35A-1241(a)(3). Provided, however, that if the ward has a health care agent appointed under a valid health care power of attorney, the health care agent has the right to make medical decisions unless the clerk has suspended his or her authority. *Id. See also* Aimee Wall, *The Guardian's Role in Health Care Decision-Making*, ON THE CIVIL SIDE: A UNC SCH. OF GOV'T BLOG (Apr. 5, 2017), https://civil.sog.unc.edu/the-guardians-role-in-health-care-decision-making/.

166. G.S. 35A-1241(a)(3).

167. *Id.*

168. *See* G.S. 35A-1241(b).

169. *Id.*

170. G.S. 35A-1241(c).

b. Duties of the GOP

The GOP is charged with certain duties, both as to the older adult and to the court. These include

- involving the older adult in decision-making to the extent possible;[171]

- permitting the older adult to exercise those rights within his or her comprehension and judgment, allowing for the possibility of error to the same degree as is allowed for persons who are not incompetent;[172]

- acting in the older adult's best interests;

- making provision for the older adult's care, comfort, and maintenance;[173]

- arranging for training, education, employment, rehabilitation, or habilitation that are appropriate for the older adult;[174]

- taking reasonable care of the ward's clothing, furniture, vehicles, and other personal effects that are with the older adult;[175]

- obeying lawful court orders pertaining to the guardianship;[176] and

- timely filing status reports with the court, when required by law or court order.[177]

These duties continue until the guardianship is terminated.[178]

E. WHAT COURT OVERSIGHT EXISTS TO PROTECT OLDER ADULTS UNDER GUARDIANSHIP?

The court retains jurisdiction following the appointment of a guardian and oversees the guardianship as the "ultimate guardian" with the authority to take action to protect the interests of the incompetent older adult.[179] The risk of the abuse of an adult under guardianship may be mitigated, in part, by effective court oversight of the guardianship.[180] This includes ensuring timely and complete status reports, inventories, and accountings are filed with the court and taking actions to compel reports, which in extreme cases may result in holding the guardian in contempt of court. It also includes holding hearings to address information presented to the court about potential abuse of the older adult, modifying the guardianship when necessary to protect the older adult or better serve the older adult's interests, and, in extreme cases, removing the guardian for failing to protect an older adult from abuse or because the guardian is the perpetrator of abuse. For purposes of this section, references to a GOE or a GOP include a GG.

---

171. G.S. 35A-1201(a)(5).
172. *Id.*
173. G.S. 35A-1241(a)(1).
174. *Id.*
175. *Id.*
176. G.S. 35A-1241.
177. G.S. 35A-1242. The duty to file status reports is discussed in further detail in Section II.E.1.
178. G.S. 35A-1295(a).
179. *In re* Thomas, 290 N.C. 410, 424–25 (1976).
180. GAO ELDER ABUSE REPORT, at 19–20.

1. STATUS REPORTS AND STATUS REPORT HEARINGS

Certain GOPs are required to file status reports with the court. These reports must be filed

- in all cases where a corporation or disinterested public agent guardian (DSS) has been appointed as a GOP and

- when a court appoints an individual to serve as an older adult's GOP and orders the individual to file status reports.[181]

> ### ✎ PRACTICE NOTE
>
> The N.C. Department of Health and Human Services maintains a form status report that is used by many county departments of social services and by corporations. This form is available at https://policies.ncdhhs.gov/divisional/aging-and-adult/guardianship/manual/guardianship-status-report.
>
> Instructions for the form are available at https://policies.ncdhhs.gov/divisional/aging-and-adult/guardianship/manual/guardianship-status-report-instructions.

If required by law or ordered by a court to file a status report, a GOP must file an initial report within six months after being appointed and then annually thereafter.[182] The status report should contain a summary of the work the guardian has performed on behalf of the ward and must include[183]

- a report or summary of recent medical and dental examinations of the ward by one or more physicians and dentists; if the guardian has made diligent but unsuccessful attempts to secure this information, the guardian must include an explanation and documentation of all actions taken to secure this information;

- a report on the guardian's performance of the duties imposed by law and in the clerk's order appointing the guardian;

- a report on the ward's residence, education, employment, and rehabilitation or habilitation;

- a report on the guardian's efforts to restore the ward's competency;

- a report on the guardian's efforts to seek alternatives to guardianship;

- a report on efforts to identify alternative guardians (if the guardian is a disinterested public agent or corporation);

- the guardian's recommendations for implementing a more limited guardianship, preserving for the ward the opportunity to exercise rights that are within the ward's comprehension and judgment;

---

181. G.S. 35A-1242(a).
182. *Id.*
183. G.S. 35A-1242(a1), (a2).

- any additional reports or information required by the clerk; and

- any additional information pertaining to the ward's best interests.

The status report must be filed with the court under the guardian's oath or affirmation or with the signature of a witness attesting that the report is complete and accurate so far as the guardian can determine.[184] The status report is not available for public inspection; it is only available to the guardian, the court, the ward, or the state or local human services agency providing services to the ward.[185]

After the report is filed with the court, the clerk, on his or her own motion, or on the motion of an interested party, may file a motion in the cause to request modification of the order appointing the guardian or guardians or for consideration of any matters contained in the status report.[186] The clerk may then hold a hearing on any matters contained in the motion and enter an order to address any issues in the status report, including ordering the guardian to take certain actions to remedy or address any deficiencies in the report.

> ### ◇ EXAMPLE
>
> *A status report is filed by a corporate GOP for an older adult. The status report fails to include information about the older adult's residence, education, employment, and rehabilitation or habilitation. It also does not identify any doctor or dentist visits by the ward in the prior year. The clerk may, on his or her own motion, calendar a hearing and notice the guardian of the hearing. The clerk could then inquire about the deficiencies in the report to ensure that the guardian is not neglecting the older adult and is carrying out its duties as GOP.*

2. INVENTORY AND ACCOUNTINGS

A GOE is required to file both an inventory and regular accountings with the court. These filings are critical to helping the court oversee the guardian and detect financial exploitation of the older adult, including whether the guardian is using the older adult's property for his or her own benefit. Some expenditures on an accounting, such as a $100 bill at a restaurant or a $500 cost for vacation travel when the incompetent adult is in a locked dementia unit, will raise red flags with the court and are not permissible uses of the incompetent adult's property by the guardian.[187]

a. Inventory

Within three months of being appointed guardian of the estate (GOE) for an older adult, a GOE must file an inventory, under oath, with the clerk of superior court listing the older

---

184. G.S. 35A-1242(b).
185. G.S. 35A-1242(c).
186. G.S. 35A-1242(d).
187. Note that some expenditures of the older adult's estate for the benefit of others are permissible, such as the expenditure of estate income for support, maintenance, and education of the ward's minor children, spouse, and dependents. G.S. 35A-1251(21).

adult's real and personal property.[188] Typically, the guardian uses Form AOC-E-510. The GOE must file a supplemental inventory when (1) the guardian becomes aware of property that was not included in the original inventory or (2) the value or description of any property or of the older adult's interest in the property is erroneous or misleading.[189] Common items on an inventory include real property, bank accounts, vehicles, household goods, jewelry, and income from benefit programs such as Social Security or veteran's benefits.

b. Accountings

The GOE has a duty to file annual accountings with the clerk for so long as any of the older adult's estate remains in the guardian's control.[190] The accounting is filed under oath with the clerk.[191] Typically, the guardian uses Form AOC-E-506. The accounting must include the amount of property received or invested by the GOE, as well as the receipts and disbursements for the preceding year.[192] The GOE is required to produce vouchers for all payments or verified proof for payments instead of vouchers.[193] The clerk has the authority to examine any person, including the guardian, on any matter related to the accounting or the estate.[194] The clerk carefully reviews and audits the account and, if the clerk approves the accounting, he or she then endorses approval on the accounting.[195]

3. CONTEMPT

If a guardian fails to file a satisfactory status report, inventory, or accounting, or if the guardian does not file a status report, inventory, or accounting at all, the clerk of court has the authority to compel the required filings.[196] This includes the authority after notice and hearing to hold a guardian in civil contempt and to imprison the guardian for so long as the deficiency exists or the filing is absent, for a period of up to one year.[197] The clerk may, in addition to or in lieu of holding the guardian in contempt, remove the guardian and appoint a new guardian.[198] Compelling timely filings is critical to ensure that any exploitation or other abuse of the older adult under guardianship does not go undiscovered or unaddressed. When a guardian fails to file required reports, inventories, and accountings, it is a warning sign for potential abuse.

4. MOTIONS IN THE CAUSE

An important mechanism for raising potential concerns about elder abuse to the court after the appointment of a guardian is through a motion in the cause. Any interested

---

188. G.S. 35A-1261. The clerk may extend the time to file the inventory to up to six months for good cause shown. *Id.*
189. G.S. 35A-1263.1.
190. G.S. 35A-1264.
191. *Id.*
192. *Id.*
193. *Id.*
194. *Id.*
195. *Id.*
196. G.S. 35A-1244 (status report); 35A-1262 (inventory or account); 35A-1265 (accounting).
197. *See* G.S. 5A-21(b2) (civil contempt statute).
198. G.S. 35A-1244; 35A-1262; 35A-1265. *See also id.* § 35A-1290 (removal by clerk).

person may file a motion in the cause in the guardianship proceeding before the clerk of superior court to ask the court to modify the guardianship or consider any matter pertaining to the guardianship.[199] The N.C. Administrative Office of the Courts (AOC) maintains a form "Motion in the Cause to Modify Guardianship" (Form AOC E-415).[200] However, an interested person is not required to use the form or to label the request to the court as a motion in the cause. The court is required to treat requests to modify the guardianship or to consider matters related to the guardianship, however labeled, as motions in the cause.[201] The clerk schedules a hearing on the motion and the movant serves the motion, together with a notice of hearing, on all other parties and any other persons on whom the clerk directs that service be made.[202]

After a guardian is appointed, if an emergency exists that threatens the physical well-being of an older adult under guardianship or constitutes a risk of substantial injury to an older adult's estate, the movant may include a request for ex parte relief in the motion.[203] If the clerk finds reasonable cause to believe that an emergency exists, the clerk may enter an ex parte order to address the emergency pending disposition of the matter at a hearing on the motion.[204]

A motion may be appropriate, in particular, if an interested person suspects that the guardian is not effectively protecting the adult against abuse or is a perpetrator of abuse.[205] In response to the motion, for example, the court could order an individual GOP to start filing regular status reports with the court to document the care, comfort, and maintenance the guardian is providing to the older adult or regarding anything else specifically requested by the court to be included in the report, such as medical visits, efforts to secure stable and appropriate housing, and efforts to secure an in-home aide. This could potentially result in the guardian taking more diligent steps to oversee the older adult's care if neglect by the guardian is a basis for the motion in the cause.

5. REMOVAL OF THE GUARDIAN

In extreme cases, when a guardian is a perpetrator of abuse or fails to take action to protect an older adult from abuse, removal of the guardian and the appointment of a successor guardian by the court may be necessary. There are two types of removal: removal in an emergency and removal after a hearing.[206]

a. Emergency Removal

The clerk may summarily remove a guardian without hearing if the clerk finds reasonable cause to believe that an emergency exists that threatens the physical well-being of the

---

199. G.S. 35A-1207(a).
200. AOC, Form E-415, "Motion in the Cause to Modify Guardianship," available at https://www.nccourts.gov/assets/documents/forms/e415-en.pdf?fY_pBR42JKVRtoiuMKdt5nBUb6BgNS3d.
201. G.S. 35A-1207(b).
202. G.S. 35A-1207(c).
203. G.S. 35A-1207(d).
204. *Id.*
205. G.S. 35A-1207; -1290.
206. G.S. 35A-1291 (summary removal); 35A-1290 (removal after a hearing).

older adult ward or constitutes a risk of substantial injury to the ward's estate.[207] This includes cases where there is evidence the guardian is subjecting the ward to ongoing abuse.

b. Removal after a Hearing

In the absence of an emergency, the clerk may remove a guardian after a hearing on the clerk's own motion or upon a motion or petition filed with the court.[208] The clerk has the authority to remove a guardian upon finding that removal will ensure the better care and maintenance of the older adult and the better management of the older adult's estate.[209] The clerk has a duty to remove the guardian or to take action necessary to protect the older adult's interests if the clerk finds that[210]

- the guardian has wasted the older adult's money or estate or converted it to the guardian's own use;

- the guardian has in any manner mismanaged the older adult's estate;

- the guardian has neglected to care for or maintain the older adult or the older adult's dependents in a suitable manner;

- the guardian or the guardian's sureties are likely to become insolvent or to become nonresidents of North Carolina;

- the original appointment was made on the basis of a false representation or mistake;

- the guardian has violated a fiduciary duty through default or misconduct;

- the guardian has a private interest, whether direct or indirect, that might tend to hinder or be adverse to carrying out his or her duties as guardian;

- the guardian has been adjudged incompetent by a court of competent jurisdiction and has not been restored to competence;

- the guardian has been convicted of a felony under the laws of the United States or of any state or territory of the United States or of the District of Columbia and the guardian's citizenship has not been restored;

- the guardian was originally unqualified for appointment and continues to be unqualified or the guardian would no longer qualify for appointment as guardian due to a change in residence, a change in the charter of a corporate guardian, or any other reason;

---

207. G.S. 35A-1291.
208. G.S. 35A-1290.
209. G.S. 35A-1290(a). *See also In re* Guardianship of Thomas, 183 N.C. App. 480, 484 (2007).
210. G.S. 35A-1290(b).

- the guardian is the older adult's spouse and has lost his or her rights under G.S. Chapter 31A;

- the guardian fails to post, renew, or increase a bond as required by law or by order of the court;

- the guardian refuses or fails without justification to obey any citation, notice, or process served on him or her in regard to the guardianship;

- the guardian fails to file required accountings with the clerk;

- the clerk finds the guardian unsuitable to continue serving as guardian for any reason;

- the guardian is a nonresident of North Carolina and refuses or fails to obey any citation, notice, or process served on the guardian or on the guardian's process agent; or

- the guardian is a licensed attorney, and the clerk is in receipt of an order entered pursuant to G.S. 84-28 enjoining, suspending, or disbarring the attorney.

Whether the guardian is removed in an emergency or after a hearing, the clerk must appoint a successor guardian to act on the older adult's behalf.[211] The clerk may, pending the resolution of any controversy regarding removal, make interlocutory orders and decrees as the clerk finds necessary for the protection of the older adult or the older adult's estate or as to the other party seeking relief through revocation.[212] For example, the clerk's order may direct the previous guardian to turn over the older adult's property to the successor guardian. The successor guardian should take steps to recover the older adult's property wrongfully conveyed or misappropriated by the previous guardian, including making a claim on the bond, and should make any necessary referrals to law enforcement for prosecution of the guardian removed by the court. If a guardian is removed and does not file a full and proper accounting with the court, the successor guardian must initiate a proceeding to compel an accounting by the former guardian.[213]

---

211. G.S. 35A-1293.
212. G.S. 35A-1291.
213. G.S. 35A-1294(a).

III. CHALLENGES OF GUARDIANSHIP

Guardianship may be an effective tool to protect an incompetent older adult from abuse. A guardian has the authority, as determined by the court, to make decisions for an older adult who lacks the capacity to make decisions. The guardian has a duty to stop ongoing abuse and to protect the older adult and the adult's property from future abuse. However, guardianship has its challenges. These challenges merit consideration before seeking guardianship on behalf of an older adult.

WARD AS A VICTIM OF ABUSE—CONNECTIONS BETWEEN ADULT PROTECTIVE SERVICES (APS) AND GUARDIANSHIP[214]

When a guardian is suspected of abusing an older adult under guardianship, it is appropriate to report the abuse to APS. The response from APS will vary depending on whether a county department of social services (DSS) is the ward's guardian and whether DSS is the alleged perpetrator.

DSS is the guardian and is not the alleged perpetrator. It is possible that DSS may "screen out" the case and not conduct a formal APS evaluation if DSS is the adult's guardian and is not the alleged perpetrator of the abuse. (See Chapter 2 of this manual for a detailed discussion of the screening process.) This is true even if there is evidence of abuse, neglect, or exploitation as defined in G.S. 108A-101. DSS will screen the case out because it is able, as the guardian of the ward, to act in an able, willing, and responsible manner to perform or obtain essential services for the adult. Therefore, the adult does not need protective services and fails to meet the criteria to be screened in as an APS report.

Where DSS is the guardian of the older adult and the alleged abuse is by a third party, such as a family member or other caregiver, DSS has the obligation as guardian to take necessary actions to protect the ward. As noted in the *Adult Protective Services, Division of Aging and Adult Services Manual* (*APS Manual*), this may include making reports to the district attorney, state Adult Home Specialists,[215] or other agencies regarding violations of laws or regulations; reviewing financial and/or medical records; authorizing and facilitating health care or mental health treatment; assisting the adult with personal hygiene; removing health and safety hazards; implementing more effective monitoring tools; and, if necessary, removing the adult from a setting where abuse may be taking place.[216]

---

214. For further discussion of adult protective services, refer to Chapter 2 of this manual.

215. N.C. Dep't of Health & Human Servs., *Adult Care Homes*, NCDHHS.GOV, https://www.ncdhhs.gov/assistance/adult-services/adult-care-homes (explaining that adult care homes are monitored by Adult Home Specialists within local DSS entities).

216. N.C. DIV. OF AGING & ADULT SERVS., ADULT PROTECTIVE SERVICES, DIVISION OF AGING AND ADULT SERVICES MANUAL III-7 (Apr. 1, 2011), https://files.nc.gov/ncdhhs/documents/files/APS_Manual.pdf (hereinafter APS MANUAL).

DSS is the guardian and is the alleged perpetrator. In some instances, DSS receives a report that meets the requisite screening criteria but the agency is the guardian of the suspected victim of elder abuse and the DSS director or a member of the director's staff or other county personnel is the alleged perpetrator of the abuse.[217] This may occur, for example, when there are allegations that DSS as the guardian has allowed the adult to live in an unsafe environment or failed to authorize medical treatment.[218] In these cases, the allegations are to be screened in as an APS report.[219] However, the county DSS that has been appointed as guardian has a conflict of interest and may not conduct the evaluation.[220] Another county is then engaged to conduct the evaluation in accordance with the APS Reciprocal Protocol.[221] An APS evaluation by another county must include an assessment of the director's performance of his or her duties as guardian.[222]

DSS is not the guardian and the guardian is not the alleged perpetrator. If the guardian is not the alleged perpetrator of the suspected abuse, DSS may screen in the case as an APS report if it is determined that the ward is a disabled adult in need of protective services because there are concerns that there is not an able, responsible, and willing person to perform or obtain essential services for the ward and thus protect the ward from such abuse. *The APS Manual* offers definitions and guidance on what it means to be an able, responsible, and willing person.[223]

It may be that the guardian is able and willing but is not responsible, in that the guardian has poor judgment, is unreliable, or does not demonstrate adequate oversight in making sure the ward's needs are met. By continuing to allow the ward to live in a possibly neglectful or exploitative situation and not taking the steps to remedy it, the guardian is not an "able, responsible, and willing person."[224]

If DSS screens in a report and substantiates an evaluation, the protective services provided to the ward may include working with the guardian to become an able, responsible, and willing person if the guardian expresses a desire to do so and consents to protective services on the ward's behalf. This could include providing planning and counseling to the guardian to assist the guardian in identifying, remedying, and preventing circumstances which result in abuse.[225] It is also possible that DSS may seek to remove the guardian and to be appointed itself as the ward's guardian.[226] After the guardian is removed and while DSS serves as guardian, the agency could work with the former guardian to improve

---

217. *Id.*
218. APS MANUAL, at III-7–8.
219. *Id.* at III-7.
220. *Id.*
221. *See* APS MANUAL app. U, at III-91–92.
222. *Id.*
223. *Id.* at III-18–19.
224. *See* G.S. 108A-101(e) (a disabled adult is in need of protective services, in part, if he or she is without an able, responsible, and willing person who can perform or obtain essential services for that person).
225. APS MANUAL, at III-19.
226. *Id.* at III-33.

the former guardian's ability to serve as guardian and to enable the former guardian to later file a motion requesting that the court re-appoint him or her as the ward's guardian if he or she becomes qualified to serve at a later date.

However, in the event the guardian does not consent to protective services on the ward's behalf and does not demonstrate a desire to become able, responsible, and willing, DSS may elect to file a motion to remove the guardian before the clerk of superior court due to the guardian's failure to protect the ward from abuse and suitably exercise his or her duties to care for the older adult.[227]

DSS is not the guardian and the guardian is the alleged perpetrator. If the guardian is the alleged perpetrator of the abuse and the report is screened in and an evaluation conducted by APS, the protective action taken by DSS may include filing a motion to remove the guardian.[228] This may be done on an emergency basis without a hearing if the clerk finds reasonable cause to believe that an emergency exists that (1) threatens the well-being of the ward or (2) constitutes a risk of substantial injury to the ward's estate.[229] If the clerk revokes a guardian's authority based on this emergency jurisdiction, the clerk may enter orders as he or she finds necessary to protect the older adult, which may include appointing DSS as guardian until such time as another individual is determined to be appropriate to serve as the older adult's guardian.[230]

A. GUARDIAN IS THE ABUSER

Just because an older adult has a guardian, it does not mean that the risks of elder abuse are eliminated. In fact, guardians may create circumstances that allow for such abuse by leaving the older adult in vulnerable situations and failing to monitor the adult's care. In addition, guardians may be the source of such abuse by taking advantage of and exploiting the authority they are given.

There are certain actions by a general guardian or guardian of the estate that are red flags for potential abuse. Some of these include when the guardian[231]

1. fails to file, or inadequately or incompletely files, inventories and accountings;
2. fails to respond to court notices or orders to complete such filings;
3. pays the older adult's bills late, irregularly, or not at all;
4. maintains a lifestyle that is more affluent than the one the guardian enjoyed prior to being appointed guardian;

---

227. *See* G.S. 35A-1290.
228. *See id.* Refer to Section II.E.5, *supra*, for further discussion of removal of the guardian.
229. G.S. 35A-1291.
230. *Id.*
231. Adapted from Nat'l Ass'n for Ct. Mgmt., Adult Guardianship Guide (2013-2014), https://nacmnet.org/sites/default/files/publications/AdultGuardianshipGuide_withCover.pdf.

5. fails to post, renew, or increase a bond or has a bond revoked;
6. has expenditures reflected on an accounting that are not appropriate for the older adult's lifestyle or setting;
7. refuses to pay for services and care the older adult is able to afford;
8. is the subject of complaints by the older adult's family or friends;
9. fails to secure the older adult's property;
10. executes transfers of the older adult's property to himself or herself as the guardian;
11. makes gifts or loans of the older adult's property without the approval of the court;
12. wastes the older adult's money; or
13. lists questionable entries on an accounting, including
    - utilities charges when the older adult is not living at home;
    - items purchased that are not present in the older adult's home, such as a television, cell phone, or other electronics;
    - checks written for cash;
    - unexplained ATM withdrawals;
    - vehicles purchased that are not appropriate for the older adult's transportation or not needed by the older adult;
    - a lack of entries for expected expenses, such as health insurance, property insurance, or taxes.

Other actions by a general guardian or guardian of the older adult's person are red flags for potential abuse by those guardians. Some of these include when the guardian

1. fails to file, or inadequately or incompletely files, any required status reports;
2. fails to respond to court notices or orders to complete such filings;
3. fails to visit the older adult regularly;
4. fails to oversee the older adult's care;
5. isolates the older adult from others;
6. induces fear of or submissiveness or unusual deference to the guardian by the older adult;
7. changes the older adult's residence without notifying the court or other family members or next of kin;
8. fails to take the older adult to necessary medical appointments;
9. refuses to allow the older adult to be interviewed alone;
10. treats the older adult like a child or in a dehumanizing way;
11. responds defensively when questioned;
12. blames the older adult for acts such as incontinence; or
13. fails to engage the older adult in decisions about the adult's day-to-day life.

WHAT TO DO IF YOU SUSPECT ELDER ABUSE BY A GUARDIAN.

- **Make an Adult Protective Services (APS) report.** Every person in North Carolina, with the singular exception of the long-term care ombudsman, must make an APS report if that person has reasonable cause to believe that a disabled adult needs protective services. This universal reporting requirement in North Carolina does not change simply because the adult has a guardian.[232] See Chapter 2 for a full discussion of the duty to report.

- **File a motion in the cause to modify the guardianship or a petition to remove the guardian.** As mentioned in Section II.E, *supra*, any interested person may file a motion in the cause before the clerk of superior court in the existing guardianship proceeding to modify the guardianship or a petition to remove the guardian if the guardian's actions (or lack thereof) result in elder abuse.

- **Make a report to law enforcement.** If there are concerns that the older adult is the victim of a crime, including one perpetrated by the guardian, the concerned person should make a report to law enforcement.

- **Make a claim on the bond.** If a guardian of the estate or a general guardian fails to perform his or her duties, the guardian may be removed and a new guardian appointed. The new guardian should make a claim on the bond (bonds are discussed in more detail in Section II.C, *supra*) with the bonding company to seek repayment for the older adult's loss due to the guardian's actions up to the amount recoverable under the bond.

- **File for civil damages.** A guardian may be held liable in civil court for breach of fiduciary duty, constructive fraud, or other offenses. Possible claims are set forth in Chapter 6. It may be necessary to seek civil damages in addition to any claim made on a bond. The bond may not cover the full amount of the damages to the older adult. Additional amounts may be recoverable through civil litigation.

---

232. *See* Aimee Wall, *Adult Protective Services: A New Reporting Requirement*, COATES' CANONS: N.C. LOC. GOV'T L. BLOG (June 23, 2015), https://canons.sog.unc.edu/adult-protective-services-a-new-reporting-requirement/.

B. LACK OF UNDERSTANDING OF GUARDIANSHIP

Most court-appointed individual guardians have had little training before taking on the responsibility of serving as someone else's guardian. This lack of understanding can leave the older adult open to abuse. Often, a spouse or family member of an older adult is told to "go get guardianship" by a hospital, a church, or some well-meaning person. Guardians are frequently unaware of the significance of their role and the breadth of decision-making they are charged with carrying out on the older adult's behalf.[233] People seeking guardianship for an incompetent adult often do not understand the scope of duties imposed on a guardian, including the duty to post a bond; maintain separate guardianship accounts; and file documents such as status reports, inventories, and accountings with the court. These filings may overwhelm an individual who has no history of managing and accounting for property or of documenting other actions taken on behalf of another person. This commonly occurs among spouses when one spouse is appointed as guardian for an incompetent spouse and the incompetent spouse was the one who handled the couple's finances prior to incompetency. In addition, the court proceedings can be costly, and costs are frequently charged against the estate of the older adult who is alleged to be incompetent.

---

233. *See* Meredith Smith, *Eight Common Mistakes Made by Guardians of an Incompetent Adult's Estate*, ON THE CIVIL SIDE: A UNC SCH. OF GOV'T BLOG (May 1, 2019), https://civil.sog.unc.edu/eight-common-mistakes-by-guardians-of-an-incompetent-adults-estate/.

RESOURCES FOR GUARDIANS.

The resources listed below will help guardians better understand the responsibilities, importance, and scope of their role.

- **Court files.** There are two court files produced when an older adult is adjudicated incompetent in North Carolina that are especially useful for guardians: the *incompetency special proceeding file* and the *guardianship estate file*. These files will contain copies of the court orders determining the type of guardian appointed and listing any limitations on the guardian's authority. In addition, the files will contain information related to the needs, assets, and liabilities of the older adult.

- ***Understanding Guardianship* video.** The North Carolina Administrative Office of the Courts (AOC) has created a video entitled "Understanding Guardianship." Guardians are advised to watch the video, which is available at https://www.nccourts.gov/about/nc-administrative-office-of-the-courts/training/understanding-guardianship.

- **Guardianship website and pamphlet.** The AOC maintains a help-topic webpage dedicated to providing information about the guardianship process in North Carolina (see https://www.nccourts.gov/help-topics/guardianship) and has created a form entitled "Responsibilities of Guardians in North Carolina" (see https://www.nccourts.gov/documents/forms/responsibilities-of-guardians-in-north-carolina).

- **Guardianship Services Manual (published for DSS and corporation guardians).** The N.C. Department of Health and Human Services' Division of Aging and Adult Services maintains a guardianship policy and procedures manual. It can be accessed at https://www.ncdhhs.gov/aging-and-adult-services-guardianship-services-policy-and-procedures-manual.

- **North Carolina Clerk of Superior Court Procedures Manual.** This manual, published by the School of Government, has two chapters on incompetency and guardianship proceedings. It is produced for clerks of superior court but is available for purchase by the public (see https://www.sog.unc.edu/publications/books/north-carolina-clerk-superior-court-procedures-manual-2012-edition-complete-set-volume-one-and).

- **Managing Someone Else's Money: Help for Court-Appointed Guardians of Property and Conservators.** The Consumer Financial Protection Bureau publishes guides to help people understand the role of a guardian of the estate or a general guardian (see https://files.consumerfinance.gov/f/documents/201310_cfpb_msem-help-for-court-appointed-guardians-of-property-and-conservators.pdf).

C. IMPACT ON AUTONOMY

Although guardianship serves an important function and may protect an older adult from abuse, it also limits the personal autonomy and legal rights of the affected older adult.[234] The law of guardianship attempts to strike a balance between preserving and protecting an older adult's legal rights, freedoms, and personal autonomy and the duty of the State to protect individuals who lack capacity, including the capacity to protect themselves or their property from harm, injury, or exploitation.[235]

It is important to note that not every older adult who lacks capacity needs a guardian. Guardianship should only be sought as a last resort when all other options, such as powers of attorney, trusts, and supportive decision-making, have failed or are not feasible. North Carolina law provides that placing limits on an older adult's rights by appointing a guardian for that adult should not be undertaken unless it is clear that a guardian will give the adult a fuller capacity for exercising his or her rights.[236]

IF NOT GUARDIANSHIP, THEN WHAT?

When an older adult appears to have some level of diminished capacity, rather than assuming that a full guardianship is needed, concerned individuals should

- consider seeking or granting a limited guardianship (Section II.C.2) or
- consider alternatives to guardianship. There are many alternatives to guardianship, such as a power of attorney, a representative payee, or a trust, that also may help protect an older adult from abuse. These alternatives empower a surrogate decision maker to act on behalf of the older adult and, in many cases, replace the need for a guardian. These and other alternatives are set out in Appendix A; powers of attorney are discussed in detail in Chapter 5.

D. INCREASING CASELOADS

The public guardianship system is dealing with increasing caseloads and limited resources to respond to the growing number of older adults in need of services. County departments of social services (DSS) are the only available disinterested public agent guardians in North Carolina and, if appointed by the court, they are required to serve.[237]

---

234. SAXON, *supra* note 2, at § 1.4, p. 8 (2008).
235. *Id.*
236. G.S. 35A-1201(a)(4).
237. G.S. 35A-1202(4); G.S. 35A-1213(d).

IDENTIFY AND CONSIDER OTHER POSSIBLE GUARDIANS.

- If DSS is not the party filing an incompetency petition for an older adult but it appears from the petition that DSS may be appointed as that adult's guardian, the court may direct the petitioner to serve of a copy of the petition and the notice of hearing on DSS at the time the incompetency petition is filed.[238] This will allow DSS to get involved in the case early to work to identify potential guardians (other than DSS) for the court to appoint.

- If DSS is appointed as an older adult's guardian, the agency will work to identify other potential guardians, such as family members and friends, and will work with those persons to prepare them to replace DSS as guardian with the approval of the court.[239]

- The clerk of superior court appoints DSS as an older adult's guardian only as a last resort.[240] The clerk, the petitioner, and the guardian ad litem each work diligently within their respective roles to identity an appropriate individual or corporation to serve as the older adult's guardian instead of DSS.

---

238. *See* G.S. 35A-1109 (allowing the clerk to designate other persons to receive notice of the incompetency petition and hearing).

239. G.S. 35A-1242(a1)(6).

240. G.S. 35A-1214.

Chapter 5
Powers of Attorney

CONTENTS

I. SCOPE OF CHAPTER

A power of attorney (POA) governed by Chapter 32C of the North Carolina General Statutes (hereinafter G.S.) grants authority to a person (the agent) to act on behalf of someone else (the principal) with respect to property and property interests. These POAs often make appearances in cases related to elder abuse. A POA may be used as a tool to protect against abuse; it also may be the source of abuse.

This chapter summarizes the parties responsible for POAs governed by G.S. Chapter 32C (also called the North Carolina Uniform Power of Attorney Act (NCUPOAA)), how these arrangements protect older adults, and how they work. It then discusses some common challenges that arise related to POAs when actors in the elder protection system seek to protect older adults from abuse. The chapter does not address health care powers of attorney (HCPOAs). G.S. Chapter 32A governs this type of POA, which is defined as "[a] written instrument . . . signed in the presence of two qualified witnesses, and acknowledged before a notary public, pursuant to which an attorney-in-fact or agent is appointed to act for the principal in matters relating to the health care of the principal."[1] The provisions of G.S. Chapter 32C specifically do not apply to a power to make health care decisions.[2]

II. OVERVIEW OF POWERS OF ATTORNEY (POAs)

A. WHO IS RESPONSIBLE?

1. PARTIES TO THE POA

Unlike guardianship, where a court appoints and oversees a guardian authorized to make decisions for someone else, a POA is a private arrangement. A POA is "[a] writing or other record that grants authority to an agent to act in the place of the principal."[3] An agent is sometimes called an "attorney-in-fact" (this is how now-repealed state law referred to agents). The term "agent" now includes an attorney-in-fact.[4] The agent may be an individual or any commercial or legal entity, such as a corporation or partnership.[5] The principal is the individual who executes the POA.[6]

---

1. Chapter 32A, Section 16(3), of the North Carolina General Statutes (hereinafter G.S.).
2. G.S. 32C-1-103(2).
3. G.S. 32C-1-102(9) (emphasis added). The term "power of attorney" does not have to be used for the writing or other record to be a power of attorney. *Id.*
4. G.S. 32C-1-102(1).
5. *Id.*; *id.* § 32C-1-102(8).
6. G.S. 32C-1-102(11).

Figure 5.1. **Parties to a POA**

The principal grants authority to the agent to act on the principal's behalf in the manner set forth in the POA with respect to some or all of the principal's property and property interests. An act by an agent under a POA has the same effect as, and binds the principal and the principal's successors in interest to the same extent as, if the principal had performed the act himself or herself.[7]

2. CAPACITY TO EXECUTE A POA

A principal must have capacity when he or she signs a POA. The standard of capacity applicable to the execution of a POA by a principal appears to be the same standard applicable to the capacity required to enter into a contract.[8] North Carolina courts have set the standard for competency to contract as follows:

> [A] person has mental capacity sufficient to contract if he knows what he is about, and that the measure of capacity is the ability to understand the nature of the act in which he is engaged and its scope and effect, or its nature and consequences, not that he should be able to act wisely or discreetly, nor to drive a good bargain, but that he should be in such possession of his faculties as to enable him to know at least what he is doing and to contract understandingly.[9]

In terms of a POA, this means that the principal must understand the nature of the act of executing a POA and the scope and effect of the POA on the agent's authority to handle the principal's property and other property interests.

3. OBTAINING A POA BY OR FOR AN OLDER ADULT

An older adult may draft and sign a POA or seek the assistance of an attorney who will prepare the POA for the older adult to sign. North Carolina law, in G.S. 32C-3-301, sets out a form POA that may be printed/duplicated and used free of charge.

---

7. G.S. 32C-2-201(h).

8. *See* Hedgepeth v. Home Sav. & Loan Ass'n, 87 N.C. App. 610, 611–12 (1987) (determining that a POA should be treated the same as a contract). *See also* O'Neal *ex rel.* Small v. O'Neal, 803 S.E.2d 184, 186-87 (N.C. Ct. App. 2017) (stating as a general matter that there is little reason to draw distinctions between POAs and contracts); 1 WIGGINS LAW OF WILLS AND TRUSTS IN NORTH CAROLINA § 20:3 (5th ed. 2020). *But see* RESTATEMENT (THIRD) OF AGENCY § 1.01 cmt. d (AM. LAW INST. 2006) (stating that an agency relationship does not always create an enforceable contract because many agents, such as family or friends of the principal, act or promise to act gratuitously).

9. Matthews v. James, 88 N.C. App. 32, 35 (1987) (quoting Sprinkle v. Wellborn, 140 N.C. 163, 181 (1905)). *See also* Ridings v. Ridings, 55 N.C. App. 630, 633, *discretionary review denied*, 305 N.C. 586 (1982).

North Carolina Statutory Form POA

The statutory form POA is available online at https://www.ncleg.gov/Laws/GeneralStatuteSections/Chapter32C.

There are also groups, such as the N.C. Bar Foundation's Wills for Heroes program and Legal Aid of North Carolina's Senior Law Project, that provide free assistance in preparing POAs for certain eligible older adults. A private attorney will frequently charge fees for preparing a POA but may under certain circumstances draft a POA for a client pro bono (without charge). There are no generally available public funds to assist with the preparation and execution of POAs.

Legal Aid of North Carolina—Senior Law Project

Legal Aid of North Carolina's Senior Law Project provides free civil legal help to North Carolinians who are 60 years of age or older.

Website

http://www.legalaidnc.org/about-us/projects/senior-law-project

Helpline:
- Toll-free: 1-877-579-7562
- Hours: Monday–Friday, 9–11 a.m. and 1–3 p.m.

There may be instances when an adult child contacts an attorney to prepare a POA for his or her parent and pays the attorney for the representation. The attorney may prepare the POA but the attorney must make clear that he or she represents the parent in that situation and has duties to the parent as the client.[10] The attorney must obtain the older adult's informed consent to the representation before accepting compensation for his or her services from the family member.[11] The attorney must determine whether the older adult wants or needs a POA; who the older adult, not the adult child, wants appointed as agent under the POA; and what powers the older adult wants the agent to be granted.[12] If the older adult has diminished capacity, Rule 1.14 of the N.C. Rules of Professional

---

10. N.C. State Bar, Preparation of Power of Attorney for Principal upon Request of Prospective Attorney-in-Fact, Formal Ethics Op. 7 (Jan. 16, 2004) (hereinafter 2003 FEO 7). Note that this rule does not apply to commercial or business transactions. *Id. See also* N.C. State Bar, Preparation of Legal Documents at the Request of Another, Formal Ethics Op. 11 (July 21, 2006) (hereinafter 2006 FEO 11). The attorney may meet with the adult child alone to discuss the representation of the parent, but the attorney must explain, in a timely and clear manner, that the attorney represents the parent and not the adult child. 2003 FEO 7. Statements given by the adult child in the initial interview may later be used by the attorney in the representation of the parent, including to defend a guardianship proceeding filed against the parent by the child. *Id.*

11. 2003 FEO 7, 2006 FEO 11, *supra* note 10.

12. 2003 FEO 7, *supra* note 10. *See also* 2006 FEO 11, *supra* note 10.

Conduct applies to guide the attorney in the representation of the older adult.[13] It requires the attorney to try to maintain a normal client-lawyer relationship, as far as this is reasonably possible, and to keep the client's interests foremost, looking to the older adult/client—and not the family member—when making decisions on the client's behalf.[14]

B. HOW DO POAs PROTECT OLDER ADULTS?

POAs empower an older adult (the principal) to grant authority to a trusted person (the agent) to act on the older adult's behalf. An older adult may execute a POA authorizing an agent to act on the older adult's behalf while the older adult has capacity or only after the adult becomes incapacitated and is unable to act. Examples of some of the different reasons why an older adult may execute a POA are provided below.

- An older adult has mental capacity but is homebound. He executes a POA granting a caregiver authority to access his bank accounts to pay bills, shop for groceries and household items, and manage other aspects of his property.

- An older adult is unavailable to attend the closing on the sale of property she owns. She executes a limited POA authorizing a family member to sign a deed on her behalf.

- An older adult executes a POA together with a will, an HCPOA, and a living will to prepare for future incapacity and death, naming his two children as co-agents.

POAs also protect older adults by preserving their autonomy and self-determination to a greater extent than more restrictive options for surrogate decision-making, such as guardianships, do.[15] Under a POA arrangement, an older adult retains legal ownership of his or her assets, as well as the authority to act when he or she has capacity. The older adult, not a court, selects the person authorized to act on his or her behalf and determines the nature and extent of an agent's authority under the POA. The agent can act without court oversight, unlike in a guardianship, and the principal's property and property interests are generally kept private. A POA may prevent the need for a court-appointed guardian of the estate or general guardian[16] if the older adult lacks capacity to make decisions or manage his or her property.

The benefits and protections provided to older adults by POAs may be outweighed in some cases by the risk of abuse. Abuse by the agent is discussed in Section III, *infra*.

---

13. N.C. R. PROF'L CONDUCT 1.14 (N.C. State Bar 1997, amended 2003, 2014). *See generally* ABA Comm'n on Law & Aging & Am. Psychol. Ass'n, *Assessment of Older Adults with Diminished Capacity: A Handbook for Lawyers* (2006), http://www.apa.org/pi/aging/resources/guides/diminished-capacity.pdf.

14. N.C. R. PROF'L CONDUCT 1.14(a) & cmt. [3]. The attorney may consult with individuals, including family members, who have the ability to take action to protect the client when the attorney reasonably believes that a client with diminished capacity is at risk of substantial physical, financial, or other harm unless action is taken and that the client cannot adequately act in his or her own interest. *Id.* at r. 1.14(b).

15. UNIF. POWER OF ATT'Y ACT, prefatory note (UNIF. LAW COMM'N 2006) (noting that a primary goal of the uniform law is to protect the principal's freedom to choose both the extent of the agent's authority and the principles to govern the agent's conduct).

16. Defined and discussed further in Chapter 4.

To ensure that a POA functions to protect an older adult and does not become a source of abuse, the older adult/principal may consider [17]

- selecting a trustworthy agent that will carry out the principal's expectations, values, and preferences and communicating those expectations, values, and preferences to the agent;

- clearly stating the agent's duties and authority, along with any limitations on the agent's authority, in the POA, including a limit on making gifts;

- including a statement in the POA that a third party may refuse to accept the POA if that party has a good faith belief that the principal is subject to abuse;

- requiring the agent, after the principal's incapacity, to account or submit regular financial statements to a third party who serves as a check on the agent's actions; and

- appointing a special fiduciary in the POA to approve any gifts made by the agent.

> ### 📖 RESOURCE
>
> The Consumer Financial Protection Bureau published a guide to assist family and friends serving as agents under POAs better understand the role of fiduciary. The guide, titled *Managing Someone Else's Money: Help for Agents under a Power of Attorney*, is available at https://files.consumerfinance.gov/f/documents/201310_cfpb_msem-help-for-agents-under-a-power-of-attorney.pdf.

C. HOW DO POAs WORK?

POAs are used often—and are often misunderstood. This section summarizes some of the basic aspects of POAs under North Carolina law, including

- what is required for a POA to be valid in North Carolina,

- when registration (recording) of the POA is required,

- third party protections for POAs accepted in good faith,

- the effect of the principal's incapacity on a POA,

- termination of the POA and an agent's authority,

- the meaning and effect of terms in a POA,

---

17. Linda S. Whitton, *Durable Powers as An Alternative to Guardianship: Lessons We Have Learned*, 37 STETSON L. REV. 7 (2007). *See generally* LORI A. STIEGEL & ELLEN VANCLEAVE KLEM, AARP PUB. POL'Y INST., POWER OF ATTORNEY ABUSE: WHAT STATES CAN DO ABOUT IT Exec. Summary, at vii–viii (2008), https://assets.aarp.org/rgcenter/consume/2008_17_poa.pdf (summarizing key provisions of the Uniform Power of Attorney Act that protect people who execute powers of attorney).

- when a POA is effective,

- the authority of an agent under a POA, and

- an agent's duties under a POA.

North Carolina passed the NCUPOAA, which took effect on January 1, 2018, and created G.S. Chapter 32C.[18] There are many POAs still in use that were created under the old law. Those POAs are still valid. The provisions of G.S. Chapter 32C discussed in this chapter generally apply to those POAs created before January 1, 2018, except in limited circumstances, such as a clear contrary intent expressed in the POA.[19]

1. REQUIREMENT FOR A POA TO BE VALID IN NORTH CAROLINA

As discussed in Section II.A.2, *supra*, in order for a POA to be valid in North Carolina, a principal must have capacity when he or she signs the POA. In addition, a POA must meet certain other technical requirements to be valid under North Carolina law. Those requirements are different depending on when and where the principal executed the POA.[20] An agent is not required to sign a POA for the POA to be valid.

A POA executed in this state on or after January 1, 2018, is valid if it is

a. signed[21] by the principal or by another individual directed by the principal to sign the principal's name on the POA in the principal's conscious presence[22] and

b. acknowledged.[23]

> ### ✎ PRACTICE NOTE
>
> A principal's signature on a POA is **presumed to be genuine** if it is acknowledged before a notary or other individual authorized to take acknowledgments.[24]

---

18. S.L. 2017-153. The General Assembly subsequently amended provisions of G.S. Chapter 32C in S.L. 2018-142 and S.L. 2019-243.

19. G.S. 32C-4-403 (setting out the effect of G.S. Chapter 32C on POAs executed prior to January 1, 2018).

20. G.S. 32C-1-105, -106. The purpose of these provisions is to promote the portability and use of POAs across jurisdictions. *See id.* § 32C-1-106, Official Cmt.

21. "Sign" means "[w]ith the present intent to authenticate or adopt a record, (i) to execute or adopt a tangible symbol or (ii) to attach to or logically associate with the record an electronic sound, symbol, or process." G.S. 32C-1-102(14).

22. "Conscious presence" under the Uniform Probate Code for the execution of wills generally requires that the signing by the person directed by the principal take place within the range of the principal's senses, such as sight or hearing; the signing need not have occurred within the testator's line of sight. Unif. Probate Code § 2-502 cmt. a (UNIF. LAW COMM'N 2010). North Carolina has not adopted the Uniform Probate Code. North Carolina probate law does not use or define the term "conscious presence," which is more expansive than the requirement under state law that the witnesses to an attested written will sign in the "presence" of the testator. G.S. 31-3.3; 32C-1-105, N.C. Cmt. To satisfy the requirement under North Carolina law that the witnesses sign in the presence of the testator, it is not necessary that the testator actually *see* the witnesses sign. *In re* Pridgen's Will, 249 N.C. 509, 512–14 (1959). It is sufficient if the signing was in the view of the testator and the testator would be capable of seeing the attesting witnesses sign the will. *Id.*; *In re* Cherry's Will, 164 N.C. 363 (1913); Graham v. Graham, 32 N.C. 219 (1849). *See also* G.S. 32C-1-105, N.C. Cmt.

23. G.S. 32C-1-105; 32C-1-106(a).

24. G.S. 32C-1-105 (emphasis added).

If a POA was executed in North Carolina prior to January 1, 2018, it is valid as long as it complied with North Carolina law at the time of its execution.[25] Under the law in effect in this state prior to January 1, 2018, a POA did not have to be acknowledged or witnessed to be valid.[26] It did have to be in writing and contain a grant of authority by the principal to an agent to act on the principal's behalf.[27]

If a POA was executed at any time in another state, it is valid in North Carolina if, when it was executed, it

- complied with the law of the jurisdiction indicated in the POA,

- without an indication of jurisdiction in the POA, complied with the law of the jurisdiction where it was executed, or

- complied with the requirements for a military POA under 10 U.S.C. § 1044b.[28]

The law of the jurisdiction indicated in a non-military POA controls over the place of execution. For example, if a POA is executed in Georgia but states that it is executed under North Carolina law, then North Carolina requirements for execution of a valid POA apply.[29]

Table 5.1. **Requirements for a POA to be Valid in North Carolina**

WHERE POA EXECUTED	WHEN POA EXECUTED	POA VALID IN NORTH CAROLINA IF IT COMPLIES WITH . . .
North Carolina	On or after January 1, 2018	G.S. 32C-1-105 (signed + acknowledged)
North Carolina	Before January 1, 2018	North Carolina law in effect at time of execution
Another state*	Before, on, or after January 1, 2018	Either 1. The law of the jurisdiction indicated in the POA; 2. If no jurisdiction is indicated in the POA, the law where the POA was executed; or 3. 10 U.S.C § 1044b (military POAs).

* The term "state" includes a state of the United States, the District of Columbia, Puerto Rico, the U.S. Virgin Islands, or "any territory or insular possession subject to the jurisdiction of" the U.S. G.S. 32C-1-102(15).

---

25. G.S. 32C-1-106(b).
26. *See generally* G.S. Ch. 32A, Arts. 1, 2 (repealed).
27. *See* N.C. Nat'l Bank v. Hammond, 298 N.C. 703, 713 (1979) (noting that G.S. 47-115.1 (which was later replaced by G.S. Chapter 32A) codified a particular subset of POAs which continued to be effective after the incapacity or mental incompetence of the principal but did not change the requirement that written authority is necessary for a POA); Howard v. Boyce, 266 N.C. 572, 577 (1966).
28. G.S. 32C-1-106(c), -107.
29. *See* G.S. 32C-1-106(c), -107.

2. WHEN REGISTRATION (RECORDING) OF THE POA IS REQUIRED

A POA does not have to be registered in a register of deeds office or with the clerk of superior court to be valid in North Carolina subsequent to a principal's incapacity.[30] This rule is stated in the NCUPOAA, which went into effect on January 1, 2018, and represents a change from prior law. Under the law previously in effect in North Carolina, no POA was valid after a principal's incapacity unless it was registered in the county register of deeds office.[31] In addition, within thirty days after registration, the agent under the POA had to file a copy of the POA with the clerk of superior court.[32] As a result of this prior law, there are many people who, in practice, may expect a POA to be recorded in order for it to be valid. But, as noted above, G.S. Chapter 32C does not require (1) registration of a POA after a principal's incapacity or incompetence or (2) later filing of the registered POA with the clerk in order for the POA to be valid.

The one exception to this rule applies when an agent desires to transfer real property under the POA. Before any transfer of real property executed by an agent under a POA, the POA, or a certified copy of it, must be registered in the register of deeds office in the county in which the principal is domiciled or where the real property lies.[33] If the principal is not a resident of North Carolina, the POA, or a certified copy of it, may be recorded in any county in this state in which the principal owns real property or has a significant business reason for registering the POA.[34]

3. THIRD-PARTY PROTECTIONS FOR POAs ACCEPTED IN GOOD FAITH

There are legal protections for third parties, such as financial institutions, who accept POAs in good faith, whether they are acknowledged or unacknowledged.[35] A third party can claim these protections provided that party does not have actual knowledge that

- the POA is void, invalid, or terminated;

- the purported agent's authority is void, invalid, or terminated; or

- the agent is exceeding or improperly exercising the agent's authority.[36]

A third party without actual knowledge of any of the circumstances listed above

- may rely on the POA as if

  □ the POA were genuine, valid, and still in effect;

  □ the agent's authority was genuine, valid, and still in effect; and

---

30. G.S. 32C-1-104, N.C. Cmt.

31. G.S. 32A-9(b) (repealed).

32. G.S. 32A-11(a) (repealed). Note that a principal or agent may present a POA for filing with the clerk under the misapprehension that it is still required. If a POA is presented for filing with the clerk and no related proceeding or request for relief is filed, the clerk opens an "E" file and places the POA in the file. *See* N.C. ADMIN. OFF. OF THE CTS., RULES OF RECORDKEEPING r. 6.1(g).

33. G.S. 47-28(a). The necessity to produce a POA in connection with the transfer of title dates far back into North Carolina law. *See* Yarborough v. Beard, 1 N.C. 117, Tay. 25 (1799) (holding that whenever a deed was executed by virtue of a POA, the POA or a copy of it must be produced).

34. G.S. 47-28(a).

35. G.S. 32C-1-119, N.C. Cmt.

36. G.S. 32C-1-119(c).

☐ the agent is not exceeding and had properly exercised the authority and

■ shall not be held responsible for any breach of fiduciary duty by the agent.[37]

The purpose of these protections is to promote the acceptance of POAs by third parties. These protections would apply, for example, to a forged POA without an acknowledgment that was accepted by a person in good faith, unless that person has actual knowledge that (1) the POA or the agent's authority is void, invalid, or terminated or (2) the agent is exceeding or improperly exercising the agent's authority.[38]

> ### ◇ EXAMPLE
>
> *An adult son forges his 85-year-old mother's signature and the acknowledgment on a POA. The mother is incapacitated and has a substantial 401K account. The son meets with the 401K account manager, who accepts the POA and allows the son to withdraw the total amount available from his mother's account, as is allowed under the terms of the POA.*
>
> - *Provided that the account manager did not have actual knowledge that the POA, or the agent's authority, was void and accepted the POA in good faith, the company for whom the account manager works may be protected against liability for allowing the son to withdraw the funds from the mother's retirement account.*
> - *The mother may have a civil cause of action against the son to recover the money or to seek monetary damages, but likely not against the company that allowed the withdrawal. Civil actions are discussed in Chapter 6.*
> - *The son may be subject to criminal prosecution for a crime such as common law forgery, obtaining property by false pretenses, or exploitation of an older adult. Criminal actions are discussed in Chapter 1.*
> - *A friend, family member, or other person may file (1) a civil action to set aside the POA, (2) a POA proceeding to remove the agent for breach of fiduciary duty, or, if necessary, (3) a guardianship proceeding to appoint a guardian to terminate the POA. These are discussed in Section III.A, infra. Civil actions are discussed in detail in Chapter 6.*

---

37. *Id.*

38. Andrew H. Hook & Thomas D. Begley, Jr., *Uniform Power of Attorney Act: Protecting Third Parties Too Much?*, 37 EST. PLAN. 36, 37 (2010). The NCUPOAA places the risk that the POA is forged on the principal rather than on a third party. G.S. 32C-1-119, Official Cmt. This includes when someone forges the principal's signature on a POA and presents an unacknowledged POA to a third party, who then accepts the POA in good faith and without actual knowledge that it is invalid. G.S. 32C-1-119(c), N.C. Cmt. (providing protections to third parties for both acknowledged and unacknowledged POAs).

4. EFFECT OF THE PRINCIPAL'S INCAPACITY ON THE POA

A POA that is durable is a POA that is not terminated by the incapacity of the principal.[39] This means that the POA continues to remain in effect and the agent may act on the principal's behalf after the incapacity of the principal. A POA is durable unless it expressly states that it is terminated by the incapacity of the principal.[40] If the POA was created prior to January 1, 2018, and it is silent regarding durability, it is durable unless such an interpretation would substantially impair the rights of a party.[41]

> ◇ **EXAMPLE**
>
> *An older adult executes a POA for the limited purpose of authorizing a family member, John, to sign a deed conveying property owned by the older adult. The older adult will be out of town when the closing is scheduled to occur and thus unable to attend the closing in person. The POA expressly states it is not durable and terminates upon the incapacity of the principal. A year later, the older adult suffers significant cognitive decline due to dementia. The county department of social services (DSS) receives a report that the adult is the subject of financial abuse. During the investigation, John tells DSS that the older adult appointed him as agent under a POA and he can take action as agent to protect the older adult from further financial abuse. DSS should obtain a copy of the POA and review it. John's statements are not consistent with the actual authority granted to him as agent under the POA. Because the POA is not durable, it terminated upon the older adult's incapacity. Therefore, John no longer has authority to act as agent under the POA. DSS risks leaving the adult without someone to act on the adult's behalf if it relies simply on John's statements about the POA and screens the case out on the mistaken belief that John has the authority to act on behalf of the older adult under the POA when, in reality, the POA terminated upon the principal's incapacity.*

5. TERMINATION OF THE POA AND THE AGENT'S AUTHORITY

a. Termination of the POA

A POA terminates when any of the following occurs:[42]
1. The principal dies.
2. The POA is not durable and the principal becomes incapacitated.
3. The principal revokes the POA.
4. The POA provides that it terminates.

---

39. G.S. 32C-1-102(2).
40. G.S. 32C-1-104.
41. G.S. 32C-4-403(a)(4).
42. G.S. 32C-1-110(a).

5. The purpose of the POA is accomplished.
6. The principal revokes the agent's authority or the agent dies, becomes incapacitated, or resigns, and the POA does not provide for another agent to act under the POA.
7. A guardian of the principal's estate or general guardian terminates the POA.

b. Termination of the Agent's Authority

An agent's authority under a POA terminates when any of the following occurs:[43]
1. The principal revokes the agent's authority in writing.
2. The agent dies, becomes incapacitated, resigns, or is removed.
3. The court enters a decree of divorce between the principal and the agent. (Note: If the POA provides that divorce does not terminate the agent's authority, then that authority is not terminated by a divorce decree.)
4. The POA terminates.
5. A guardian of the principal's estate or general guardian terminates the agent's authority.

c. Effect of Termination on the Agent

If an agent does not have actual knowledge of the termination of (1) a POA or (2) the agent's authority under the POA, then the termination is not effective as to that agent, so long as the agent acts in good faith.[44] Any acts performed after termination by the agent in good faith and without actual knowledge of the termination bind the principal and the principal's successors in interest.[45] This is true unless the agent's act is otherwise invalid or unenforceable, such as any act that exceeds the scope of authority granted in the POA.[46]

> ◇ **EXAMPLE**
>
> *John, the principal under a POA, dies at the age of 65. The agent under the POA is a local credit union. No one alerts the credit union that John died. Any acts conducted by the credit union, as agent under the POA, on behalf of John after his death still bind John's estate, so long as the acts are conducted in good faith and are not otherwise invalid or unenforceable.*

---

43. G.S. 32C-1-110(b)
44. G.S. 32C-1-110(d).
45. *Id.*
46. *Id.*

d. Effect of Termination on a Third Party

If a third party does not have actual knowledge of the termination of (1) a POA or (2) the agent's authority under the POA, then the termination is not effective as to the third party, so long as the third party acts in good faith and the transaction is not otherwise invalid or unenforceable.[47] The principal and the principal's successors in interest are bound by such transactions.[48] This is true even if the agent has actual knowledge of the termination, as long as (1) the third party acts in good faith, (2) the third party does not have actual knowledge of the termination, and (3) the transaction is not otherwise invalid or unenforceable.[49]

> ### ◇ EXAMPLE
>
> *Sally, the principal under a non-durable POA, becomes incapacitated (note that this terminates a POA under G.S. 32C-1-110(a)(2), as discussed above). Sally's agent under the POA is her son, Frank. Frank knows that Sally is incapacitated but continues to conduct transactions on Sally's behalf as agent under the POA. Frank sells Sally's car to a third-party purchaser for value. The non-durable POA authorizes Frank to sell Sally's car while Sally has capacity. Frank does not alert the third-party purchaser that Sally is now incapacitated and that the non-durable POA is therefore terminated. The sale of the car by Frank to the third-party purchaser binds Sally and Sally's successors in interest, provided that the sale is conducted by the third-party purchaser in good faith and is not otherwise invalid or unenforceable.[50]*

6. MEANING AND EFFECT OF TERMS IN A POA

To analyze and construe the terms of a POA, it is necessary to first determine what law applies to the POA—whether the law of North Carolina applies to give meaning and effect to the POA or whether the law of another jurisdiction controls. This is first determined by looking at the POA itself.[51] If the POA expressly indicates that the law of a certain jurisdiction applies to give meaning and effect to the POA, then that law applies.[52] If the POA lacks an indication of jurisdiction, then the law of the jurisdiction in which the POA was executed applies.[53]

---

47. *Id.*

48. *Id.*

49. G.S. 32C-1-110, Official Cmt. (citing RESTATEMENT (THIRD) OF AGENCY § 3.11 (2006), which provides that termination of actual authority does not end any apparent authority held by the agent). *See also* G.S. 32C-1-119(c) (providing protections for any third party who accepts a POA in good faith without actual knowledge that the POA is terminated, including the protection that the third party may rely on the POA and the agent's authority as if they were genuine, valid, and still in effect).

50. G.S. 32C-1-110(e).

51. G.S. 32C-1-107.

52. *Id.*

53. *Id.*

⬦ **EXAMPLE**

A POA grants an agent the authority "to make gifts" on behalf of the principal, an older adult. The principal's in-home aide is the agent under the POA. The aide makes gifts of the older adult's property to the aide's wife in the amount of $335,000. A friend of the older adult makes a report to law enforcement that the aide is "stealing" from the older adult. To determine whether the gift by the aide is authorized by the POA or whether it exceeds the scope of his authority, the investigator will need to review the POA to determine what law—North Carolina law or the law of another state—applies to give meaning and effect to the term "make a gift."

Under North Carolina law, an agent may make a gift of the principal's property only if the POA expressly states that the agent has the authority to make a gift.[54] The nature and extent of the agent's gifting authority depends on what is set out in the POA. If the POA only states that the agent has the authority to "make a gift," then the nature and extent of the agent's authority to make a gift is limited by North Carolina statute.[55] Under those circumstances, an agent may not make a gift that exceeds the greater of (1) the amount determined to be in accordance with the principal's history of making or of joining in the making of gifts or (2) the annual dollar limit of the federal gift tax exclusion.[56] If North Carolina law gives the POA meaning and effect, and if the aide's gift exceeds the scope of authority granted to the agent in the POA, then the aide may be guilty of a crime, such as embezzlement or exploitation of an older adult or disabled adult (discussed in more detail in Chapter 3).

7. WHEN A POA IS EFFECTIVE

The default rule is that a POA is effective when it is executed.[57] This reflects the idea that any agent that can be trusted to act as an agent should be trusted enough to hold an immediate power, even if the principal still retains the desire and capacity to manage his or her own property and business affairs.[58] This rule also ensures that an agent can act immediately when needed by the principal. But a principal may instead desire to make a POA effective upon a future date or upon the occurrence of a future event or contingency,[59] such as the principal's incapacity.

---

54. G.S. 32C-2-201(a)(1)a.

55. G.S. 32C-2-217(b).

56. G.S. 32C-2-217(b)(1)a.

57. G.S. 32C-1-109(a). Note that although the POA may be effective, an agent does not accept appointment under a POA, and thus the agency relationship does not commence, until the agent exercises authority, performs duties, takes some other act, or makes some other assertion that indicates acceptance, unless the POA states otherwise. *Id.* § 32C-1-113. There is no statutory requirement that the POA must be actually delivered to the agent for the agent to have the authority to act on the principal's behalf. *See id.*

58. G.S. 32C-1-109, Official Cmt.

59. G.S. 32C-1-109(a).

> ## 💬 KEY TERM
>
> *A POA effective upon the occurrence of a future event or contingency is often called a* **springing POA**.

If the POA is effective upon a future event or contingency, the principal may authorize one or more persons in the POA to determine in a writing or other record that the event or contingency has occurred.[60] For example, the POA may state that it becomes effective upon the principal's incapacity. Once the principal becomes incapacitated, the authorized person(s) designated in the POA may write, date, and sign a statement that the principal is incapacitated and indicate that the agent's authority under the POA is activated or "sprung" into effect.[61]

> ## 💬 KEY TERM
>
> **Incapacity** *under the North Carolina Uniform Power of Attorney Act (NCUPOAA) is defined as the inability of an individual to manage his or her property or business affairs because he or she*
>
> a. *has "[a]n impairment in the ability to receive and evaluate information or make or communicate decisions even with the use of technological assistance"[62] or*
>
> b. *"[i]s missing, detained, including incarcerated in a penal system, or outside the United States and unable to return."[63]*

If the POA is effective upon the principal's incapacity and the principal has not authorized a person to determine whether the principal is incapacitated, or if the person authorized is unable or unwilling to make the determination, the POA becomes effective upon a determination in a writing or other record by either

- two individuals, who are either a physician, a licensed psychologist, or both, and after a personal examination, that the principal is unable to manage his or her property or business affairs because he or she has an impairment in the ability to receive and evaluate information or make or communicate decisions, even with the use of technological assistance, or[64]

- an attorney-at-law, a judge, or an appropriate governmental official[65] that the principal is unable to manage his or her property or business affairs because he or

---

60. G.S. 32C-1-109(b).

61. There is no requirement in G.S. Chapter 32C that the statement signed by the designated person be in the form of an affidavit or otherwise made under oath.

62. G.S. 32C-1-102(6)a.

63. G.S. 32C-1-102(6)b.

64. G.S. 32C-1-109(c)(1), -102(6)a.

65. If the principal is incarcerated in North Carolina, for example, the appropriate governmental official is likely the district or superior court judge who presided over the principal's case. If the principal is detained, such as by

she is missing; detained, including incarcerated in a penal system; or outside the United States and unable to return.[66]

> ◇ **EXAMPLE**
>
> *Joan executes a POA appointing her son, Frank, as her agent. The POA states that it does not become effective until Joan is incapacitated, as determined in writing by her personal doctor, Dr. Betty Smith. Two years later, Joan is struggling with some of her day-to-day activities due to a stroke. Frank takes Joan to see Dr. Smith, but Dr. Smith refuses to state in writing that Joan is incapacitated, in part because she does not trust Frank. Frank then takes Joan to an urgent care clinic and gets the nurse practitioner there to put in writing that Joan is incapacitated. Frank then uses the POA to change the beneficiaries on Joan's retirement accounts, to sell Joan's home and move her to an assisted living facility, and to open a new credit card in Joan's name and make charges on the card. Each action may have been authorized under the POA but, because Frank did not obtain a letter from Joan's personal doctor, the POA never "sprung" into effect. Frank therefore lacked the authority to act as agent under the POA. Frank may be subject to civil or criminal liability for his unauthorized acts.*

8. THE AUTHORITY OF AN AGENT UNDER A POA

The nature and extent of the agent's authority are set by the principal in the POA and will vary from POA to POA. When the court or a third party is presented with a POA, it is important to read the POA to determine the scope of and any limitations on an agent's authority.[67] An agent under one POA likely does not have the same authority as an agent under another POA. Furthermore, an agent may have the authority to act with respect to some areas of an older adult's property and property interests but not as to all areas. Granting one type of authority to an agent does not mean that the older adult has consented to all acts by the agent.

The NCUPOAA sets out various kinds of authority a principal may grant to an agent under a POA, which fall into four different categories:

1. general authority,
2. specific authority,
3. the authority to make a gift, and
4. incidental authority.

---

immigration officials, or precluded from entering the United States, then a statement from the federal officials with custody of the principal would seem appropriate. If the principal is missing, the appropriate governmental official may be a federal or state law enforcement officer. If the principal is unavailable due to military service, then the appropriate governmental official may be a person in the uniformed services of the United States. *See* G.S. 32C-1-109, Official Cmt.

66. G.S. 32C-1-109(c)(2); 32C-1-102(6)b.

67. *See* SunTrust v. C & D Custom Homes, LLC, 223 N.C. App. 347, 350–51 (2012).

a. General Authority

If a POA states that an agent has the authority "to do all of the acts a principal could do" or that the agent has general authority to act on the principal's behalf, then the agent has general authority to act/enter into transactions in the areas listed below, as set forth in the corresponding provisions of G.S. Chapter 32C.[68]

AREA	STATUTE (G.S.)
Real property	32C-2-204
Tangible personal property	32C-2-205
Stocks and bonds	32C-2-206
Commodities and options	32C-2-207
Banks and other financial institutions	32C-2-208
Operation of entity	32C-2-209
Insurance and annuities	32C-2-210
Estates, trusts, and other beneficial interests	32C-2-211
Claims and litigation	32C-2-212
Personal and family maintenance	32C-2-213
Benefits from governmental programs or civil or military service	32C-2-214
Retirement plans	32C-2-215
Taxes	32C-2-216

The drafter of a POA may incorporate by reference all or some of these provisions of general authority when establishing an agent's authority in the POA. The drafter may choose to grant the general authority to the agent by listing a descriptive term, such as "real property," or the related statutory citation, such as "G.S. 32C-2-204." [69] A reference in a POA to either a descriptive term for a subject or a citation to G.S. 32C-2-204 through -216 incorporates the entire section as if it were set out in full in the POA.[70] The drafter of a POA may modify in the POA any authority incorporated by reference.[71] Note that if a POA was created before January 1, 2018, using the statutory short form authorized under the now-repealed G.S. 32A-1, the powers conferred by the former G.S. 32A-2 apply.[72]

If the POA references some but not all of the descriptive terms or statutory citations listed above, then it does not incorporate all of the areas of general authority, and the agent only has general authority with regard to the areas listed. For example, if a POA

---

68. G.S. 32C-2-201(d).
69. G.S. 32C-2-202(a).
70. G.S. 32C-2-202(b). Note that inclusion of the descriptive term "make a gift" or the citation G.S. 32C-2-217 also incorporates the entire section as if it were set out in full in the POA. *Id.* Gifting authority is treated as both specific and general authority under the POA and is discussed separately in Section II.C.8.c, *infra.*
71. G.S. 32C-2-202(c).
72. G.S. 32C-4-403(d).

states that the agent has only general authority over real property, then the agent has all of the authority set out in G.S. 32C-2-204 but lacks the authority over any of the other areas of general authority, such as taxes, insurance, or any of the other subjects set out in G.S. 32C-2-205 through -216.

b. Specific Authority

Specific authority is authority that must be expressly granted in the POA in order for the agent to act; it may not be inferred from a general grant of authority.[73] The actions by an agent that require an express grant of specific authority in the POA under G.S. 32C-2-201(a)(1) include the authority to

- create or change rights of survivorship;

- create or change a beneficiary designation;

- delegate authority granted under the POA;

- waive the principal's right to be a beneficiary of a joint and survivor annuity, including a survivor benefit under a retirement plan;

- exercise fiduciary powers that the principal has authority to delegate;

- renounce or disclaim property, including a power of appointment; and

- exercise authority over the content of electronic communication, as defined in 18 U.S.C. § 2510(12), sent or received by the principal.

Furthermore, an agent may do the following only if the POA or the terms of a trust expressly grant such authority to the agent:

- exercise the powers of the principal as settlor of a revocable trust in accordance with G.S. 36C-6-602.1[74] or

- exercise the powers of the principal as settlor of an irrevocable trust to consent to the trust's modification or termination in accordance with G.S. 36C-4-411(a).[75]

These actions require a specific grant of authority because of the risk they pose to the principal's property and estate plan.[76] Despite the risk, it may be necessary to grant the agent the authority in order to effectuate the principal's property management and estate-planning objectives.[77] These areas of specific authority are often called "hot powers" because of the risks associated with them. A principal may further define or limit the specific authority granted in a POA.[78] For example, if a principal grants an agent the specific

---

73. UNIF. POWER OF ATTY ACT, Authority, General Cmt. (UNIF. LAW COMM'N 2006).
74. G.S. 32C-2-201(a)(2)a.
75. G.S. 32C-2-201(a)(2)b.
76. G.S. 32C-2-201, Official Cmt. The Official Comment also notes that these are areas where the principal would ideally seek advice before granting authority to the agent. *Id.*
77. *Id.*
78. *Id.*

authority to change survivorship rights or beneficiary designations, the principal may choose to restrict that authority to specifically-identified property interests, accounts, or contracts.[79]

c. Authority to Make a Gift

i. POA Is Silent Regarding Gifts

Gifting authority is in a category all its own because it is referred to throughout G.S. Chapter 32C as requiring general and specific authority.[80] If a POA is silent about gifts, then the agent lacks the authority to make gifts without a court order authorizing the particular gift.[81] This rule applies even when a POA states that the agent has the general authority to "do all of the acts a principal could do" or otherwise states that the agent has the broad authority to manage the principal's property.[82] This broad language does not confer gifting authority on the agent.

ii. POA Grants General Authority to Make a Gift

If the POA (1) expressly states that the agent is authorized to make a gift, (2) grants the agent general authority with respect to gifts, or (3) grants the agent only the authority under G.S. 32C-2-217, then the agent's gifting authority is not unlimited.[83] The agent may only make gifts under G.S. 32C-2-217, which provides, in part, that the agent may not make a gift to an individual that exceeds the greater of the amount determined to be in accordance with the principal's history of making or of joining in making of gifts or the annual dollar limit of the federal gift tax exclusion.[84]

iii. POA Grants Specific Authority to Make a Gift

Any authority that enlarges, modifies, or limits the agent's general authority to make a gift under G.S. 32C-2-217 requires specific, express language in the POA.[85] For example, if the goal is for the agent to be able to make unlimited gifts to a trust but the principal does not have a history of making such gifts, then the POA must expressly state this authority.

---

79. *Id.*

80. *See* G.S. 32C-2-201(a)(1)a (the specific authority to make a gift), -217 (gifts authorized by general authority).

81. G.S. 32C-2-218. *See also id.* §§ 32C-2-201(a), (d), -217.

82. G.S. 32C-2-201(d). This is unlike prior law under G.S. 32A-14.1 (repealed), which was enacted in 1995 and stated in subsection (a) that an express grant of power was not required to make gifts to individuals or charitable organizations in accordance with the principal's history of making gifts. *Id.* § 32C-2-201, N.C. Cmt.

83. G.S. 32C-2-201(a)(1)a; -217; -217, Official Cmt.

84. G.S. 32C-2-217(b)(1).

85. G.S. 32C-2-217, Official Cmt.

Table 5.2. **An Agent's Authority to Make a Gift under the NCUPOAA**

LANGUAGE IN THE POA	AGENT'S GIFT AUTHORITY
POA is silent or says that the agent has all of the powers of the principal	No authority to make a gift
POA only says that the agent has the authority to make a gift or references G.S. 32C-2-217	Agent ONLY has the authority to make gifts set forth in G.S. 32C-2-217, subject to G.S. 32C-2-201(b) and (c)
Any other authority to make gifts	Must be specifically set forth in the POA, subject to G.S. 32C-2-201(b) and (c), unless the POA states otherwise

Author's Note: The court may authorize any gift that is reasonable under the circumstances, including a gift that is in addition to or different from a gift authorized by the POA. G.S. 32C-2-218.

iv. Gifts Must Be Made in Accordance with the Principal's Objectives, if Known

Unless the POA states otherwise, the agent has a duty to make gifts in accordance with the principal's objectives, if these are known by the agent.[86] If the principal's objectives are not known by the agent, then the agent has a duty to make gifts consistent with the principal's best interests based on all relevant factors, which may include, but are not limited to,

- the value and nature of the principal's property;

- the principal's foreseeable obligations and need for maintenance;

- minimization of taxes, including income, estate, inheritance, generation-skipping transfer, and gift taxes;

- eligibility for a benefit, a program, or assistance under a statute or regulation;

- the principal's personal history of making or of joining in the making of gifts; and

- the principal's existing estate plan.[87]

Furthermore, under G.S. 32C-2-201(c), unless the POA states otherwise, the agent may not exercise authority under a POA to create in the agent, or in an individual to whom the agent owes a legal obligation of support, an interest in the principal's property, whether by gift or otherwise.

---

86. G.S. 32C-2-201(b).
87. G.S. 32C-2-201(b), (e).

d. Incidental Authority

Incidental authority is the authority that comes with or "tags along" when the principal executes a POA that (1) grants the agent any general authority, (2) grants the agent the authority to make a gift, or (3) states that the agent may do all of the acts the principal could do.[88] By granting an agent one of these types of authority, a principal also authorizes the agent to do the other "incidental acts" to exercise or implement that authority. Areas of incidental authority are set out below.[89]

1. Demand, receive, and obtain by litigation or otherwise, money or another thing of value to which the principal is, may become, or claims to be entitled, and conserve, invest, disburse, or use anything so received or obtained for the purposes intended.

2. Contract in any manner with any person, on terms agreeable to the agent, to accomplish a purpose of a transaction and perform, rescind, cancel, terminate, reform, restate, release, or modify the contract or another contract made by or on behalf of the principal.

3. Execute, acknowledge, seal, deliver, file, or record any instrument or communication the agent considers desirable to accomplish a purpose of a transaction, including creating at any time a schedule listing some or all of the principal's property and attaching it to the POA.

4. Initiate, participate in, submit to alternative dispute resolution, settle, oppose, or propose or accept a compromise with respect to a claim existing in favor of or against the principal or intervene in litigation relating to the claim.

5. Seek on the principal's behalf the assistance of a court or other governmental agency to carry out an act authorized in the POA.

6. Engage, compensate, and discharge an attorney, accountant, discretionary investment manager, expert witness, or other advisor.

7. Prepare, execute, and file a record, report, or other document to safeguard or promote the principal's interest under a statute or regulation.

8. Communicate with any representative or employee of a government or governmental subdivision, agency, or instrumentality, on behalf of the principal.

9. Access communications intended for, and communicate on behalf of the principal, whether by mail, electronic transmission, telephone, or other means.

10. Do any lawful act with respect to the subject and all property related to the subject.

---

88. G.S. 32C-2-203.
89. *Id.*

9. THE AGENT'S DUTIES UNDER A POA

An agent under a POA is a fiduciary concerning matters that are within the scope of the agency.[90] A fiduciary relationship is one of trust and confidence and carries with it certain legal responsibilities or duties.[91] To determine whether an agent has violated a duty under a POA and whether, as a result, the older adult/principal may have a claim for civil damages or a court should remove the agent for breach, it is necessary to identify the agent's duties to the principal under the POA. There are three sources for an agent's duties under a POA: (1) the POA, (2) statutory law, and (3) the common law of agency.[92]

The statutory duties imposed on an agent under G.S. Chapter 32C fall into two categories: (1) mandatory duties that may not be altered by the principal in a POA and (2) default duties that may be altered or eliminated by the principal in the POA.[93]

The agent's duties apply only when the agent exercises authority under a POA.[94] An agent has no affirmative duty to exercise powers or to continue to exercise powers granted to the agent by the POA, unless the POA states otherwise.[95]

Because a POA may expressly alter or omit any of the default duties of an agent, it is important to review every POA to determine the nature and extent of the agent's duties, particularly in a proceeding before a court alleging breach of an agent's duty. The principal may impose certain duties on the agent in the POA beyond what is set forth in G.S. Chapter 32C, such as the duty to account to the principal or to another person designated in the POA.

---

90. Albert v. Cowart, 219 N.C. App. 546, 554 (2012) ("The relationship created by a power of attorney between the principal and the attorney-in-fact is fiduciary in nature . . . ."); SNML Corp. v. Bank of N.C., 41 N.C. App. 28, 37 (1979); Honeycutt v. Farmers & Merchs. Bank, 126 N.C. App. 816, 820 (1997); G.S. 32C-1-114, Official Cmt. *See also* Meinhard v. Salmon, 249 N.Y. 458, 464 (1928) (stating that many forms of conduct permissible for those acting at arm's length are forbidden to those bound by fiduciary ties; a fiduciary "is held to something stricter than the morals of the market place").

91. Estate of Graham v. Morrison, 168 N.C. App. 63, 74 (2005); Dallaire v. Bank of Am., N.A., 367 N.C. 363, 367 (2014) (discussing different fiduciary relationships and providing that common to all fiduciary relationships is a heightened level of trust).

92. Linda S. Whitton, *Understanding Duties and Conflicts of Interest—A Guide for the Honorable Agent*, 117 Penn. St. L. Rev. 1037, 1040–41 (2013) (noting that the drafters of the uniform law "chose to enumerate specific duties because neither the common law nor existing state statutes provided a cohesive fiduciary standard for the [POA] relationship"). *See also In re* Skinner, 370 N.C. 126, 144 (2017) (noting that the question of whether a fiduciary violated a duty is a broader question than simply whether the fiduciary violated the written instrument governing the relationship, and that additional duties may be imposed by law).

93. G.S. 32C-1-114.

94. The duties imposed on an agent under G.S. Chapter 32C do not apply until the agent accepts the appointment as agent and exercises authority under the POA. G.S. 32C-1-114(a), (b).

95. G.S. 32C-1-114(b).

Table 5.3. **Mandatory and Default Duties of an Agent under G.S. Chapter 32C-1-114(a) and (b)**

MANDATORY DUTIES (May NOT Be Altered in the POA)	DEFAULT DUTIES (May Be Altered or Eliminated in the POA)
1. Act in accordance with the principal's reasonable expectations, to the extent they are actually known by the agent; otherwise, act in the principal's best interests.	1. Act loyally for the principal's benefit.
2. Act in good faith.	2. Act so as not to create a conflict of interest that impairs the agent's ability to act impartially in the principal's best interests.
3. Act only within the scope of authority granted in the POA.	3. Act with the care, competence, and diligence ordinarily exercised by agents in similar circumstances.
	4. Keep a record of all receipts, disbursements, and transactions made on behalf of the principal.
	5. Cooperate with any person who has authority to make health care decisions for the principal to carry out the principal's reasonable expectations, to the extent they are actually known by the agent; otherwise, act in the principal's best interests.
	6. Attempt to preserve the principal's estate plan, to the extent it is actually known by the agent, if preserving the plan is consistent with the principal's best interests based on all relevant factors.

III. CHALLENGES FOR POAs

A. ABUSE BY THE AGENT UNDER A POA

POAs are often recommended to older adults because of their flexibility, convenience, low cost, and lack of court involvement.[96] But POAs may also be a source of abuse against older adults. They have been referred to by some commentators as a "license to steal."[97] Common categories of abuse related to POAs include when a POA is improperly obtained and when an agent exceeds the scope of authority granted in a POA.

1. COMMON TYPES OF ABUSE

a. POA Improperly Obtained

Because POAs are private arrangements, an unscrupulous individual may write a POA and present it to an older adult to sign. The individual may use the older adult's lack of capacity or fraud, duress, undue influence, or misrepresentation to induce the older adult to sign the POA.

> ◇ **EXAMPLE**
>
> *Jane Smith was a 98-year-old woman who lived alone in Florida after her husband died. She had no children. She had dementia and needed assistance with her care. A distant relative of Mrs. Smith appeared and offered to help her with her day-to-day needs. He moved Mrs. Smith from Florida to Alabama and had her sign a POA appointing him as her agent. He told her that she needed to sign the POA to lease her new apartment in Alabama. The POA was drafted by the relative's girlfriend. The relative then proceeded to exploit Mrs. Smith by using her money to gamble, to buy a house for himself, and to purchase large items such as motorcycles, a bulldozer, and a convenience store. In total, the relative spent around $53,000 per month and a total sum of $2.3 million.[98]*

b. Agent Exceeds Scope of Authority

The agent has only the authority granted in the POA. If the agent exceeds the scope of that authority, the agent may be subject to civil or criminal liability.

---

96. *See* STIEGEL & VANCLEAVE KLEM, *supra* note 17, at 5.

97. *Id.*

98. Adapted from a May 16, 2015, story by Kym Klass in the *Montgomery Advertiser* describing the case of Virginia Freck that is available here: https://www.montgomeryadvertiser.com/story/life/project7/2015/05/17/project-elder-abuse/27479125/.

◇ EXAMPLE

Tom executes a POA that gives the agent, Sarah, general authority over "real property." This means that Sarah has all of the authority set out in G.S. 32C-2-204, including the authority to sell, mortgage, and lease all real property owned by Tom. Sarah then cashes out Tom's retirement accounts, life insurance, and bank accounts. Sarah has exceeded the scope of her authority under the POA.

◇ EXAMPLE

Fred executes a POA stating that his agent, John, has the authority to do all of the acts Fred could do. This means that John has all of the general authority set out under G.S. 32C-2-204 through -216 related to real property, personal property, taxes, insurance, retirement plans, and other areas described in those statutes. John then makes a gift of Fred's property and changes the beneficiary designations on Fred's retirement accounts. John exceeded the scope of his authority under the POA because the authority to make a gift and the authority to change beneficiary designations are not expressly set forth in the POA, which is required for an agent to have those types of specific authority.

WHAT TO DO IF YOU SUSPECT THAT AN AGENT FOR AN OLDER ADULT IS ABUSING AUTHORITY GRANTED UNDER A POA.

In such circumstances, the older adult, or someone acting with or on behalf of the older adult, could consider taking the following actions:

    a. get a copy of the POA,

    b. gather information/evidence,

    c. refuse to accept the POA,

    d. make a report to APS or law enforcement,

    e. terminate the POA or the agent's authority, and

    f. seek judicial relief.

Each of these actions is discussed in detail below.

2. POSSIBLE WAYS TO RESPOND TO ABUSE

a. Get a Copy of the POA

There is no standardized form POA that every individual who executes a POA must use. Although there is a form POA set out in statute, that form may be modified or ignored completely by the drafter of a POA. Each POA is unique. A POA is drafted to reflect the needs and wishes of a particular principal. It is imperative for any person who seeks to understand the authority granted to an agent by a principal in a POA to have a copy of the POA. This includes a law enforcement officer investigating a crime, a county social worker investigating reports of elder abuse, and a court seeking to determine whether an agent under a POA committed a breach of fiduciary duty.

> **✏️ PRACTICE NOTE**
> 1. **Treat each POA as unique**—it is not a requirement that the available statutory form be used; if the form is used, it may be modified.
> 2. **Get a copy of the POA**—ask the principal, check with family and friends, and search the county register of deeds office for a recorded copy of the POA (note that the POA does not have to be recorded to be valid; see Section II.C.1, *supra*).
> 3. **Review the POA for the agent's authority to act and the extent of the agent's duties**—determine what acts are authorized by the POA and what duties it imposes on the agent (see Sections II.C.8 and 9, *supra*).

Reviewing the POA will enable the law enforcement officer, the county social worker, or the court to begin to answer key questions about whether the agent's actions on behalf of the principal were authorized or whether the agent's actions constitute elder abuse.

b. Gather Information/Evidence

There may be instances in which abuse of an older adult by an agent under a POA is suspected but not confirmed. Unless the POA states otherwise, the agent must keep a record of all receipts, disbursements, and transactions made on behalf of an older adult/principal.[99] The agent must disclose receipts, disbursements, or transactions conducted on behalf of the principal when

1. ordered to do so by a court or
2. a request to do so is made by
   a. the principal or a person designated by the principal in the POA;
   b. a guardian of the estate (GOE);
   c. a general guardian (GG); or,
   d. upon the death of the principal, by the personal representative or successor in interest of the principal's estate.[100]

---

99. G.S. 32C-1-114(b)(4).
100. G.S. 32C-1-114(h).

Any interested person may file a petition with the court asking it to enter an order compelling an accounting by the agent that includes the production of evidence substantiating any expenditure by the agent of the principal's assets.[101] The proceeding is commenced before the clerk of superior court as prescribed for in, and conducted in accordance with, estate proceedings under G.S. 28A-2-6.[102] There is no form available to initiate the proceeding.[103] There is a fee collected by the court to file the action unless the costs are waived because the petitioner is indigent (see Chapter 6 for discussion of suing as indigent).[104]

c. Refuse to Accept the POA

A person, including, in this context, a financial institution, is never required to accept and is not liable for refusing to accept a POA that is not duly acknowledged.[105]

If a POA is acknowledged, a person may refuse to accept the POA, for example, if the person

- believes in good faith that the POA is not valid;

- believes in good faith that the agent under the POA does not have the authority to perform the act requested;

- has reasonable cause to question the authenticity or validity of the POA or the appropriateness of its exercise by the agent; or

- makes, or has actual knowledge that another person has made, a report to adult protective services (APS) or law enforcement stating a good faith belief that the principal may be subject to physical or financial abuse, neglect, exploitation, or abandonment by the agent or a person acting for or with the agent.[106]

d. Make a Report
i. Adult Protective Services (APS)

Every person in North Carolina, with the singular exception of the long-term care ombudsman, must make an APS report if that person has reasonable cause to believe that a disabled adult needs protective services, including as a result of abuse by an agent under a POA.[107] Refer to Chapter 2 for a full discussion of the duty to report and the steps APS will take in response to a report.

---

101. G.S. 32C-1-116(a)(1), (c).

102. G.S. 32C-1-116(c).

103. For a discussion of the procedure applicable to estate proceedings before the clerk, refer to Ann M. Anderson, *Estate Proceedings in North Carolina*, EST. ADMIN. BULL. No. 1, 8–18 (Dec. 2012), https://www.sog.unc.edu/sites/www.sog.unc.edu/files/reports/eab01.pdf.

104. G.S. 7A-307(a).

105. G.S. 32C-1-120(a).

106. G.S. 32C-1-120(c) (listing the circumstances when a person is not required to accept an acknowledged POA).

107. G.S. 108A-102; 143B-181.20(f). *See* Aimee Wall, *Adult Protective Services: A New Reporting Requirement*, COATES' CANONS: NC LOC. GOV'L. BLOG (June 23, 2015), https://canons.sog.unc.edu/adult-protective-services-a-new-reporting-requirement/.

ii. Law Enforcement

An agent under a POA is not immune from prosecution; a report or referral to law enforcement may be appropriate if the agent engaged in criminal activity. Possible crimes that may apply to abuse by an agent under a POA include

- obtaining property by false pretenses (G.S. 14-100),

- obtaining signature by false pretenses (G.S. 14-101),

- common law forgery (G.S. 14-119 and -120),

- embezzlement by an agent or fiduciary (G.S. 14-90), and

- exploitation of an older adult or disabled adult (G.S. 14-112.2).

e. Terminate the POA or the Agent's Authority

An older adult, as principal under a POA, has the authority to revoke the POA or the agent's authority under it.[108] If the older adult seeks to revoke the agent's authority, the revocation must be in writing, unless the POA states otherwise.[109] The termination of the agent's authority is not effective until the agent has actual knowledge of it.[110] If the older adult is incapacitated, then judicial action may be necessary to terminate the POA or the agent's authority.

f. Seek Judicial Relief

There are various types of judicial relief that may be available to protect an older adult in the event of abuse by an agent under a POA. The type of judicial action filed will depend upon the facts of a particular case. Possible judicial actions include (1) a POA proceeding, (2) a civil action, or (3) a guardianship proceeding.

---

108. G.S. 32C-1-110(a)(3), (b)(1).
109. G.S. 32C-1-110(b)(1), (c).
110. G.S. 32C-1-110(d).

Table 5.4. Judicial Relief Available Related to POAs in Elder Abuse Cases

TYPE OF ACTION	WHO PRESIDES?	POSSIBLE REMEDIES
POA proceeding	Clerk of superior court or superior court judge (on transfer from the clerk under G.S. 32C-1-116(a)(4))	• Compel an accounting by the agent • Remove the agent • Suspend the agent's authority • Reduce or deny the agent's compensation • Other relief set forth in G.S. 32C-1-117, except as limited by G.S. 32C-1-116(b)
Civil action	District or superior court judge or magistrate (in certain small claims)	• Set aside or rescind the POA based on undue influence or lack of capacity • Modify or amend the POA • Monetary damages • Recovery of property conveyed by an agent with the intent to hinder, delay, or defraud the principal's creditors • Other civil remedies (discussed in Chapter 6)
Guardianship proceeding	Clerk of superior court	For an older adult who lacks capacity, the appointment by the court of a guardian of the estate or general guardian who • takes action to terminate the POA and the agent's authority, • takes control of and secures the older adult's property, and • takes action to recover the older adult's property and seeks civil damages or other relief on behalf of the older adult.

i. POA Proceeding to Remove an Agent or Seek Other Relief before the Clerk

The term "POA proceeding" includes proceedings under G.S. Chapter 32C. Examples of POA proceedings that may be filed when an older adult is the subject of abuse include a proceeding to terminate a POA after the appointment of a guardian of the estate or a general guardian, a proceeding to determine compensation for an agent, and a proceeding to determine whether and to what extent a POA must be accepted by a third party.[111]

POA proceedings are commenced before the clerk and conducted in accordance with the procedures for estate proceedings under G.S. 28A-2-6.[112] Some POA proceedings initiated before the clerk will be transferred to superior court upon the request of a party.[113]

The person who files the petition and brings the POA proceeding is called the *petitioner*.

---

111. G.S. 32C-1-116(a).

112. G.S. 32C-1-116(c). The procedures for estate proceedings are set out in G.S. 28A-2-6. For further discussion of estate proceedings, refer to Anderson, *supra* note 103.

113. G.S. 32C-1-116(a)(4).

The following persons have standing to bring a POA proceeding:

- the principal under a POA;

- the agent under a POA;

- the principal's general guardian, guardian of the estate, or guardian of the person;

- the personal representative of the estate of a deceased principal;

- a person authorized to make health care decisions for the principal; and

- any other interested person, including a person asked to accept a POA.[114]

The term "interested person" is not defined in the statutes governing POA proceedings. Examples of persons who may qualify as interested persons are an heir or beneficiary under a will or trust, a caregiver, or a county department of social services (DSS) that has the authority to protect a principal from financial exploitation. A county DSS, for example, may choose to file a proceeding to compel an accounting from an agent to determine whether and to what extent an incapacitated adult is subject to financial exploitation by the agent. The county would likely have standing to file such an action as an interested person.[115]

Notwithstanding the broad authority of the clerk to hear POA proceedings, certain actions are carved out of the clerk's jurisdiction and must be filed in superior court. These are civil actions by nature or are otherwise matters traditionally adjudicated before the superior court.[116] They include any action[117]

- to modify or amend a POA;

- by or against creditors or debtors of an agent or a principal;

- involving claims for monetary damages;

- to set aside a POA based on undue influence or lack of capacity; or

- to recover property transferred or conveyed by an agent on behalf of a principal with the intent to hinder, delay, or defraud the principal's creditors.

It may be appropriate in some cases involving abuse by an agent of a principal/older adult to file a POA proceeding before the clerk of superior court rather than a civil action. A civil action in district or superior court may take longer to reach a final judgment and be more expensive than a POA proceeding initiated before the clerk. The relief sought to protect the older adult may be available through a more expeditious POA proceeding.

---

114. G.S. 32C-1-116(c).

115. G.S. 32C-1-116, Official Cmt. (noting that the uniform law sets forth broad categories of persons who have standing to petition the court for the primary purpose of protecting vulnerable or incapacitated principals against financial abuse). *But see id.* § 32C-1-116, N.C. Cmt. (stating that a "person that demonstrates sufficient interest in the principal's welfare" should be disregarded from the broad category of persons identified in the Official Comment as having standing to bring an estate proceeding).

116. Anderson, *supra* note 103.

117. G.S. 32C-1-116(b).

For example, it may be that instead of monetary damages, a principal/older adult's family member or friend, or another interested person, wants to compel an accounting, remove an agent, or compel an agent to return property to the principal, which can be done through a POA proceeding.[118]

A POA proceeding may also stop ongoing abuse of an older adult and prevent the need for a guardianship proceeding under G.S. Chapter 35A. In some cases where an older adult has a POA that is subject to abuse by an agent, the older adult may also lack capacity to make decisions or to manage his or her affairs. Family, friends, or other persons may consider seeking a court-appointed guardian who will take action to terminate the agent's authority.[119] However, the older adult may not need a guardian if the POA names a willing, responsible successor agent to act.[120] The family member, friend, or other interested person may instead choose to file a POA proceeding to remove an agent and stop abuse by the agent.[121] Once the agent is removed, the successor agent may act on behalf of the older adult, including taking steps to secure the older adult's property and recover any property improperly taken by the agent if authorized under the POA.[122]

> ◇ **EXAMPLE**
>
> *Fran appointed her son, John, as her agent under a POA. Her other son, Jeff, is named as the successor agent. Jeff learns that John gifted much of Fran's property to John's wife, in violation of the authority granted to John under the POA, which restricts gifts and self-dealing. Jeff files a POA proceeding to remove John as agent. The clerk finds that John breached his fiduciary duty and removes him as the agent. The order removing John as agent then allows Jeff, as successor agent named in the POA, to act on Fran's behalf.*

ii. Civil Action to Rescind a POA and for Civil Damages and Other Relief

If a POA is improperly obtained or an agent exceeds the scope of his or her authority, there are a number of civil remedies that may be obtained by initiating a civil action. For example, an older adult, or an authorized person acting on his or her behalf, may file a civil action in superior court to rescind, or set aside the POA, if the POA was signed when the older adult lacked capacity or as a result of undue influence.[123] Civil actions, including an action to set aside a document, are explained in Chapter 6.

A civil action may be the appropriate action to file when an older adult seeks monetary damages from an agent. The clerk of superior court in a POA proceeding lacks the

---

118. G.S. 32C-1-116(a) (stating that proceedings under G.S. Chapter 32C fall under the original jurisdiction of the clerk, except as set forth in G.S 32C-1-116(c)); 32C-1-117(b) (listing the types of relief the court may grant when an agent violates G.S. Chapter 32C).

119. Guardianship is discussed further in Chapter 4.

120. G.S. 32C-1-111(b).

121. G.S. 32C-1-116(a); 32C-1-117(b)(6).

122. G.S. 32C-1-111(b).

123. G.S. 32C-1-116(b)(4).

authority over claims for monetary damages.[124] Claims that do not involve monetary damages related to a POA, including claims that otherwise fall under the exclusive jurisdiction of the clerk, may be joined in the civil action by a party.[125] Furthermore, when there is a civil action before the superior court and a POA proceeding before the clerk that involve a common question of law or fact, on the court's motion or the motion of a party, the superior court judge may order consolidation of the POA proceeding and the civil action and decide all matters.[126]

iii. Proceeding to Appoint a Guardian; Termination of POA by Guardian

When an older adult lacks capacity and is subject to abuse by an agent under a POA, it may be necessary to seek the appointment of a guardian for the older adult, particularly where other supports, services, or alternatives to guardianship will not enable the adult to remain free from abuse. Guardianship is discussed in Chapter 4. A guardian of the estate (GOE) and a general guardian (GG) appointed by the court have the authority to terminate a POA without any further order from the court.[127] A guardian of the person (GOP) lacks the authority to terminate a POA.[128]

(a) Process for Termination of POA by GOE or GG

The process for terminating a POA by a GOE or GG appointed by the court is different depending on whether the POA was previously registered in a North Carolina register of deeds office.

(1) Termination by GOE or GG of POA Previously Registered in a North Carolina Register of Deeds Office

If a POA was previously registered in a North Carolina register of deeds office, the GOE or GG can terminate the POA by registering an instrument of revocation in the same office where the POA is registered.[129] The GOE or GG must execute and acknowledge the instrument of revocation.[130] The instrument must be registered along with proof of service on the agent under the POA being revoked.[131] Service of the instrument of revocation on the agent must be completed pursuant to Rule 5 of the state Rules of Civil Procedure, which requires

- handing a copy of the revocation to the agent,

- mailing a copy to the agent at the agent's last known address, or

- filing a copy with the clerk of court if the agent's address is not known.[132]

---

124. G.S. 32C-1-116(b)(3).
125. G.S. 32C-1-116(c); 28A-2-6(g).
126. G.S. 32C-1-116(c); 28A-2-6(f).
127. G.S. 32C-1-110(a)(7). The GOE and GG also have the authority to terminate the agent's authority under a POA. *Id.* § 32C-1-110(b)(5).
128. *See* G.S. 32C-1-110(a)(7).
129. G.S. 32C-1-110(h).
130. *Id.*
131. *Id.*
132. *Id.; id.* § 1A-1, Rule 5. Rule 5 allows for service on a party's attorney of record in some cases. The GOE or GG is not required to file a court action to terminate the POA, therefore Rule 5 service discussed herein addresses service on the agent.

Service by mail is complete once a copy of the revocation is placed in a pre-paid envelope or other wrapper, properly addressed, and deposited with the U.S. Postal Service.[133]

Typically, a certificate of service accompanies any paper served pursuant to Rule 5 and suffices for purposes of showing proof of service; a certificate of service is a way to show that service was effected in order to satisfy the requirements of G.S. 32C-1-110(h).[134] A certificate must

- include the date and method of service or the date of acceptance of service,

- include the name and service address of the agent served with the revocation, and

- be signed in accordance with and subject to Rule 11 of the N.C. Rules of Civil Procedure.[135]

The statute governing the termination of POAs requires proof of service of the revocation on "the agent."[136] An agent as defined in G.S. Chapter 32C includes an original agent, co-agent, successor agent, and any person to whom an agent's authority is delegated.[137]

✎ PRACTICE NOTE

Steps to Revoke a Previously Registered POA by a GOE or GG

1. The GOE or GG executes and acknowledges an instrument of revocation.
2. The GOE or GG serves the instrument of revocation on the agent under Rule 5 of the N.C. Rules of Civil Procedure.
3. The GOE or GG registers the instrument of revocation along with proof of service on the agent (i.e., the certificate of service) with the register of deeds in the same county where the POA being revoked is registered.

---

(2) Termination by GOE or GG of POA Not Registered in a North Carolina Register of Deeds Office

G.S. Chapter 32C does not provide a procedure for a court-appointed GOE or GG to follow to terminate a POA if the POA was not previously registered with a North Carolina register of deeds office. The GOE or GG may choose to execute and acknowledge a written instrument of revocation and then serve a copy of that revocation on the agent, any co-agent, and any successor agents named in the POA. The GOE or GG could then file a copy of the written revocation along with proof of service on the agent(s) in the court's guardianship "E" file. This would make clear to the agent(s) and the court that the GOE or GG terminated the POA, and it would make the date of termination clear as well. A termination of a POA

---

133. G.S. 1A-1, Rule 5(b)(2) ("Service by mail shall be complete upon deposit of the pleading or paper enclosed in a post-paid, properly addressed wrapper in a post office or official depository under the exclusive care and custody of the United States Postal Service").

134. G.S. 1A-1, Rule 5(b1).

135. *Id.*

136. G.S. 32C-1-110(h).

137. G.S. 32C-1-102(1).

is not effective as to any agent(s) or third parties who, without actual knowledge of the termination, act in good faith under the POA.[138]

(b) Termination of POA by Interim Guardian

After a petition for adjudication of incompetence is filed but before the appointment of a GOE, GG, or GOP under G.S. Chapter 35A, the clerk may appoint an interim GOE, GG, or GOP on the clerk's own motion or on the motion of the petitioner or guardian ad litem.[139] An interim guardian is a guardian appointed when (1) there is or reasonably appears to be an imminent or foreseeable risk of harm to the older adult/respondent's physical well-being (interim GOP), estate (interim GOE), or both (interim GG) that requires immediate intervention and (2) there is reasonable cause to believe that the older adult is incompetent.[140] Interim guardians are discussed in detail in Chapter 4.

G.S. Chapter 32C does not expressly state that a G.S. Chapter 35A interim GOE or GG has the authority to terminate a POA. Because the powers of a plenary GOE and GG include the power to terminate a POA, it is likely that the clerk may specifically authorize an interim GOE or interim GG to terminate a POA in the clerk's order appointing an interim guardian.[141] It is advisable for the clerk to specifically state that termination authority in the order appointing the interim guardian.[142] It may be necessary for an interim GOE or GG to have that authority where there is an imminent risk of harm to an older adult/respondent's estate that arises from abuse or exploitation by an agent under a POA.

Unlike a GOE or GG, the powers of a GOP do not include the power to terminate a POA. Therefore, an interim GOP lacks the authority to terminate a POA.

B. LACK OF UNDERSTANDING ABOUT POAs

Law enforcement and others who work in criminal law may be inclined to view a report involving a POA as a "civil matter" or one where there is not criminal activity because the principal gave the agent consent to act. But just as in other, more familiar criminal cases like sexual assault, consent to one act does not mean consent to all acts. The principal may have granted the agent authority with regard to some of the principal's property but not all of it, and a criminal charge, such as embezzlement, may be appropriate against the agent under a POA. A list of crimes that may be implicated in elder abuse cases is available in Appendix C.

---

138. G.S. 32C-1-110(d).

139. G.S. 35A-1112(b1) (appointment on the clerk's own motion); 35A-1114(a) (appointment pursuant to a motion of the petitioner or the guardian ad litem).

140. G.S. 35A-1114(b), (d).

141. *See* G.S. 32C-1-110(a)(7).

142. *See* G.S. 35A-1114(e) (requiring the court to set forth the interim guardian's powers and duties in the order appointing the interim guardian). The court typically uses Form AOC-SP-900, "Order on Motion for Appointment of Interim Guardian," when appointing an interim guardian. The form is available at https://www.nccourts.gov/assets/documents/forms/459.pdf?Sf_GqOc97Vu6lMNzyFOP5UHCVSO8qlrg.

> **TIPS FOR HANDLING REPORTS OF ELDER ABUSE INVOLVING POAS.**
>
> 1. Learn the foundational law governing POAs. Some abuses will be relatively easy to identify once a person has a basic understanding of the law governing POAs.
> 2. Always obtain a copy of a POA and review it to determine the nature and extent of the agent's authority to act under it.
> 3. Avoid making assumptions about POAs, including that a POA gives an agent unlimited authority to act for the principal or that if a person acted under a POA there is nothing law enforcement or APS can do to prosecute the agent or protect the older adult's property.
> 4. Develop relationships with local elder law attorneys. They may be willing to review and advise on the scope and limitations of specific POAs.

C. DIFFICULT TO DETECT ABUSE

POAs are private arrangements when they are executed and are likely to remain private during the time the agent acts on the principal's behalf. The agent does not have a duty to account to the principal, the court, or any other person, unless the POA provides otherwise or the court orders an accounting. Abuse under a POA can go undetected for long periods of time, as shown by the case of Virginia Freck, one of the most extreme examples of elder abuse and exploitation in recent years.[143] A distant relative of the 98-year-old appeared when Mrs. Freck started showing signs of dementia and needing assistance with her care. She had no children and lived alone. The relative moved Mrs. Freck from Florida to Alabama and had Mrs. Freck sign a POA appointing him as her agent. The POA was drafted by the relative's girlfriend. The relative then proceeded to exploit Mrs. Freck by using her money to gamble, to buy a house for himself, and to purchase large items, such as motorcycles, a bulldozer, and a convenience store. In total, he spent around $53,000 per month and a total sum of $2.3 million. The abuse did not come to light until Mrs. Freck's bank account was overdrawn and she was almost evicted from her apartment.

---

143. Klass, *supra* note 98.

TIPS FOR EARLY DETECTION OF ABUSE UNDER A POA.

- **Learn the signs of financial abuse or exploitation.** Individuals who work with older adults should be aware of the different types of abuse and remain alert to potential signs of financial abuse and exploitation. A list of signs of abuse is presented in Chapter 1.

- **Promote and use trusted persons lists.** Financial institutions are encouraged (but not required) by law to offer older adult customers the opportunity to submit and periodically update a list of trusted persons to be contacted in case of suspected abuse.[144] Adult protective services (APS) and others working with older adults should encourage them to submit such a list to financial institutions so that there is someone in place for the financial institution to reach out to if there is any indication of abuse.

- **Make an APS report.** Every person in North Carolina, with the singular exception of long-term care ombudsmen, must make an APS report if there is reasonable cause to believe that a disabled adult needs protective services, including as a result of abuse by an agent under a POA.[145] Refer to Chapter 2 for a full discussion of the duty to report and the steps APS will take in response to a report.

---

144. G.S. 108A-114.
145. G.S. 108A-102. *See* Wall, *supra* note 107.

Chapter 6
Civil Actions, Domestic Violence, and Housing

CONTENTS

I. SCOPE OF CHAPTER

The district attorney may criminally prosecute a perpetrator of elder abuse. An adult protective services (APS) investigation may lead to the mobilization of essential services to protect an older adult from abuse. A court may appoint a guardian for an older adult who lacks capacity and needs a surrogate decision-maker to take action to protect him or her from abuse. But the older adult still may not be made financially whole or may require additional legal protections to stop the abuse.

There are other remedies available through North Carolina courts to protect the older adult and his or her property. This chapter identifies some of these other civil judicial remedies, including remedies available (1) through civil litigation, (2) in cases involving domestic violence or unwanted contact, and (3) related to housing. It begins with a summary of how these remedies protect older adults. It then identifies who is responsible for bringing these types of actions. Next it provides details about each category of remedy and how it may provide compensation or relief for older adults in cases involving elder abuse. The chapter concludes with a discussion of some of the key challenges to seeking these civil remedies to address elder abuse and possible ways to tackle those challenges.

II. OVERVIEW OF CIVIL REMEDIES

A. HOW DO CIVIL LEGAL REMEDIES PROTECT OLDER ADULTS?

A door-to-door home repairman defrauds an older adult out of her life savings. A friend gets an older adult who lacks capacity to sign a deed conveying the older adult's property to the friend. A grandchild pushes an older adult to the ground trying to get the older adult's debit card. A caregiver refuses to move out of the older adult's home when asked. The civil remedies described in this chapter protect older adults in these types of situations by enabling the older adult to

- recover money or property or seek civil damages or other relief—for example, rescission of documents such as a will, a power of attorney, or a deed;

- obtain a civil protective order, such as a domestic violence protective order or a civil no-contact order; and

- remove someone from his or her residence, such as through summary ejectment or civil trespass.

B. WHO IS RESPONSIBLE?

1. WHO FILES THE ACTION?

In civil actions in North Carolina, claims and defenses must be brought in the name of the real party in interest.[1] A real party in interest is a party who has benefited or been injured by the judgment in a case and who by substantive law has the legal right to enforce the claim in question.[2] A person with a general interest in, or someone who will be indirectly impacted by, the outcome of a case is typically not a real party in interest.[3] Generally, the real party in interest is "the one entitled to receive the fruits of the litigation," such as damages.[4]

a. When the Older Adult Has Capacity

If an older adult is the aggrieved party and has capacity, then the older adult files the civil action and prosecutes the claim(s) as the real party in interest.[5] The older adult is the named plaintiff or petitioner in the action and has the right to prosecute the action with or without the assistance of an attorney.

b. When the Older Adult Is Incompetent

If an older adult is the aggrieved party and is incompetent, the general rule is that (1) claims may be prosecuted in the name of the older adult as the real party in interest or (2) if the older adult has a guardian, claims may be brought by the guardian in the guardian's own name without joining the older adult as a party subject to certain limitations discussed below.[6]

i. Older Adult Is the Real Party in Interest

If the claim is brought in the name of the incompetent older adult as the real party in interest, then, under Rule 17(b) of the North Carolina Rules of Civil Procedure, the older adult must appear by either

- a general guardian (GG)[7] appointed by the clerk pursuant to G.S. Chapter 35A or

- a guardian ad litem (Rule 17 GAL).[8]

---

1. Chapter 1, Section 57, of the North Carolina General Statutes (hereinafter G.S.); G.S. 1A-1, Rule 17(a) (N.C. Rules of Civil Procedure). *See* Reliance Ins. Co. v. Walker, 33 N.C. App. 15, 18 (1977) (stating that although Rule 17 by its terms applies only to "parties plaintiff," the rule is applicable to "parties defendant" as well (citing 3A MOORE'S FEDERAL PRACTICE § 17.07, at 226–27)).

2. *See Reliance*, 33 N.C. App. at 18–19; Energy Inv'rs Fund, L.P. v. Metric Constructors, Inc., 351 N.C. 331, 337 (2000) (quoting Parnell v. Nationwide Mut. Ins. Co., 263 N.C. 445, 448–49 (1965)).

3. *See* John L. Saxon, *Who Are the Parties in IV-D Child Support Proceedings? And What Difference Does it Make?* FAM. L. BULL. No. 22, at 5 (Jan. 2007). The concept of real party in interest is closely related to the concept of standing to commence and prosecute an action or proceeding before a court. *Id. See also* G. GRAY WILSON, NORTH CAROLINA CIVIL PROCEDURE § 17-1 (3d ed. 2007).

4. WILSON, *supra* note 3, at § 17-1.

5. G.S. 1A-1, Rule 17(a).

6. *Id.*

7. A general guardian is both a guardian of the person and a guardian of the estate. G.S. 35A-1101(7).

8. G.S. 1A-1, Rule 17(b)(1).

The appointment of a Rule 17 GAL must be made at any time prior to, or at the time of, the commencement of the action.[9] The appointment is made on the application of any relative or friend of the incompetent older adult or by the court on its own motion.[10] The written application is generally filed, and the appointment is typically made, by the clerk at the time the complaint initiating the action is presented for filing with the court. If the claim is brought in the name of the incompetent older adult as the real party in interest and the older adult has a GG, the court may still appoint a Rule 17 GAL if the court deems it expedient to have the older adult represented by a Rule 17 GAL.[11]

> ### ✎ PRACTICE NOTE
>
> **_Things to Keep in Mind about a Rule 17 GAL_**
>
> - Any "relative or friend" may file a written application seeking the appointment of a Rule 17 GAL for an older adult who is (1) the plaintiff in a civil action or special proceeding and (2) incompetent.[12]
> - A court may appoint a Rule 17 GAL on its own motion.[13]
> - The Rule 17 GAL appointed by the court does not have to be an attorney and is not the older adult's lawyer.[14] Any competent adult may serve as a Rule 17 GAL.
> - The Rule 17 GAL either serves pro bono or the Rule 17 GAL's fees may be taxed to a party as part of the costs if allowed by law.[15]

The role of the Rule 17 GAL, appointed when the incompetent older adult is the named party to the action, is one of substitution.[16] The North Carolina Court of Appeals has stated that the "[a]ppointment of a GAL under Rule 17 for an incompetent person 'will divest the [incompetent party] of their fundamental right to conduct his or her litigation according to their own judgment and inclination.'"[17] The Rule 17 GAL has a duty to file and timely serve pleadings.[18] If a party has a Rule 17 GAL, the court may proceed to final judgment, order, or decree as if the party had been under no legal disability.[19]

---

9. G.S. 1A-1, Rule 17(c)(1).

10. _Id._

11. G.S. 1A-1, Rule 17(b)(3).

12. G.S. 1A-1, Rule 17(c)(1).

13. _Id._

14. _See_ N.C. State Bar, Formal Ethics Op. 11 (2004) (discussing the difference in ethical duties owed to the ward by a lawyer representing the ward as a client versus a lawyer who is appointed solely as a GAL). An exception to this rule is a GAL appointed to represent a respondent in a G.S. Chapter 35A incompetency and guardianship proceeding. The GAL is appointed pursuant to Rule 17 but is also the respondent's lawyer in the proceeding unless the respondent retains his own counsel, in which event the GAL may be discharged. G.S. 35A-1101(6); 35A-1107.

15. _See_ N.C. Off. of Indigent Def. Servs. & Admin. Off. of the Cts., North Carolina Proceedings That Involve Guardians ad Litem (GALs) (revised Oct. 2014), http://www.ncids.org/Rules%20&%20Procedures/GAL_Chart.pdf (hereinafter IDS GAL Chart).

16. _In re_ P.D.R., 224 N.C. App. 460, 467 (2012) (quoting _In re_ J.A.A. & S.A.A., 175 N.C. App. 66, 71 (2005)).

17. _J.A.A. & S.A.A._, 175 N.C. App. at 71.

18. G.S. 1A-1, Rule 17(e).

19. _Id._

ii. Guardian Sues in His or Her Own Name

Under Rule 17(a) of the North Carolina Rules of Civil Procedure, a claim may be brought by a guardian in the guardian's own name on behalf of the incompetent older adult without joining the older adult as a party.[20] The clerk of superior court appoints a guardian in a separate proceeding under G.S. Chapter 35A after a judicial determination of incompetency (discussed in more detail in Chapter 4).[21] The clerk may appoint

- a guardian of the person (GOP), who is a guardian with authority over the care, custody, and control of the incompetent older adult;

- a guardian of the estate (GOE), who is a guardian with authority over the property, estate,[22] and business affairs of the incompetent older adult; or

- a general guardian (GG), who is a guardian of the estate and the person.[23]

A GOP does not have authority to initiate an action on behalf of the older adult in the GOP's own name.[24] Both a GOE and a GG have the authority to initiate actions related to the incompetent older adult's estate in their own names without joining the older adult as a party.[25] A GOE generally may not initiate an action in his or her own name that relates to the care, custody, or control of the older adult, such as one to obtain a domestic violence protective order (DVPO).[26]

If there is any doubt as to whether a GOE or GG may commence the action in the guardian's own name without joining the incompetent older adult as a party, such as in the case of a DVPO or other action that does not involve the estate of the older incompetent adult, the action may be filed in the name of the older adult as the real party in interest, as discussed above, and the GG could appear on behalf of the incompetent older adult in the proceeding or a "relative or friend" could seek the appointment of a Rule 17 GAL to appear

---

20. G.S. 1A-1, Rule 17(a).

21. G.S. 35A-1120; 35A-1203(a); 35A-1210.

22. "Estate" means "[a]ny interest in real property, choses in action, intangible personal property, and tangible personal property, and includes any interest in joint accounts or jointly held property." G.S. 35A-1202(5).

23. G.S. 35A-1202(10), (9), (7). A clerk in a G.S. Chapter 35A proceeding may also appoint a limited GOP, GOE, or GG or an interim GOP, GOE, or GG. These types of guardians are discussed in more detail in Chapter 4. If the clerk appoints a limited GOE or GG or an interim GOE or GG, that guardian's authority to initiate an action in the guardian's own name on behalf of the incompetent older adult may be limited by the clerk's order appointing the limited or interim guardian.

24. G.S. 35A-1241 (listing the powers of the guardian of the person, which include the duty to give consent or approval to enable the incompetent adult to receive legal counsel but do not include the power to initiate legal action). *See* Clawser v. Campbell, 184 N.C. App. 526, 529 (2007) (holding that the guardian of the person lacks the power to maintain an action); Granville v. Yeddo, 199 N.C. App. 318 (2009) (unpublished) (stating that "[t]he power to initiate legal action lies with the general guardian, guardian of the estate, or guardian ad litem" and not with the guardian of the person).

25. G.S. 35A-1251(3) ("[A] general guardian or guardian of the estate has the power to perform . . . every act . . . incident to the collection, preservation, management, and use of the ward's estate . . . including but not limited to the . . . specific powers . . . [t]o maintain any appropriate action or proceeding to recover possession of any of the ward's property, to determine the title thereto, or to recover damages for any injury done to any of the ward's property; also, to compromise, adjust, arbitrate, sue on or defend, abandon, or otherwise deal with and settle any other claims in favor of or against the ward"); Stern v. Cinoman, 221 N.C. App. 231, 233–34 (2012) (stating that a guardian of the estate has the authority to bring a medical malpractice suit in his own name as guardian).

26. G.S. 35A-1251 (describing the authority of the guardian of the estate as limited to "the collection, preservation, management, and use of the ward's estate" and listing specific powers under that umbrella of authority as including the power to sue on or defend any claims in favor of or against the ward).

on his or her behalf.[27] If the relief granted does not relate to the older adult's estate, such as the relief in a DVPO proceeding, significant confusion may arise in the enforcement of the order or judgment if the action is brought in the name of the guardian rather than the older adult.[28]

c. Effect of the Death of the Older Adult on the Action

After the death of an older adult, the personal representative (PR) or collector of the adult's estate may bring an action as the real party in interest if the cause of action survives the death of the older adult.[29] Causes of action that do not survive death include those alleging libel and slander (except slander of title) or false imprisonment, and those where the relief sought could not be enjoyed, or where the granting of relief would be of no value or importance, after the older adult's death.[30]

If the action is pending at the time of the older adult's death and the cause of action survives, the action may be continued by the PR or collector of the adult's estate.[31] However, substitution of the PR or the collector is not automatic.[32] First, a PR or a collector must be appointed by the clerk of superior court as part of the administration of the older adult's estate.[33] Once a PR or a collector is appointed by the clerk, the court where the action is pending may, in response to a motion, order the PR or collector substituted in as the real party in interest.[34] The motion for substitution must be made within the time specified for the presentation of claims in the estate under G.S. 28A-19-3, which generally is around ninety days, as specified in the notice to creditors of the estate to file claims.[35]

d. Child's Right to Bring an Action on Behalf of a Parent

An adult child does not have the right to bring an action on behalf of a parent unless the parent is incompetent and the child brings the action as the parent's legal representative, as discussed in Section II.B.1.b, *supra*.[36]

There may be instances when an older adult changes a long-held estate plan later in life. This may include when the older adult revokes a will and executes a new will naming new beneficiaries who are not the adult's children. This may be a result of, for example, undue influence or fraud perpetrated by a caregiver, distant relative, or other person

---

27. G.S. 1A-1, Rule 17(b).

28. *See* Cheryl Howell, *Minor Parties in 50B Cases*, ON THE CIVIL SIDE: A UNC SCH. OF GOV'T BLOG (Mar. 13, 2015), https://civil.sog.unc.edu/minor-parties-in-50b-cases/ (explaining that, in cases involving minors, the child's name should be listed as plaintiff rather than the GAL's name).

29. G.S. 1A-1, Rule 17(a); 28A-18-1(a); 1-22.

30. G.S. 28A-18-1(b).

31. G.S. 28A-18-1(a); 1A-1, Rule 25(a).

32. Purvis v. Moses H. Cone Mem'l Hosp. Serv. Corp., 175 N.C. App. 474, 483 (2006).

33. Refer to G.S. Chapter 28A, related to the administration of decedents' estates, for the law governing the appointment of a personal representative and a collector. *See* Ragan v. Hill, 337 N.C. 667, 674 (1994) (noting that once a personal representative was appointed, the action could proceed); Pierce v. Johnson, 154 N.C. App. 34, 40 (2002) (explaining that at death the deceased person no longer had legal standing because the person transformed into the estate of the decedent).

34. G.S. 1A-1, Rule 25(a).

35. *Id.*; *id.* § 28A-19-3(a).

36. G.S. 1A-1, Rule 17; Hauser v. Hauser, 252 N.C. App. 10, 14 (2017).

who recently became involved in the older adult's life. A child who is disinherited by these changes may have a claim as a plaintiff in a civil action for wrongful interference with an expected inheritance *after* the death of his or her parent. North Carolina law recognizes a right of action, after the death of a person who makes a will (testator), when a third party wrongfully interferes with the beneficiary's expected inheritance through, for example, fraud or undue influence.[37] But an expected beneficiary such as a child of an older adult has no claim *during* the lifetime of the older adult who makes a will.[38] The North Carolina Supreme Court has stated that this is because a child has no interest in the property of a living parent, only an intangible hope of succession.[39] The child's right to inherit does not exist during the parent's lifetime.[40] A parent has an absolute right to dispose of property as he or she pleases and may make distributions or no distributions to children, with or without reason.[41]

Another legal ground to challenge changes to an older adult's will after the death of the older adult is through a caveat proceeding. A child or other interested person may challenge the validity of a will admitted to probate by the clerk of superior court by entering a caveat to the will.[42] The purpose of a caveat is to determine whether the will admitted to probate is in fact the last will and testament of the decedent.[43] Possible grounds for a caveat include undue influence, duress, fraud, forgery, mistake, revocation, and lack of testamentary capacity.[44]

2. TIME TO BRING THE ACTION

There are limits imposed by law on how long from the time of the events giving rise to the cause of action or from the discovery of such events a plaintiff has to file a civil lawsuit.[45] This is known as a statute of limitations. Once the statute of limitations expires, the plaintiff is time-barred from filing the lawsuit.

If an older adult is under a disability when the cause of action accrues, the statute of limitations is tolled (meaning, essentially, that the time for bringing suit is paused).[46] An older adult is under a disability if he or she is "insane" or "incompetent" as defined in G.S. Chapter 35A.[47] An adjudication of incompetency by the court under G.S. Chapter 35A is not required to toll the statute of limitations.[48] The statute of limitations is tolled until the

---

37. Bohannon v. Wachovia Bank & Tr. Co., 210 N.C. 679 (1936).

38. *Hauser*, 252 N.C. App. at 14.

39. *Id.* (quoting Holt v. Holt, 232 N.C. 497, 500–01 (1950)).

40. *Id.*

41. *Id.*

42. G.S. 31-32.

43. Wilder v. Hill, 175 N.C. App. 769, 772 (2006).

44. *See* Ann Anderson, *Will Caveats, in* NORTH CAROLINA SUPERIOR COURT JUDGES' BENCHBOOK (Sept. 2012), https://benchbook.sog.unc.edu/sites/default/files/pdf/Will%20Caveats.pdf.

45. G.S. 1-15(a).

46. G.S. 1-17(a).

47. *Id.* An "incompetent adult" is defined in G.S. 35A-1101(7) as an adult or emancipated minor who "lacks sufficient capacity (1) to manage his or her own affairs or (2) to make or communicate important decisions concerning his or her person, family, or property, regardless of whether the lack of capacity is due to mental illness, intellectual disability, epilepsy, cerebral palsy, autism, inebriety, senility, disease, injury, or similar cause or condition."

48. Ragsdale v. Whitley, 257 N.C. App. 336, 341–42, *review denied*, 371 N.C. 447 (2018).

disability is removed.[49] A disability may be removed generally, as to all causes of action. This happens, for example, if the older adult has a general guardian (GG) when the cause of action accrues or upon the appointment of a GG by the clerk of superior court in a Chapter 35A proceeding.[50] A disability may be removed as to a specific cause of action, for example, upon the appointment of a guardian ad litem (GAL) in the action.[51]

If the older adult is under a guardianship, and the guardian is the perpetrator of financial exploitation or other abuse against the older adult, the statute of limitations may be tolled with respect to claims the older adult has against the guardian until a successor guardian is appointed.[52] This is because both the GG and a guardian of the estate (GOE) have the authority to initiate actions related to the incompetent older adult's estate.[53] An exploitative or abusive guardian would not sue himself or herself, and the incompetent adult could not reasonably be expected to bring a lawsuit.[54]

If an older adult dies before the statute of limitations runs for an action and the cause of action survives the death of the older adult, the action may be commenced by the personal representative or collector of the older adult's estate up until the statute of limitations runs.[55] If the statute of limitations expires within one year after the death of the older adult, the statute of limitations is extended to one year from the date of death of the older adult.[56]

3. WHERE THE SUIT IS FILED

With limited exceptions, the district and superior courts in North Carolina generally have concurrent (shared) authority to hear matters of a civil nature.[57] This means that a plaintiff could file a civil action in either court. For judicial efficiency, however, state statutes prescribe the proper divisions for bringing civil actions.[58] For example, the district court is the proper division for the trial of all civil actions in which the amount in controversy is $25,000 or less, while the superior court is the proper division where the amount exceeds $25,000.[59]

---

49. G.S. 1-17(a).

50. *See* King *ex rel.* Small v. Albemarle Hosp. Auth., 370 N.C. 467, 472 (2018); Teele v. Kerr, 261 N.C. 148, 150 (1964); Fox v. Health Force, Inc., 143 N.C. App. 501, 507 (2001) (holding that once the general guardian was appointed to represent the plaintiff's interests, the limitation period began to run).

51. Jefferys v. Tolin, 90 N.C. App. 233, 235 (1988); *Teele*, 261 N.C. at 150. Note that the scope of the authority of the GAL is determined by the terms of the complaint, which means that those terms determine whether a GAL can join or bring a particular suit, which, in turn, will affect the operation of a statute of limitations. Genesco, Inc. v. Cone Mills Corp., 604 F.2d 281, 286 (4th Cir. 1979). *See also* Rowland v. Beauchamp, 253 N.C. 231, 234–36 (1960) (appointing a new GAL did not restart the statute of limitations, which began to run at the appointment of the first GAL).

52. *See* State *ex rel.* Duckett v. Pettee, 50 N.C. App. 119, 124–25 (1980).

53. *Id.* at 124. *See* note 25, *supra*.

54. *Id.*

55. G.S. 1-22.

56. *Id. See also* 2 JAMES B. MCLAUGHLIN, JR. & RICHARD T. BOWSER, WIGGINS WILLS & ADMINISTRATION OF ESTATES IN N.C. § 20:7 (4th ed.).

57. G.S. 7A-240.

58. G.S. 7A-242.

59. G.S. 7A-243.

Small claims are a subset of civil actions; these claims are heard by magistrates.[60] A special set of statutes governs the trial of small claims. A small claim is any civil action in which

1. the amount in controversy does not exceed $10,000;
2. the principal relief sought is money, the recovery of specific personal property, summary ejectment, or some combination of these things; and
3. the plaintiff (the person who files the civil action) requests that the action be assigned to a magistrate.[61]

The plaintiff initiates a small claims action by filing a complaint.[62] The clerk of superior court then issues a magistrate summons, which is served on the defendant. The N.C. Administrative Office of the Courts (AOC) maintains a number of small claims forms, including three complaint forms and a magistrate summons; all are available for free online at nccourts.gov.

Table 6.1. **Select AOC Small Claims Complaint Forms**

FORM	NAME
CVM-100	Magistrate Summons
CVM-200	Complaint for Money Owed
CVM-201	Complaint in Summary Ejectment
CVM-202	Complaint to Recover Possession of Personal Property

The small claims complaint must be filed in the county where at least one of the defendants (the persons being sued) resides.[63] The chief district court judge ultimately determines whether cases are assigned to a magistrate by a specific order or by a general rule.[64] The chief typically does this by a general administrative order directing the clerk to calendar specified cases to be heard by a magistrate.[65] Based on this order, the clerk calendars the case to be heard by a magistrate as soon as it is filed. The procedure for small claims is intended to be simpler than the procedural rules governing claims heard in district or superior courts. The small claims procedures are largely set out in G.S. Chapter 7A, Article 19.[66] Many litigants in small claims proceedings are not represented by attorneys. There are a number of free resources available to assist parties to small claims actions.

---

60. G.S. 7A, Article 19.

61. G.S. 7A-210. A request for claim and delivery as a remedy or an order from the clerk for relinquishment of property subject to a lien pursuant to G.S. 44A-4(a) does not prevent an action that otherwise qualifies as a small claim from qualifying. *Id.*

62. G.S. 7A-213.

63. *Id.*

64. G.S. 7A-211.

65. JOAN G. BRANNON, NORTH CAROLINA SMALL CLAIMS LAW 13 (2009) (hereinafter SMALL CLAIMS LAW).

66. *Id.*

C. HOW DO CIVIL LEGAL REMEDIES WORK?

This section provides a basic overview of how three types of civil legal remedies may provide relief or protection to older adults who are subject to elder abuse: (1) causes of action and remedies available through traditional civil litigation, including remedies available before a final judgment is entered by a court; (2) remedies available to protect an older adult from domestic violence or unwanted contact; and (3) remedies available when the older adult wants to remove an unwanted occupant from a home owned by the older adult, as well as remedies available when an older adult is a tenant of property owned by someone else.

1. CAUSES OF ACTION AND REMEDIES THROUGH CIVIL LITIGATION

An older adult, or an older adult's legal representative (as discussed above), may file a civil lawsuit against the perpetrator of abuse seeking monetary damages or other relief, such as the reformation or rescission of a deed or contract or an order for the return of personal property. Unlike other states, North Carolina does not have a specific civil private right of action for elder abuse and exploitation.[67] Many of these elder abuse and financial exploitation civil actions in other states have "heightened remedies and penalties to encourage enforcement and deter abuse."[68]

This section begins by providing examples of pre-judgment remedies that may be available to stop ongoing elder abuse while a civil action is pending and before a judgment is entered. It then catalogues common civil causes of action, together with the elements of each action, that may be relevant in cases of elder abuse.

---

67. *See, e.g.*, UTAH CODE ANN. § 62A-3-314; ARIZ. REV. STAT. ANN. § 46-455 and -456; CAL. WELF. & INST. CODE §§ 15657–15657.8 ("Civil Actions for Abuse of Elderly or Dependent Adults"); CONN. GEN. STAT. ANN. § 17b-462.

68. Jeff Aidikoff & Ashley Rivkin, *States with A Civil Private Right of Action for Financial Elder Abuse and Exploitation*, 24 PIABA B.J. 29 (2017).

> **✏ PRACTICE NOTE**
>
> When an older adult is the victim of financial exploitation, it is likely that the perpetrator will attempt to hide the older adult's property or cause it to disappear. The faster the older adult or someone assisting the older adult is able to locate the property and seek a pre-judgment remedy, such as freezing a bank account through an attachment, the better the chances are for the older adult to be made whole through a final judgment in a civil action.

a. Pre-Judgment Civil Remedies to Stop Ongoing Abuse/Exploitation

Certain remedies may be sought while a civil action is pending and before a final judgment related to the alleged abuse of the older adult is entered. An underlying civil action must have been commenced in order for any of these remedies to be sought. A *temporary restraining order* or *injunctive relief* may be necessary to preserve the status quo while litigation is pending. An *attachment* may be necessary to secure the defendant's property to ensure that there will be assets available to satisfy any judgment ultimately entered against the defendant. A *claim and delivery action* may be sought to obtain possession of personal property while the litigation is pending. The older adult may file a *lis pendens* to restrain the defendant from transferring real property and to notify third parties that there is litigation pending related to the real property. Each of these pre-judgment remedies is detailed below, along with examples about how each may apply in a case involving elder abuse.

i. Preliminary Injunction; Temporary Restraining Order[69]

A preliminary injunction is an order of the court preventing a party from doing specified acts. Its purpose is to preserve the status quo or, far less commonly, to direct a party to take certain action(s), during an underlying litigation.[70] A request for a preliminary injunction may be included in the original complaint initiating the civil action or made as a separate motion filed with the court.[71] A prerequisite of a preliminary injunction is notice to the party to be restrained.[72] To obtain a preliminary injunction, the person seeking the injunction (the movant) must show that

1. there is a likelihood of success on the merits of the underlying case and
2. the movant will likely suffer "irreparable loss unless the injunction is issued"[73] or that issuance of the injunction "appears reasonably necessary to protect [the] plaintiffs' rights during the litigation."[74]

---

69. For more information on preliminary injunctions and TROs, refer to Ann Anderson, *Temporary Restraining Orders and Preliminary Injunctions (Rule 65)*, in NORTH CAROLINA SUPERIOR COURT JUDGES' BENCHBOOK (Feb. 2011) (hereinafter *TRO Chapter*).
70. *Id.* at 1.
71. *Id.* at 2.
72. G.S. 1A-1, Rule 65(a).
73. Ridge Cmty. Inv'rs, Inc. v. Berry, 293 N.C. 688, 701 (1977).
74. Setzer v. Annas, 286 N.C. 534, 537 (1975).

The movant must post a bond in an amount the judge finds proper.[75] The purpose of the bond is to protect the restrained party against costs and damages it may suffer if the injunction is dissolved or otherwise found to have been wrongful.[76]

A temporary restraining order (TRO) is an emergency measure that *precedes* a hearing on a preliminary injunction and serves the same function.[77] It may be granted without notice (oral or written) to the restrained party, which may be important in a case involving ongoing financial abuse of an older adult.[78] A party seeking a preliminary injunction does not have to also seek a TRO but may choose to do so at the start of litigation to prevent being harmed while waiting for a hearing on a preliminary injunction.[79]

Figure 6.1. Relative Order of a TRO to a Preliminary Injunction

To obtain a TRO, the person seeking the TRO (the applicant) must show to the court

1. that it clearly appears from specific facts shown by affidavit or by verified complaint that immediate and irreparable injury, loss, or damage will result to the applicant before the adverse party or that party's attorney can be heard in opposition and
2. a written certification from the applicant's attorney to the court detailing (a) the efforts, if any, that have been made to give notice to the other party or (b) the reasons supporting the claim that notice should not be required.[80]

A TRO granted without notice to the restrained party must expire within the time after entry as the judge sets in the TRO, not to exceed ten days.[81] The TRO may be extended before the original duration expires (1) for a like period for good cause shown or (2) for longer if the restrained party consents.[82] If the court issues a TRO without notice, the matter must be set for hearing at the earliest possible time.[83] At the hearing, the restraining party "shall proceed with a motion for a preliminary injunction."[84] If the restraining party does not

---

75. G.S. 1A-1, Rule 65(c). The amount of the bond is in the court's discretion. Schulz v. Ingram, 38 N.C. App. 422, 430 (1978).
76. G.S. 1A-1, Rule 65(c).
77. *TRO Chapter*, at 2.
78. G.S. 1A-1, Rule 65(b).
79. *TRO Chapter*, at 2.
80. G.S. 1A-1, Rule 65(b).
81. *Id.*
82. *Id.*
83. *Id.*
84. *Id.*

proceed, the judge "shall dissolve the temporary restraining order."[85] If the restraining party proceeds, the judge may grant a preliminary injunction or dissolve or modify the TRO.[86]

With limited exceptions, just as with a preliminary injunction, the party seeking a TRO must post a bond "in such sum as the judge deems proper" to protect the restrained party against costs and damages it may suffer if the TRO is dissolved or otherwise found to have been wrongful.[87]

◇ **EXAMPLE**

Injunctive Relief

Frank is 75 years old and a retired farmer. He was diagnosed with dementia. Frank owns farm equipment worth more than $50,000. He let a former employee borrow the equipment. When Frank's daughter, who is his agent under a power of attorney, asks the employee to return the equipment, he refuses and asserts that Frank sold him the equipment. Frank's daughter applies to be appointed as guardian ad litem for Frank (see Section II.B.1.b, supra) and files a civil action to recover personal property (discussed in Section II.C.1.b.i.(b), infra) on Frank's behalf. Frank's daughter also includes in her verified civil complaint a request for both a TRO and a preliminary injunction preventing the employee from selling the property during the litigation. Frank's daughter has evidence that the employee listed the property for sale on a farming equipment auction site.

---

ii. Attachment

If an older adult has concerns that the defendant in a civil action will transfer, assign, or dispose of his or her property before entry of a final money judgment to avoid paying the judgment, the older adult could seek an attachment.[88] An attachment is an order entered by the court directing the sheriff to seize and hold the defendant's property pending the outcome of a lawsuit so that the property, should the plaintiff win a judgment, will be available to satisfy that judgment.[89]

All of a defendant's real or personal property in North Carolina that is subject to levy under an execution or that can be reached through a supplemental proceeding is subject to being attached.[90] A key feature of this remedy is that the property subject to being attached does not have to be related to the lawsuit.[91] Attachment is ancillary to an underlying pending action; the purpose of the underlying action must be, in whole or in part,

---

85. *Id.*
86. *Id.*
87. G.S. 1A-1, Rule 65(c).
88. Procedures for attachment may be found in G.S. Chapter 1, Article 35.
89. G.S. 1-440.1. For additional information on attachments, see JOAN G. BRANNON & ANN M. ANDERSON, NORTH CAROLINA CLERK OF SUPERIOR COURT PROCEDURES MANUAL ch. 34 (2012) (hereinafter CSC MANUAL).
90. G.S. 1-440.4.
91. *Id.*

to secure a money judgment, alimony, or child support.[92] Attachment is not available in a small claims action.[93] An attachment order is typically entered by the clerk of superior court.[94]

The clerk may enter an attachment order when it is shown by affidavit or by a verified complaint that the defendant is

1. a North Carolina resident with an intent to avoid service of summons who has departed or is about to depart the state or who is keeping himself or herself concealed;
2. a person or domestic corporation with an intent to default creditors that has removed or is about to remove property from North Carolina or has assigned, disposed of, or secreted property, or is about to do the same;
3. a nonresident.[95]

The plaintiff must furnish a bond before the clerk enters an order of attachment.[96] The clerk sets the bond amount at an amount necessary to afford reasonable protection to the defendant for the property to be taken.[97]

> ◇ **EXAMPLE**
>
> *Attachment*
>
> *Jane is 82 years old and lives alone in North Carolina. Thomas, a handyman who lives in Virginia, came to her home and offered to repair her leaky roof. Jane wrote him a check for $10,000 up front, and Thomas left and did not return. Jane filed a civil action in North Carolina against Thomas for fraud. Jane may consider filing an affidavit of attachment when she files the complaint against Thomas if Thomas has property in North Carolina, including bank accounts. (In practice, it will be necessary to know which bank Thomas uses in order to seize bank accounts.) If he does not have property in this state, then a North Carolina sheriff will not be able to seize any property.*

---

92. G.S. 1-440.1(a); 1-440.2.
93. G.S. 7A-231.
94. G.S. 1-440.5. The trial judge may also enter the order. *Id.*
95. G.S. 1-440.3.
96. G.S. 1-440.10.
97. G.S. 1-440.10(1).

Table 6.2. **AOC Attachment Forms**[98]

FORM	NAME
CV-300	Affidavit in an Attachment Proceeding
CV-301	Order of Attachment
CV-901M	Defendant's Motion to Discharge Attachment
CV-302	Summons to Garnishee and Notice of Levy

iii. Claim and Delivery

If an older adult files an action to recover personal property, then the adult may consider filing a claim and delivery action in the underlying lawsuit.[99] A civil action to recover personal property is discussed in detail in Section II.C.1.b.i.(b), *infra*. Claim and delivery allows a plaintiff to get immediate possession of personal property pending the outcome of an underlying lawsuit.[100] The underlying lawsuit determines the right of permanent possession.[101] A claim and delivery order gives the plaintiff the right to possess the property until the lawsuit is decided.[102]

The claim and delivery action may be filed at any time after the complaint is filed and before judgment is entered in the principal action related to the property.[103] The clerk of superior court typically presides over the claim and delivery hearing. A claim and delivery action may be filed in connection with a civil action for recovery of personal property before a district or superior court judge or before a magistrate in a small claims action.[104] It may be more likely to be filed in a district or superior court civil action. It is rarely used in small claims actions because the trial before the magistrate on the underlying action may be heard more quickly than the claim and delivery before the clerk.[105]

A plaintiff initiates a claim and delivery action by filing an affidavit.[106] The affidavit must show

1. facts showing that the plaintiff is the owner of the property claimed (and the property must be particularly described) or is entitled to possession of it;
2. that the property is being wrongfully detained by the defendant;
3. the alleged cause(s) of the detention, according to the plaintiff's best knowledge, information, and belief;

---

98. The N.C. Judicial Branch's website features a "Forms" page where users may search for or download forms. *See* https://www.nccourts.gov/documents/forms.
99. Procedures for claim and delivery may be found in G.S. Chapter 1, Article 36. For additional information on claim and delivery, see CSC MANUAL, at ch. 35.
100. G.S. 1-472.
101. CSC MANUAL, at ch. 35, § 35.1.
102. *Id.*
103. *Id.*
104. G.S. 7A-231.
105. CSC MANUAL, at ch. 35, § 35.1.
106. G.S. 1-473.

4. that the property has not been
   a. taken for tax, assessment, or fine, pursuant to a statute;
   b. seized under an execution or attachment against the property of the plaintiff; or
   c. if so seized, that it is, by statute, exempt from the seizure; and
5. the actual value of the property.[107]

⬦ **EXAMPLE**

Claim and Delivery

Molly is 75 years old and was diagnosed with dementia this year. She owns a diamond ring and necklace worth $40,000. While visiting Molly, her daughter, Sara, notices that the jewelry is no longer in Molly's home. Sara confronts Molly's neighbor, Patricia, about the jewelry. Patricia says that Molly gave her the jewelry two years ago to show how grateful she was that Patricia cared for and checked on her each day. Patricia says that Molly told her that she was her "real daughter" when she gave her the jewelry. Sara is appointed as Molly's guardian ad litem and files a lawsuit to recover possession of the jewelry. Sara includes in the suit an action for claim and delivery.

After the affidavit is filed, the clerk will issue a notice of hearing.[108] The plaintiff may request that the clerk include an order in the notice enjoining the defendant (1) from willfully disposing of the property in any way, (2) from removing or permitting the removal of the property from North Carolina, or (3) from causing or permitting willful damage or destruction of the property.[109] If the defendant violates the order and the plaintiff is entitled to possession of the property, then the defendant may be held in contempt and fined or imprisoned by the court.[110]

The hearing date may not be less than ten days from the date the notice is served; service of the notice and a copy of the affidavit must be made on the defendant pursuant to Rule 4 of the N.C. Rules of Civil Procedure.[111] If the clerk finds that probable cause[112] exists to enter an order for seizure of the property, then he or she will enter an order of seizure.[113] The plaintiff must give a bond for double the value of the property to be recovered.[114] The defendant, within certain time limits, may object to the surety on the plaintiff's bond or

---

107. *Id.*
108. G.S. 1-474.1(a).
109. *Id.*
110. *Id.*
111. *Id.*
112. CSC MANUAL, at ch. 35, § 35.6. Note that G.S. Chapter 1, Article 36, regarding claim and delivery does not refer to the standard of proof.
113. *See* G.S. 1-474(a).
114. G.S. 1-475.

post a bond to allow the defendant to keep the property until the underlying lawsuit to recover possession of the personal property is decided.[115]

Table 6.3. **AOC Claim and Delivery Forms**[116]

FORM	NAME
CV-200	Affidavit and Request for Hearing in Claim and Delivery
CV-201	Notice of Hearing in Claim and Delivery
CV-202	Findings on Application for Claim and Delivery Order
CV-203	Order of Seizure in Claim and Delivery
CV-900M	Defendant's Bond in Claim and Delivery
CV-901M	Voluntary Waiver of Hearing in Claim and Delivery

iv. Lis Pendens

A lis pendens is a notice of pending litigation filed by a party to a civil action with the clerk of superior court in cases affecting title to real property.[117] A lis pendens may also be filed where an order of attachment is issued and real property is attached.[118] The lis pendens is cross-indexed by the clerk in a record called the "Record of Lis Pendens."[119] Once the lis pendens is cross-indexed, it provides constructive notice to any future purchaser or creditor seeking to secure a debt with the real property.[120] Any person who takes title to or a lien on the real property after the indexing of the lis pendens takes it subject to the outcome of the underlying civil action as if the person was a party to the civil action.[121] The lis pendens restricts the transfer or encumbrance of the real property during the litigation and ensures that the real property is available post-judgment; it preserves the status quo during the litigation.

> ◇ **EXAMPLE**
>
> *Lis Pendens*
>
> *Mary Jones is 85 years old. She has an adult son, John Jones, who is 45. John goes to Mary with three deeds transferring unencumbered real property owned by Mary to the "Jones Family Trust." John tells Mary that the purpose of the transfer is to create tax savings for Mary. John is the only one of Mary's children who visits her often, and she is afraid that if she does not sign the deeds, he will stop*

---

115. G.S. 1-475; -477.
116. *See* note 98, *supra*
117. G.S. 1-116(a)(1). Procedures for lis pendens may be found in G.S. Chapter 1, Article 11.
118. G.S. 1-116(a)(3). Other cases where a lis pendens is permissible are (1) actions to foreclose any mortgage or deed of trust or to enforce any lien on real property, (2) actions seeking injunctive relief under G.S. 113A-64.1 or -65 regarding sedimentation and erosion control for any land-disturbing activity that is subject to the requirements of Article 4 of G.S. Chapter 113A, and (3) actions for asset freezing or seizure under G.S. 14-112.3. *Id.* § 1-116(a).
119. G.S. 1-117.
120. G.S. 1-118.
121. *Id.*

visiting her. John tells Mary that she is the beneficiary of the trust when in real-ity, John is the trustee and the sole beneficiary of the trust. After the deeds are recorded, John immediately takes out a loan on all three properties in the amount of $250,000. Mary's daughter, Jill, becomes suspicious and does some investigat-ing. Jill helps Mary hire an attorney, who files a civil action to undo the transac-tions conducted by John and recover the real property. During the litigation, Mary may consider filing a lis pendens with the court to put third parties on construc-tive notice that the real property is the subject of a pending lawsuit and to hinder further transfers or encumbrances by John.

b. Civil Causes of Action

There are numerous civil causes of action that may be available to an older adult seeking redress for elder abuse or exploitation. This section does not provide an exhaustive list but instead provides a basis for thinking about what may be available depending on the facts of a particular case. If the action relates to personal property, the older adult may seek recovery of the value of the property wrongfully taken or of the property itself. The older adult may seek monetary damages based on other claims, such as breach of fiduciary duty, constructive fraud, actual fraud, negligent misrepresentation, unfair and deceptive trade practices, breach of contract, unjust enrichment, breach of trust, or civil torts. If a deed, power of attorney, trust, will, or other document was obtained from an older adult based on undue influence, duress, fraud, or lack of mental capacity on the part of the older adult, there may be a cause of action for rescission of the document. Each of these types of actions are discussed below.

i. Actions Related to Personal Property

(a) Conversion

If an item of personal property is wrongfully taken from an older adult who is the owner of the property, or taken with permission and then wrongfully detained, the older adult may bring either an action for conversion or an action to recover the personal property, discussed in more detail, *infra*.

The **elements** of an action for conversion are as follows.

1. The plaintiff is the lawful owner of personal property that has been taken and is entitled to repossess it immediately.
2. The defendant converted the property by
   a. wrongfully taking it from the plaintiff or
   b. rightfully taking it from the plaintiff but wrongfully retaining it after a demand was made to return it.
3. The fair market value of the property at the time it was wrongfully taken or wrongfully retained is ascertainable. [122]

---

122. SMALL CLAIMS LAW, at 122. *See also* Variety Wholesalers, Inc. v. Salem Logistics Traffic Servs., LLC, 365 N.C. 520,

Conversion is sometimes called a "forced sale" because if the plaintiff succeeds in the lawsuit, the defendant is effectively forced to buy the property from the plaintiff.[123] The plaintiff does not recover the property but recovers the fair market value of the property from the defendant plus interest from the date of the wrongful taking.[124]

A plaintiff is generally not required to demand return of his or her property from a defendant who has wrongfully taken possession of it.[125] But if the defendant took possession lawfully but failed to return the property, the property is not deemed converted until the plaintiff demands return of the property.[126] This is true even if the defendant was supposed to return the property at a specific time.

The **statute of limitations** for conversion is three years from when the unauthorized assumption and exercise of ownership occurs.[127]

> ◇ **EXAMPLE**
>
> *Conversion*
>
> *While 83-year-old Susie is in a rehabilitation facility recovering from a fall she suffered at home, her caregiver, Frank, goes to her house and takes the keys to her car (worth more than $15,000). He uses the car for months while Susie is in rehab. While using the car, Frank gets in an accident and causes $1,000 worth of damage to the car. When Susie returns home, she has to rent a car while her car is being repaired. Susie could sue Frank for conversion. If successful, she would recover damages equal to $15,000 (the value of the car when it was taken) plus interest from the time it was taken until judgment is entered.*

(b) Action to Recover Personal Property

If an item of personal property is wrongfully taken from an older adult who is the owner of the property, or taken with permission and then wrongfully detained, instead of filing a claim for conversion, the older adult may bring an action to recover the personal property.

The **elements** of an action to recover personal property are as follows.

1. Plaintiff is the lawful owner of personal property and is entitled to repossess it immediately.
2. The property was wrongfully taken from the plaintiff or was lawfully taken but wrongfully retained after a demand was made for its return.

---

523 (2012) (citing Peed v. Burleson's, Inc., 244 N.C. 437, 439 (1956)) (stating that conversion is "an unauthorized assumption and exercise of the right of ownership over goods or personal chattels belonging to another, to the alteration of their condition or the exclusion of an owner's rights").

123. SMALL CLAIMS LAW, at 121.

124. *Id.* Fair market value is measured at the time the property was taken or not returned. *Id.*

125. *Id.* at 122.

126. *Id.*

127. G.S. 1-52(4); Stratton v. Royal Bank of Canada, 211 N.C. App. 78 (2011). As a general rule, the statute of limitations begins to accrue when the unauthorized assumption and exercise of ownership occurs—not when the plaintiff discovers the conversion. *Stratton*, 211 N.C. App. at 83. G.S. 1-52(9), which states that the cause of action shall not be deemed to have accrued until the discovery by the aggrieved party of the facts constituting the fraud or mistake, does not apply to a claim for conversion. *Id.*

3. The defendant is in possession of the property.
4. The amount of damages, if any, for loss of use of the property and physical damage to it are ascertainable.[128]

In this action, the plaintiff asks the court to order the return of the personal property, pay the plaintiff for damage done to the property while in the defendant's possession, and compensate the plaintiff for loss of use of the property while in the defendant's possession.[129] The plaintiff may file a separate action for damages once the property is returned and the plaintiff can assess the damages to it.[130] A form "Complaint to Recover Possession of Personal Property (Small Claims)" (CVM-202) is available from the N.C. Administrative Office of the Courts (AOC).[131] The form is designed for use in small claims court, discussed in Section II.B.3, *supra*.

The action is filed against the person in possession of the property.[132] If the person who wrongfully took or kept the property is no longer in possession of it, the plaintiff may consider an action for conversion instead of an action to recover possession.[133] The older adult may be entitled to payment of costs by the defendant, including reasonable attorneys' fees, in an action to recover possession of personal property.[134]

The **statute of limitations** for an action to recover personal property is three years from the taking or wrongful retention of the property.[135]

> ⬦ **EXAMPLE**
>
> *Action to Recover Personal Property*
>
> *Rather than bring an action for conversion, Susie (see example immediately above) could bring an action to recover personal property (the car). If she prevails, her relief will be return of the property plus damages ($1,000 to repair the car and $500 to rent a car).*

ii. General Claims Involving Monetary Damages

An older adult may have a claim against a perpetrator of abuse that could yield monetary damages and compensate the older adult for a loss resulting from the actions of the perpetrator. Damages may be strictly compensatory or, in some cases, may also include punitive damages.[136] Punitive damages (damages exceeding compensation and intended to punish and deter the defendant) may be available if the older adult can show

---

128. SMALL CLAIMS LAW, at 123.
129. *Id.* at 122.
130. *Id.*
131. *See* note 98, *supra*.
132. *Id.*
133. *Id.*
134. G.S. 6-18(2).
135. G.S. 1-52(4).
136. *See* Watson v. Dixon, 352 N.C. 343, 347–48 (2000) (discussing the different purposes of compensatory versus punitive damages).

that the defendant is liable for compensatory damages and there is an aggravating factor (as shown by clear and convincing evidence).[137] Aggravating factors include fraud, malice, and willful or wanton conduct.[138] Punitive damages are unavailable in cases solely for breach of contract.[139]

(a) Breach of Fiduciary Duty

The **elements** of a claim for breach of fiduciary duty are as follows.

1. The defendant owed the plaintiff a fiduciary duty.
2. The defendant breached that fiduciary duty.
3. The breach of fiduciary duty was a proximate cause of injury to the plaintiff.[140]

The existence of a fiduciary relationship is an essential element of a claim for breach of fiduciary duty. There are certain legal fiduciary relationships recognized by North Carolina law, including

- attorney-client,[141]

- spouse-spouse,[142]

- executor-beneficiary (decedent's estate),

- administrator-heir (decedent's estate),[143]

- guardian-ward (guardianship),[144]

- principal-agent (power of attorney),[145] and

- trustee-beneficiary (trust).[146]

In each relationship, there is a heightened level of trust and a duty imposed on the fiduciary to act in the best interests of the other party.[147]

---

137. G.S. 1D-1; -15(a), (b). Punitive damages may not exceed three times the amount of compensatory damages or $250,000, whichever is greater. *Id.* § 1D-25(b). If a trier of fact returns a verdict for punitive damages in excess of the maximum amount, the trial court must reduce the award and enter judgment for punitive damages in the maximum amount. *Id.*

138. G.S. 1D-15(a). The aggravating factor must be present and related to the injury for which the compensatory damages were awarded. *Id. See* Collier v. Bryant, 216 N.C. App. 419 (2011) (awarding punitive damages for constructive fraud); Lacey v. Kirk, 238 N.C. App. 376 (2014), *writ denied, review denied*, 368 N.C. 250 (2015) (awarding punitive damages in case of breach of fiduciary duty).

139. G.S. 1D-15(d).

140. Green v. Freeman, 367 N.C. 136, 141 (2013).

141. Fox v. Wilson, 85 N.C. App. 292, 299 (1987).

142. Eubanks v. Eubanks, 273 N.C. 189, 195–96 (1968) ("[t]he relationship between husband and wife is the most confidential of all relationships, and transactions between them, to be valid, must be fair and reasonable."); Dallaire v. Bank of Am., N.A., 367 N.C. 363, 367 (2014).

143. Collier v. Bryant, 216 N.C. App. 419, 432 (2011).

144. *In re* Estate of Armfield, 113 N.C. App. 467, 474 (1994).

145. *See* G.S. 32C-1-117(a); -114(a), (b) (duties of an agent to a principal).

146. Wachovia Bank & Trust Co. v. Johnston, 269 N.C. 701, 711 (1967).

147. *Dallaire*, 367 N.C. at 367. *See also* Hager v. Smithfield E. Health Holdings, LLC, ___ N.C. App. ___, ___, 826 S.E.2d 567, 571–74 (2019) (discussing fiduciary relationships generally and declining to find that a fiduciary relationship exists as a matter of law between assisted living facilities with memory wards and their residents).

A fiduciary relationship may also arise in other relationships, such as between an older adult and a caregiver, where "there has been a special confidence reposed in one who in equity and good conscience is bound to act in good faith and with due regard to the interests of the one reposing confidence[.]"[148] Such a relationship "extends to any possible case in which a fiduciary relationship exists in fact, and in which there is confidence reposed in one side, and resulting domination and influence on the other."[149] But "[o]nly when one party figuratively holds all the cards—all the financial power or technical information, for example—have North Carolina courts found that the special circumstance of a fiduciary relationship has arisen."[150]

The **statute of limitations** applicable to a claim for breach of fiduciary duty is three years from when the plaintiff either discovers the facts giving rise to the claim or with reasonable diligence could have discovered the facts.[151]

◇ EXAMPLE

Breach of Fiduciary Duty

Sam is 78, a widower, and lives alone. He has two children who live outside North Carolina. Sam meets a young woman at church, Anna, who offers to run errands for him and help him out around the house. Sam is showing early signs of cognitive impairment but has not been diagnosed. After a few months of helping Sam out, Anna tells Sam it would be easier for her to keep helping him if he signs a power of attorney (POA) naming her as his agent, which Sam then does. The POA gives Anna broad authority but does not give her the authority to make gifts or to change rights of survivorship. Anna then executes a deed granting an 11-acre tract of land owned by Sam to herself. She then executes a second deed conveying another tract of land to her son, Brandon. The combined value of the properties is more than $500,000. This set of facts likely meets the requirements for breach of fiduciary duty. Anna owed Sam a fiduciary duty as agent under the POA. She breached that duty by conveying the land to herself and to her son without any consideration (payment). Sam lost significant assets as a result of her breach. Even if Anna were to argue that the transfers were made as consideration for her caregiving services, the value of the services likely would not reflect a fair and reasonable price for the properties.[152]

148. Dalton v. Camp, 353 N.C. 647, 651 (2001) (internal quotation marks omitted) (quoting Abbitt v. Gregory, 201 N.C. 577, 598 (1931). *See also* Meinhard v. Salmon, 249 N.Y. 458, 464 (1928) (describing fiduciaries as being held to a standard "stricter than the morals of the market place" and adding that "[n]ot honesty alone, but the punctilio of an honor the most sensitive, is then the standard of behavior").

149. *Dalton*, 353 N.C. at 651 (internal quotations and emphasis omitted) (quoting *Abbitt*, 201 N.C. at 598).

150. Lockerman v. S. River Elec. Membership Corp., 250 N.C. App. 631, 636 (2016) (internal quotation marks omitted) (quoting S.N.R. Mgmt. Corp. v. Danube Partners 141, LLC, 189 N.C. App. 601, 613 (2008). *See also Hager*, ___ N.C. App. at ___, 826 S.E.2d at 572.

151. Toomer v. Branch Banking & Tr. Co., 171 N.C. App. 58, 66 (2005) (holding that allegations of breach of fiduciary duty that do not rise to the level of constructive fraud are governed by the three-year statute of limitations applicable to contract actions contained in G.S. 1–52(1)).

152. *See* Estate of Graham v. Morrison, 168 N.C. App. 63, 69 (2005).

(b) Constructive Fraud

The **elements** of a claim for constructive fraud are as follows.

1. A relationship of trust and confidence existed between the plaintiff and the defendant.
2. The defendant took advantage of that position of trust to benefit himself or herself.
3. The plaintiff was, as a result, injured.[153]

Constructive fraud and breach of fiduciary duty are often pled together in the same complaint. Constructive fraud is similar to, but is a separate claim from, breach of fiduciary duty.[154] The primary difference between a claim for constructive fraud and one for breach of fiduciary duty is that constructive fraud requires that the defendant benefit himself or herself.[155] For example, if the actions by the defendant lead to a loss to the plaintiff but do not ultimately benefit the defendant, then there may be claim for breach of fiduciary duty but not a claim for constructive fraud.

Fraud may be *actual* or *constructive*. The elements of actual fraud are set out below. Constructive fraud differs from actual fraud in that "it is based on a confidential relationship rather than a specific misrepresentation."[156] It is the relationship between the parties that enables the defendant to take advantage of his or her position of trust to hurt the plaintiff.[157] An intent to deceive, an element of actual fraud, is not an element of constructive fraud.[158]

When the superior party obtains a possible benefit through the alleged abuse of the confidential or fiduciary relationship, the aggrieved party is entitled to a presumption that constructive fraud occurred.[159] The alleged fiduciary may rebut the presumption by showing, for example, that the confidence placed in the fiduciary was not abused.[160]

The **statute of limitations** applicable to a claim for constructive fraud is ten years after the cause of action accrues or ten years from when the aggrieved party either discovers the fraud or with reasonable diligence could have discovered it.[161] While there is no duty to investigate, a plaintiff may not remain willfully ignorant.[162]

---

153. Hauser v. Hauser, 252 N.C. App. 10, 16 (2017).

154. White v. Consol. Planning, Inc., 166 N.C. App. 283, 293 (2004).

155. *Id.* at 294.

156. Barger v. McCoy Hillard & Parks, 346 N.C. 650, 666 (1997) (internal quotation marks omitted) (quoting Terry v. Terry, 302 N.C. 77, 85 (1981).

157. Forbis v. Neal, 361 N.C. 519, 528 (2007).

158. *Id.* at 529.

159. *Id.*; Collier v. Bryant, 216 N.C. App. 419, 432 (2011).

160. *Forbis*, 361 N.C. at 529.

161. NationsBank of N.C., N.A. v. Parker, 140 N.C. App. 106, 113 (2000); Shepherd v. Shepherd, 57 N.C. App. 680, 682 (1982) ("An action for fraud accrues when the aggrieved party discovers the facts constituting the fraud, or when, in the exercise of due diligence, such facts should have been discovered.").

162. Honeycutt v. Weaver, 257 N.C. App. 599, 606 (2018) (quoting Vail v. Vail, 233 N.C. 109, 116–17 (1951) ("[w]here a confidential relationship exists between the parties, the aggrieved party 'is under no duty to make inquiry until something occurs to excite his suspicions, so long as he does not purposefully remain ignorant of such facts' ").

> ⬦ **EXAMPLE**
>
> *Constructive Fraud*
>
> *Along with a claim for breach of fiduciary duty, Sam (see example immediately above) may also have a claim for constructive fraud against Anna for transferring the property to herself. Sam had a relationship of trust and confidence with Anna, his caregiver and agent under the POA. Anna exploited her position to benefit herself by transferring the property for no/inadequate consideration to herself. As a result, Sam incurred an injury, which was loss of a valuable asset without receiving adequate consideration.*

(c) Fraud

The **elements** of a claim for actual fraud are

- false representation or concealment of a material fact

- that was reasonably calculated to deceive,

- made with intent to deceive,

- that did in fact deceive an injured party, and

- resulted in damage to that party.[163]

The proof required for an actual fraud claim is more exacting than that required in constructive fraud cases, and thus these types of claims are often harder to win.[164] Fraud must be pled with particularity.[165] The claim is not based on the relationship between the parties but, rather, on an intent to deceive. To prove fraud, a plaintiff must show that the defendant made a specific misrepresentation, the defendant intended to deceive the plaintiff and the plaintiff was in fact deceived, and as a result, the plaintiff was damaged. The plaintiff's reliance on the allegedly false representations must be reasonable.[166] Damages in a fraud case "is the amount of loss caused by the difference between what was received and what was promised through a false representation."[167]

The **statute of limitations** applicable to an action for actual fraud is three years after the cause of action accrues or three years from when the aggrieved party either discovers the fraud or with reasonable diligence could have discovered it.[168]

---

163. Jones v. Harrelson & Smith Contractors, LLC, 194 N.C. App. 203, 229 (2008), *aff'd*, 363 N.C. 371 (2009).
164. Watts v. Cumberland Cty. Hosp. Sys., Inc., 317 N.C. 110, 115–16 (1986).
165. Terry v. Terry, 302 N.C. 77, 84 (1981).
166. *Forbis*, 361 N.C. at 527.
167. First Atl. Mgmt. Corp. v. Dunlea Realty Co., 131 N.C. App. 242, 256 (1998).
168. *Forbis*, 361 N.C. at 524.

◇ **EXAMPLE**

Fraud

Along with conveying property to herself and her son, Anna (see the example immediately above) also transferred the money in Sam's checking account to a joint account with a right of survivorship with Anna and Sam as the owners of the account. Anna had the authority to manage Sam's account as agent under the POA but lacked the authority to change ownership and survivorship rights. Anna told Sam that she needed access to his account to help pay for things she purchased for him when she ran errands for him and that the new account had a better rate of return than his sole checking account and carried fewer penalties. Anna did not tell Sam that she added herself to the account and made it a survivorship account. Anna then used the funds in the account for her own personal needs. She concealed the true nature of the account from Sam to deceive him about her rights to the account and ownership in the account. She then used the account funds for her own benefit and not Sam's benefit, causing him injury.[169] As a result, Sam may also have a claim for fraud.

(d) Negligent Misrepresentation

The **elements** of a claim for negligent misrepresentation are that

- a party justifiably relies

- to his or her detriment

- on information prepared without reasonable care

- by one who owed the relying party a duty of care.[170]

Unlike fraud, which requires an intent to deceive, negligent misrepresentation only requires justifiable reliance by the plaintiff on information prepared without reasonable care by someone who owed the plaintiff a duty of care. To succeed in a claim for negligent misrepresentation, a plaintiff must show that the defendant owed a duty to provide "complete and accurate information" and that such duty was breached.[171] In addition, the plaintiff must have actually relied, justifiably, on the false information supplied by the

---

169. *See Forbis*, 361 N.C. at 527.

170. Simms v. Prudential Life Ins. Co. of Am., 140 N.C. App. 529, 532 (2000) (quoting Raritan River Steel Co. v. Cherry, Bekaert & Holland, 322 N.C. 200, 206 (1988), *rev'd on other grounds*, 329 N.C. 646 (1991)), *discretionary review denied*, 353 N.C. 381 (2001).

171. *Simms*, 140 N.C. App. at 533 (2000). North Carolina courts have described a breach by a defendant of a duty of care as involving a situation where "[o]ne who, in the course of his business, profession or employment, or in any other transaction in which he has a pecuniary interest, supplies false information for the guidance of others in their business transactions, [and thus] is subject to liability for pecuniary loss caused to [those others] by their justifiable reliance upon the information, if [that person] fails to exercise reasonable care or competence in obtaining or communicating the information." *Id.* at 534 (emphasis omitted).

defendant.[172] A plaintiff cannot establish justified reliance on an alleged misrepresentation if the plaintiff fails to make reasonable inquiry regarding the alleged statement.[173]

The **statute of limitations** applicable to an action for negligent misrepresentation is three years after the cause of action accrues or three years from when the aggrieved party either discovers the misrepresentation or with reasonable diligence could have discovered it.[174]

(e) Unfair and Deceptive Trade Practices

The **elements** of a claim for unfair and deceptive trade practices (UDTP) are as follows.

1.   The defendant committed an unfair or deceptive act or practice.
2.   The action in question was in or affected commerce.
3.   The act proximately caused injury to the plaintiff.[175]

A claim for UDTP may be appropriate in the case of elder abuse, particularly when asserted together with other claims, such as breach of fiduciary duty and/or constructive fraud.[176] A trade practice is *unfair* "when the practice is immoral, unethical, oppressive, unscrupulous, or substantially injurious to consumers."[177] A trade practice is *deceptive* if it "possessed the tendency or capacity to mislead or created the likelihood of deception."[178] A plaintiff must show that the defendant's misrepresentation proximately caused him or her to suffer injury.[179] "A party may be guilty of unfair or deceptive acts or practices when it engages in conduct that amounts to an inequitable assertion of its power or position."[180]

One of the benefits of a UDTP claim to a victim of elder abuse is that a successful claim will result in an award of automatic treble (triple) damages to the plaintiff.[181] Furthermore, the judge may award reasonable attorneys' fees, which are taxed as part of the costs to the defendant.[182]

---

172. Walker v. Town of Stoneville, 211 N.C. App. 24, 31 (2011); Brinkman v. Barrett Kays & Assocs., P.A., 155 N.C. App. 738, 742 (2003).

173. Pinney v. State Farm Mut. Ins. Co., 146 N.C. App. 248, 256 (2001) (citation omitted) ("It has also been held that when a party relying on a 'misleading representation could have discovered the truth upon inquiry, the complaint must allege that he was denied the opportunity to investigate or that he could not have learned the true facts by exercise of reasonable diligence.'"), *discretionary review denied*, 356 N.C. 438 (2002).

174. Carlisle v. Keith, 169 N.C. App. 674, 684 (2005) (referencing G.S. 1-52).

175. Capital Res., LLC v. Chelda, Inc., 223 N.C. App. 227, 239 (2012).

176. Compton v. Kirby, 157 N.C. App. 1, 20 (2003) (noting that North Carolina case law has held that conduct which constitutes a breach of fiduciary duty and constructive fraud is sufficient to support a UDTP claim).

177. Marshall v. Miller, 302 N.C. 539, 548 (1981).

178. *Capital Res.*, 223 N.C. App. at 239 (internal quotation marks omitted) (quoting Overstreet v. Brookland, Inc., 52 N.C. App. 444, 425–53 (1981).

179. Tucker v. Blvd. at Piper Glen LLC, 150 N.C. App. 150, 154 (2002).

180. *Compton*, 157 N.C. App. at 20 (quoting Edwards v. West, 128 N.C. App. 570, 575, *cert. denied*, 348 N.C. 282 (1998)).

181. G.S. 75-16.

182. G.S. 75-16.1. To award attorneys' fees, the judge must find that (1) the party charged with the violation has willfully engaged in the act or practice and that there was an unwarranted refusal by such party to fully resolve the matter which constitutes the basis of such suit; or (2) the party instituting the action knew, or should have known, the action was frivolous and malicious. *Id.*

The applicable **statute of limitations** requires that the UDTP claim must be commenced within four years after the cause of action accrues or within four years of the date the plaintiff discovers or should have discovered the defendant's wrongful conduct.[183]

> ◇ **EXAMPLE**
>
> *Unfair and Deceptive Trade Practices*
>
> *John is 89 and owns a home in a desirable neighborhood in an urban area. He has owned the home for sixty years. John suffers from memory loss. He has no family who lives close by and is pretty lonely on a day-to-day basis. One day, a real estate broker knocks on his door and John invites him in. The broker says that he has clients who would like to purchase the house. He tells John that he can also serve as his agent for the sale. The broker tells John that he has conducted an appraisal of the house and that it is worth $50,000. In reality, the house is worth more than $250,000. The broker handles the closing and conveys the property to himself. There was no third-party purchaser of the house. As a result, John may have a claim for UDTP against the broker.*

(f) Other Possible Claims

There are other claims that might be appropriate for an older adult to bring depending on the facts of his or her case. Such claims can be brought either separate from or along with other claims.

(1) Breach of Contract

If the older adult enters into a valid contract and the other party to the contract breaches the contract, then the older adult may have a claim for breach of contract. A claim for breach of contract requires the showing of a valid contract and breach of that contract.[184] For example, assume that an older adult enters into a contract with a man who knocked on her door and claimed she needed a new roof. The older adult may assert breach of contract if the man fails to complete the project according to the contract.

(2) Unjust Enrichment

A claim for unjust enrichment might be available when a plaintiff has rendered services or made expenditures for someone else without an express contract to pay. When the other party was enriched by the plaintiff's actions, the law will imply a promise to pay a fair compensation for the services or expenditures. It is a claim for a contract that the law implies.[185] If there is a contract that governs the claim, then the appropriate claim would be for breach of contract, not for unjust enrichment.[186] The elements of a claim for unjust

---

183. G.S. 75-16.2; Hunter v. Guardian Life Ins. Co. of Am., 162 N.C. App. 477, 485 (2004).
184. Poor v. Hill, 138 N.C. App. 19, 26 (2000).
185. *See* Shelter Corp. v. BTU, Inc., 154 N.C. App. 321, 330–31 (2002).
186. *Id.* at 331.

enrichment are (1) the plaintiff conferred a benefit on another party, (2) the other party consciously accepted the benefit, and (3) the benefit was not conferred gratuitously or by an interference in the affairs of the other party.[187]

(3) Breach of Trust

If an older adult has a trust in place and the trustee breaches a duty the trustee owes under the trust, the older adult may have a claim for breach of trust.[188] The trustee may be held liable for the greater of: (1) the amount required to restore the value of the trust property and trust distributions to what they would have been had the breach not occurred or (2) the profit the trustee made because of the breach.[189] A proceeding against a trustee for breach of trust may be commenced up to five years after the earliest of the date on which

- the trustee is removed, resigns, or dies;

- the beneficiary's interest in the trust is terminated; or

- the trust is terminated.[190]

(4) Torts

A tort is a civil wrong for which a remedy may be obtained, usually in the form of damages.[191] Torts include cases resulting from intentional acts, such as assault, battery, and intentional infliction of emotional distress, and from the failure to observe a standard of care, such as negligent infliction of emotional distress and negligence. These civil claims may be brought in addition to any criminal action related to the same conduct.

> **(A) CIVIL ASSAULT AND BATTERY.** An older adult may have a claim against a perpetrator of physical or sexual abuse for civil assault and battery. The tort of assault occurs when a person is put in reasonable apprehension of imminent harmful or offensive contact.[192] Words alone generally are not enough to constitute assault unless they are coupled with other acts or circumstances that put the older adult in reasonable fear of such contact.[193] Battery occurs when an older adult is offensively touched against his or her will.[194]

> **(B) INFLICTION OF EMOTIONAL DISTRESS.** There are two types of infliction of emotional distress: intentional and negligent. Either may be an appropriate cause of action for an older adult to bring in the event of emotional abuse. The elements of intentional infliction of emotional distress (IIED) are

---

187. *Id.* at 330.
188. G.S. 36C-10-1001(a).
189. G.S. 36C-10-1002(a).
190. G.S. 36C-10-1005(a).
191. *Tort*, BLACK'S LAW DICTIONARY (11th ed. 2019).
192. *See* Dickens v. Puryear, 302 N.C. 437, 445 (1981); McCraney v. Flanagan, 47 N.C. App. 498, 499 (1980). "Imminent" in this context has been found to not mean immediate. *Dickens*, 302 N.C. at 445–46. Rather, it means "that there will be no significant delay." *Id.* at 446.
193. *Id.* at 446.
194. Lynn v. Burnette, 138 N.C. App. 435, 439 (2000).

(1) extreme and outrageous conduct by the defendant/perpetrator, (2) that is intended to cause severe emotional distress to the victim, and (3) that does in fact cause such severe emotional distress.[195]

The elements of a claim for negligent infliction of emotional distress (NIED) are (1) the defendant negligently engaged in conduct, (2) it was reasonably foreseeable that the conduct would cause the plaintiff severe emotional distress (often called mental anguish), and (3) the conduct did in fact cause the plaintiff severe emotional distress.[196] Unlike IIED, a claim for NIED does not require a showing of extreme and outrageous conduct.

For both IIED and NIED, *severe emotional distress* means "any emotional or mental disorder, such as, for example, neurosis, psychosis, chronic depression, phobia, or any other type of severe and disabling emotional or mental condition" which a professional may diagnose.[197] Punitive damages may be available for a claim for intentional or negligent emotional distress if the older adult can show that the actions of the perpetrator were done with malice or willful or wanton conduct.[198]

(C) FALSE IMPRISONMENT. False imprisonment is an intentional tort. The elements of false imprisonment are (1) the illegal restraint of the plaintiff by the defendant, (2) by force or by an implied threat of force, and (3) against the plaintiff's will.[199] Even a brief restraint of the plaintiff's freedom is sufficient for this tort.[200] This cause of action may be appropriate, for example, against a caregiver who moves an older adult who requires the use of a wheelchair to a second floor bedroom against the older adult's will. The caregiver may be trying to prevent the older adult from leaving the home and reporting the caregiver's abusive actions to others.

(D) NEGLIGENCE; GROSS NEGLIGENCE. The elements of negligence in the context of a situation involving an older adult are (1) the defendant owes a duty of care to the older adult, (2) the defendant breaches that duty of care, and (3) the breach proximately causes injury to the older adult.[201] Negligence may be easier to prove than a breach of fiduciary duty claim, and a negligence cause of action can be applied to more relationships than just fiduciary relationships. For example, if an adult care home fails to provide adequate care or to keep the premises reasonably safe and an older adult is

---

195. Holleman v. Aiken, 193 N.C. App. 484, 501 (2008) (citation omitted).
196. Wilkerson v. Duke Univ., 229 N.C. App. 670, 675 (2013).
197. *Id. at* 675–76 (internal quotation marks omitted).
198. G.S. 1D-15(a); Burgess v. Busby, 142 N.C. App. 393, 409–10 (2001) (intentional infliction of emotional distress); Shaw v. Goodyear Tire & Rubber Co., 225 N.C. App. 90, 94–95 (2013) (discussing what constitutes "willful or wanton" negligence and stating that the jury was properly instructed on what to find before punitive damages could be awarded in claim for negligent infliction of emotional distress).
199. *Wilkerson*, 229 N.C. App. at 674.
200. *Id.*
201. Lynn v. Burnette, 138 N.C. App. 435, 439 (2000).

injured as a result, the older adult may have a claim against the adult care home for negligence. Recovery in a negligence action is limited to compensatory damages.[202] Gross negligence requires the same showing as a negligence action but also requires the added element of "wanton conduct done with conscious or reckless disregard for the rights and safety of others."[203] A successful claim for gross negligence would entitle the older adult to punitive damages along with compensatory damages.[204]

iii. Rescission of Documents

An older adult may sign or modify a document such as a will, trust, deed, or contract as a result of undue influence,[205] duress, or fraud imposed by another person, or the older adult may lack capacity when the document was signed. As a result, the older adult, or a person legally acting on behalf of the older adult (discussed in Section II.B.1, *supra*), can seek a court order to rescind the document or the changes made to the document.[206] If the action involves the rescission of a deed, the older adult may also be entitled to payment of costs by the defendant, including reasonable attorneys' fees.[207]

(a) Undue Influence

The **elements** required to show undue influence are as follows.

1. A person is subject to influence.
2. The perpetrator has an opportunity to exert influence.
3. The perpetrator has a disposition to exert influence.
4. There is a result that indicates undue influence.[208]

To show undue influence in the execution of a document, a party must show that something operated on the mind of the older adult subject to influence that had "a controlling effect sufficient to destroy the person's free agency and to render the instrument not properly an expression of the person's wishes, but rather the expression of the wishes of

---

202. *See, e.g.,* King v. Britt, 267 N.C. 594, 597–98 (1966) (stating that in personal injury cases resulting from negligence, the plaintiff is entitled to recover damages resulting from the negligence).

203. Clayton v. Branson, 170 N.C. App. 438, 445 (2005) (internal quotation marks omitted).

204. G.S. 1D-15.

205. "Undue influence" is defined by North Carolina law as a "fraudulent influence over the mind and will of another to the extent that the professed action is not freely done but is in truth the act of the one who procures the result." *In re* Loftin's Estate, 285 N.C. 717, 722 (1974).

206. *See* Hinson v. United Fin. Servs., Inc., 123 N.C. App. 469, 473–74 (1996) (discussing statute of limitations for claim for rescission based on duress); Matthews v. James, 88 N.C. App. 32 (1987) (involving action for rescission based on lack of mental capacity and undue influence); Caudill v. Smith, 117 N.C. App. 64 (1994) (involving undue influence in the execution of a deed by a 90-year-old man; deed was set aside).

207. G.S. 6-18(1).

208. *In re* Will of Smith, 158 N.C. App. 722, 726 (2003).

another or others."[209] Undue influence may be shown by proving several factors, including

- the old age and physical and mental weakness of the person executing the instrument,

- that the person signing the paper is in the home of the beneficiary of the paper and is subject to his or her constant association and supervision,

- that others have little or no opportunity to see the person signing the paper,

- that the newly signed instrument is different from and revokes a prior instrument,

- that the new instrument has been made in favor of one with whom the signing party has no ties of blood,

- that the paper disinherits the natural objects of the signer's bounty, or

- that the beneficiary of the document has procured its execution.[210]

Undue influence is generally shown by several facts that, were they to be asserted individually, would not be enough to make a case but that, taken together, may be sufficient evidence of undue influence.[211] Undue influence need not be due to bad motives; even good motives may result in undue influence.[212]

> ◇ **EXAMPLE**
>
> *Undue Influence*
>
> *James was 73 years old and a chronic alcoholic with bipolar disorder. He originally named his wife and son as beneficiaries of his pension and profit-sharing plans administered by his employer. He then changed the beneficiary to his caregiver. Less than one month prior to the change, he attempted to take his own life, and two weeks after the change he did just that. James lived in his own home but for two months before signing the forms was subject to the constant association and supervision of the caregiver. Prior caregivers noted that James could not care for himself—he could not use the bathroom unassisted or care for his other personal hygiene needs. When anyone had contact with James, he was always accompanied by the caregiver.[213] James depended on the caregiver for his basic needs and was lonely because the caregiver isolated him from others most of the time. These facts likely support a claim to rescind the beneficiary designations based on undue influence of James by the caregiver.*

---

209. Matthews v. James, 88 N.C. App. 32, 37 (1987) (quoting Hardee v. Hardee, 309 N.C. 753, 756 (1983)) (internal quotation marks omitted) (civil action to rescind change in beneficiary designations on pension and profit-sharing plans administered by an employer).

210. Hardee v. Hardee, 309 N.C. 753, 756–57 (1983).

211. *See In re* Will of Jones, 362 N.C. 569, 575 (2008) (stating that a determination of undue influence is highly fact-specific and inherently subjective).

212. *Id.* at 574.

213. *See Matthews*, 88 N.C. App. at 38–39 (similar facts sufficient to allow the question of undue influence to go to the jury).

(b) Duress

An older adult may have grounds to rescind a contract, deed, will, or other document based on duress. The **elements** required to show duress are that

- by the unlawful act(s) of another,

- an older adult is induced to make a contract or to perform or forego some act

- under circumstances that deprive the adult of his or her free will.[214]

A wrongful act or threat is a key element of duress. Whereas fraud rests on deception by misrepresentation or concealment, duress results from coercion and may exist even though the older adult is fully aware of all of the material facts of the situation.[215]

(c) Fraud

The elements of a fraud claim are set out in Section II.C.1.b.ii.(c), *supra*. Rather than seek compensatory damages for fraud, the older adult alleging fraud in connection with the execution of documents may elect the remedy of rescission.[216] This prevents double redress for a single wrong.[217] The election of rescission rather than damages does not preclude an award for punitive damages.[218]

(d) Lack of Mental Capacity

An older adult may have grounds to rescind an agreement or other document for lack of capacity.

(1) Mental Capacity to Contract

"[A] person has mental capacity sufficient to contract if he knows what he is about, and that the measure of capacity is the ability to understand the nature of the act in which he is engaged and its scope and effect, or its nature and consequences, not that he should be able to act wisely or discreetly, nor to drive a good bargain, but that he should be in such possession of his faculties as to enable him to know at least what he is doing and to contract understandingly."[219]

(2) Mental Capacity to Make a Will

The standard for capacity to make (or modify) a will (known as testamentary capacity) is different from the capacity to contract.[220] Testamentary capacity requires that a person be of *sound mind*, meaning that the person understands the natural objects of his or her bounty; understands the kind, nature, and extent of his or her property; knows the manner in which he or she desired the act to take effect; and realizes the effect that the act would have upon his or her estate.[221]

---

214. Radford v. Keith, 160 N.C. App. 41, 43–44 (2003), *aff'd*, 358 N.C. 136 (2004).
215. Link v. Link, 278 N.C. 181, 191 (1971).
216. Mehovic v. Mehovic, 133 N.C. App. 131, 135 (1999).
217. *Id.*
218. *Id.* at 135–37.
219. Sprinkle v. Wellborn, 140 N.C. 163 (1905) (internal citations omitted).
220. *In re* Will of Maynard, 64 N.C. App. 211, 224–25 (1983).
221. *Id.* at 224.

2. PROTECTION FROM DOMESTIC VIOLENCE OR UNWANTED CONTACT

There may be situations when an older adult is the victim of domestic violence perpetrated by someone with whom the adult has a personal relationship, such as a child, grandchild, or intimate partner. The older adult may also be the victim of sexual misconduct or stalking by someone with whom he or she does not have a personal relationship, such as an adult care home worker.

Two types of civil protective orders are available under North Carolina law to protect older adults in these situations. G.S. Chapter 50B authorizes the court to enter civil domestic violence protective orders (often referred to as DVPOs, 50B orders, or restraining orders) to protect victims of domestic violence. Chapter 50C authorizes the court to enter civil no-contact orders (no-contact or 50C orders) to protect victims of sexual misconduct and stalking who do not have the personal relationship with the perpetrator required for DVPOs. Actions to secure these orders may be initiated by an older adult himself or herself or by the older adult's authorized legal representative (persons authorized to act on behalf of an older adult are discussed in Section II.B, *supra*).

📖 RESOURCES

- If the adult is in immediate danger, call 911.
- The telephone number of the National Domestic Violence Hotline is 1-800-799-7233 (SAFE); for TTY accessibility: 1-800-787-3224.
- Text HOME to 741741 at any time and from anywhere in the United States to talk by text about any type of crisis, including domestic violence.
- The N.C. Coalition Against Domestic Violence maintains a list of local domestic violence service providers in the state. The list can be accessed on the organization's website at https://nccadv.org/get-help.

A DVPO or 50C order may be obtained instead of or along with a criminal prosecution.[222] Neither type of order is tantamount to a criminal conviction, but a criminal conviction may result from the violation of a DVPO (but not from the violation of a 50C order). Similarly, obtaining a DVPO or 50C order does not preclude an older adult from obtaining relief through a civil lawsuit for tort claims, such as assault, battery, or intentional infliction of emotional distress.[223] A victim of domestic violence/unwanted contact may not, however, obtain both a DVPO and a 50C order. The two actions are mutually exclusive because, to obtain a DVPO, the victim and perpetrator must have a personal relationship with one another. By contrast, to obtain a 50C order, the parties need not have a personal relationship.

---

222. G.S. 50B-7; 50C-11.
223. *Id.*

a. Domestic Violence Protective Order

A DVPO is a court order that requires a perpetrator of domestic violence to stop committing domestic violence.[224] Domestic violence is defined[225] as

1. causing or attempting to cause bodily injury to someone;
2. putting someone in fear of imminent serious bodily injury;
3. putting someone in fear of continued harassment that inflicts substantial emotional distress; or
4. committing rape, sexual offense, sexual battery, or another act defined in G.S. 14-27.21 through -27.33.

📖 RESOURCE

The North Carolina Administrative Office of the Courts maintains information on its website about how to get a protective order. See https://www.nccourts.gov/help-topics/domestic-violence/how-to-get-a-protection-order.

To obtain a DVPO, an older adult must have a personal relationship with the perpetrator of domestic violence.[226] If the older adult does not have a personal relationship with the perpetrator, the older adult may be able to obtain a 50C civil no-contact order in some cases (discussed in more detail below).[227] A "personal relationship" in the DVPO context means that the parties

- are current or former spouses,

- are persons of the opposite sex who live together or have lived together,

- are related as parents and children or as grandparents and grandchildren (a parent or grandparent may not obtain a protective order against a child or grandchild under the age of 16),

- have a child in common,

- are current or former household members, or

- are persons of the opposite sex who are in or have been in a dating relationship (defined as "romantically involved over time and on a continuous basis during the course of the relationship").[228]

---

224. G.S. 50B-1(c) (defining "protective order"); 50B-3 (describing the relief available in an order as directed by the court).
225. G.S. 50B-1.
226. G.S. 50B-1(a), (b).
227. G.S. 50C-1(8) (defining "victim" for purposes of civil no-contact orders as a person against whom an act of unlawful conduct, as defined by statute, has been committed by someone not involved in a personal relationship with that person).
228. G.S. 50B-1(b). A dating relationship does not include a casual acquaintance or ordinary fraternization between persons in a business or social context. *Id.* § 50B-1(b)(6).

i. Filing for a DVPO

Any person residing in North Carolina may seek a DVPO by filing a civil action or by filing a motion in any existing G.S. Chapter 50 action; the act of violence does not have to occur in North Carolina.[229] A form "Complaint and Motion for DVPO" (CV-303) is available from the N.C. Administrative Office of the Courts (AOC).[230] The form includes instructions on how to initiate and maintain a DVPO action. There are several local domestic violence agencies that will help victims with the process of filing for DVPOs. A list of these agencies is available at https://nccadv.org/get-help.

If an older adult is the aggrieved party in a domestic violence situation, and if the adult has capacity, then he or she files for the DVPO himself or herself and prosecutes the action as the real party in interest.[231] If the older adult in such circumstances lacks capacity, then he or she is named as the real party in interest to the proceeding but appears in the action through a general guardian or through a guardian ad litem (GAL) appointed by the court.[232] This process is explained in Section II.B.1.b, *supra*.

An older adult may file for a DVPO without the assistance of legal counsel.[233] The clerk of superior court of each county in the state must provide to any person without legal counsel who is seeking a DVPO all forms that are necessary or appropriate to enable the person to proceed without counsel.[234] The clerk must, whenever feasible, provide a private area for complainants to fill out forms and make inquiries.[235] No court costs or attorneys' fees are assessed for a DVPO.[236]

After the DVPO complaint is filed, a summons will be issued by the court and served by the sheriff. The summons requires the defendant to answer the complaint within ten days of the date of service.[237] The law does not specify the time within which the hearing on the order must be held, unless an ex parte DVPO has been entered. In any case, the hearing may be held only when the defendant has been served. If an ex parte DVPO has been entered, the hearing must be held within ten days of the issuance of the ex parte order or within seven days of the date of service of process on the defendant, whichever is later.[238] The hearing may be continued by consent of the parties or by the court for good cause.[239]

ii. Ex Parte DVPO Hearing and Order

Between the time the complaint or motion is filed in a DVPO matter and the hearing on the request for a DVPO, an older adult victim of domestic violence may seek a temporary

---

229. G.S. 50B-2(a).

230. *See* note 98, *supra*.

231. G.S. 1A-1, Rule 17(a).

232. G.S. 1A-1, Rule 17(a), (b)(1).

233. G.S. 50B-2(a).

234. G.S. 50B-2(d).

235. *Id.*

236. G.S. 50B-2(a). There is an exception to this rule for costs and attorneys' fees pursuant to G.S. 1A-1, Rule 11.

237. *Id.* This time period may be shortened by G.S. 50B-2(c)(5) if there is the issuance of an ex parte DVPO, which requires a hearing to be held within ten days from the date of issuance of the order or within seven days from the date of service of process on the other party, whichever occurs later, unless the hearing is continued by consent or for good cause. *Id.* § 50B-2(c)(5).

238. G.S. 50B-2(c)(5).

239. *Id.*

order, known as an *ex parte DVPO*, to protect himself or herself while the matter is pending. The older adult may request ex parte relief any time before the hearing on the DVPO complaint.[240] An ex parte order is relief granted by the court without the defendant being present and typically before service has been made on the defendant.

The hearing on the ex parte order is conducted by a judge or a magistrate in person or through a video conference.[241] The hearing is typically held at or shortly after the time the complaint is filed.[242] If the judge determines that there is a danger of acts of domestic violence being committed against the older adult, the judge may grant an ex parte DVPO, deeming it necessary for the protection of the older adult (this includes the relief available for a DVPO set forth below, including, in certain circumstances, surrender of firearms, ammunition, and permits after asking the older adult about the presence of or the defendant's access to or ownership of these items).[243]

If the ex parte DVPO is entered by a judge, as opposed to a magistrate, it will not expire unless the order includes a specific expiration date.[244] An ex parte order entered by a magistrate expires by the end of the next day that the district court is in session in the county in which the action was filed.[245] The magistrate must schedule a second ex parte hearing before a district court judge before the order expires.[246] In practice, the ex parte DVPO typically remains in effect for a brief time—until either the entry or denial of the DVPO.[247]

iii. DVPO Hearing and Order

The hearing for a DVPO is held before a district court judge who will either grant or deny the DVPO. The parties may also consent to the entry of a DVPO. For the court to enter a DVPO, it must find that the parties had a personal relationship and that an act of domestic violence has occurred.[248] If the court grants the DVPO, its order must dictate that the defendant must not commit further acts of domestic violence.[249] The DVPO may also include any of the following types of relief:[250]

1. granting a party possession of the residence or household of the parties and excluding the other party from the residence or household;

---

240. G.S. 50B-2(c)(1).

241. G.S. 50B-2(e).

242. If the older adult seeking the DVPO does not have an attorney, the clerk must schedule the ex parte hearing within seventy-two hours of the filing for relief or by the end of the next day on which the district court is in session, whichever occurs first. G.S. 50B-2(c)(6). If the district court is not in session, the older adult may contact the clerk in any other county in the judicial district, who then must schedule an ex parte hearing by the end of the next day with the district court in that county. *Id.*

243. G.S. 50B-2(c)(1).

244. G.S. 50B-2(c) does not specify a date or time for expiration of an ex parte order issued by a district court judge. For further discussion, *see* CHERYL D. HOWELL & JAN S. SIMMONS, NORTH CAROLINA TRIAL JUDGES' BENCHBOOK 7-22 (2019 ed.) (hereinafter BENCHBOOK).

245. G.S. 50B-2(c1).

246. *Id.*

247. BENCHBOOK, at 7-11.

248. G.S. 50B-1, -3(a).

249. G.S. 50B-3(a).

250. For a complete list, refer to G.S. 50B-3(a).

2. requiring a party to provide a spouse and his or her children suitable alternate housing;
3. ordering the eviction of a party from the residence or household and providing assistance to the victim in returning to it;
4. ordering either party to make payments for the support of a spouse as required by law;
5. providing for the possession of personal property of the parties, including the care, custody, and control of any animal owned, possessed, kept, or held as a pet by either party or any minor child residing in the household;
6. ordering a party to refrain from doing any or all of the following:
    a. threatening, abusing, or following the other party;
    b. harassing the other party, including by telephone, visiting the other party's home or workplace, or by some other means;
    c. cruelly treating or abusing any animal owned, possessed, kept, or held as a pet by either party or any minor child residing in the household;
    d. otherwise interfering with the other party;
7. awarding attorneys' fees to either party;
8. prohibiting a party from purchasing a firearm for a time fixed in the order;
9. ordering any party the court finds is responsible for acts of domestic violence to attend and complete an abuser treatment program if the program is approved by the Domestic Violence Commission; or
10. including in the order any additional prohibitions or requirements the court finds necessary to protect any party or any minor child.

Under certain circumstances, the court must order the defendant to surrender to the sheriff all firearms, ammunition, and permits that are in the care, custody, possession, ownership, or control of the defendant.[251] At the DVPO hearing, the court must ask the defendant about (1) the presence of, the defendant's ownership of, or the defendant's access to firearms, ammunition, or permits to purchase firearms or to carry concealed firearms and (2) identifying information for those items, such as a description of each item, the total number owned, and the location of each.[252] If the court orders the defendant to surrender firearms, ammunition, and permits, it must inform the plaintiff and the defendant of the terms of the DVPO and include these terms on the face of the order, including that the defendant is prohibited from possessing, purchasing, or receiving a firearm (or attempting to do any of these things) for so long as the protective order or any successive protective order is in effect.[253]

---

251. G.S. 50B-3.1. The court must order the defendant to surrender firearms, ammunition, and permits if it finds any of the following: (1) the use or threatened use of a deadly weapon by the defendant or a pattern of prior conduct involving the use or threatened use of violence with a firearm against any person(s), (2) threats made by the defendant to seriously injure or kill the aggrieved party or a minor child, (3) threats by the defendant to commit suicide, or (4) serious injuries inflicted upon the aggrieved party or a minor child by the defendant. G.S. 50B-3.1(a).
252. G.S. 50B-3.1(c).
253. G.S. 50B-3.1(d)(1).

The protective order may not exceed one year.[254] Before expiration of the current order, the court may renew a DVPO for good cause for a fixed period not to exceed two years, including an order that has previously been renewed.[255]

Table 6.4. **AOC G.S. Chapter 50B Domestic Violence Forms**[256]

FORM	NAME
CV-303	Complaint and Motion for Domestic Violence Protective Order; Instructions for Domestic Violence Forms
CV-304	Ex Parte Domestic Violence Order of Protection
CV-305	Notice of Hearing on Domestic Violence Protective Order
CV-306	Domestic Violence Order of Protection
CV-307	Motion for Order to Show Cause Domestic Violence Protective Order
CV-308	Order to Appear and Show Cause for Failure to Comply with Domestic Violence Protective Order
CV-309	Contempt Order Domestic Violence Protective Order
CV-311	Notice of Ex Parte Hearing before District Court Judge
CV-312	Identifying Information about Defendant Domestic Violence Action
CV-313	Motion to Renew/Modify/Set Aside Domestic Violence Protective Order Notice of Hearing
CV-314	Order Renewing Domestic Violence Protective Order; Order Setting Aside Domestic Violence Protective Order
CV-315	Request and Affidavit to Register and Registration of Out-of-State Domestic Violence Protective Order
CV-316	Order Continuing Domestic Violence Hearing and Ex Parte Order
CV-317	Civil Summons Domestic Violence
CV-319	Motion for Return of Weapons Surrendered under Domestic Violence Protective Order and Notice of Hearing
CV-320	Order Upon Motion to Return Weapons Surrendered under Domestic Violence Protective Order
CV-321	Motion and Notice of Hearing for Disposal of Weapons Surrendered under Domestic Violence Protective Order
CV-322	Order Upon Motion for Disposal of Weapons Surrendered under Domestic Violence Protective Order
CV-323	Victim Information Sheet
CV-326	Modified Domestic Violence Order of Protection

---

254. G.S. 50B-3(b).
255. *Id.*
256. *See* note 98, *supra.*

iv. Enforcement of a DVPO

A valid protective order, including a DVPO and an ex parte DVPO, must be enforced by all North Carolina law enforcement agencies without further order of the court.[257] Violation of a DVPO is a crime and may be reported to law enforcement. The defendant may be prosecuted for the crime of violating a protective order.[258] In the alternative, the protective order may be enforced through a motion filed with the court for contempt.[259] A form "Motion for Order to Show Cause DVPO" (CV-307) is available from the N.C. Administrative Office of the Courts (AOC). An older adult may use this form to initiate a contempt proceeding.

b. G.S. Chapter 50C Civil No-Contact Order

When an older adult who is subject to domestic violence does not have the type of personal relationship with the perpetrator that is defined in G.S. Chapter 50B, the older adult may be able to obtain a Chapter 50C civil no-contact order against a perpetrator. Chapter 50C allows the court to enter a civil no-contact order when an older adult proves that he or she is a victim of "unlawful conduct."[260] Unlawful conduct in this context means an act by a person who is 16 years or older of

- nonconsensual sexual conduct or

- stalking.[261]

✎ PRACTICE NOTE

1. The statutory definition of "stalking" does not require the victim to give prior notice to the perpetrator to stop the behavior before the action may be legally considered stalking.
2. The definition of stalking in G.S. Chapter 50C does not exactly mirror the criminal definition of stalking in G.S. 14-277.3A.

To obtain a 50C order, the act of unlawful conduct must occur in North Carolina.[262]

---

257. G.S. 50B-4(c).
258. G.S. 50B-4.1(b).
259. G.S. 50B-4(a).
260. G.S. 50C-2(a).
261. G.S. 50C-1(7). "Sexual conduct" is defined as "[a]ny intentional or knowing touching, fondling, or sexual penetration by a person, either directly or through clothing, of the sexual organs, anus, or breast of another, whether an adult or a minor, for the purpose of sexual gratification or arousal." G.S. 50C-1(4). "Stalking" is defined as, "[o]n more than one occasion, following or otherwise harassing, as defined in G.S. 14-277.3A(b)(2), another person without legal purpose with the intent to do any of the following: (a) [p]lace the person in reasonable fear either for the person's safety or the safety of the person's immediate family or close personal associates[, or] (b) [c]ause that person to suffer substantial emotional distress by placing that person in fear of death, bodily injury, or continued harassment and that in fact causes that person substantial emotional distress." *Id.* § 50C-1(6). More than one incident of following or harassing is needed to constitute stalking. *Id.*
262. G.S. 50C-2(a).

i. Filing for a No-Contact Order

An older adult who is the victim of unlawful conduct may seek a 50C order by filing a verified complaint in district court or by a filing a motion in any existing civil action.[263] A competent adult who resides in North Carolina may file a complaint or motion for a 50C order on behalf of an incompetent adult.[264] A form "Complaint for No-Contact Order for Stalking or Nonconsensual Sexual Conduct" (Form AOC-CV-520) is available from the AOC.[265]

Once the 50C complaint is filed, the court will issue a summons, and the summons, the complaint, a notice of hearing, and any temporary civil no-contact order must then be served personally on the respondent/perpetrator by the sheriff.[266] If the respondent fails to answer the complaint or fails to appear after having been served, the court may enter a 50C order by default.[267]

ii. Entry of a No-Contact Order

If the court finds that an older adult who has filed a 50C complaint has suffered unlawful conduct committed by the respondent named in the complaint, the court may issue a permanent or temporary no-contact order.[268] Physical injury to the victim is not required to enter either order.[269] A temporary order may not exceed ten days' duration; it may be extended during the time the original temporary order is in effect, upon good cause, for ten days or for a longer period if the respondent consents.[270]

The court may issue an ex parte temporary order, meaning without notice to the respondent, in limited instances.[271] If an ex parte temporary order is entered, the hearing for the permanent order must be set for hearing within ten days from the date of the motion for the permanent order.[272]

If the court enters a no-contact order, whether temporary or permanent, it may also enter any or all of the following forms of relief:[273]

1. ordering the respondent not to visit, assault, molest, or otherwise interfere with the victim;
2. ordering the respondent to cease stalking the victim, including at the victim's workplace;

---

263. G.S. 50C-2(a)(1).
264. G.S. 50C-2(a)(2).
265. *See* note 98, *supra.*
266. G.S. 50C-3(a), (b). If the respondent cannot with due diligence be served by the sheriff by personal delivery, the respondent may be served by publication by the complainant in accordance with Rule 4(j1) of the Rules of Civil Procedure. *Id.*
267. G.S. 50C-3(c).
268. G.S. 50C-5(a).
269. *Id.*
270. G.S. 50C-8(a).
271. G.S. 50C-6(a). To enter an ex parte temporary no-contact order, the court must find (1) that it clearly appears that immediate injury, loss, or damage will result to the victim before the respondent can be heard in opposition and (2) either, (a) that the older adult certifies to the court in writing the efforts, if any, that have been made to give the notice and the reasons supporting the claim that notice should not be required or (b) that the older adult certified to the court that there is good cause to grant the remedy because the harm that the remedy is intended to prevent would likely occur if the respondent were given any prior notice of the complainant's efforts to obtain judicial relief. *Id.*
272. G.S. 50C-6(b)(4); 50C-8(a).
273. G.S. 50C-5(b).

3. ordering the respondent to cease harassment of the victim;

4. ordering the respondent not to abuse or injure the victim;

5. ordering the respondent not to contact the victim by telephone, written communication, or electronic means;

6. ordering the respondent to refrain from entering or remaining present at the victim's residence, school, place of employment, or other specified places at times when the victim is present; or

7. ordering other relief deemed necessary and appropriate by the court, including assessing attorneys' fees to either party.

iii. Enforcement of a No-Contact Order

A violation of a civil no-contact order is punishable as contempt of court, which may lead to a fine or imprisonment.[274] A form "Motion for Order to Show Cause" (CV-528) is available from the AOC. An older adult may use this form to initiate a contempt proceeding.[275]

Table 6.5. **AOC G.S. Chapter 50C Civil No-Contact Forms**[276]

FORM	NAME
CV-520	Complaint for No-Contact Order for Stalking or Nonconsensual Sexual Conduct
CV-522	Notice of Hearing on No-Contact Order for Stalking or Nonconsensual Sexual Conduct
CV-523	Temporary No-Contact Order for Stalking or Nonconsensual Sexual Conduct
CV-524	No-Contact Order for Stalking or Nonconsensual Sexual Conduct
CV-525	Motion to Renew/Set Aside No-Contact Order for Stalking or Nonconsensual Sexual Conduct
CV-526	Order Renewing No-Contact Order for Stalking or Nonconsensual Sexual Conduct
CV-527	Order Continuing No-Contact Hearing and Temporary Order
CV-528	Motion and Order to Show Cause for Failure to Comply with No-Contact Order for Stalking or Nonconsensual Sexual Conduct
CV-529	Contempt Order No-Contact Order for Stalking or Nonconsensual Sexual Conduct

274. G.S. 50C-10; *see also id.* § 50C-5(c).
275. *See* note 98, *supra.*
276. *See* note 98, *supra.*

3. HOUSING[277]

a. The Older Adult Is the Homeowner

The overwhelming majority of older adults are homeowners. A recent study showed that the homeownership rate for individuals in their early 70s was 81 percent.[278] This was higher than the national rate of 64 percent for all ages.[279] It is expected that homeowner households headed by a person age 80 or older will more than double—from 6 to 12 million—by 2035.[280]

It is a fairly common scenario, in cases involving elder abuse, for an older adult to have agreed to allow another person to live in the adult's home, only to later regret that decision. These situations are sometimes complicated. The older adult may be afraid or unwilling to change the status quo because he or she relies on the person living with him or her for food, companionship, or other assistance. The older adult (and those who support him or her) may face the difficult choice of whether to pursue judicial action to remove the person from the home or to continue living in an abusive situation because of fear, reliance, or a desire not to upset the person living with the older adult.

If the older adult decides that legal action is necessary to remove an unwanted occupant, the next step is to identify the correct legal procedure. In almost all cases, the occupant will be either a guest or a live-in paid companion or caregiver. In either situation, the available procedures include (1) seeking criminal charges for unlawful trespass and/or (2) filing a civil lawsuit for trespass in which the relief sought is a court order directing the occupant to leave. Both of these procedures will be discussed below.

Rarely, the unwanted occupant is a tenant, rather than a guest or current or former employee. When the occupant is a tenant, the procedure for removal is entirely different: the older adult, or someone legally authorized to act on the older adult's behalf,[281] must file a summary ejectment action, typically in small claims court.[282] Summary ejectment is an action by a landlord asking the court to terminate the lease of a tenant in breach and award possession of the premises to the landlord.[283] This lawsuit is available only when parties are involved in a landlord-tenant relationship. A summary ejectment action filed by a homeowner against an occupant other than a tenant, such as a guest or employee, will be dismissed,[284] with the homeowner losing time and court costs with no corresponding benefit. On the other hand, a residential tenant who refuses to vacate rental premises when legally obligated to do so may be evicted only by summary ejectment.[285] Landlords who change the locks or otherwise try to oust a tenant without going to court violate

---

277. This subsection was written by UNC School of Government faculty member Dona Lewandowski.

278. Joint Ctr. for Hous. Studies of Harvard Univ., Projections & Implications for Housing a Growing Population: Older Households 2015–2035, 7 (2016), https://www.jchs.harvard.edu/sites/default/files/harvard_jchs_housing_growing_population_2016_1_0.pdf

279. *Id.*

280. *Id.*

281. See Section II.B.1, *supra,* for a discussion of who is authorized to bring an action on behalf of an older adult.

282. G.S. 7A-210(2).

283. G.S. 42-26(a).

284. Marantz Piano Co., Inc. v. Kincaid, 108 N.C. App. 693 (1993).

285. G.S. 42-25.6.

the law and may themselves be civilly liable as a result.[286] Consequently, even though unwanted occupants are more often guests or employees than tenants, the first step in the process of forcing them to leave is to evaluate whether the law classifies them as tenants.

i. Is the Occupant a Tenant?

When a person entitled to possession of property agrees to transfer possession to another person temporarily in exchange for compensation such as money or services, a lease agreement is created between a landlord and a tenant.[287] Most of the time, the answer to whether the parties are involved in a lease is quite clear, but there are a few situations that sometimes cause confusion.[288]

One common misconception is that summary ejectment is required if the unwanted occupant is a legal resident. In fact, there is no legal relationship between tenancy and residency.[289] A person may receive mail at the residence, be registered to vote based on the address of the premises, obtain a library card on that basis, or even have children enrolled in school in that district—none of these facts are related to whether the occupant is a tenant.[290]

A second misconception is that a landlord-tenant relationship is created automatically if the occupant helped pay household expenses or provided services such as routine household maintenance. Such contributions may indeed be suggestive of a landlord-tenant relationship, but they occur in other contexts as well.[291] An appreciative guest, grateful for the generosity of a host, will often return that generosity, with neither party having any intention of establishing a contractually binding landlord-tenant relationship. People involved in romantic relationships or an older adult and an adult child sometimes decide to live together in a home owned by one of them with no notion of creating a landlord-tenant relationship, even if they agree to share expenses. The agreement between the parties in these cases lacks two requirements for a valid lease: first, the parties' agreement is usually indefinite, rather than for a specific period of time or an agreed-upon notice period for termination.[292] Second, the agreement between the parties is not to accomplish transfer

---

286. G.S. 42-25.9.

287. Carolina Helicopter Corp. v. Cutter Realty Co., 263 N.C. 139, 143–44 (1964).

288. When the parties have entered into a written lease agreement, the relationship is clear. Confusion arises, when it does, because the parties have entered into an oral agreement or, quite often, never had a frank, clear discussion about their expectations related to the person's occupancy. For more information on interpreting leases, see Dona Lewandowski, *A Lease Is a Contract*, ON THE CIVIL SIDE: A UNC SCH. OF GOV'T BLOG (Aug. 23, 2017), https://civil.sog.unc. edu/a-lease-is-a-contract/.

289. *See, e.g.*, Jones v. Swain, 89 N.C. App. 663 (1988) (although woman and son resided in plaintiff's home for a year, there was no landlord-tenant relationship where she had never been required to pay rent and there was no evidence of any contract or lease, actual or implied, between the parties).

290. *See id.*

291. *See* Jackson v. United States, 357 A.2d 409 (D.C. 1976) (boyfriend's evidence that he contributed furniture and food to his girlfriend's apartment not sufficient to establish a tenancy where he admitted he paid no rent and that there was no agreement to share the expenses of the apartment). *See also* Young v. District of Columbia, 752 A.2d 138 (D.C. 2000) (eviction upheld of man who argued that he was a subtenant because he occasionally paid some expenses despite not paying rent and having no agreement beyond a temporary stint as a guest).

292. For information on types of leases, see JOAN G. BRANNON, NORTH CAROLINA SMALL CLAIMS LAW 155–57 (2009).

of a property interest to the occupant for the occupant's exclusive possession and enjoyment but, to the contrary, is aimed at sharing the home.[293] In situations such as these, the occupant's right to occupy the premises is based on the homeowner's permission and ends when that permission is withdrawn.[294]

A third—and especially challenging—fact situation arises when the occupant is a live-in employee. A misconception in this situation is that an employee's right to live on the premises ends when the employment ends. In fact, the answer depends on whether the employee is also a tenant.[295] North Carolina appellate courts have established a test for categorizing the occupant in situations such as these. If residing on the premises is (1) reasonably necessary for the effective performance of the employee's job, (2) inseparable from the job, or (3) required by the employer, occupancy is assumed to be incidental to employment.[296] On the other hand, if the employee could perform the responsibilities of the job just as well while residing off premises, a landlord-tenant relationship is assumed, and summary ejectment is the required method of forcing the employee to leave.[297]

ii. The Occupant Is Not a Tenant

When an occupant who is not a tenant refuses to leave an older person's home after being asked to do so, there are two legal actions for removing the occupant from the adult's home: (1) seeking criminal charges for criminal trespass and (2) filing a civil action for civil trespass.

To pursue **criminal trespass**, an older adult would have to make a report to law enforcement or, in the alternative, visit the local magistrate's office in the county where the property is located to request that criminal charges be filed.

> ### ✐ PRACTICE NOTE
>
> Law enforcement officers sometimes believe that criminal charges are not appropriate under the circumstances and advise the homeowner to seek summary ejectment instead. An older adult who believes that the evidence does not support a landlord-tenant relationship and that, therefore, summary ejectment is not appropriate, might consider going directly to a magistrate to ask for a determination of whether probable cause exists to charge the occupant with trespass.

If the older adult visits the magistrate's office, the older adult should bring any written or other evidence related to the agreement between the parties. The magistrate will consider any such evidence in addition to the sworn testimony of the older adult in deciding whether criminal charges are appropriate. If the magistrate does find probable cause, the magistrate will issue either a warrant for the occupant's arrest or a summons requiring

---

293. *See, e.g., Young*, 752 A.2d at 143 (evicted man had been invited to live in apartment temporarily as a guest).
294. *See id. See also Jackson*, 357 A.2d at 411–12.
295. Simons v. Lebrun, 219 N.C. 42 (1941).
296. *Id.*
297. *Id.*

the occupant to appear at trial on the offense charged. The older adult's testimony at trial is likely to be required as evidence supporting a conviction of the criminal charge.

Whether a report is made to law enforcement or the action is initiated by visiting the magistrate, the failure of a person to leave the premises of another when told to do so may lead to a conviction for first-degree trespass under G.S. 14-159.12, which prohibits a person from entering or remaining in a building belonging to another without authorization.[298] Even when the person initially enters the property with the owner's consent, that person becomes a trespasser if the owner withdraws consent and tells the person to leave.[299]

To pursue a claim for **civil trespass** against an unwanted occupant, an older adult or someone legally authorized to act on the older adult's behalf[300] would file a civil complaint in district or superior court for civil trespass, asking the court to order the defendant to vacate the premises.[301] In addition to the order requiring the defendant to leave, the older adult is entitled to recover money damages resulting from the defendant's actions.[302] This lawsuit is not eligible for small claims court.

The elements of a claim for civil trespass to real property are

1. possession of the property by the older adult when the alleged trespass was committed,
2. an unauthorized entry that interferes with the older adult's ownership or possession of that property, and
3. damage to the older adult from the trespass.[303]

Similar to criminal trespass, just because an older adult consented to a person's initial entry onto the older adult's premises does not automatically defeat a claim for civil trespass.[304] If the person later commits wrongful acts that abuse or are in excess of his or her authority to enter the premises, the person may be held liable for civil trespass if the other elements set out immediately above are met.[305] Furthermore, actual damages do not have to be proven; any unauthorized entry entitles the property owner to, at minimum, nominal damages.[306]

iii. The Occupant Is a Tenant

When an unwanted occupant is a tenant, the tenant's right to continue living in the older adult's home is governed by the lease agreement. If the tenant violates the lease in a way that justifies eviction according to the lease, or if the tenant breaches in certain other ways, such as by failing to pay rent or engaging in criminal activity, summary ejectment is

---

298. G.S. 14-159.12. For further information, refer to Chapter 18 of *North Carolina Crimes: A Guidebook on the Elements of Crime* by Jessica Smith (7th ed., UNC School of Government, 2012).

299. Miller v. Brooks, 123 N.C. App. 20, 27–28 (1996) (citing Blackwood v. Cates, 297 N.C. 163, 167 (1979)).

300. *See* Section II.B.1, *supra*, for the process for seeking civil relief by someone acting on the older adult's behalf.

301. *See* Singleton v. Haywood Elec. Membership Corp., 357 N.C. 623 (2003).

302. Matthews v. Forrest, 235 N.C. 281, 283 (1952).

303. Keyzer v. Amerlink, Ltd., 173 N.C. App. 284, 289 (2005), *aff'd*, 360 N.C. 397 (2006). *See also* Batts v. Batts, 219 N.C. App. 650 (2012) (unpublished) (affirming a trial court's order entering a judgment finding that the defendant was a trespasser against the plaintiff's land).

304. *Keyzer*, 173 N.C. App. at 290.

305. *Id.*

306. Taha v. Thompson, 120 N.C. App. 697, 704 (1995).

the appropriate remedy.[307] This lawsuit may be filed in small claims court by filing a complaint.[308] A form "Complaint in Summary Ejectment" (Form AOC-CVM-201) is available from the N.C. Administrative Office of the Courts (AOC) in summary ejectment actions.[309] In cases involving residential leases, landlords may not use self-help remedies (e.g., forcibly removing a tenant, padlocking the premises, or rendering the premises uninhabitable by cutting off electricity or water).[310]

b. The Older Adult Is the Tenant

The previous section of this chapter focuses on situations when an older adult is a homeowner. In other cases, the older adult may be a tenant. One study estimates that by 2035, the number of households headed by renters age 65 and older will increase by 80 percent, up to 11.5 million.[311] Tenants have rights and protections under both federal and North Carolina law.

i. Federal Law: The Federal Fair Housing Act[312]

The federal Fair Housing Act does not provide protections based on age.[313] It does, however, prohibit discrimination based on physical or mental disability.[314] As applied to older adults, this means that a landlord may not[315]

1. refuse to rent a dwelling to an older adult with a disability;
2. require different lease terms because of an older adult's disability;
3. refuse to permit reasonable modification to the premises, such as the installation of a wheelchair ramp or grip rails in a bathroom, if the modification is necessary to allow a disabled older adult's full use of the dwelling; or
4. refuse to make reasonable exceptions to rules, policies, practices, or services when doing so may be necessary to afford an older adult with a disability equal opportunity to occupy and enjoy the full use of the dwelling.

ii. North Carolina Law
(a) The N.C. Residential Rental Agreement Act (RRAA)[316]

North Carolina law requires a landlord to provide residential tenants with fit and habitable premises.[317] This obligation is not subject to waiver or modification by the

---

307. G.S. 42-26(a); G.S. Chapter 42, Article 7 ("Expedited Eviction of Drug Trafficking and Other Criminals").

308. G.S. 7A-210(2); -213.

309. *See* note 98, *supra.*

310. Dona Lewandowski, *A Judgment for Possession Is Only Step 1 in Summary Ejectment Cases,* ON THE CIVIL SIDE: A UNC SCH. OF GOV'T BLOG (May 31, 2018), https://civil.sog.unc.edu/a-judgment-for-possession-is-only-step-1-in-summary-ejectment-cases/; G.S. 42-25.6 (stating that a residential tenant may only be evicted by the procedures set forth in Article 3 or 7 of G.S. Chapter 42).

311. Joint Ctr. For Hous. Studies of Harvard Univ., *supra* note 278, at 34.

312. 42 U.S.C. Ch. 45. See also G.S. Chapter 41A, the North Carolina Fair Housing Act, which provides similar protections.

313. 42 U.S.C. § 3604.

314. *Id.* The FHA uses the term "handicap." "Handicap" means a physical or mental impairment that substantially limits one or more major life activities of a person. 42 U.S.C. § 3602(h). This includes a person with a record of an impairment or a person who is regarded as having an impairment. *Id.* This manual uses the term "disability" to replace the term "handicap" to align with common practice.

315. 42 U.S.C. § 3604(f).

316. G.S. Ch. 42, Art. 5.

317. G.S. 42-42(a)(2).

tenant's agreement and is not affected by a landlord's agreement to lower the rent to reflect the fair rental value of the premises in their noncompliant condition.[318] Furthermore, under the RRAA, the landlord[319] must

1. comply with current applicable building and housing codes;
2. make all repairs and do whatever is necessary to put and keep the premises in a fit and habitable condition;
3. keep all common areas of the premises in safe condition;
4. maintain in good and safe working order and promptly repair all electrical, plumbing, sanitary, heating, ventilating, air conditioning, and other facilities and appliances supplied or required to be supplied by the landlord, provided that notification of needed repairs is made to the landlord in writing by the tenant, except in emergency situations; and
5. comply with the other requirements set forth in G.S. 42-42(a)(5) through (8).

(b) Other Tenant Consumer Protections under N.C. Law[320]

North Carolina law provides tenants with other protections as well. G.S. 42-46 regulates late fees in residential rental agreements. A landlord's obligations regarding security deposits is governed by G.S. Chapter 42, Article 6.

Several statutes regulate eviction of residential tenants. Landlords are prohibited from changing the locks, cutting off utilities, or otherwise rendering the premises uninhabitable to force tenants to leave.[321] Instead, a landlord must file a summary ejectment lawsuit. Landlords are not allowed to retain possession of tenants' personal property in an attempt to coerce payment of overdue rent,[322] and they must follow legal procedures before disposing of property belonging to evicted tenants.[323] Residential tenants may not be evicted in retaliation for making a good faith complaint or request for repairs, or because of other grounds set forth in G.S. Chapter 42, Article 4A ("Retaliatory Eviction," sections 42-37.1 through -37.3). If the older adult is a tenant of publicly assisted housing, including public housing and Section 8 housing, the older adult is entitled to additional protections and may only be evicted for good cause.[324] Finally, G.S. 42-46 restricts fees a landlord may assess connected with eviction.

---

318. G.S. 42-42(b). *See also* Mendenhall-Moore Realtors v. Sedoris, 89 N.C. App. 486 (1988).

319. "Landlord" is defined in G.S. 42-40(3) as any owner and any rental management company, rental agency, or any other person having the actual or apparent authority of an agent to perform the duties imposed by Article 5 of G.S. Chapter 42.

320. Dona G. Lewandowski, *A Lease Is a Contract, But . . .*, ON THE CIVIL SIDE: A UNC SCH. OF GOV'T BLOG (Oct. 11, 2017), https://civil.sog.unc.edu/a-lease-is-a-contract-but/.

321. G.S. 42-25.6. *See also* Dona G. Lewandowski, *Don't Try This at Home: Self-Help Evictions*, ON THE CIVIL SIDE: A UNC SCH. OF GOV'T BLOG (Apr. 25, 2018), https://civil.sog.unc.edu/dont-try-this-at-home-self-help-evictions/.

322. G.S. 42-25.7.

323. G.S. 42-36.2; 42-25.9.

324. *See* BRANNON & ANDERSON, *supra* note 89, at 184–86.

III. CHALLENGES TO PURSUING PRIVATE CIVIL REMEDIES

A. COST OF CIVIL LITIGATION

Litigation can be expensive. While an older adult may file a civil action without an attorney, matters are often complicated and challenging without an attorney's assistance. Filing fees start with the cost of filing a civil complaint—$96 for certain proceedings before a magistrate, $150 for certain ones before the district court, and around $200 in superior court—and add up from there. The cost of litigation may—and often does—prevent older adults from seeking civil legal remedies.

RESOURCES FOR OLDER ADULTS WHO WISH TO PURSUE CIVIL REMEDIES.

1. Seek advice from and/or representation by an attorney.

An older adult (or someone legally acting on his or her behalf) who is thinking about filing a civil suit may choose to seek legal advice from an attorney. The North Carolina Bar Association has a lawyer referral system that will help older adults find local attorneys with whom they can consult. Contact information is provided below.

> **N.C. Bar Association Lawyer Referral Service (LRS)**
>
> **Website:** http://www.ncfindalawyer.org/
>
> **LRS by phone:**
>
> **1-800-662-7660 (toll-free) or 919-677-8574**
> *Note that there is a charge for an initial consultation.

If an older adult cannot afford an attorney, he or she may be eligible for legal services through a local office of Legal Aid, an organization that assists people free of charge with various legal problems, provided they meet certain eligibility guidelines based on household income and type of legal issue involved. Legal Aid maintains a Senior Law Project, which focuses specifically on assisting people age 60 and older.[325] Contact information is provided below.

---

325. Legal Aid of North Carolina, *Senior Law Project*, LEGALAIDNC.ORG, http://www.legalaidnc.org/about-us/projects/senior-law-project (last visited Aug. 6, 2019).

Legal Aid of North Carolina—Senior Law Project

Website: http://www.legalaidnc.org/about-us/projects
/senior-law-project

Legal Aid of North Carolina—Senior Legal Helpline:
Toll-free: 1-877-579-7562
Hours: Monday–Friday, 9–11 a.m. and 1–3 p.m.

Several law schools in North Carolina operate elder law clinics that accept cases involving older adults and allow law students to obtain practical experience under the supervision of a licensed attorney. Two of these clinics, along with contact information, are listed below.

Wake Forest University Elder Law Clinic

Services are available to any person age 60 or older with a monthly household income of less than $2,200 for a household of one or $2,900 for a household of two.

This clinic serves Forsyth County and surrounding counties.

Website: http://elder-clinic.law.wfu.edu/
Phone: 336-758-5061

Senior Law Clinic, Campbell University

Services are available to any person age 60 and above with a monthly household income below $1,897 if single and $2,572 if married.

This clinic serves the greater Raleigh area.

Website: https://law.campbell.edu/advocate/clinical-programs
/the-senior-law-clinic/
Phone: 919-865-4693

2. Use the free court forms provided by the state court system.

A number of forms are available online at no charge from the N.C. Administrative Office of the Courts (AOC) at https://www.nccourts.gov/documents/local-rules-and-forms. Using AOC forms is not a legal requirement, but it may help ensure compliance with law and established standards of practice. Using these forms also may help reduce the cost of litigation for an older adult, as the court is often familiar with AOC forms and may be able to process them more efficiently than litigant-drafted documents. Applicable civil forms are referenced throughout this chapter.

If an older adult (or any other person) is seeking a DVPO but cannot afford to hire an attorney, the clerk of superior court of each county in North Carolina must provide the adult with all of the forms that are necessary or appropriate to enable the adult to proceed without counsel.[326] The clerk must also, whenever feasible, provide a private area for DVPO complainants to fill out forms and make inquiries.[327] No court costs or attorneys' fees are assessed in connection with filing for a DVPO.[328]

3. Petition to sue as indigent.

While a person seeking a DVPO will not be assessed court costs or attorneys' fees, as mentioned above, for other civil matters a judge or clerk may authorize the person filing the claim to sue as indigent in the appropriate court.[329] To sue as indigent, a person must file an affidavit with the court stating that he or she is unable to advance court costs.[330] Typically, a person filing an action who is seeking an indigency classification will use the AOC's Form "Petition to Proceed as an Indigent" (G-106).[331] The clerk of superior court must authorize a person to sue as indigent if the person makes the required affidavit and

- receives electronic food and nutrition benefits, such as those offered through the Supplemental Nutrition Assistance Program (SNAP/food stamps);
- receives Work First Family Assistance, such as Temporary Assistance for Needy Families (TANF);
- receives Supplemental Security Income (SSI); or
- is represented by a legal services organization, such as Legal Aid of North Carolina, that has as its primary purpose the furnishing of legal services to indigent persons or by private counsel working on behalf of such an organization.

For all other persons, it is up to the discretion of the judge or the clerk whether to authorize a person to sue as an indigent based on the information presented in the affidavit.[332]

4. Seek recovery of attorneys' fees.

The default rule in North Carolina is that each party to a civil action is responsible for his or her own attorneys' fees. But there are exceptions to this rule. For example, where specifically authorized by statute, a court may award reasonable attorneys' fees to one party as costs taxed against the other party. This exception permitting the recovery of attorneys' fees applies to some of the civil actions referenced in this chapter, including

- actions for the recovery of personal property (*see* Section II.C.1.b.i.(b), *supra*),
- claims for unfair and deceptive trade practices (*see* Section II.C.1.b.ii.(e), *supra*), and
- claims for rescission of a deed (*see* Section II.C.1.b.iii, *supra*).

---

326. G.S. 50B-2(d).
327. *Id.*
328. G.S. 50B-2(a). There is an exception to this rule for costs and attorneys' fees pursuant to G.S. 1A-1, Rule 11.
329. G.S. 1-110(a).
330. *Id.*
331. This form is available at https://www.nccourts.gov/documents/forms/petition-to-proceed-as-an-indigent.
332. G.S. 1-110(a). For further discussion of determining indigency, refer to John Rubin, Phil Dixon Jr., and Allison Grine, *North Carolina Defender Manual* vol. 1 (2d edition 2013), at Section D, pages 12-26 to 12-27.

B. PERPETRATOR HAS NO MONEY OR OTHER PROPERTY TO SATISFY A JUDGMENT

By the time elder abuse is discovered, a perpetrator may have already spent (or hidden) the money or other property taken from the older adult. An often-heard refrain is that it is not worth the time and effort to file a civil action to go after the perpetrator because he or she "doesn't have anything anyway."

ADVICE FOR OLDER ADULT VICTIMS IN CASES WHERE RECOVERY AGAINST A PERPETRATOR MAY NOT BE POSSIBLE.

1. **Make a report to adult protective services (APS).**

   Even if a perpetrator has already moved on to another victim and is no longer in the affected older adult's life, the adult may fall prey to abuse again. In response to a report, APS may be able to connect the older adult with community supports and services that will enable the adult, or those acting on his or her behalf, to be free from abuse in the future.

2. **Make a report to law enforcement.**

   Although the older adult may not be able to recover from the perpetrator in a particular case, the perpetrator may move on to other victims. If a report is made to law enforcement, this may lead to a decision by law enforcement to investigate the perpetrator and take appropriate action against him or her—including criminal prosecution—to stop the perpetrator from committing more acts of elder abuse. Furthermore, if the perpetrator is found guilty in criminal court, he or she may be ordered to pay restitution to the older adult. "[C]ivil settlement agreements and restitution awards are separate and distinct remedies."[333] A civil settlement does not bar criminal restitution, and vice versa.[334] The civil settlement is intended to compensate the victim for a civil wrong, while criminal restitution serves the additional "rehabilitative, deterrent, and retributive goals of the criminal justice system" by "forc[ing] the defendant to confront, in concrete terms, the harm his actions have caused."[335] Criminal restitution in excess of $250 must be docketed as a civil judgment for offenses covered under the N.C. Crime Victims' Rights Act (G.S. 15A-830).[336]

---

333. State v. Williams, No. COA18-994, 2019 WL 2344858, at *3 (N.C. Ct. App. June 4, 2019).

334. G.S. 15A-1340.37(a); *Williams*, 2019 WL 2344858, at *3.

335. *Williams*, 2019 WL 2344858, at *3 (quoting Kirby v. Florida, 863 So. 2d 238 (Fla. 2003)). For further discussion, refer to Jamie Markham, *Civil Settlements and Criminal Restitution*, N.C. CRIM. L.: A UNC SCH. OF GOV'T BLOG (June 6, 2019), https://nccriminallaw.sog.unc.edu/civil-settlements-and-criminal-restitution/.

336. For further discussion of docketing a criminal monetary obligation as a civil judgment, refer to Jamie Markham, *I'm Just a Civil Judgment*, N.C. CRIM. L.: A UNC SCH. OF GOV'T BLOG (Oct. 19, 2017), https://nccriminallaw.sog.unc.edu/im-just-civil-judgment/.

3. Consider the nature of a civil money judgment.

Given the nature of civil money judgments, it may still be helpful for an older adult to obtain a judgment even if the perpetrator does not currently have assets.

- **A judgment draws interest.** Money judgments draw interest at the legal rate on the principal.[337]

- **A judgment is good for ten years (longer if extended).** An older adult may win a case against a perpetrator/defendant and obtain a money judgment. Once the judgment is entered, the older adult has ten years to try to collect on it. If the defendant does not have sufficient property to satisfy the judgment when it is entered, the judgment does not go away. Instead, it is docketed for any amount unpaid. If the defendant later comes into property, the judgment may attach to the property and the older adult, or someone acting on his or her behalf, including the older adult's estate after the older adult's death, could execute on the judgment at that time. Furthermore, the judgment may be extended for an additional ten years. The legal mechanism for obtaining an extension is for the older adult to bring a second lawsuit for the amount remaining due on the original judgment.[338]

- **A judgment attaches generally to real and personal property owned by the defendant.** A monetary judgment attaches to more than the specific property taken by the defendant from the older adult. It may attach to other real and personal property. Note, however, that a judgment debtor may claim certain property he or she owns as exempt (or free) from the enforcement of a monetary judgment or a judgment for possession of household goods.[339]

C. UNABLE TO LOCATE THE PERPETRATOR

Financial scams against older adults may be committed by perpetrators located outside the United States or across state lines.[340] The perpetrator may travel door to door offering bogus or unnecessary services, such as home repairs, to older adults. As soon as the perpetrator has drained the older adult's accounts, or if there is a hint of skepticism from a neighbor or friend of the older adult, the perpetrator takes off. The task of trying to track down the perpetrator, or the feeling that it would be impossible to locate him or her, may prevent an older adult (or someone legally acting on his or her behalf), from seeking civil remedies.

---

337. G.S. 24-1, -5. The one exception to this rule is for money judgments arising out of a contract that is not for consumer purposes. *Id.* Then it draws interest at the contract rate if the contract specifically provides that the contract rate applies after judgment. *Id.*

338. Dona Lewandowski, *Action to Renew a Judgment—But Not Really*, ON THE CIVIL SIDE: A UNC SCH. OF GOV'T BLOG (Feb. 24, 2017), https://civil.sog.unc.edu/action-to-renew-a-judgment-but-not-really/.

339. CSC MANUAL, at ch. 37, § 37.1; G.S. Chapter 1C.

340. David Kirkman, *Fraud, Vulnerability, and Aging – When Criminals Gang Up on Mom and Dad*, N.C. STATE BAR J., 15 (Winter 2013) (noting that the elder fraud industry is "diverse and global" and includes mobsters from the former Soviet Union; Caribbean criminal gangs; groups from the Middle East, South Asia, and western Africa; and groups in the western United States who target seniors with home-based Internet marketing programs), https://www.ncbar.gov/media/121117/journal-18-4.pdf.

WHAT TO DO WHEN THE PERPETRATOR CANNOT BE LOCATED.

1. Make a report to federal and state agencies.

Certain federal and state agencies receive and respond to cases of elder abuse, particularly cases that impact commerce and more than one victim. Many of these agencies and their roles related to elder abuse, including how to make a report, are explained in Chapter 7. Two specific tools are available through the U.S. Department of Justice to assist people with reporting and connecting to resources related to financial abuse and fraud, including scams where the perpetrator cannot be located.

- The **Elder Abuse Resource Roadmap** is designed to help victims of financial abuse identify the proper agencies to contact to report, and to receive assistance in connection with, abuse. It is available at https://www.justice.gov/elderjustice/roadmap.

- The **National Elder Fraud Hotline** is available for people to report fraud against anyone age 60 or older and to connect to a case manager who will provide assistance with the reporting process. The phone number for the hotline is **833-FRAUD-11 (833-372-8311)**. It is open seven days a week, from 6 a.m. to 11 p.m.

2. Act to protect the adult from repeat offenders.

It may not be possible for a victim of elder abuse to seek civil remedies if the perpetrator of the abuse cannot be found. Older adults who are victims of elder abuse may (and likely will) be scammed more than once.[341] Once an older adult falls prey to elder abuse, particularly financial fraud and exploitation, it is crucial that the adult (or others acting on his or her behalf) try to protect the adult from further abuse. This may include, for example, adding the older adult's phone number to the National Do Not Call Registry (https://www.donotcall.gov/). A number of other steps are outlined in the guide, Money Smart for Older Adults, available at https://www.consumerfinance.gov/practitioner-resources/resources-for-older-adults/protecting-against-fraud/.

D. RELATIONSHIP TO THE PERPETRATOR

The relationship between an older adult and a perpetrator of abuse on the adult may cause the adult to resist seeking civil remedies such as a monetary judgment, a protection order, or summary ejectment. This may be because the older adult is protective of family members or caretakers who are abusing them. In such situations, the older adult wants some relief but does not want his or her loved one to be the defendant in a court proceeding or "to get them in trouble." The older adult may be lonely and want the continued

---

341. Kirkman, *supra* note 340, at 15.

attention and contact from a phone scammer. The older adult may be unwilling to recognize that the transaction he or she has engaged in is a scam and that the perpetrator committed abuse against him or her.

> **TIPS FOR HELPING A VICTIM OF ELDER ABUSE WHO HAS A RELATIONSHIP WITH THE PERPETRATOR OF THE ABUSE.**
>
> - **Engage adult protective services and other family and friends to support the older adult's participation in a civil action.** A broader network of support may reduce the older adult's perceived dependence on the abuser.
> - **Contact an ombudsman.** If the older adult lives in a state-licensed adult care home or other facility, contact the ombudsman who serves as the facility's patient advocate. The role of the ombudsman is discussed in Chapter 7.
> - **Connect with community services and supports that will engage the older adult in activities and connect with others in the community.** An area authority on aging serving the older adult's community may be able to assist the adult in getting plugged into community networks. Area authorities are discussed in Chapter 7. The Eldercare Locator is a nationwide service that connects older adults and caregivers to local support resources. It is available at https://eldercare.acl.gov/Public/Index.aspx or **1-800-677-1116**.

E. NATURE OF THE VICTIM AND THE ROLE OF CONSENT

A defense often raised in civil proceedings involving property brought by older adults is that the adult had capacity and consented to the transfer of his or her property, either as a gift or as consideration for caregiving services or for property of the defendant. Either the older adult lacked capacity at the time of the incident or the older adult's capacity declines so significantly between the incident and the trial on the civil claim that the older adult is unable to testify and refute the defense of consent.

TIPS FOR HANDLING CASES WHERE AN OLDER ADULT'S CONSENT IS ASSERTED AS A DEFENSE BY THE PERPETRATOR.

- **Gather evidence to refute capacity to consent.** Evidence that might help show an older adult's inability to consent at the time of a disputed transaction may include medical records and witness testimony.

- **Obtain a professional evaluation of the older adult's cognitive abilities.** An older adult's medical records may not include a recent cognitive assessment. It may be critical to litigation brought by the adult (or brought on the adult's behalf) to have evidence of the adult's lack of capacity at the time of the disputed transaction in order to refute the defense of consent. This lack of capacity could be documented through a geriatric psychiatric or other cognitive evaluation of the older adult.

- **Take the older adult's deposition as soon as possible after the incident at issue.** Depositions are used in civil actions to obtain evidence in preparation for trial.[342] An older adult's condition may decline between the time of the incident at the heart of the abuse claim and the trial. The older adult may be unavailable to testify at the trial as a witness. Live witness testimony is "more desirable" at trial and, generally speaking, witness testimony must be taken orally in open court, unless otherwise provided by law.[343] In "sharply limited" circumstances, some of which are set out in Rule 32 of the N.C. Rules of Civil Procedure, deposition testimony may be used at trial.[344] Under Rule 32, deposition testimony may be used at trial if it meets the following three criteria:

  - it is being used against a party who was present or represented at, or who had reasonable notice of, the deposition;

  - it falls within one of the categories set out in Rule 32(a)(1) through (a)(4), including that the deposition is of a witness who is unavailable because the witness is dead or is unable to testify due to age, illness, infirmity, or imprisonment;[345] and

  - it is admissible under the Rules of Evidence (applied as though the witness were present and testifying).[346]

Depending on the facts of the particular case, Rule 32 may provide an avenue for admitting the older adult's deposition testimony at the civil trial.

---

342. Ann Anderson, *Use of Deposition Testimony at Trial*, ON THE CIVIL SIDE: A UNC SCH. OF GOV'T BLOG (Nov. 9, 2016), https://civil.sog.unc.edu/use-of-deposition-testimony-at-trial/.

343. Investors Title Ins. Co. v. Herzig, 330 N.C. 681, 690 (1992); G.S. 1A-1, Rule 43. Anderson, *supra* note 342.

344. Warren v. City of Asheville, 74 N.C. App. 402, 408-10 (1985). Anderson, *supra* note 342.

345. If the witness is unavailable due to death, age, illness, infirmity, imprisonment, or some other category in G.S. 1A-1, Rule 32(a)(4), the deposition testimony must also comply with N.C. Rule of Evidence 804(b)(1), which states that the party against whom it is used "had an opportunity and similar motive to develop the testimony by direct, cross, or redirect examination." Pleasant Valley Promenade v. Lechmere, Inc., 120 N.C. App. 650, 659 (1995); *see also Investors Title*, 330 N.C. at 692 (opposing party had been given requisite opportunity). Anderson, *supra* note 342.

346. G.S. 1A-1, Rule 32. Anderson, *supra* note 342.

Chapter 7
Other Critical Components of the Elder Protection System

CONTENTS

I. SCOPE OF CHAPTER

The term "elder protection system" encompasses not only the agencies, individuals, and options identified in the first several chapters of this manual. It extends to many other public and private actors who are essential to preventing abuse; providing protection, care, and services; and enforcing other applicable laws. This chapter provides an overview of several of the components that play a major role in this system. It is not intended to be comprehensive but, rather, representative. There are certainly many other essential partners involved with protecting older adults in North Carolina.

II. OVERVIEW OF OTHER COMPONENTS

A. HEALTH CARE PROVIDERS

Health care providers play an important role in identifying and reporting elder abuse. This includes primary care physicians, hospitals, mental health providers, dentists, pharmacists, chiropractors, nurses, home health providers, physical therapists, and any other person providing medical care. Health care providers may be the first people to interact with an older adult after an incident and, possibly, the only people outside of family who the older adult sees regularly.[1]

A health care provider is mandated to report suspected elder abuse if the provider has reasonable cause to believe that a disabled adult is in need of protective services.[2] This duty to report is described in detail in Chapter 2 of this manual. Despite this mandatory duty, studies show underreporting by health care providers.[3] This lack of reporting may be due to a reluctance to acknowledge abuse, lack of protocols for acknowledging abuse, lack of protocols for identifying abuse, fear of liability, and limited services to respond to abuse.[4] Physicians specifically may be concerned about the impact on patient rapport and trust, patient quality of life, and physician control.[5] Studies suggest that cases go undetected because of a lack of knowledge about elder abuse, the prevalence of elder abuse, signs and symptoms, risk factors, and information on perpetrators.[6]

---

1. *See* Amy N. Schmeidel et al., *Healthcare Professionals' Perspectives on Barriers to Elder Abuse Detection and Reporting in Primary Care Settings*, 24(1) J. ELDER ABUSE & NEGLECT 17–36 (2012), https://www.ncbi.nlm.nih.gov/pmc/articles/PMC3298114/.

2. Chapter 108A, Section 102, of the North Carolina General Statutes (hereinafter G.S.).

3. Schmeidel et al., *supra* note 1.

4. *Id.*

5. *Id.*

6. *Id.*

B. N.C. DEPARTMENT OF HEALTH AND HUMAN SERVICES

The North Carolina Department of Health and Human Services (DHHS) is a state agency with an expansive mission that encompasses many programs, divisions, and offices that are involved with providing services to and protecting older adults.[7] Of the sixteen service divisions within the agency, five have a significant role in supporting older adults.

Table 7.1. **Overview of Selected DHHS Divisions Involved with Elder Protection**

DHHS DIVISION	ROLE
Aging and Adult Services	Oversees adult protective services (APS) and other aging programs provided by county departments of social services and area agencies on aging; administers the long-term care ombudsman program and the state-county special assistance program
Health Service Regulation	Responsible for regulation and oversight of health care facilities such as hospitals, nursing homes, and adult care homes
Medical Assistance (Medicaid)	Manages administration of health insurance program that is available to many low-income and disabled adults
Mental Health, Substance Abuse, and Developmental Disabilities	Oversees regional managed care program providing publicly funded services, primarily funded through Medicaid
Social Services	Oversees administration of economic services programs relied upon by older adults, such as food and nutrition services (e.g., food stamps, energy assistance)

Other divisions and offices involved with protecting the safety and welfare of older adults include public health, rural health, services for the deaf and hard of hearing, and services for the blind. Rather than provide detailed information about the roles of each of these divisions within DHHS, the discussion below highlights several specific and important functions that may overlap or intersect regularly with other components of the state's elder protection system.

Each area of work comes equipped with different bodies of law, including different tools and processes designed to support compliance with laws and policies. For example, a particular agency may, in the case of elder abuse, be able to impose a fine or other financial penalty, take action on a facility or individual license or permit, or require a regulated

---

7. The agency's mission statement provides: "In collaboration with our partners, DHHS provides essential services to improve the health, safety and well-being of all North Carolinians." Its vision statement goes further to explain that the agency intends to advance "innovative solutions that foster independence, improve health and promote well-being for all North Carolinians." N.C. Dep't of Health & Human Servs., *Mission Vision*, NCDHHS.GOV, https://www.ncdhhs.gov/about/dhhs-mission-vision-values-and-goals/mission-vision.

entity or person to take corrective action within a specified period. Many types of inspection reports and penalties are public record and may be available upon request.

1. SUPERVISION OF COUNTY SOCIAL SERVICES AGENCIES

North Carolina operates a state-supervised, county-administered system to deliver social service programs, including adult services. In this model, local social services agencies take on the primary role of day-to-day program administration. The state provides supervision, direction, and support to the local agencies.[8] For adult services, including adult protective services (APS) and guardianship by a county department of social services (DSS), the state's Division of Aging and Adult Services (DAAS) provides oversight and supervision for the county departments providing direct services. Supervision includes developing policies and forms, offering training, collecting data, and compliance monitoring. In most situations, other components of the elder protection system will work directly with a county DSS but occasionally it may be appropriate and necessary to contact the DAAS for assistance as well.

2. REGULATION OF LONG-TERM CARE FACILITIES

An older adult may be the subject of physical, emotional, or sexual abuse or neglect while a resident in a long-term care facility. Consider the following examples.

- A resident with Alzheimer's disease may be seriously injured after leaving the facility unsupervised.

- A resident may be sexually or physically abused by another resident or by a member of the staff.

- Staff may not administer pain medication as ordered or provide appropriate wound care, causing the resident to suffer unnecessarily.

DHHS has a role in both (1) trying to prevent this type of harm and (2) investigating and penalizing facilities where such harm has or may have occurred.

On the prevention side, DHHS's Division of Health Service Regulation (DHSR) is responsible for licensure and certification of nursing homes, adult care homes, and facilities for individuals with intellectual disabilities, developmental disabilities, mental illness, and substance abuse issues. These facilities must apply for a license, pass inspections, and be approved before serving patients. During this process, the government agency's role is to determine whether the facility complies with all applicable federal and state laws and policies, including the applicable resident "bill of rights." (See resource below.) After a license is issued, the facility remains subject to regular inspections and oversight by the government.[9] For example, DHSR has the authority to inspect most adult care homes at any time

---

8. *See* SOC. SERVS. REG'L SUPERVISION & COLLABORATION WORKING GROUP, STAGE ONE FINAL REPORT (UNC School of Government, Mar. 2018), https://www.sog.unc.edu/resources/microsites/social-services/reports.
9. G.S. 131D-2.11(a).

and is required to do so at least annually.[10] County departments of social services (DSS) are required to work with DHSR to support this oversight function.[11] If problems are identified in the course of standard oversight and monitoring, the agency will work with the facility to remedy the problem, impose fines, or take action on the facility's license.[12]

💬 KEY TERMS

Key Terms: Adult Care Home vs. Nursing Home

Term	Definition
Adult Care Home[13]	A facility that provides twenty-four-hour personal care services, such as eating, dressing, bathing, toileting, and grooming, to two or more residents Medical care is usually occasional or incidental, with supervised administration of medication[14] Adult care homes that provide care to two to six unrelated residents are referred to as "family care homes"
Nursing Home[15]	A facility that provides nursing or convalescent care for three or more persons Nursing homes generally provide care for people who are not sick enough to require general hospital care but who require nursing care to address chronic or rehabilitative needs The general term "nursing home" encompasses more specific types of facilities, such as skilled nursing and intermediate care facilities
Combination Home[16]	A facility may be a "combination home" that offers various levels of care, including both adult care home services and nursing home services

If DHSR or DSS receives a complaint regarding a licensed facility, an investigation must be initiated within certain timeframes.[17] For adult care homes, the county DSS will be responsible for conducting the investigation. This investigation is in addition to any adult protective services (APS) process that DSS may initiate (see Chapter 2 for more details about APS). If DSS finds a violation, the agency will inform both the facility and DHSR

---

10. G.S. 131D-2.11(a), (a1). DHSR may waive an annual inspection for an adult care home that achieved the highest performance rating the previous year; however, the agency must inspect the adult care home at least once every two years. *Id.* § 131D-2.11(a1).

11. G.S. 131D-2.11(b).

12. *See* G.S. 131D-34(a).

13. G.S. 131D-2.1(3) (definition of "adult care home" in the context of adult care home regulation); 131E-101(1) (definition of "adult care home," in contrast to definition of "nursing home").

14. G.S. 131D-2.2(a). There is an exception for when a physician certifies that appropriate care can be provided on a temporary basis to meet the resident's needs and prevent unnecessary relocation. *Id.* Adult care homes also do not care for (1) individuals who are dependent on ventilators, (2) individuals whose physician certifies that placement is no longer appropriate, (3) individuals whose health needs cannot be met in the specific adult care home as determined by the residence, and (4) such other medical and functional care needs as the Medical Care Commission determines cannot be properly met in an adult care home. *Id.*

15. G.S. 131E-101(6).

16. G.S. 131E-101(1a).

17. G.S. 131D-26(a1) (adult care homes); 131E-124(a1) (nursing homes).

of the violation, what corrective action must be taken, and a date by which the violation must be corrected.[18] DSS may request assistance from DHSR in resolving complaints.[19] If the complaint involves a nursing home, DHSR rather than the county DSS will be responsible for conducting the investigation.[20] DHSR must reply to the complaint within a reasonable time, which must not exceed sixty days.[21]

📖 **RESOURCE**

Long-Term Care Residents' Bill of Rights

Adult care homes and nursing homes are required by law to treat their residents in accordance with a residents' bill of rights.[22] The facilities may not require residents to waive these rights.[23] For example, residents have the right

- to be treated with consideration and respect;
- to be free of mental and physical abuse;
- to be free of neglect and exploitation (adult care homes);
- except in emergencies, to be free from chemical and physical restraint, unless authorized for a specified period of time by a physician according to clear and indicated medical need; and
- to be encouraged to exercise their rights as residents and citizens and to be permitted to make complaints and suggestions without fear of coercion or retaliation (adult care homes).

For a more detailed comparison of the bills of rights for adult care homes and nursing homes, see Comparing Residents' Bills of Rights, available at protectadults.unc.edu.

DHSR has the authority to take action if it finds that a facility is out of compliance with applicable laws, including the residents' bill of rights.[24] The penalty DHSR may impose depends on the severity of the violation committed.[25] For example, in the context of adult care homes, the agency has the authority to

- revoke, suspend, or summarily suspend a license;[26]

---

18. G.S. 131D-26(b).
19. G.S. 131D-26(c).
20. G.S. 131E-124(a).
21. *Id.*
22. G.S. 131D-21 (adult care homes); 131E-117 (nursing homes).
23. G.S. 131D-23 (adult care homes); 131E-119 (nursing homes).
24. G.S. 131D-34 (adult care homes); 131E-124 (nursing homes).
25. G.S. 131D-34.
26. G.S. 131D-2.7; -29.

- require a court-appointed temporary manager for the facility;[27] and

- impose an administrative penalty, which may include a corrective action plan and fines up to $20,000 for each violation and up to $1,000 each day the violation continues beyond the specified deadline.[28]

Penalties will vary based on the severity of the violation. The most severe violations (known as Type A violations) are those that result in or create a substantial risk[29] of death or serious physical harm, abuse, neglect, or exploitation.[30] Less severe violations (known as Type B violations) include those that are detrimental to the health, safety, or welfare of any resident but do not create a substantial risk that death or serious physical harm, abuse, neglect, or exploitation will occur.[31]

Table 7.2. **Examples of Violations in Adult Care Homes**

VIOLATION	EXAMPLE
Type A	"A confused resident who is not properly supervised, wanders away from the facility and as a result, his or her safety is endangered or the resident suffers serious physical harm."
	"A wrong medication is given to a resident by facility staff which has the strong potential of adversely affecting the resident or the resident suffers serious physical harm."
Type B	"Several resident[s] have orders to receive over the counter pain medications every morning but on one morning, staff forget to give the residents the medication. The residents suffer no ill consequence from the missed doses and subsequent doses are given as ordered."
	"The facility's pest management program is not effective and insects are noted in a couple of resident rooms on one out of two halls in the facility."

Source: N.C. Div. of Health Serv. Regulation (DSHR), Adult Care Licensure Sec., *Adult Care Home Violations and Penalties*, "Regarding Adult Care Home Inspections," NCDHHS.GOV, https://info.ncdhhs.gov/dhsr/acls/adultcarehomefines.html.

---

27. G.S. 131D-34(a)(3).

28. G.S. 131D-34(a) (adult care homes); 131E-129 (nursing homes).

29. Substantial risk means the risk of an outcome that is substantially certain to materialize if immediate action is not taken. G.S. 131D-34(2b).

30. G.S. 131D-34(a)(1), (1a).

31. G.S. 131D-34(a)(2).

> ### ✎ PRACTICE TIP
> *Find information about particular facilities, including the facts listed below.*
> - **Adult care homes.** Investigate "star ratings" (rankings of homes based on one to four stars), penalties imposed, and information gathered by the state Department of Health and Human Services in the course of inspections of family care homes and adult care homes. For more information on star ratings, see DSHR, *Star Rating Program*, NCDHHS.GOV, https://www2.ncdhhs.gov/dhsr/acls/star/search.asp#search.
> - **Nursing homes.** Nursing homes certified by Medicare or Medicaid are listed in a comparison tool developed by the U.S. Department of Health and Human Services that includes star ratings, staffing information, and quality of care information. For more on this tool, see U.S. Dep't of Health & Human Servs., *Nursing Home Compare*, "Find a Nursing Home," MEDICARE.GOV, https://www.medicare.gov/nursinghomecompare/search.html?.

In addition to filing a complaint with DHSR, a resident of a facility (or the resident's legal representative) may file a civil action for injunctive relief to enforce the applicable bill of rights.[32] See Chapter 6 for further discussion of private civil actions.

3. LONG-TERM CARE OMBUDSMAN PROGRAM

The Long-term Care Ombudsman Program provides another avenue for promoting the well-being of older adults who are residents in long-term care facilities, including both nursing homes and adult care homes.[33] One purpose of the Ombudsman Program is to advocate on behalf of residents of long-term care facilities.[34] There is a State Ombudsman located within the DHHS Division of Aging and Adult Services and Regional Ombudsmen throughout the state in each of the Area Agencies on Aging.[35] In 2016, the state's program reported receiving 3,769 complaints and closing almost 2,000 cases.[36]

Upon receiving a complaint, the ombudsman will typically attempt to resolve the problem using informal techniques such as mediation, conciliation, and persuasion.[37] If those

---

32. G.S. 131D-28 (adult care homes); 131E-123 (nursing homes).

33. G.S. 143B, Art. 3, Pt. 14D.

34. G.S. 143B-181.15. *See also* DHHS, ADULT HOME AND NURSING HOME LONG TERM CARE ADVISORY COMMITTEES (CACS): THE ESSENTIAL GUIDE 1 (June 2009), https://files.nc.gov/ncdhhs/documents/files/CAC_Essential_Guide.pdf. A list of State and Regional Ombudsman contact information may be accessed online. *See* DHHS, *Long Term Care Ombudsman (Advocacy for Residents in Long Term Care Facilities)*, NCDHHS.GOV, https://www.ncdhhs.gov/assistance/adult-services/long-term-care-ombudsman (last visited Aug. 12, 2019).

35. G.S. 143B-181.17; -181.18(3a).

36. Data is from U.S. Department of Health and Human Services, Administration for Community Living's *AGing Integrated Database* (AGID), "State Profiles," https://agid.acl.gov/StateProfiles/Profile/Compare/?id=35&compareid=109&variable=7&years=2016 (last visited Aug. 12, 2019).

37. G.S. 143B-181.21(a).

methods are unsuccessful, the ombudsman will refer the matter to DHSR if the complaint relates to an adult care home or nursing home.[38] The ombudsman has the authority to[39]

- enter any long-term care facility at any time during regular visiting hours, or at any other time when access may be required by the circumstances to be investigated, and may have related authority to obtain access to any resident;

- communicate privately and confidentially with residents of the facility, individually or in groups; and

- access residents' files, records, and other information.[40]

The ombudsman must identify himself or herself as such to the resident about whom a complaint was filed. The resident may be unable to or may refuse to communicate with the ombudsman, but that does not diminish the authority of the ombudsman to gather information about the complaint.[41] The resident has the right to participate in planning any actions proposed by the ombudsman and ultimately retains the right to approve or disapprove any proposed action.[42]

If the subject of the complaint involves suspected abuse, neglect, or exploitation, the Regional Ombudsman may only notify the Adult Protection Services (APS) section of the county department of social services (DSS) after obtaining either the written informed consent of the resident or authorization by the State Ombudsman.[43] This is an exception to the general APS reporting obligations discussed in Chapter 2.

Another way the State Ombudsman works to promote quality of care in both nursing homes and adult care homes is through community advisory committees (CACs).[44] Members of each CAC serve as representatives of the State Ombudsman.[45] A CAC exists in each county where there is an adult care home or nursing home.[46] The CAC works to serve the best interests of the residents, assist persons who have grievances with the facility, and attempt to facilitate the resolution of grievances at the local level.[47]

---

38. G.S. 143B-181.21(b).
39. G.S. 143B-181.20(a).
40. Access is allowed as permitted under the Older Americans Act of 1965, as amended, 42 U.S.C. §§ 3001 *et seq.*, and regulations promulgated thereunder, and under procedures established by the State Ombudsman pursuant to G.S. 143B-181.18(6).
41. G.S. 143B-181.20(b).
42. G.S. 143B-181.20(c).
43. G.S. 143B-181.20(f).
44. G.S. 131D-31 (adult care home CAC); 131E-128 (nursing home CAC).
45. G.S. 131D-31 (adult care home CAC); 131E-128 (nursing home CAC).
46. G.S. 131D-31(b)(1) (adult care homes); 131E-128(b)(1) (nursing homes).
47. G.S. 131D-32(e) (adult care homes); 131E-128(h)(1) (nursing homes).

Table 7.3. **Contacting Agencies about Concerns Related to a Long-Term Care Facility**

GOVERNMENT AGENCY	INVESTIGATIVE AUTHORITY	CONTACT INFORMATION
Department of Health Services Regulation (DHSR)	• Investigate complaints related to nursing homes • Refer complaints related to adult care homes to local DSS • Assist local DSS with adult care home investigations as necessary	• (800) 624-3004 (N.C. calls only) • (919) 855-4500 • https://www2.ncdhhs.gov/dhsr/
Local DSS	• Investigate complaints related to adult care homes in the county or region	Local DSS directory: https://www.ncdhhs.gov/divisions/social-services/local-dss-directory
State Ombudsman	• Refer complaints related to long-term care facilities to regional offices • Assist regional ombudsman with complaint investigations as necessary	• (919) 855-3400 • http://www.ncdhhs.gov/aging/ombud.htm
Regional Ombudsman	• Investigate complaints related to long-term care facilities in the region	Regional office directory: https://files.nc.gov/ncdhhs/Ombudsman-Contact%20List_2.pdf

4. HEALTH CARE PERSONNEL REGISTRY

Doctors, nurses, and some other health care personnel are subject to regulation by their professional licensing boards. Any suspected misconduct can be reported directly to those boards, which have the authority to take disciplinary action.[48] In addition, an individual may be charged with a crime for failing to comply with the standards that apply to his or her profession.[49]

Many staff working in health care facilities are not licensed and not subject to the same type of oversight as the personnel listed above. Therefore, DHHS maintains a registry of "health care personnel" who have been found by the agency to have committed certain types of misconduct in a health care facility.[50] The term "health care facility" is defined

---

48. *See, e.g.*, G.S. 90-14 (Medical Board); -171.37 (Board of Nursing); *see also* N.C. Med. Bd., *Resources & Information*, "Filing a Complaint with the NC Medical Board," NCMEDBOARD.ORG, https://www.ncmedboard.org/resources-information/consumer-resources/complaint-process (last visited Aug. 12, 2019).

49. *See, e.g.*, G.S. 90-18 (crime to practice medicine or surgery without a license); -171.45 (crime to fail to comply with the Nursing Practice Act).

50. G.S. 131E-256; Title 10A, Subchapter 13O, of the North Carolina Administrative Code (N.C.A.C.).

broadly to include hospitals, adult care homes, nursing homes, home health care agencies, and agencies providing in-home aide. Examples include

- neglect or abuse of a resident in a health care facility or upon a person who is receiving home care or hospice care;

- misappropriation of a resident's property, including home care and hospice care patients;

- diversion of drugs belonging to a patient or client of a health care facility; and

- fraud against a patient or client for whom the employee is providing services.[51]

In addition, the registry includes any personnel who have been accused of misconduct if DHHS "has screened the allegation and determined that an investigation is required."[52] The law provides opportunities for personnel to challenge their placement on the registry and, in limited circumstances, request removal from the registry.

This registry includes "health care personnel," which is defined to mean "any unlicensed staff of a health care facility that has direct access to residents, clients, or their property."[53] It also includes nurse aides, who are also included on a separate registry.[54] Health care facilities are required to (1) notify DHHS of potential misconduct within twenty-four hours of the facility becoming aware of it, (2) investigate the circumstances, and (3) promptly report to DHHS about the findings of the investigation.[55] Facilities are also required to check the Health Care Personnel Registry before hiring health care personnel.[56] Federal and state law prohibit facilities from hiring a nurse's aide or medication aide who has a substantiated finding against him or her on a registry.[57]

> ### ✐ PRACTICE NOTE
>
> Identifying information on a registry is not a public record,[58] but the information may be disclosed pursuant to a subpoena or court order. Prosecutors, clerks of court, social services staff, and others may want to request information from a registry in the course of an elder abuse investigation.

---

51. G.S. 131E-256(a)(1).
52. G.S. 131E-256(a)(2).
53. G.S. 131E-256(c).
54. G.S. 131E-255.
55. G.S. 131E-256(g); 10A N.C.A.C. 13O, § .0102.
56. G.S. 131E-256(d2).
57. 42 U.S.C. § 1395i-3(g)(1)(C); *id.* § 1396r(g)(1)(C); 42 C.F.R. § 483.35(d)(4) (nurse aides); G.S. 131E-270 (medication aides).
58. G.S. 131E-256(g1).

C. OTHER STATE AGENCIES

In addition to the N.C. Department of Health and Human Services (DHHS), there are several other state agencies involved with elder protection. Each has a unique area of emphasis and different powers and duties. It is helpful for other components of the elder protection system to have an understanding of the scope of authority for each agency because it may be necessary to collaborate with one or more in order to provide the best possible protection to an older adult. Below is a brief overview of the elder protection role played by three key state agencies: the Department of Justice, the Secretary of State, and the Department of Insurance.

1. DEPARTMENT OF JUSTICE

A key civil function of the North Carolina Department of Justice (DOJ) is protecting consumers, including older adults, from frauds and scams. DOJ does this primarily through public education and responding to consumer complaints. In 2018, one-fifth of the approximately 20,000 consumer complaints received related to elder fraud.

DOJ has the authority to investigate corporations and persons who do business in the state in violation of law, such as those related to unfair competition and unfair and deceptive trade practices. In response to a complaint, the agency will typically contact the business for a response and may work to resolve the dispute directly. It may also refer the complaint to another state or federal agency or to a local prosecutor. In some cases, DOJ may suggest that the consumer consult a private attorney or file a small claims action. See Chapter 6 for more details on these types of civil actions.

If DOJ identifies a pattern of illegal business practices, it may file a civil lawsuit in the name of the State on behalf of all North Carolina consumers against a corporation and any of the corporate officers, agents, and employees. In the civil action, DOJ may seek to recover money and property for victims, cancellation of contracts, civil money damages, and attorneys' fees.

Table 7.4. **Common Scams Targeting Older Adults under DOJ Authority**

TYPE	THE SCAMMER . . .
Sweetheart	• Creates a fake online profile, posing as someone working out of state or overseas • Develops a friendship with the older adult which, in turn, develops into a romantic relationship and, in some cases, a marriage proposal • Asks the older adult to wire money immediately to help with a financial crisis
Home repair	• Comes to the older adult's house • Identifies unnecessary repairs that need to be made to the roof, driveway, or other parts of the house • After starting the work, may identify more and more repairs or problems, such as toxic mold • Collects series of payments from the older adult • Disappears before the work is complete or completes shoddy repairs
IRS	• Calls the older adult demanding payment of a bogus tax bill • States that the adult will be sent to jail unless the payment is made immediately through a wire transfer or debit card • May require the adult to stay on the phone while completing the wire transfer
Grandparent	• Calls the older adult claiming to be a grandchild or a friend of a grandchild • Asks the older adult to wire money immediately to pay for medical care or get the grandchild out of jail
Lottery	• Calls the older adult and says that the adult won the lottery or a contest • Asks the older adult to wire money to cover fees and taxes so that the adult can claim the winnings

In addition to this role in consumer protection, DOJ also takes the lead on investigating potential fraud involving the Medicaid program. Examples of potential signs of this type of fraud include

- a patient being pressured to receive unnecessary or excessive services,

- a patient's medical records being altered,

- a medical provider claiming to provide services for free, and

- a medical provider dispensing excessive amounts of controlled substances.[59]

DOJ is able to both criminally prosecute those involved with fraud and also pursue a civil suit to recover program funds.

---

59. N.C. Dep't of Just., Att'y Gen., *How to Spot Medicaid Fraud & Abuse*, NCDOJ.GOV, http://ncdoj.gov/responding-to-crime/health-fraud (last visited Oct. 16, 2019).

Information maintained by DOJ may be useful to assist other components of the elder protection system, such as local prosecutors and adult protective services.

2. SECRETARY OF STATE

The N.C. Secretary of State (SOS) has specific authority related to the regulation and oversight of the securities industry and of charities.

> ◇ **EXAMPLE**
>
> *Bob, an 82-year-old widower, receives a call from an unknown investment broker. The broker explains that he is reaching out to a small group of people to offer an opportunity to get in on a new investment. He describes it as a "once-in-a-lifetime opportunity." Bob thinks the broker sounds really bright and trustworthy. He's excited about growing his retirement nest egg. The broker persuades Bob to transfer $5,000 to an investment account the same day.*

> ◇ **EXAMPLE**
>
> *Linda receives a letter asking her to donate money to raise funds to feed local children. She writes a check for $200 and mails it to the organization. She later finds out that the charity does not exist.*

The SOS plays a role in trying to prevent the types of fraud discussed in the examples above through education. The agency also registers investment salespersons, advisors, securities, and charities. A consumer who has questions about a particular opportunity may contact the SOS to learn about the organization or individual offering the opportunity.

If someone has a negative experience with a regulated individual, organization, or entity, he or she can file a consumer complaint with the SOS. While the agency is not able to represent individuals or recover money for private persons, it does have the authority to enforce the state laws regulating these activities and individuals.

The SOS also maintains a voluntary online registry of advance health care directives. The registry is password-protected and allows a family member or doctor to access the directives of an individual once the individual has given the family member/doctor the correct file number and password. Alternatively, an individual may keep a registry card containing that information in a location where it can be found in the event it is needed by a family member, caregiver, or medical professional.

3. DEPARTMENT OF INSURANCE

The N.C. Department of Insurance (DOI) regulates the insurance industry, which encompasses all types of insurance, such as health, life, long-term care, disability, homeowners, and auto insurance, and oversees collection agencies, among other duties. The DOI assists consumers with questions about insurance and the filing of claims. It also investigates complaints and allegations of insurance fraud. In 2016, the agency's Criminal Investigation Division handled more than 4,500 cases and recovered in excess of $4.8 million.

> ◇ **EXAMPLE**
>
> *After a big hailstorm, a roofing company representative knocks on Dan's door. The representative explains that his company can inspect the roof, repair it, and get reimbursed from Dan's homeowner's insurance. Dan, who is 85 years old, signs paperwork authorizing the company to collect directly from his insurer. The company never repairs his roof.*

> ◇ **EXAMPLE**
>
> *An insurance agent contacts Mary, who is 82 years old, and explains that she can use her existing insurance policy's cash value to pay for a newer policy. In order to generate a commission, the agent "may 'twist' the truth and 'churn' a new, 'better' or 'cheaper' policy to the customer. This new policy may, in fact, have less favorable terms or fewer benefits. This is illegal."*[60]

---

60. N.C. Dep't of Ins. Crim. Investigations Unit, Insurance Fraud: Recognize It. Report It. Protect Yourself, http://ncdoi.com/_Publications/Insurance%20Fraud%20in%20North%20Carolina_CIF1.pdf.

Which State Agency Should an Older Adult Call for Assistance?

TYPE OF COMPLAINT	AGENCY	CONTACT
Consumer fraud or scam	DOJ	• (919) 716-6000 • (877) 5-NO-SCAM (only N.C. calls) • (919) 716-0058 (Spanish) • www.ncdoj.gov
• Securities (investment) professionals • Securities (investment) offerings • Charities	SOS	• (800) 688-4507 • www.sosnc.gov
Insurance fraud	DOI	• (919) 807-6840 • (888) 680-7684 (only N.C. calls) • reportfraud@ncdoi.gov • www.ncdoi.gov
Medicaid recipient fraud	DHHS	• (800) 862-7030 • (877) DMA-TIP1 (362-8471)
Medicaid provider fraud	DOJ	• (919) 881-2320
Tax fraud	Revenue	• (800) 232-4939 • www.ncdor.gov

D. AREA AGENCIES ON AGING

The federal government provides funding to the states to establish Area Agencies on Aging (AAA). North Carolina has sixteen of these regional agencies in place, which are co-located with the regional Councils of Government. Each agency is home to a regional Long-Term Care Ombudsman, described above. In addition, each agency plays an important role in its community by working with local officials and others to identify needs of older adults in the community and then contracting with service providers to meet those needs. The Land of Sky AAA describes its role as promoting

> the highest level of well being of older adults and their families by partnering with organizations to provide a comprehensive system of opportunities, services, and protective services. The AAA is a leader and catalyst in helping older adults in our four county region lead more independent, vibrant lives. As part of a national network of aging agencies established by the Older Americans Act, we work to strengthen home and community care for older adults.[61]

---

61. LAND OF SKY REGIONAL COUNCIL, http://landofsky.org/aaa.html (last visited Aug. 12, 2019).

An AAA may have contracts with organizations that provide home meal delivery or congregate meals, transportation services, adult day care services, recreation, or wellness activities. AAAs are also involved with advocacy for older adults in the community, both individually and collectively. Except for the ombuds program, each agency is involved with different types of programs and services.

Agency staff or contractors who interact with older adults may identify suspected elder abuse and report it to adult protective services and law enforcement. The agency may also be able to help other components of the elder protection system identify resources and supports within the community to improve the quality of life for an older adult who has been abused.

> ### ✎ RESOURCE
>
> Identify the AAA in your region and determine what services and supports it may have available. If there are service gaps for older adults in your community, share those with the AAA. This will help the staff to integrate those needs into the regional planning efforts and advocate for them in the community. A list of agency locations can be found at https://files.nc.gov/ncdhhs/documents/files/aging/AAA-Locations.pdf

E. FEDERAL AGENCIES

In 2010, Congress enacted a law that established the Elder Justice Coordinating Council (EJCC).[62] The EJCC is housed in the U.S. Department of Health and Human Services (DHHS) and is required to include representatives from "each Federal department or agency or other governmental entity identified by [DHHS] as having responsibilities, or administering programs, relating to elder abuse, neglect, and exploitation."[63] The EJCC includes representation from approximately sixteen different federal agencies and programs[64] (see sidebar for the complete list).

---

62. 42 U.S.C. § 1397k(b)(1).

63. *Id.*

64. U.S. Dep't of Health & Human Servs., Admin. for Cmty. Living, Fall 2018 EJCC Meeting, "Elder Justice Coordinating Council Membership List" (last modified Mar. 29, 2019), https://acl.gov/programs/elder-justice/fall-2018-ejcc-meeting.

Membership of the Federal Elder Justice Coordinating Council

- Department of Health and Human Services (chair of council)
- Consumer Financial Protection Bureau
- Corporation for National and Community Service
- Federal Trade Commission
- Department of Agriculture
- Department of Housing and Urban Development
- Department of the Interior
- Department of Justice
- Postal Inspection Service
- Department of Labor
- Social Security Administration
- Department of the Treasury
- Department of Veterans Affairs
- Securities and Exchange Commission

A full overview of the role of each agency is beyond the scope of this manual, but below are brief overviews of the roles played by six key agencies that may interact more frequently with components of North Carolina's elder protection system.

1. U.S. DEPARTMENT OF HEALTH AND HUMAN SERVICES

The U.S. Department of Health and Human Services (US DHHS) is involved in funding and supporting quite a few initiatives focused on elder abuse. For example, the agency provides support and funding to

- states for training, education, and coalition-building;

- the National Center for Elder Abuse, which provides information, training, and consultation for professionals involved with elder protection;

- the National Center on Law and Elder Rights, which provides tools and support for legal and aging provider organizations;

- organizations providing legal services to older adults;

- states, in the form of grants, to support adult protective services (APS) programs;

- states for the operation of their long-term care ombudsman programs; and

- researchers examining topics related to elder abuse.[65]

In 2016, US DHHS worked with a wide range of professionals to develop "Voluntary Consensus Guidelines for State APS Systems."[66] The guidelines are intended to "provide

---

65. U.S. DEP'T OF HEALTH & HUMAN SERVS. (DHHS), ELDER JUST. COORDINATING COUNCIL, 2014–2016 REPORT TO CONGRESS 6–15, https://acl.gov/sites/default/files/programs/2017-11/2017%20EJCC%20Report.pdf.
66. U.S. DHHS, Admin for Cmty. Living, *Voluntary Consensus Guidelines for State APS Systems* (2016), https://acl.gov/programs/elder-justice/final-voluntary-consensus-guidelines-state-aps-systems.

a core set of principles and common expectations for APS programs, and to encourage consistency in the policies and practices of APS across the country."[67]

US DHHS also recently started gathering data from states on adult mistreatment on a voluntary basis. The new database is called the National Adult Mistreatment Reporting System (NAMRS) and it began receiving data submissions from states in 2017. It is described as "aspirational" because many states, including North Carolina, do not have robust electronic APS systems and therefore are not able to contribute some or all of the data elements.[68]

2. U.S. DEPARTMENT OF JUSTICE

The U.S. Department of Justice (US DOJ) has focused significant resources on disseminating information; providing training, education, and technical assistance; and, in conjunction with US DHHS, supporting the provision of direct legal services to older adults. The Elder Justice Initiative website includes a tremendous amount of information for public agencies involved with elder protection and citizens, including

- written materials, videos, and websites specifically designed for law enforcement officials and prosecutors;

- webinars and other training materials for other types of elder abuse professionals;

- community outreach materials;

- tools and resources for multidisciplinary teams; and

- curated research on elder abuse topics.

The website includes an "Elder Abuse Resource Roadmap" for victims of financial exploitation.[69] The roadmap is a tool that walks users through a series of questions and answers that ultimately guide them to the government agency or connection that may be able to receive a report or provide assistance. Through the Office for Victims of Crime, the US DOJ also maintains the National Elder Fraud Hotline. The hotline allows people to report fraud against anyone age 60 or older and to connect to case managers who will provide assistance with the reporting process at the federal, state, and local levels. The phone number for the hotline is 833-FRAUD-11 (833-372-8311).

The US DOJ also has a role in leading, coordinating, and assisting with investigations and prosecutions when federal laws are violated. For example, in 2018, the department worked with state and local law enforcement to conduct an elder fraud "sweep."

The cases involve more than two hundred and fifty defendants from around the globe who victimized more than a million Americans, most of whom were elderly.

---

67. ELDER JUST. COORDINATING COUNCIL, *supra* note 65, at 8.

68. U.S. DHHS., Admin. for Cmty. Living, *NAMRS (Nat'l Adult Maltreatment Reporting Sys.)*, "FAQ: What Else Do I Need to Know?," https://namrs.acl.gov/FAQ.aspx (last visited Aug. 12, 2019).

69. U.S. Dep't of Just., *Elder Abuse Resource Roadmap: Financial*, JUSTICE.GOV, https://www.justice.gov/elderjustice/roadmap (last visited Aug. 12, 2019).

The cases include criminal, civil, and forfeiture actions across more than 50 federal districts. Of the defendants, 200 were charged criminally.[70]

A map of the federal prosecutions resulting from the sweep is also available online, including available court documents.[71]

3. CONSUMER FINANCIAL PROTECTION BUREAU

This agency focuses entirely on consumer financial protection.[72] It has the authority to adopt rules and enforce federal consumer financial laws. It also receives consumer complaints, promotes financial education, researches consumer behavior, and monitors financial markets for risks to consumers.[73] One office within the agency is dedicated to protecting older adults. It generates outreach and educational materials for consumers and financial institutions and conducts research on issues that impact older adults (such as reverse mortgages).[74]

4. FEDERAL TRADE COMMISSION

One role of the Federal Trade Commission (FTC) is to "combat unfair, deceptive, abusive and fraudulent practices that impact older adults."[75] Like many of the other federal agencies, the FTC has developed outreach and training materials for both consumers and professionals. The agency also plays an active role in enforcement. For example, it prosecutes scams, such as those involving international sweepstakes, government imposters, and unnecessary computer technical support. It also accepts consumer complaints.

Additionally, the FTC plays a central role in the federal government's identity theft–prevention efforts and in helping victims build "personal recovery plans" that are tailored to their circumstances.[76] These plans help victims (1) determine who they need to call and what steps they should take to protect their assets going forward and (2) possibly recover assets that may have been lost.

5. U.S. DEPARTMENT OF THE TREASURY

The charge of the Financial Crimes Enforcement Network (FinCEN) within the U.S. Department of the Treasury is to safeguard "the financial system from illicit use, combat money laundering, and promote national security through the strategic use of financial authorities and the collection, analysis, and dissemination of financial intelligence."[77]

---

70. U.S. Dep't of Just., *Justice News*, "Justice Department Coordinates Nationwide Elder Fraud Sweep of More Than 250 Defendants," JUSTICE.GOV (Feb. 22, 2018), https://www.justice.gov/opa/pr/justice-department-coordinates-nationwide-elder-fraud-sweep-more-250-defendants.

71. U.S. Dep't of Just., *February 22, 2018 Elder Fraud Sweep Map*, JUSTICE.GOV, https://www.justice.gov/opa/february-22-2018-elder-fraud-sweep/map (last visited Aug. 12, 2019).

72. Consumer Fin. Prot. Bureau, CONSUMERFINANCE.GOV, https://www.consumerfinance.gov/ (last visited Aug. 12, 2019).

73. ELDER JUST. COORDINATING COUNCIL, *supra* note 65, at 21.

74. Research reports are available on the Consumer Financial Protection Bureau's website at https://www.consumerfinance.gov/data-research/research-reports/ (last visited Aug. 12, 2019).

75. ELDER JUST. COORDINATING COUNCIL, *supra* note 65, at 24.

76. U.S. Fed. Trade Comm'n, *Report Identity Theft and Get a Recovery Plan*, IDENTITYTHEFT.GOV, https://Identity-Theft.gov (last visited Aug. 12, 2019).

77. U.S. Dep't of Treasury, Fin. Crimes Enf't Network, *Mission*, FINCEN.GOV, https://www.fincen.gov/about/mission (last visited Aug. 12, 2019).

In this role, FinCEN provides support for financial institutions, such as banks and credit unions, collects data from those institutions, and links the data from various sources to provide system oversight. Since 2013, financial institutions have been required to submit "Suspicious Activity Reports" (SARs) to FinCEN. With these reports, federal and state law enforcement officials are able to both investigate individual cases and identify trends. A financial institution may be required to file a SAR if it knows, suspects, or has reason to suspect that a transaction conducted or attempted by, at, or through the financial institution

- involves funds derived from illegal activity or attempts to disguise funds derived from illegal activity,

- is designed to evade regulations promulgated under the Bank Secrecy Act (BSA),

- lacks a business or apparent lawful purpose, or

- involves the use of the financial institution to facilitate a criminal activity.[78]

There has been significant growth in the reporting of SARs related to elder financial exploitation since the reporting mandate went into effect. See Figure 7.1.

Figure 7.1 **Number of Suspicious Activity Reports (SARs) Submitted by Financial Institutions in North Carolina Identified by the Institution as Involving "Elder Financial Exploitation," 2012–2018[79]**

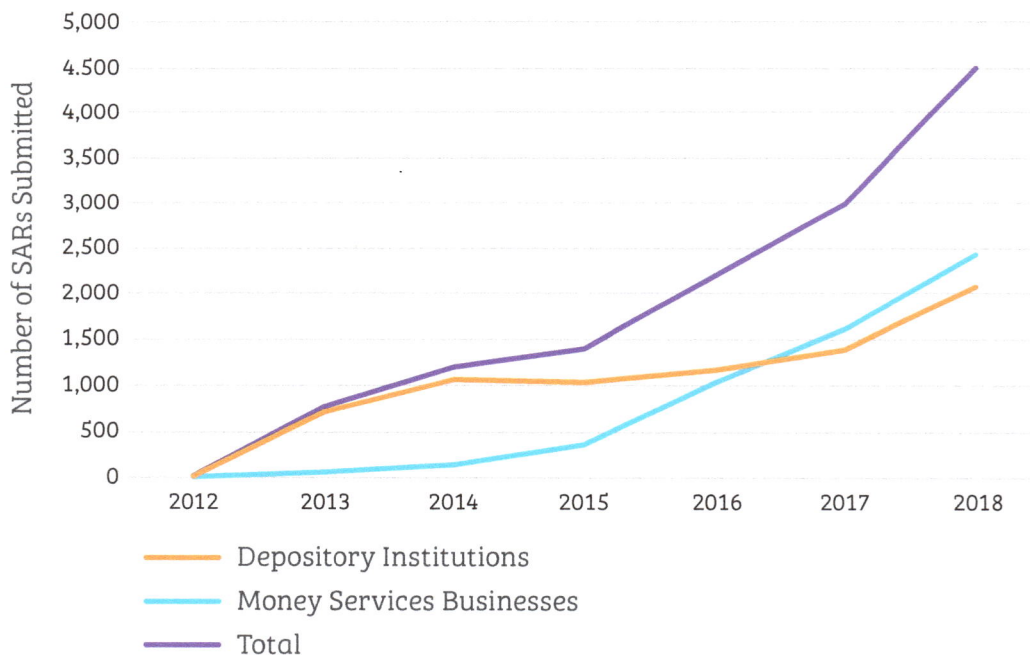

---

78. CONSUMER FIN. PROT. BUREAU & U.S. DEP'T OF TREASURY, FIN. CRIMES ENF'T NETWORK, MEMORANDUM ON FINANCIAL INSTITUTION AND LAW ENFORCEMENT EFFORTS TO COMBAT ELDER FINANCIAL EXPLOITATION (Aug. 30, 2017), https://files.consumerfinance.gov/f/documents/201708_cfpb-treasury-fincen_memo_elder-financial-exploitation.pdf.

79. U.S. Dep't of Treasury, Fin. Crimes Enf't Network, *Suspicious Activity Report Statistics (SAR Stats)*, https://www.fincen.gov/ (searchable database) (last visited Aug. 12, 2019).

The federal Consumer Financial Protection Bureau (*see* Section II.E.3, *supra*) studied the SARs data for elder financial exploitation and identified patterns. For example,

- the majority (51 percent) of the suspects listed in the reports were strangers;

- financial losses were greater if the suspect was known to the older adult victim; and

- more than half of the reports related to a money transfer.

Information collected by FinCEN through SARs reporting is protected by federal confidentiality laws, but law enforcement officials can initiate a FinCEN query after a criminal investigation has been opened or in connection with reviews conducted by a task force or group charged with proactively reviewing SARs to identify potential exploitation.[80]

> ### ✐ PRACTICE NOTE
>
> The SARs reporting requirement is based in federal law. The financial institution must still comply with reporting requirements under **state** law. See Chapter 2, Section II.C.I, for more details regarding the APS reporting obligations.

6. SOCIAL SECURITY ADMINISTRATION

Many older adults receive Social Security income every month. The federal Social Security Administration (SSA) is responsible for paying these benefits and has a strong interest in ensuring that payments are received and used by or on behalf of the older adults who have earned them. One of the best tools available from SSA to help older adults who may be cognitively impaired is the representative payee program.[81]

In short, the program allows another individual to apply to the SSA to serve as a recipient's representative payee. If SSA approves the application, benefit payments will go directly to the payee, and the payee is expected to spend them only for the benefit of the recipient. In some instances, it may be appropriate to appoint an organization, such as a nursing home, or an agency, such as DSS, to serve as the representative payee. The payee is required to keep records of how the benefits are used and saved and to provide an accounting to SSA upon request.[82]

---

80. 31 C.F.R. § 1010.950(b) ("The Secretary may make any information set forth in any report received pursuant to this chapter available to another agency of the United States, to an agency of a state or local government or to an agency of a foreign government, upon the request of the head of such department or agency made in writing and stating the particular information desired, the criminal, tax or regulatory purpose for which the information is sought, and the official need for the information."); *id.* § 1010.950(e) (placing restrictions on redisclosure of information received). *See also* U.S. Dep't of Just., *Suspicious Activity Reports (SARs) and Their Role in Investigations of Elder Financial Exploitation*, JUSTICE.GOV (Nov. 2, 2017), https://www.justice.gov/elderjustice/video/suspicious-activity-reports-sars-and-their-role-investigations-elder-financial.

81. *See, e.g.*, Soc. Sec. Admin., *Frequently Asked Questions (FAQs) for Representative Payees*, SSA.GOV, https://www.ssa.gov/payee/faqrep.htm (describing the role of a representative payee) (last visited Aug. 12. 2019).

82. Justice in Aging, *Fact Sheet: SSA's Representative Payee Program*, JUSTICEINAGING.ORG (2016), https://www.justiceinaging.org/our-work/economic-security/rep-payee-program/.

Unfortunately, this program has the potential to be abused. If a payee has misused benefits, SSA has the authority to pursue both civil and criminal penalties.[83]

> **RESOURCE**
>
> The federal government has invested significant resources in developing training materials and other resources related to elder protection. Some of the most comprehensive materials include the following:
>
> - DOJ Elder Justice Initiative (EJI): https://www.justice.gov/elderjustice
> - National Center on Elder Abuse: https://ncea.acl.gov/
> - Consumer Financial Protection Bureau: https://www.consumerfinance.gov/
> - Federal Trade Commission: https://www.ftc.gov/ and https://IdentityTheft.gov
> - National Center on Law and Elder Rights: https://ncler.acl.gov/

F. FINANCIAL INSTITUTIONS

Banks, credit unions, and other financial institutions are critical components of the elder protection system with respect to financial exploitation.[84] They have expertise in identifying irregular financial activity and offer tools to monitor accounts and transactions when necessary. These institutions (1) identify potential exploitation and make reports, (2) provide access to records, and (3) freeze accounts. Below is a brief overview of their connection to the system in each of these three areas.

1. IDENTIFY AND REPORT

Financial institutions are subject to several federal and state confidentiality laws that can at times be perceived as barriers to information-sharing (see further discussion below). Even with these rigorous laws in place, financial institutions, and their officers and employees, are clearly allowed to comply with the reporting requirements for adult protective services (APS), law enforcement, "trusted persons," and the federal government (SARs).

- **Duty to report all abuse, neglect, and exploitation to APS.** Financial institutions must comply with the universal mandated APS reporting law, which requires all individuals who have reasonable cause to believe that a *disabled* adult is in need of services to provide protection from abuse, neglect, or exploitation.[85]

- **Duty to report financial exploitation to APS.** Financial institutions are also subject to a more specific (and likely redundant) law that requires them to report to

83. 42 U.S.C. § 408(a)(5); *id.* § 405(j)(7).

84. CONSUMER FIN. PROT. BUREAU & U.S. DEP'T OF TREASURY, FIN. CRIMES ENF'T NETWORK, *supra* note 79. *See also* Quick Reference: Legal Framework for the Role of Financial Institutions in Elder Protection, available at protectadults. sog.unc.edu.

85. G.S. 108A-102.

APS if they have reasonable cause to believe that a *disabled* adult is the victim or target of financial exploitation.[86] See Chapter 2 for further discussion of APS reporting laws.

- **Duty to report to law enforcement.** If a financial institution has reasonable cause to believe that a *disabled adult or older adult* (65 years and older) is the victim or target of financial exploitation, the institution must make a report to local law enforcement.[87]

- **Trusted persons list.** Under state law, financial institutions are encouraged to offer disabled adults and older adults an opportunity to submit to the institutions a list of "trusted persons" and to update the lists periodically.[88] If the institution has reasonable cause to believe that the adult is the victim or target of financial exploitation, it must report the suspicion to any "trusted person" identified by the customer, unless the institution "suspects that [the trusted person is] financially exploiting the disabled adult or older adult."[89]

- **Duty to report to federal government (SARs).** As discussed above, financial institutions are required to file Suspicious Activity Reports with the U.S. Department of the Treasury in some circumstances.

2. PROVIDE ACCESS TO RECORDS

As mentioned above, financial institutions are subject to several complex federal and state confidentiality laws.[90] While strict confidentiality is a high priority, these laws also recognize the need to share information in order to protect older adults from exploitation. A financial institution may, in some circumstances, provide access to an older adult's financial records to (1) APS, (2) law enforcement, and (3) a party to a court proceeding.

A full review of the confidentiality laws governing financial institutions is beyond the scope of this manual, but a brief overview is important to help orient the other components of the elder protection system to the legal framework.

The first thing to keep in mind is that an older adult with capacity, or an adult's legal representative (such as a general guardian, guardian of the estate, or interim guardian), may authorize a financial institution to provide access to an official, agency, or individual at any time.[91] If the older adult lacks capacity or there is a need to obtain access without asking for the older adult's authorization, there are some tools and processes available to the three entities listed above to obtain access to information from financial institutions.

---

86. G.S. 108A-115(a)(3).

87. G.S. 108A-115(a)(2).

88. G.S. 108A-114.

89. G.S. 108A-115(a)(1).

90. *See* 15 U.S.C. § 6801(a) ("It is the policy of the Congress that each financial institution has an affirmative and continuing obligation to respect the privacy of its customers and to protect the security and confidentiality of those customers' nonpublic personal information."); G.S. 53B-3 ("It is the public policy of this State that financial records should be treated as confidential and that no financial institution may provide to any government authority and no government authority may have access to any financial records except in accordance with the provisions of [Chapter 53].").

91. 15 U.S.C. § 6802(e)(2); 12 C.F.R. § 332.15(a)(1); G.S. 35B-4(1); *id.* § 35A-1251. Note that an interim guardian of the estate (GOE) or general guardian (GG) has only the authority set forth in the order appointing the interim guardian. G.S. 35A-1114(e).

- **APS.** In the course of an APS investigation, social services officials have three tools available to obtain information from a financial institution: subpoenas, freeze and inspect orders, and search warrants. See Chapter 2 for an overview of each of these tools.

- **Law enforcement.** In a criminal investigation, law enforcement officials may use search warrants, court orders, or subpoenas[92] to obtain information from financial institutions. See Chapter 2 for an overview of each of these options.

- **Party to a court proceeding.** A party to a court proceeding, such as a petitioner in a guardianship proceeding, may rely on traditional discovery under the rules of civil procedure to gain access to an older adult's financial records. This includes a request for production of documents. The downside to relying on civil discovery is that it can be costly and time-consuming. If an older adult is the subject of financial exploitation, quick action may be necessary to protect the adult, and civil discovery may be an inadequate tool to stop ongoing exploitation.

As a general rule, a financial institution is required to (1) provide every customer with notice that it plans to disclose the customer's information to a third party and (2) provide the customer with an opportunity to opt out of the disclosure.[93] This requirement is based on both federal and state law, although the parameters for each body of law are slightly different.

A governmental authority requesting access to records from a financial institution may request that the notice to the customer be delayed. A judge (not the clerk or magistrate) may order delayed notice to the customer if the request is relevant to a legitimate governmental inquiry and if notice to the customer will

- endanger the life or physical safety of any person,

- result in flight from prosecution,

- lead to intimidation of a witness,

- result in destruction of or tampering with evidence, or

- otherwise seriously jeopardize the governmental inquiry or an official proceeding or investigation.[94]

If the disclosure is being made pursuant to a subpoena issued by a district court judge, that judge has the authority to authorize the delay.[95] If the disclosure is being made pursuant to other process, such as a court order or search warrant, the order delaying notice must be issued by a superior court judge (not a clerk or magistrate).[96]

---

92. G.S. 108A-116 (authorizing law enforcement to request a subpoena for financial records).
93. 15 U.S.C. §§ 6803(a), (b); 6802(a), (b).
94. G.S. 53B-6.
95. G.S. 108A-117(b).
96. G.S. 53B-6.

3. FREEZE ACCOUNTS

If government officials find it necessary to freeze the assets of either an older adult or a defendant in a criminal case, then the involvement of financial institutions will be necessary.

- **Assets of an older adult.** In the course of investigating potential financial exploitation, adult protective services (APS) is authorized to petition a district court judge to issue an order freezing the adult's assets and allowing APS to inspect them.[97] See Chapter 2 for more details about this process.

- **Assets of a criminal defendant.** A district attorney may ask the court to freeze the assets of a defendant if "it appears by clear and convincing evidence that [the] defendant is about to or intends to divest himself or herself of assets in a manner that would render the defendant insolvent for the purposes of restitution."[98] See Chapter 3 for more details about this process.

G. CREDIT REPORTING AGENCIES

An older adult, like anyone else, may be the victim of identity theft. Some common identity theft scams targeting older adults involve (1) telephone calls that persuade the adult to share personal or financial information in exchange for the promise of time-limited, too-good-to-be-true deals and (2) emails asking the adult to confirm account information by clicking on a link.[99]

If an older adult's identity is stolen, one of the most important steps the adult or the adult's representative can take is to freeze the victim's credit temporarily. All consumers have the authority to put a security freeze on credit accounts.[100] Once the freeze is in place, a credit reporting agency may not release the consumer's credit report or information to a third party without the express authorization of the consumer.[101] The effect of a freeze is that it stops someone from opening a new account in the consumer's name or increasing an existing credit line.[102] A credit freeze is a tool that helps lessen the impact of identity theft.

---

97. G.S. 108A-106(f).

98. G.S. 14-112.3(b).

99. FBI, *Scams and Safety,* "Common Fraud Schemes," FBI.GOV, https://www.fbi.gov/scams-and-safety/common-fraud-schemes/telemarketing-fraud (last visited Aug. 13, 2019).

100. G.S. 75-63(a). *See* N.C. Att'y Gen., *Free Security Freeze*, NCDOJ.GOV, https://ncdoj.gov/protecting-consumers/protecting-your-identity/free-security-freeze (providing instructions for placing a security freeze) (last visited Aug. 13, 2019).

101. G.S. 75-63(a). Note that an agency may notify a third party that a freeze is in place. *Id.*

102. *See* N.C. Att'y Gen., *supra* note 100.

An older adult may be incapacitated and, as a result, unable to place a credit freeze without assistance. State law allows a representative of a "protected consumer" to place a security freeze with a credit reporting agency.[103] A protected consumer includes both

- an incapacitated adult (note that the adult does not first have to be adjudicated incompetent to qualify as a protected consumer) and

- an adult for whom a guardian or guardian ad litem has been appointed.[104]

To be authorized to place the freeze, the representative must be able to document his or her authority to act on behalf of the protected consumer.[105] Acceptable documentation includes

- a court order;

- a valid power of attorney; and

- a written, notarized statement signed by the protected consumer that expressly describes the authority of the representative to act on behalf of the consumer.[106]

The representative places the freeze by contacting the credit reporting agency by mail, phone, or through a secure website.[107] The three nationwide credit reporting agencies are Equifax, TransUnion, and Experian. [108] To place the freeze, the representative must do all of the following:[109]

- follow the instructions for submitting the report specified by the agency;

- provide sufficient identification for both himself or herself and for the protected consumer;

- provide sufficient proof of authority to act on the protected consumer's behalf; and

- pay a reasonable fee, not to exceed $5.00, for placement or removal of the freeze.[110]

Charging a fee is prohibited if the protected consumer is over age 62 or if the representative submits a copy of a report or complaint to law enforcement about the unlawful use of the consumer's identifying information by another person.[111]

---

103. G.S. 75-63.1. For a detailed discussion of this law and some of the practical questions raised by it, see Kate Mewhinney, *The Protected Consumer Credit Freeze: A New Tool to Prevent and Stop Financial Exploitation of Incapacitated Adults*, Wake Forest University School of Law Elder Law Clinic (2016), http://elder-clinic.law.wfu.edu/files/2016/09/Protected-Consumer-Security-Freeze-.pdf.

104. G.S. 75-61(11a). The statute does not make clear what type of guardian may place the freeze—a general guardian, a guardian of the estate, or a guardian of the person.

105. G.S. 75-61(13a) (defining "representative"), (16) ("sufficient proof of authority").

106. G.S. 75-61(16)b.

107. G.S. 75-63.1(a)(1).

108. *See* N.C. Att'y Gen., *Children's Security Freezes*, NCDOJ.GOV, https://www.ncdoj.gov/protecting-your-identity/childrens-security-freezes/ (providing contact information for each of the three national credit bureaus) (last visited Aug. 13, 2019).

109. G.S. 75-63.1(a)(2).

110. G.S. 75-63.1(d).

111. G.S. 75-63.1(d)(2)a., c.

Once these requirements are satisfied, the credit reporting agency must place the freeze within thirty days.[112] The freeze remains in effect until the protected consumer (or his or her representative) submits a request to the agency to remove the freeze and pays the fee (unless the consumer is over age 62 or submits a law enforcement report or complaint of unlawful use of identifying information, in which case no fee can be charged).[113] If a protected consumer himself or herself asks for the freeze to be removed, he or she must provide identification and proof that the representative no longer has valid authority to act on his or her behalf.[114] If the representative asks for the removal of the freeze, he or she must provide identification and proof of authority to act on the protected consumer's behalf.[115] The credit reporting agency has up to thirty days to remove the freeze.[116]

III. CHALLENGE FOR OTHER ELDER PROTECTION SYSTEM COMPONENTS

Perhaps the greatest challenge facing these other players in the elder protection system is the one that underlies the system as a whole: fragmentation. Each component has limited resources, knowledge, and legal authority. With these limitations, it is difficult to develop the resource-intensive connections and collaborations that are often needed to provide adequate services and supports to victims of elder abuse.

TIPS FOR COMBATTING SYSTEM FRAGMENTATION.

- Develop a list of contact people in your jurisdiction who are involved with elder protection. Update the list regularly.
- Develop multidisciplinary teams and convene information-sharing meetings and other types of collaborative initiatives.[117] See Chapter 1 for more information about multidisciplinary teams.
- Participate in online forums, either through protectadults.unc.edu or locally. These types of virtual communities can support collaboration and communication and help the overall elder protection system become more consistent and cohesive.

---

112. G.S. 75-63.1(a).
113. G.S. 75-63.1(c), (d).
114. G.S. 75-63.1(c)(1)b.
115. G.S. 75-63.1(c)(1)c.
116. G.S. 75-63.1(c).
117. Consumer Fin. Prot. Bureau, Off. for Older Americans, Report and Recommendations: Fighting Elder Financial Exploitation through Community Networks (2016), https://files.consumerfinance.gov/f/documents/082016_cfpb_Networks_Study_Report.pdf.

With tremendous demographic shifts on the horizon, agencies, organizations, and individuals involved with the protection of older adults have an opportunity to take critical steps now to build an effective elder protection system. Components of the system identify partners, develop relationships, and work together. As demonstrated throughout this manual, the "elder protection system" depends on meaningful and productive connections across disciplines, borders, and authority.

Appendix A
Alternatives to Guardianship

Every older adult who lacks capacity does not need a guardian. Guardianship removes fundamental rights, inhibits autonomy, and is indefinite and difficult to terminate, particularly for older adults with a condition like dementia that will continue to decline over time. There are legal and practical alternatives to guardianship of the person and of the estate that empower surrogate decision makers to act on an older adult's behalf (guardianship is discussed in detail in Chapter 4). The most effective of these alternatives may be powers of attorney, which require advance planning and are discussed in detail in Chapter 5. But, even without advance planning, there are supports that may be put in place for an older adult after a cognitive decline occurs that may prevent or, at the very least, delay the need for a guardian.

I. HEALTH AND PERSONAL CARE DECISION-MAKING ALTERNATIVES TO A GUARDIANSHIP OF THE PERSON (GOP)

A. HEALTH CARE POWER OF ATTORNEY (HEALTH CARE POA)

A health care POA is a written instrument, signed in the presence of two qualified witnesses and acknowledged before a notary public, pursuant to which an attorney-in-fact or agent is appointed to act for an older adult in matters relating to health care.[1] This may include the power to authorize withholding or discontinuing life-prolonging measures and to authorize providing or withholding mental health treatment.[2] Any person who is 18 years of age or older and has an understanding and capacity to make and communicate health care decisions may make a health care POA.[3] If a court appoints a guardian of the person or general guardian for an older adult, the agent's authority under a health care POA continues until suspended by court order for good cause.[4] The order suspending the health care POA should direct whether the guardian must act consistently with the health care POA and whether and to what extent the guardian may deviate from it.[5] A form health care POA is set forth in G.S. 32A-25.1.

B. LIVING WILL

A living will is a type of health care advanced directive that allows an individual to give future instructions to health care providers to withhold or withdraw life-prolonging measures, such as a feeding tube, in certain situations.[6] A living will states the choices an individual would make if the individual were able to communicate. It must be signed in

---

1. Chapter 32A, Section 16(3), of the North Carolina General Statutes (hereinafter G.S.).
2. G.S. 32A-19(a).
3. G.S. 32A-17.
4. G.S. 32A-22(a).
5. *Id.*
6. G.S. 90-321.

the presence of two qualified witnesses and acknowledged before a clerk, assistant clerk, or notary public.[7] A form living will is set forth in G.S. 90-321.

C. ADVANCE INSTRUCTION FOR MENTAL HEALTH TREATMENT

An advance instruction for mental health treatment is a written instruction signed in the presence of two qualified witnesses and acknowledged before a notary public.[8] In an advance instruction, a principal makes a declaration of instructions, information, and preferences regarding mental health treatment to be followed when the principal is incapable of giving or refusing consent.[9] It may include the authority to administer medications, to deliver shock treatment, and to admit the individual to a facility for care.[10] A form advance instruction is set forth in G.S. 122C-77.

D. INFORMED CONSENT STATUTE

A health care provider may not treat a patient without consent in most non-emergency situations.[11] Consent must be voluntarily given by a person with the legal authority and the decisional capacity to make health care decisions.[12] In addition, consent must be informed.[13] When a person lacks capacity to make or communicate health care decisions, North Carolina law sets out a list of persons who may consent to medical treatment on the person's behalf.[14] Priority is first given to a guardian of the person or a general guardian, then to a health care agent under a health care POA, and then an agent with powers to make health care decisions for the patient.[15] If there is no guardian or agent authorized to make decisions, the patient's spouse is first in line.[16] The list continues with other relatives and involved individuals.[17]

E. ADULT PROTECTIVE SERVICES (APS)

An APS unit exists in every county in North Carolina and serves to protect disabled adults, including older adults who lack capacity, who are abused, neglected, or exploited.[18] APS may help an older adult resolve a crisis situation and avoid the need for a more permanent guardianship by connecting the older adult to essential services in the community or initiating court action to protect the adult under G.S. Chapter 108A. A more in-depth discussion of APS is presented in Chapter 2.

---

7. G.S. 90-321(c)(3), (4).
8. G.S. 122C-72(1).
9. *Id.*
10. G.S. 122C-72(5).
11. *See* G.S. 90-21.13 (describing the standards a health care provider must meet in obtaining informed consent).
12. *Id.*
13. *Id.*
14. G.S. 90-21.13(c).
15. *Id.* Note that if a patient has a health care POA and a general guardian or guardian of the person, the health care agent under a valid health care POA has the right to exercise the authority in the health care POA unless the clerk suspends the authority of the health care agent. *Id.* § 90-21.13(c)(1).
16. *Id.*
17. *Id.*
18. *See* G.S. Ch. 108A, Art. 6 (Protection of the Abused, Neglected, or Exploited Disabled Adult Act).

F. SUPPORTS AND SERVICES

There may be a number of public and private supports and services that can be put in place to help older adults who lack capacity navigate their day-to-day needs. This includes meal delivery programs, such as Meals on Wheels; transportation services;[19] in-home aides and home health managers; housing locators;[20] and placement services[21] and technologies that are geared toward older adults, such as medical alert systems, smart pillboxes, and remote patient monitoring devices.

II. FINANCIAL DECISION-MAKING ALTERNATIVES TO A GUARDIAN OF THE ESTATE (GOE)

A. DURABLE POWER OF ATTORNEY (POA)

A POA is a common planning tool that is employed when an individual with capacity, the principal, wants to authorize another person, the agent, to act on his or her behalf.[22] It is typically used with regard to property and property affairs. An individual may execute a POA for any reason, including for convenience or mental or physical incapacity. The POA may become effective immediately or upon the occurrence of a future event, such as the mental or physical incapacity of an individual.[23] A POA subject to G.S. Chapter 32C is durable by default, meaning that it survives the incapacity of the principal unless it expressly states otherwise.[24] The principal determines the nature and extent of the agent's authority under the POA.[25] The principal may give the agent the authority over just a certain tract of real property or over all of his or her financial affairs. A POA is not typically subject to court oversight and is susceptible to abuse, particularly where the agent exceeds the scope of the agent's authority or conducts transactions under the POA for the agent's own benefit or otherwise not in the best interests of the principal. A form POA is set forth in G.S. 32C-3-301. POAs are discussed further in Chapter 5.

B. TRUST

A trust is a fiduciary relationship in which one person (the trustee) holds a property interest subject to an obligation to keep or use that interest for the benefit of another (the beneficiary).[26] Typically, there is a trust instrument that sets out the terms of the

---

19. *See* N.C. Dep't of Health & Human Servs. (DHHS), *Transportation Services for Older Adults*, NCDHHS.GOV, https://www.ncdhhs.gov/assistance/adult-services/transportation-services-for-older-adults (last visited Aug. 13, 2019).

20. DHHS, *Elder Housing Locator*, NCDHHS.GOV, https://www.ncdhhs.gov/assistance/adult-services/elder-housing-locator (last visited Aug. 13, 2019).

21. DHHS, *Adult Placement Services*, NCDHHS.GOV, https://www.ncdhhs.gov/assistance/adult-services/adult-placement-services (last visited Aug. 13, 2019).

22. G.S. 32C-1-102(9) (defining "power of attorney").

23. G.S. 32C-1-109.

24. G.S. 32C-1-104.

25. G.S. Chapter 32C, Article 2.

26. *See* G.S. 36C-4-402(a). The North Carolina Uniform Trust Code is contained in G.S. Chapter 36C and applies to any express trust no matter how created. *Id.* § 36C-1-102.

trust.[27] A common type of trust used to avoid guardianship for an older adult is a revocable living trust, which may be modified or revoked by the older adult.[28] The older adult may create the trust naming himself or herself as the trustee but then name a successor trustee to take over the management of the trust in the event of the adult's incapacity.

C. REPRESENTATIVE PAYEE

A representative payee is a person or an organization appointed by a federal governmental agency to receive benefits for a person who is unable to manage or direct the management of his or her benefits.[29] A representative payee may be appointed after an individual loses capacity. The payee must use the benefits to pay for the current and future needs of the beneficiary and save any benefits not required to meet current needs. A payee must keep records of expenses and provide an accounting upon request by the agency. Federal agencies with representative payee programs include the Social Security Administration (for Social Security benefits such as Medicaid and Medicare and supplemental Social Security benefits (commonly referred to as disability benefits)), the Veteran's Administration, the Department of Defense, and the Office of Personnel Management.

D. CLERK ADMINISTRATION OF FUNDS

A clerk of superior court may receive $5,000 or less from any person for an incapacitated adult who does not have a guardian and is domiciled in the clerk's county.[30] In addition, if an incapacitated adult is entitled to insurance proceeds that do not exceed $5,000, the proceeds may be paid to the clerk in the county of the adult's domicile.[31] The clerk may receive, administer, and, upon finding that it is in the best interest of the incapacitated adult, disburse the funds to a creditor, relative, or some "discreet and solvent neighbor" or friend for the purpose of handling the property and affairs of that adult.[32] The clerk will require receipts or paid vouchers showing that the money disbursed was used for the exclusive benefit of the incapacitated adult.[33]

E. JOINT PROPERTY

An older adult may own property, such as a house, car, or bank accounts, jointly with a spouse or other family member or friend. The joint ownership allows continued use of the assets for the older adult's benefit after one joint owner's incapacity. This type of ownership may prevent the need for a guardian, particularly in those situations involving one

27. G.S. 36C-1-103(21).

28. *See* G.S. Ch. 36C, Art. 6 (Revocable Trusts).

29. *See, e.g.*, Soc. Sec. Admin., *Frequently Asked Questions (FAQs) for Representative Payees*, SSA.GOV, https://www.ssa.gov/payee/faqrep.htm (describing the role of a representative payee).

30. G.S. 7A-111(b).

31. *Id.*

32. *Id.*

33. *Id.*

spouse with capacity who is a joint owner with a spouse who lacks capacity. If spouses hold property as tenants by the entirety and one or both of the spouses is/are mentally incompetent to execute a conveyance of the property when it is necessary or desirable that the property be mortgaged or sold, a special proceeding may be brought to authorize a sale or mortgage of the property.[34] This process is available when a spouse has not been adjudicated incompetent but is not competent to convey property.

F. SUPPORTS AND SERVICES

An older adult who lacks capacity may avoid the need for guardianship through supports and services, such as a daily money management (DMM) program. A DMM helps older adults with personal household finances, and services can range from comprehensive financial management to maintaining financial records to reminders to pay bills.[35] These types of services may be most helpful in situations where one spouse dies and the living spouse has not had a history of or experience with managing finances and needs some assistance and support.

---

34. G.S. 35A-1310.

35. Lynnette Khalfani-Cox, *Need Help Managing Day-to-Day Finances?*, AARP.ORG (July 1, 2016), https://www.aarp.org/money/budgeting-saving/info-2016/money-management-on-a-budget.html/.

Appendix B
Techniques and Tips for Interviewing Older Adults

A law enforcement officer interviews an older adult who is the victim of a crime. An adult protective services (APS) social worker interviews an older adult as part of an APS investigation. An attorney interviews an older adult as part of the attorney's representation of the adult in a guardianship case or civil litigation.

This appendix provides information for these professionals and others to consider when interviewing older adults in connection with elder abuse cases.

I. SELECTING THE INTERVIEW LOCATION

The interviewer may

- conduct the interview in the older adult's home or at a location that is comfortable to the older adult (note: conducting interviews in the homes of older adults allows interviewers to assess living conditions and ask questions about what they see around them);

- ensure that the location is free from distractions for both the older adult and the interviewer; and

- ask about and be aware of any physical limitations the older adult might have, such as hearing or sight impairment, and make sure that the older adult has access to accommodations that will empower him or her to participate meaningfully in the interview.

II. CONDUCT OF THE INTERVIEWER

The interviewer may

- provide his or her name and contact information to the older adult;

- explain the role of the interviewer and the purpose of the interview to the adult;

- develop a rapport with the older adult by asking about the adult's life and daily routine;

- ask the older adult whether he or she has any questions, needs, or concerns before going into the substance of the interview;

- make sure that cell phones, televisions, and other electronic devices that will distract from the interview are turned off and/or put away;

- treat the older adult with respect;

- ask the older adult how he or she prefers to be addressed;

- refrain from stereotyping the older adult; and

- be prepared to offer the older adult referrals to supports and services in the community, including protective services against further abuse.

III. SPECIAL CONSIDERATIONS FOR OLDER ADULTS WITH COGNITIVE IMPAIRMENTS

The interviewer may

- remember that a cognitive impairment does not always prevent an older adult from relaying what happened (i.e., don't discount what the older adult has to say because of a cognitive impairment);

- ask short, open-ended but specific questions;

- ask about one thing at a time, building on what the older adult has already disclosed;

- give the older adult time to answer each question without interrupting the adult but redirect as necessary;

- speak slowly and clearly but not condescendingly;

- speak at eye level with the older adult and maintain eye contact;

- NOT correct the older adult; and

- consider the timing of the interview, asking, for example, whether the older adult is more or less alert because the interview is occurring

    - after a meal,

    - after the adult has taken medication(s),

    - after physical exercise, or

    - earlier in the day.

Older adults with dementia may experience "sundowning," which is a restlessness, agitation, and confusion that worsens later in the day as the sun goes down. A caregiver may be able to provide information about the best time of day to conduct the interview with the older adult.

IV. JOINT INTERVIEWS WITH OTHER PROFESSIONALS

There are advantages and disadvantages of conducting joint interviews of older adults with other professionals. For example, consider the case of law enforcement joining an APS social worker to interview an older adult.

A. ADVANTAGES

- The older adult only has to give a statement once.

- The interview may be more comprehensive; one interviewer may ask a question another interviewer had not thought to ask.

B.   DISADVANTAGES

- APS and law enforcement serve different societal purposes. APS provides protection to older adults who are victims of elder abuse, while law enforcement conducts investigations to prosecute perpetrators.

- An older adult may be wary of sharing information needed by APS to provide protective services to the adult if law enforcement is present, particularly if the perpetrator is a family member or caregiver of the older adult.

- The presence of law enforcement may be intimidating to the older adult and could make the adult afraid that he or she did something wrong.

V.   PRESENCE OF FAMILY, FRIEND, OR CAREGIVER

It may be necessary, for confidentiality purposes or for other legal reasons, to conduct an interview of an older adult alone. Doing so also helps build trust with the older adult and ensures that the adult's story, and not another person's version of it, is told to the interviewer. It may be necessary for the older adult to have a support person present for some of the interview, until the adult feels comfortable. The support person may leave after introducing the older adult to the interviewer, so that the older adult may be interviewed alone.

VI. RESOURCES

- Elder Abuse Guide for Law Enforcement (EAGLE): Interviewing Older Adults, available at http://eagle.trea.usc.edu/law-enforcement-resources/interviewing-older-adults/.

- American Bar Association & American Psychological Association, Assessment of Older Adults with Diminished Capacity: A Handbook for Lawyers, available at https://www.apa.org/pi/aging/resources/guides/diminished-capacity.pdf.

- San Diego Elder and Dependent Adult Abuse Blueprint 2018, main document without addenda available at https://www.sdcda.org/helping/elder-abuse-blueprint.pdf.

- National Institute on Aging, Alzheimer's Care: Tips for Coping with Sundowning, available at https://www.nia.nih.gov/health/tips-coping-sundowning.

- Sheri Gibson, U.S. Dep't of Justice, Elder Justice Initiative, Forensic Interviewing of Older Adults (Dec. 8, 2017), webinar presentation slides available at https://www.justice.gov/file/1064541/download.

- Kay de Vries, Communicating with Older People with Dementia, 25(4) Nursing Older People 30–37 (May 2013), available for purchase at https://www.ncbi.nlm.nih.gov/pubmed/23789241.

- Gerontological Society of America, Communicating with Older Adults: An Evidence-Based Review of What Really Works (2012), see https://geron.org/publications/communicating-with-older-adults.

Appendix C
Crimes That May Be Implicated in Elder Abuse Cases

The table below identifies some of the crimes that may be charged in cases involving elder abuse. It is a more detailed version of Table 3.3 in Chapter 3.

CRIMES SPECIFIC TO ELDER AND DISABLED ADULTS

CRIME	STATUTE (G.S.)	ELEMENTS
Assault on Handicapped Person	14-32.1	(1) The defendant commits an assault or battery (2) on a handicapped person (3) knowing or having reason to know that the person is handicapped • No age requirement for victim • "Handicapped person" has definition specific to this crim
Aggravated Assault on a Handicapped Person	14-32.1(e)	(1) The defendant commits an assault or battery (2) on a handicapped person (3) knowing or having reason to know that the person is handicapped and (4) (a) uses a deadly weapon or other means of force like to cause serious injury or serious damage to a handicapped person, (b) inflicts serious injury on a handicapped person, o (c) intends to kill a handicapped person
Patient Abuse and Neglect There are four levels of conduct, resulting in different felony classifications depending on the nature of the conduct and the harm to the victim: (1) Willful or Culpably Negligent Pattern of Conduct Causing Bodily Injury (2) Willful or Culpably Negligent Conduct Causing Serious Bodily Injury (3) Culpably Negligent Conduct Causing Death (4) Intentional Conduct Causing Death	14-32.2	(1) The defendant physically abuses (2) (a) a patient of a health care facility or (b) a resident of a residential care facility and **Lowest level of offense:** (3) the abuse evinces a pattern of conduct (4) that is (a) willful or (b) culpably negligent and (5) proximately causes (6) bodily injury to a patient or resident **Next-higher levels of offense:** (3) the abuse is (a) willful or (b) culpably negligent and (4) proximately causes (5) serious bodily injury/death to a patient or resident **Highest level of offense:** (3) the abuse constitutes intentional conduct (4) that proximately causes (5) the death of the patient or resident • No age requirement for victim

CRIME	STATUTE (G.S.)	ELEMENTS

Abuse of a Disabled or Elder Adult	14-32.3	(1) The defendant is a caretaker of
		(2) (a) a disabled adult or
		    (b) an elder adult
		(3) who is residing in a domestic setting and
		(4) with malice, knowingly and willfully
		(5) (a) assaults the adult,
		    (b) fails to provide medical care or hygienic care to the adult, or
		    (c) confines or restrains the adult in a place or under a condition that is cruel or unsafe and
		(6) as a result the adult suffers mental or physical injury
		• If the mental or physical injury is serious, the crime is elevated from a Class H to a Class F felony

Neglect of a Disabled or Elder Adult	14-32.3(b)	(1) The defendant is a caretaker of
		(2) (a) a disabled adult or
		    (b) an elder adult
		(3) who is residing in a domestic setting and
		(4) wantonly, recklessly, or with gross carelessness
		(5) (a) fails to provide medical or hygienic care to the adult or
		    (b) confines or restrains the adult in a place or under a condition that is unsafe and
		(6) as a result, the adult suffers mental or physical injury
		• If the mental or physical injury is serious, the crime is elevated from a Class I to a Class G felony

Exploitation of a Disabled or Elder Adult through a Position of Trust or Business Relationship	14-112.2(b)	(1) The defendant
		    (a) stands in a position of trust and confidence or
		    (b) has a business relationship
		(2) with an elder or disabled adult and
		(3) knowingly
		(4) by deception or intimidation
		(5) obtains, uses, or endeavors to obtain or use an elder or disabled adult's funds, assets, or property
		(6) with the intent to
		    (a) deprive temporarily or permanently the elder or disabled adult of the use, benefit, or possession of the funds, assets, or property or
		    (b) benefit someone other than the elder or disabled adult

Exploitation of a Disabled or Elder Adult Lacking Capacity	14-112.2(c)	(1) The defendant knows or reasonably should know that
		(2) an elder or disabled adult lacks the capacity to consent and
		(3) obtains, uses, endeavors to obtain or use, or conspires with another to obtain or use an elder or disabled adult's funds, assets, or property
		(4) with the intent to
		    (a) deprive temporarily or permanently the elder or disabled adult of the use, benefit, or possession of the funds, assets, or property or
		    (b) benefit someone other than the elder or disabled adult

RAPE AND OTHER SEX OFFENSES

CRIME	STATUTE (G.S.)	ELEMENTS

First-Degree Forcible Rape	14-27.21	(1) The defendant has vaginal intercourse
		(2) with a person
		(3) by force and
		(4) against that person's will and
		(5) the defendant
		  (a) uses, threatens to use, or displays a dangerous or deadly weapon (or what reasonably appears to be a dangerous or deadly weapon),
		  (b) inflicts serious personal injury on the victim,
		  (c) inflicts serious personal injury on another person, or
		  (d) is aided and abetted by one or more other persons

Second-Degree Forcible Rape	14-27.22	(1) The defendant has vaginal intercourse
		(2) with a person
		(3) and the intercourse is
		  (a) by force and against the person's will or
		  (b) with someone who is
		    (i) mentally disabled,
		    (ii) mentally incapacitated, or
		    (iii) physically helpless and
		(4) the defendant knew or should have known that the victim was mentally disabled, mentally incapacitated, or physically helpless

First-Degree Forcible Sexual Offense	14-27.26	(1) The defendant engages in a sexual act other than vaginal intercourse
		(2) with a person
		(3) by force and
		(4) against that person's will and
		(5) the defendant
		  (a) uses, threatens to use, or displays a dangerous or deadly weapon (or what reasonably appears to be a dangerous or deadly weapon),
		  (b) inflicts serious personal injury on the victim,
		  (c) inflicts serious personal injury on another person, or
		  (d) is aided and abetted by one or more other persons

Second-Degree Forcible Sexual Offense	14-27.27	(1) The defendant engages in a sexual act other than vaginal intercourse
		(2) with a person and
		(3) the act is
		  (a) by force and against the person's will or
		  (b) with someone who is
		    (i) mentally disabled,
		    (ii) mentally incapacitated, or
		    (iii) physically helpless and
		(4) the defendant knew or should have known that the victim was mentally disabled, mentally incapacitated, or physically helpless

Sexual Battery	14-27.33	(1) The defendant, for the purpose of sexual arousal, sexual gratification, or sexual abuse (2) engages in sexual contact with another person (3) (a) by force and against the will of the other person or (b) who is mentally disabled, mentally incapacitated, or physically helpless and the defendant knows or should reasonably know that the other person is mentally disabled, mentally incapacitated, or physically helpless
Crime Against Nature	14-177	(1) Commits a crime against nature • This crime requires penetration of, or by, a sexual organ, as illustrated by examples from case law

ASSAULTS*

CRIME	STATUTE (G.S.)	ELEMENTS	
Assault with Deadly Weapon with Intent to Kill Inflicting Serious Injury	14-32(a)	(1) (2) (3) (4) (5)	The defendant commits an assault on another with a deadly weapon and with intent to kill and inflicts serious injury
Assault with Deadly Weapon Inflicting Serious Injury	14-32(b)	(1) (2) (3) (4)	The defendant commits an assault on another with a deadly weapon and inflicts serious injury
Assault with Deadly Weapon with Intent to Kill	14-32(c)	(1) (2) (3) (4)	The defendant commits an assault on another with a deadly weapon with intent to kill
Assault Inflicting Serious Bodily Injury	14-32.4(a)	(1) (2) (3)	The defendant commits an assault on another and inflicts serious bodily injury
Assault by Strangulation	14-32.4(b)	(1) (2) (3) (4)	The defendant commits an assault on another and inflicts physical injury by strangulation
Simple Assault	14-33(a)	(1) (2)	The defendant commits an assault on another
Assault Inflicting Serious Injury; Assault with Deadly Weapon	14-33(c)(1)	(1) (2) (3)	The defendant commits an assault on another and inflicts serious injury
Assault with a Deadly Weapon	14-33(c)(1)	(1) (2) (3)	The defendant commits an assault on another with a deadly weapon
Assault on Female	14-33(c)(2)	(1) (2) (3) (4)	The defendant is a male, at least 18 years old, and commits an assault on a female
Habitual Misdemeanor Assault	14-33.2	(1) (2) (3)	The defendant (a) (i) violates G.S. 14-33 and (ii) causes physical injury or (b) violates G.S. 14-34 and has two or more prior felony or misdemeanor assault convictions and the earlier of the convictions occurred no more than fifteen years before the date of the offense in Element (1)

* The term "assault" is defined by common law.

KIDNAPPING

CRIME	STATUTE (G.S.)	ELEMENTS
First-Degree Kidnapping	14-39	(1) The defendant (a) confines, (b) restrains, or (c) removes from one place to another (2) a person (3) (a) without the person's consent or, (b) if the person is under 16, without consent of the person's parent or guardian (4) for the purpose of (a) holding the victim as hostage, (b) holding the victim for ransom, (c) using the victim as a shield, (d) facilitating the commission of a felony, (e) facilitating flight following the commission of a felony, (f) doing serious bodily harm to the victim or any other person, (g) terrorizing the victim or any other person, (h) holding the victim in involuntary servitude, (i) trafficking another person, or (j) subjecting or maintaining the victim for sexual servitude and (5) (a) does not release the victim in a safe place, (b) seriously injures the victim, or (c) sexually assaults the victim
Second-Degree Kidnapping	14-39	Consists of elements (1) through (4) from First-Degree Kidnapping
False Imprisonment	Common law	(1) The defendant intentionally and unlawfully (2) (a) restrains or (b) detains (3) a person (4) without the person's consent
Felonious Restraint	14-43.3	(1) The defendant unlawfully restrains (2) a person (3) (a) without the person's consent or, (b) if the person is under 16, without consent of the person's parent or guardian and (4) transports the person by motor vehicle or other conveyance from the place of the initial restraint

BURGLARY AND OTHER HOUSEBREAKINGS

CRIME	STATUTE (G.S.)	ELEMENTS
First-Degree Burglary	14-51	(1) The defendant breaks and (2) enters (3) without consent (4) the dwelling house or sleeping apartment (5) of another (6) while it is actually occupied (7) at night (8) with the intent to commit any felony or larceny therein
Second-Degree Burglary	14-51	(1) The defendant breaks and (2) enters (3) without consent (4) the dwelling house or sleeping apartment, or any building within the curtilage of the dwelling, (5) of another (6) at night (7) with the intent to commit any felony or larceny therein
Breaking or Entering Building with Intent to Commit Felony or Larceny	14-54(a)	(1) The defendant breaks or (2) enters (3) without consent (4) any building (5) with the intent to commit any felony or larceny therein
Breaking or Entering Building with Intent to Terrorize or Injure Occupant	14-54(a1)	Consists of elements (1) through (4) of Breaking or Entering Building with Intent to Commit Felony or Larceny, plus (5) with the intent to terrorize or injure an occupant of the building
Misdemeanor Breaking or Entering	14-54(b)	(1) The defendant breaks or (2) enters (3) without consent (4) any building
Break or Enter Motor Vehicle with Intent to Commit Felony or Larceny	14-56	(1) The defendant breaks or (2) enters (3) without consent (4) any railroad car, motor vehicle, trailer, aircraft, boat, or other watercraft (5) containing goods, wares, freight, or anything of value (6) with the intent to commit any felony or larceny therein

LARCENY AND ROBBERY

CRIME	STATUTE (G.S.)	ELEMENTS

Felony Larceny	14-72	(1) The defendant takes
		 (2) personal property
		 (3) in the possession of another and
		 (4) carries it away
		 (5) without the consent of the possessor and
		 (6) with the intent to deprive the possessor of its use permanently,
		 (7) knowing that he or she was not entitled to it and
		 (8) the larceny was
		    (a) of property worth more than $1,000;
		    (b) from the person;
		    (c) committed pursuant to burglary, breaking out of a dwelling, breaking or entering a building, breaking or entering a building that is a place of religious worship, or burglary with explosives;
		    (d) of an explosive or incendiary device;
		    (e) of a firearm;
		    (f) of a record or paper in the custody of the N.C. State Archives; or
		    (g) of a horse, mule, swine, cattle, or dog

Misdemeanor Larceny	14-72	(1) The defendant takes (2) personal property (3) in the possession of another and (4) carries it away (5) without the consent of the possessor and (6) with the intent to deprive the possessor of its use permanently, (7) knowing that he or she was not entitled to it
Larceny, Concealment, or Destruction of Wills	14-77	"If any person, either during the life of the testator or after his death, shall steal or, for any fraudulent purpose, shall destroy or conceal any will, codicil or other testamentary instrument, he shall be guilty of a Class 1 misdemeanor."
Robbery with a Dangerous Weapon	14-87	(1) The defendant commits or attempts to commit larceny (2) from the person or from the person's presence (3) by the possession, use, or threatened use of a firearm or other dangerous weapon (4) that endangers or threatens the life of a person
Common Law Robbery	Common law; *see* 14-87.1	(1) The defendant commits larceny (2) from the person or from the person's presence (3) by violence or intimidation
Extortion	14-118.4	(1) The defendant threatens or communicates a threat to another (2) with the intent to obtain wrongfully (3) anything of value, any acquittance, any advantage, or any immunity

OTHER FINANCIAL AND RELATED CRIMES

CRIME	STATUTE (G.S.)	ELEMENTS
Embezzlement by an Agent or Fiduciary	14-90	(1) The defendant fraudulently or knowingly and willingly (2) uses for a purpose other than that for which the defendant received it (3) the property of another (4) held by the defendant under his or her care • Applies to fiduciaries, including a guardian, administrator, executor, trustee, or any receiver • Requires that the property be entrusted to the defendant; if no entrustment, the taking is larceny or obtaining property by false pretenses
Obtain Property by False Pretenses	14-100	(1) The defendant makes a representation about a past or existing fact or a future event (2) that is false and (3) is calculated and intended to deceive, and (4) the representation does in fact deceive another person, and (5) the person thereby obtains, or attempts to obtain, money, goods, property, services, choses in action, or any other thing of value from that other person
Theft of Financial Transaction Card	14-113.9 (a)(1)	(1) The defendant (a) takes, (b) obtains, or (c) withholds (2) a financial transaction card (3) from another (4) without the cardholder's consent and (5) with the intent to use it
Forgery of Financial Transaction Card	14-113.11	(1) The defendant (a) falsely makes or embosses a purported financial transaction card or utters a falsely-made or falsely-embossed financial transaction card; (b) falsely encodes, duplicates, or alters existing encoded information on a financial transaction card or utters a falsely-encoded, -duplicated, or -altered card; or (c) not being the cardholder or a person authorized by the cardholder, signs a financial transaction card (2) with the intent to defraud
Financial Transaction Card Fraud	14-113.13	(1) The defendant, with the intent to defraud, (2) uses a financial transaction card (3) (a) obtained or retained, or received with knowledge that it was obtained or retained, in violation of 14-113.9 or 14-113.11; (b) that he or she knows is forged, expired, revoked, or altered; or (c) that he or she knows was obtained by a fraudulent application in violation of 14-113.13(c) (4) for the purpose of obtaining money, goods, services, or anything else of value

CRIME	STATUTE (G.S.)	ELEMENTS
Financial Identity Theft	14-113.20	(1) The defendant knowingly (2) (a) obtains, (b) possesses, or (c) uses (3) identifying information of another person, living or dead, (4) with the intent to fraudulently represent the person is the other person (5) for the purpose of (a) making financial or credit transactions in the other person's name; (b) avoiding legal consequences; or (c) obtaining anything of value, benefit, or advantage
Common Law Forgery	*See* 14-119, -120	Common law elements: (1) The defendant makes a false writing (2) that is apparently capable of effecting a fraud (3) with the intent to defraud
Common Law Uttering	See 14-120	Common law elements: (1) The defendant utters as true (2) a false writing (3) that is apparently capable of effecting a fraud (4) with the intent to defraud and (5) knowing that the writing is false
Forgery and Counterfeiting of Instruments	14-119	(1) The defendant (a) forges or (b) counterfeits (2) an instrument (3) with the intent to injure or defraud (4) a person, financial institution, or governmental unit
Uttering Forged Instruments	14-120	(1) The defendant utters, publishes, passes, delivers, or attempts to pass or deliver (2) an instrument (3) (a) that is false, forged, or counterfeit or (b) that contains a false, forged, or counterfeit endorsement (4) (a) for the sake of gain or (b) with the intent to defraud or injure another and (5) knowing that (a) it was falsely forged or counterfeited or (b) falsely endorsed
Forging an Endorsement on Checks and Securities	14-120	(1) The defendant falsely makes, forges, or counterfeits (2) an endorsement (3) on an instrument (4) (a) for the sake of gain or (b) with the intent to defraud or injure another

MISCELLANEOUS

CRIME	STATUTE (G.S.)	ELEMENTS

Communicating Threats	14-277.1	(1) The defendant, without lawful authority,
		  (a) willfully threatens to physically injure
		    (i) another person or
		    (ii) that person's child, sibling, spouse, or dependent or
		  (b) willfully threatens to damage another's property and
		(2) communicates that threat to the other person
		(3) in a manner that would make a reasonable person believe it is likely to be carried out and
		(4) the threat is believed by the threatened person

Using Threatening Language on the Telephone	14-196(a)(2)	(1) The defendant, in a telephonic communication,
		(2) uses words or language
		(3) (a) threatening to inflict bodily harm to any person,
		  (b) threatening physical injury to another's property, or
		  (c) for the purpose of extorting something of value from another

Repeated Telephone Calls to Harass, etc.	14-196(a)(3)	(1) The defendant telephones
		(2) another
		(3) repeatedly
		(4) for the purpose of
		  (a) abusing,
		  (b) annoying,
		  (c) threatening,
		  (d) terrifying,
		  (e) harassing, or
		  (f) embarrassing
		(5) a person at the called number

Using Electronic Mail or Communication to Threaten or Extort	14-196(b)(1)	(1) The defendant uses, in
		  (a) electronic mail or
		  (b) electronic communication,
		(2) words or language
		(3) (a) threatening to inflict bodily harm to any person,
		  (b) threatening physical injury to the property of another, or
		  (c) for the purpose of extorting money or other things of value from any person

CRIME	STATUTE (G.S.)	ELEMENTS
Stalking	14-277.3A	(1) The defendant, willfully and (2) without legal purpose, (3) (a) harasses another person on more than one occasion or 　　(b) engages in a course of conduct directed at a specific person (4) when the defendant knows or should know that the harassment or course of conduct would cause a reasonable person to 　　(a) fear for the safety of 　　　(i) him or herself, 　　　(ii) his or her immediate family, or 　　　(iii) his or her close personal associates or 　　(b) suffer substantial emotional distress by placing that person in fear of 　　　(i) death, 　　　(ii) bodily injury, or 　　　(iii) continued harassment • This constitutes a misdemeanor • A repeat offense is punishable as a felony
Interfering with Emergency Communication	14-286.2	(1) The defendant 　　(a) intentionally interferes 　　　(i) with an emergency communication, 　　　(ii) knowing that the communication is an emergency communication, and 　　　(iii) while not making an emergency communication himself or herself and 　　(b) interferes 　　　(i) with a communication instrument or other emergency equipment 　　　(ii) with the intent to prevent an emergency communication
Violation of a Domestic Violence Protective Order	50B-4.1	(1) The defendant knowingly (2) violates a valid protective order entered pursuant to 　　(a) Chapter 50B of the General Statutes, 　　(b) a court of another state, or 　　(c) a court of an Indian tribe • This constitutes a misdemeanor • A repeat offense is punishable as a felony

Note: The list of crimes in this appendix is from the *Alamance County Elder A/N/E Legal Resources and Remedies Booklet*. The elements are from Jessica Smith, *North Carolina Crimes: A Guidebook on the Elements of Crime* (7th ed. 2012).